A Preface to the 'Nibelungenlied'

Theodore M. Andersson

A Preface to the
NIBELUNGENLIED

 STANFORD UNIVERSITY PRESS 1987
STANFORD, CALIFORNIA

Stanford University Press
Stanford, California
© 1987 by the Board of Trustees of the
Leland Stanford Junior University
Printed in the United States of America

CIP data appear at the end of the book

Published with the assistance of
the National Endowment for the Humanities

Foreword

THE FOLLOWING pages attempt to provide the necessary background for an informed reading of the *Nibelungenlied*. Although there are introductory works in English as well as German, no book undertakes to establish the literary-historical setting of the epic for general students of medieval literature. To fill this need I have tried to trace antecedent literary developments (Part I) and to suggest the immediate literary context of the poem at the time it was written (Part II). I have also appended translations and summaries of previously untranslated materials that are crucial to an understanding of the *Nibelungenlied*. Such Norse analogues as the *Poetic Edda* and *Vǫlsunga saga* are already easily available.

My aim has been to bridge the traditional gap between those scholars who have studied the *Nibelungenlied* against the background of Germanic heroic legend and those who have sought to locate the poem in the literary situation at the end of the twelfth century. Neither approach precludes the other. Although the *Nibelungenlied* poet drew the story itself from earlier heroic poems, it is clear that he absorbed impulses from other types of literature as well. Accordingly, I survey the more important types of narrative that determined the shape of the *Nibelungenlied* before I turn to an analysis of the text in Part II of the book. Chapters 1 and 2 trace the development of Germanic heroic poetry from the Migration Age on, for heroic poetry is the most immediate generic context of the *Nibelungenlied*. Chapters 3 and 4 then trace the emergence of narrative practice in the twelfth century, in historical and legendary epic on the one hand and romance on the other. These developments can only be sketched in broad outline, but a few initial bearings may serve to suggest how the *Nibelungenlied* can eventually be plotted more accurately on the literary map of the twelfth century. It is in any event my hope to lay aside the contention between students of the heroic tradition and students of classical Middle High German literature. The *Nibelungenlied* belongs to both, and the proprietary campaigns waged in the past have resulted in unnecessarily one-sided views of the poem. It is time now to think in terms of collaborative traditions rather than competing claims.

Since the focus of the book is literary, I have not discussed such specialized matters as the poetic language, the unresolved relationships among the main redactions, the dating problems, or the author's identity. Information on these and other questions may be found in W. Hoffmann's *Das Nibelungenlied* (1982). It will emerge from my presentation that I consider redaction B to be anterior to C and that, in contrast to Berta Lösel-Wieland-Engelmann (1980), I assume the author to be male. This assumption leads me to refer to the anonymous poet with the masculine pronoun.

My analysis presupposes a reader who is familiar with the *Nibelungenlied* in the original or in translation but has no prior knowledge of Germanic or Middle High German literature. The notes accordingly include references to basic critical works and to English or German translations of the relevant medieval texts. Such references are superfluous for scholars in the field but may serve to guide the first explorations of students. Further information on general topics and individual authors or works may be found in the *Dictionary of the Middle Ages* now being published by Charles Scribner's Sons (1982–). A useful annotated list of first readings on the *Nibelungenlied* is provided by W. McConnell, *The Nibelungenlied* (pp. 132–37). With respect to my own bibliographical coverage, the customary demurral obtains: I have read what I could, and wish I had read more. Much of the technical literature is reviewed in a previous book and articles and has therefore been omitted here, but despite many years of study I will still have overlooked important items.

The book was drafted from July to November of 1984 with the aid of a Fellowship for Independent Study and Research from the National Endowment for the Humanities. I am grateful to the NEH and to a generous provision of sabbatical leave from Stanford for the opportunity to complete the project. I am also indebted to an anonymous reader for the Stanford University Press who gave me a number of helpful bibliographical leads.

T.M.A.

Contents

I The Background

1. The Germanic Heroic Lay

At the time the *Nibelungenlied* was written, around 1200, it was a bold literary experiment, but the tale it told was traditional. On the one hand the *Nibelungenlied* is associated with the new rise of romance in twelfth-century France, the *romans d'antiquité*, the romances of Chrétien de Troyes, and the German adaptations of these works by Heinrich von Veldeke, Hartmann von Aue, and Wolfram von Eschenbach. On the other hand the story antedates romance and owes its formation to a sequence of lost oral and written poems reaching back as much as six centuries. This dual orientation has been the stuff of much controversy. Before World War II the epic was studied primarily in terms of its relationship to the antecedent heroic poems. When study resumed in the late 1940's and 1950's, the outlook had shifted, and subsequent critics have dealt with the *Nibelungenlied* almost exclusively in terms of its position in contemporary literature.

Although the native heroic tradition has often been ignored, it continues to be prerequisite to our understanding of the *Nibelungenlied*. We have, as a matter of course, based our literary assessments of Hartmann's and Wolfram's work on a comparison with Chrétien's corresponding romances. It is no less incumbent on us to study the *Nibelungenlied* in relation to its immediate models. This procedure is problematical because the models are lost and can be recovered only hypothetically, but approximate reconstructions are possible and tell us much about the final epic. To ascertain the older forms of the legend is also to understand the poetic options.

The study of Germanic heroic poetry is in itself a largely hypothetical exercise based on fragmentary evidence. We have only a handful of poems in three Old Germanic dialects, references to lost heroic stories in early medieval chronicles, and epic elaborations of a late period that presuppose the earlier lays—*Beowulf*, *Waltharius*, and the *Nibelungenlied* itself.[1] The most proximate remnants of the ancestral form are a fragmentary Old English lay (*The Fight at Finnsburg*), a rather more complete Old High German lay partially and superficially recast in Old Saxon forms (the *Hildebrandslied*), a few lays in Old Icelandic preserved in the *Poetic Edda* (most importantly *Brot af Sigurðarkviðu, Atlakviða,* and *Hamðismál*), and a lay preserved in part in the Icelandic legendary tale *Hervarar saga* (*Hlǫðskviða* or *The Battle of the Goths and the Huns*).

The Fight at Finnsburg survives only in an eighteenth-century transcript of a lost manuscript and is assumed to date from the eighth century, with allowance to be made for the uncertainties that attach to the dating of all Old English poetry. The *Hildebrandslied* is extant in a Carolingian manuscript and can be dated to around 800. The Eddic poems are preserved in a unique manuscript (Codex Regius 2365, 4°) from the second half of the thirteenth century, and *Hervarar saga* dates from around 1300. Despite the dispersion in time (eighth to thirteenth century) and place (England, Bavaria, Iceland), these heroic survivals have so many common features that they are assumed to derive from a single prototypical form earlier than all the extant examples.

They share, first of all, a metrical system. All the lays mentioned so far are composed in Germanic alliterative meter, that is, short verses bearing two stresses and paired into long verses by means of alliteration in two or three of the stressed syllables, as marked in the following examples.

Finnsburg (vv. 13–14)
> Ða aras mænig góldhladen ðégn, gýrde hine his swúrde;
> ða to dúra eódon drihtlice cémpan.
>
> (Then many a gold-laden thane arose and girded himself with his sword; then to the door went the noble warriors.)

Hildebrandslied (vv. 6–7)
> gárutun se iro gúðhamun, gúrtun sih iro suért ana,
> hélidos, ubar [h]ringa, do sie to dero hiltiu rítun.
>
> (They readied their battle dress, girded their swords on, the warriors, over their ring-mail when they rode to battle.)

Hamðismál (stanza 31)
> Þar féll Sǫrli at sálar gáfli,
> enn Hámðir hné at húsbáki.
>
> (There Sǫrli fell at the hall gable and Hamðir sank at the back of the house.)

The poems are of similar length, ranging from something under a hundred lines to almost two hundred. Of the *Finnsburg Fragment* only forty-eight lines survive, but the more nearly complete *Hildebrandslied* runs to sixty-eight. *Hamðismál* runs to 112 lines and *Atlakviða* to 176.

In addition to common meter and analogous dimensions, these poems subscribe to the same style and outlook. Cast partly in narrative and partly in dialogue, they center on a dramatic confrontation with an emphasis on steadfast conduct and a tragic conclusion. The *Hildebrandslied* recounts the meeting in battle of a father and son separated since the son's infancy, the son's stubborn refusal to recognize or acknowledge his father, and his insistence on single combat, which, judging from the far-flung analogues and a later Icelandic stanza, ends in his death at the hands of his grieved parent.[2] *The Fight at Finnsburg* deals with an episode in the longstanding hostility between Danes and Frisians. A temporary truce finds them sharing a hall during a long winter, but when spring comes the hostilities flare up again and battle breaks out. As we know from *Beowulf* (v. 1,152), this battle ends in the death of the Frisian king Finn.[3]

The northern material is richer. Several poems tell us of Sigurd's youthful adventures, his betrothal to Brynhild, the administration of a potion of forgetfulness that makes him oblivious to Brynhild and susceptible to Gudrun, his subsequent wooing of Brynhild for his brother-in-law Gunnar, and Brynhild's outraged contrivance of his murder. *Atlakviða* continues the story. After Sigurd's death his widow Gudrun marries the Hunnish king Atli, who covets Sigurd's treasure and seeks to acquire it by luring Gudrun's brothers to his court with a perfidious invitation to a banquet. Stouteartedness precludes caution, and the brothers accept the invitation, only to be seized and executed by Atli. The story concludes with Gudrun's vengeance for her slain brothers. She serves Atli a Thyestean banquet prepared from the bodies of his infant sons, then murders him in his sleep.

Though originally separate, the heroic tale of Hamðir and Sǫrli is appended to the catastrophe of *Atlakviða* in the *Poetic Edda*. The connecting figure is Svanhildr, conceived of by the evolving legend as Gudrun's daughter by Sigurd. After Atli's murder Gudrun marries once again and has two more children, the sons Hamðir and Sǫrli, by King Jónakr of Denmark. Svanhildr is in turn married to King Jǫrmunrekkr of the Goths, but she betrays him with his son Randvér and is trampled to death by horses when the deception is revealed. Gudrun dispatches her sons Hamðir and Sǫrli to avenge their half sister; they invade Jǫrmunrekkr's hall, succeed in severing his hands and feet, but succumb before they can finish the task.

Our final example, the fragmentary *Hlǫðskviða*, is not connected to this cycle. Together with the prose in which it is embedded, it tells the story of two half brothers, Hlǫðr and Angantýr. The illegitimate Hlǫðr contests the Gothic succession with the legitimate Angantýr, is rejected, falls in a pitched battle, and is mourned by his victorious brother.[4]

The drift of these pieces is similar enough to suggest a narrowly circumscribed genre. Typically the situation is highly charged and the issue compressed to an impossible but inescapable choice. All the poems are rich in family tensions and are peopled by men and women living under the remorseless constraints of duty, courage, honor, contempt for life, and the imperative necessity of revenge. Hengest must finally break the truce between Danes and Frisians because the ancient hostility will not recede and the demand for vengeance prevails. Some coercion that is not quite clear (loyalty to his military lord?—an obligation to vindicate his warrior's honor even against his son?) causes Hildebrand to kill Hadubrand. Jealousy and slighted honor lead Brynhild to arrange the murder of the man she loves. Some sense of impeached courage obliges the Burgundian brothers to fall in with Atli's treacherous invitation and sacrifice their realm.[5] Gudrun in turn sacrifices children and husband to gain a suitably harsh vengeance for her betrayed brothers. In the sequel she is equally willing to sacrifice her sons Hamðir and Sǫrli in a hopeless attempt to avenge her daughter Svanhildr. *Hlǫðskviða* is not unlike the *Hildebrandslied*; near kin are forced into conflict by their vision of what honor requires.

The chief instrument for focusing the dramatic intensity of these situations is dialogue. What remains of the *Hildebrandslied* is almost exclusively a strangely oblique dialogue between father and son, a conversation that fails to remove the fateful barrier to recognition. *Atlakviða* begins with a similarly oblique dialogue between Atli's messenger and the Burgundian brothers, a dialogue in which everyone seems aware of the underlying issues but no one enunciates them clearly. As time went on, this lapidary and repressed style was transformed into an increasingly full and explicit form of dialogue. Thus *Hamðismál* was prefaced with a semi-independent exchange between Gudrun and her sons as she urges them on their mission of vengeance (*Guðrúnarhvǫt*). The poet of *Atlamál* methodically expanded the dialogue of the older *Atlakviða*, and Gudrun acquired two independent laments (*Guðrúnarkviða I* and *II*).

Along with the original allusiveness in dialogue went a spare account of the action in a rapid sequence of sharply etched peaks. There is just one scene in the *Hildebrandslied*, which achieves its effects largely by exposition, but there may be half a dozen or more scenes in other poems. *Atlakviða* finds space for the interview with the Hunnish messenger, a farewell scene, the ride to Hunland, the struggle between Burgundians and Huns, the execution of Hǫgni and Gunnar, Atli's loathsome feast, his murder, and Gudrun's firing of the hall. In all these poems detail is kept to a minimum, serving only to visualize a given scene in one or two quick flashes. These moments are memorable, often drastic: the nighttime attack under scudding clouds in *The Fight at Finnsburg*, the excision of Hǫgni's heart and Gunnar's death in a snake pit in *Atlakviða*, the severing of hands and feet in *Hamðismál*, the stemming of rivers and filling of valleys with corpses in *Hlǫðskviða*.

The isolable features of the surviving poems—meter, narrative interspersed with dialogue, allusive brevity, rapid pace, compressed style, drastic effects, reduced scenic repertory, small cast, and the pervasive tension between a tyrannical code and human affections—all combine to suggest the dimensions of the common Germanic form that must have preceded the extant texts. These features also allow us to identify certain prose epitomes of heroic tales not preserved in vernacular originals but alluded to by early medieval historians writing in Latin. One of these writers, the eighth-century Langobard Paul the Deacon, a member of Charlemagne's literary circle, recorded the history of his own people and recounted, among other episodes, the tale of Rosimund and Alboin.[6]

The ominous background of the story is the marriage of the Gepid princess Rosimund to King Alboin of the Langobards, the slayer of his bride's father. Despite this latent strain the marriage appears to work well enough until one evening Alboin, his wits dimmed by drink, takes a goblet fashioned from his slain father-in-law's skull, has it filled with wine, and bids Rosimund drink cheerfully with her father. She is inflamed with a passion for revenge, but requires accomplices to carry out her plan. She therefore approaches one of Alboin's retainers, a certain Helmichis, who in turn enlists Peredeo. Peredeo, however, declines to enter into the conspiracy. In order to win him over, Rosimund substitutes herself in the bed of his mistress. Giving him time to "accomplish the evil deed," the queen asks him captiously who he thinks his bedmate is, then reveals the truth and demands his cooperation on pain of betraying their illicit intercourse to Alboin. The final stage is set while Alboin naps. Rosimund ties his sword fast to his bedpost, then Helmichis invades the bedchamber and kills him after he puts up a stout resistance with a footstool.

Although we have no other traces of a Langobardic poem on this theme, the earmarks of Paul's account are clearly those of heroic poetry. The domestic group, the sequence of vivid moments, the conflict between family bonds and the vengeance imperative, the drastic gestures (drinking from a skull and cold adultery), the scenery of hall and bedchamber, the dramatic dialogue—these elements are too remote from chronicle style and too reminiscent of the heroic lay to allow for much doubt about their origin in an oral poem current among the Langobards. The existence of fully formed heroic poetry in Langobardic Italy is thus established for the eighth century. This additional evidence is helpful because it buttresses the uncertain dating of the Old English documents. Taken together with the English material and the *Hildebrandslied*, the Langobardic story shows a distribution of heroic poetry on the Continent and in England a century before the settlement of Iceland, the focus of our later evidence. Heroic poetry was clearly a form the Icelanders brought with them when they settled their new home.

But how much older than the eighth century is Germanic heroic poetry? We are in possession of an invaluable document that enables us to roll the history of the genre back a full two centuries. In 551 the Goth Jordanes reduced twelve books of Cassiodorus' Gothic history to a slender epitome entitled *Getica*. In the course of this history he relates the circumstances surrounding the death of the Ostrogothic king Ermanaric in the year 380.[7] We are told that when Ermanaric was pondering the attack of the Huns, the tribe of the Rosomoni took advantage of the crisis to betray him. In reprisal Ermanaric seized the wife of one of their number, Sunilda by name, and ordered her bound hand and foot between two chariots, which he caused to be driven in opposite directions. Her brothers, Ammius and Sarus, sought vengeance and buried a sword in Ermanaric's side. He then succumbed both to the wound and to the agony inflicted by the Hunnish invasion.

Jordanes' Ermanaric is the Jǫrmunrekkr of the Icelandic *Hamðismál*, Sunilda is Svanhildr, and Ammius and Sarus are her avenging brothers Hamðir and Sǫrli. The motifs are not identical but very similar. Sunilda's death is explained by national treachery rather than marital infidelity. She is executed by being torn asunder rather than being trampled to death. Her brothers effect a partial revenge by piercing Ermanaric's side with a sword rather than by severing his hands and feet. These discrepancies in detail have been interpreted in different ways. For the most part critics have held that Jordanes' account reproduces exactly the content of a lay that had not yet shed the historical circumstances of Ermanaric's death 170 years earlier. It is therefore not a fully evolved heroic lay that has freed itself from fact in the process of becoming legend, but a semi-historical form lying halfway between fourth-century reality and the heroic fiction of *Hamðismál*.[8]

Contrary to the view of these critics, the version reported by Jordanes is likely to be a fully fictionalized account with only the most tenuous hold on historical reality. The elements that appear to be historical (the fear of the Huns, the betrayal of the otherwise unknown Rosomoni) were added from the contemporary account of Ammianus Marcellinus (*Res gestae*, 31.3.1–2) and the classical commonplace that alleged national perfidy to explain away embarrassing defeats. The defection of Sunilda's husband and her dismemberment between chariots were modeled specifically on a passage in Livy (*Ab urbe condita*, 1.27.9–10). This combination of Roman ideology with the Gothic lay was presumably effected in Jordanes' source, the lost Gothic history of Cassiodorus, and is symptomatic of Cassiodorus' viewpoint.[9] When the Roman features are stripped away, the remaining skeleton does not conflict with *Hamðismál*. It therefore seems likely that Jordanes or Cassiodorus was working from a version of the story essentially identical with *Hamðismál*. If so, we may conclude that heroic poetry was fully formed in the sixth century.

The passage from Jordanes is also valuable because it suggests the nature of the affinities between history and heroic legend. Whatever the precise circumstances of Ermanaric's death, he was a real figure and reigned over the Ostrogoths in the fourth century. His person is not a later fiction, although there is no reason to believe that the details of his death reported by Jordanes and later sources have any foundation in fact. This rule seems to hold true for a number of the stories in the Germanic repertory. The Gunnar of *Atlakviða* may be identified as the fifth-century Burgundian king Gundicarius (d. 435), and the name of Gunnar's father, Gjúki, is phonologically equivalent to the name given Gundicarius' father, Gibica, in the *Leges Burgundionum*. Gunnar's antagonist Atli is the Hunnish king Attila (d. 454).[10] The Dietrich of German legend, first mentioned in the *Hildebrandslied* and later an important figure in the *Nibelungenlied*, is identifiable as Theodoric the Great (d. 526), Ostrogothic king of Italy.

In contrast to such verifiable personal identities, the stories that clustered around these figures cannot be traced to any ultimate source and may be much older than the heroes themselves. The tragic meeting between father and son in the *Hildebrandslied*, for example, has narrative analogues in Persian, Irish, and Russian, and is often taken to reflect a common Indo-European tale. Regardless of their origins, the tales became attached to known kings sometime after their deaths. Ermanaric (d. 380) is the earliest of these prominent figures, and Alboin (d. 572), whose story was told by Paul the Deacon, is the latest. If a century or two were required to articulate the lays, we may assume that the formative period for Germanic heroic poetry was between 400 and 700. Important kings living after that period were not absorbed into heroic legend. Charlemagne, for example, acquired his legendary cycle only in the later French *chansons de geste*.

Because it is quite possible, as in the case of the *Hildebrandslied*, that the stories antedate their protagonists, we are not establishing literary history by positing the period 400–700 as the classical age of Germanic heroic poetry—we are merely recovering the earliest ascertainable layer. Jordanes' summary of the Ermanaric story provides assurance that the form did exist at this period; there is no definite evidence that it existed earlier. It is in any event to this layer that the surviving examples point; the period 400–700 is early enough to account for a common Germanic ancestry and for the unified prototype that spread from the Continent to England and Scandinavia.

Onomastic evidence guarantees Continental derivation. Native English and North Scandinavian heroes did not have a part in the original stock, only Continental Danes such as Hengest or Hrólfr kraki. Scholars have often supposed that heroic poetry originated specifically with the Goths, but Burgundians, Franks, and Langobards also figure prominently in the repertory. This concentration makes it clear that the central Germanic tribes were the point of diffusion for the development of the genre.

Any effort to trace the roots of heroic poetry beyond the Germanic Iron Age (400–800 A.D.) is bound to be speculative. Tacitus' informative treatise on the early Germans, *Germania* (98 A.D.), produces no evidence of the heroic poetry we know from the Migration Age. He refers only to "ancient songs" in which the Germans celebrate the god Tuisto, born from the earth (*Germania* 2), battle songs about a hero equated with the Roman Hercules (*Germania* 3), and other songs, the performance of which was called *barditus*, used to rouse courage and augur the outcome of impending battle (*Germania* 3).[11]

In a much-debated passage in his *Annales* (2.88) Tacitus also reports that Arminius, the German hero of the battle against the Romans in the Teutoburg Forest (9 A.D.), "caniturque adhuc barbaras apud gentes" (is still celebrated—in song?—among the barbarian peoples). This phrasing has often been understood to mean that Arminius was the subject of heroic poetry, but the assumption is very doubtful.[12] In the first place, the locution echoes a phrase used by Xenophon in his *Cyropaedia* (1.2.1) and may be a literary commonplace. Furthermore, as R. Reitzenstein pointed out, "the word *canere* need not mean anything more than *celebrare*."[13] The meaning would then be simply that Arminius still (something less than a century later) had a great reputation among the Germans. Such a usage is borne out by a distich in Ovid's *Ars amandi* (2.739–40), in which *cantare* (largely identical in meaning with *canere*) is used as a synonym for *celebrare*:

> Me vatem celebrate, viri, mihi dicite laudes,
>   Cantetur toto nomen in orbe meum.

> (Celebrate me as a poet, men, and utter my praises; let my name be sung in all the world.)

The same sense of *canere* may be found at the beginning of book 4 of Fredegar's *Chronicle*, referring to the fame of King Guntramn: "tante prosperetatis regnum tenuit ut omnes etiam uicinas gentes ad plinitudinem de ipso laudis canerent" (he maintained a reign of such prosperity that even the neighboring peoples sang his praises in abundance).[14]

It is in the light of this usage that we must also understand a passage from Cassiodorus frequently read as evidence of heroic poetry (*Variae* 8.9—from 526): "Extat gentis Gothicae huius probitatis exemplum: Gensimundus ille toto orbe cantabilis, solum armis filius factus, tanta se Hamalis devotione coniunxit, ut heredibus eorum curiosum exhibuerit famulatum" (there is a model of such probity among the Gothic people: Gensimundus, worthy of praise in the whole world, although adopted as a son only in arms, joined the cause of the Amali with such devotion that he performed a selfless service for their heirs).[15]

Other early allusions to Germanic song and verse are of no assistance.[16] Jordanes is the first to shed real light on the subject. In addition to his epitome of the Ermanaric story, he relates that the Gothic conquest of Scythia was told in song, that the Goths sang of the deeds of their ancestors Eterpamara, Hanala, Fritigern, and Vidigoia, and that they sang dirges for King Theodorid and Attila.[17] The most interesting item in this group is the mention of Vidigoia, of whom we learn elsewhere that he was the bravest of the Goths and perished "by the guile of the Sarmatians."[18] His name is close to that of the Witege (in MHG; OE Wudga or Widia, ON Viðga) whose role in early Germanic poetry is obscure but who came to figure prominently in the Dietrich epics of the twelfth and thirteenth centuries.[19]

After Jordanes' testimony we find no further evidence until the eighth century. *Beowulf*, customarily dated to that century, presupposes the recital of heroic lays, and a small group of references from around 800 confirms the practice. Paul the Deacon, whose knowledge of a heroic poem dealing with Alboin and Rosimund is evident in the style of his retelling, notes in another passage that Alboin acquired such fame that his glory, success in war, and bravery were still celebrated in song among the Bavarians, Saxons, and other men of the same language.[20] Since Alboin is a protagonist of a known heroic plot, we may safely assume that Paul's statement pertains to heroic poetry.

In Altfrid's *Life of Liudger* we are told that during his missionary work in Frisia around 793 Liudger was approached by a blind man named Bernlef, who was very popular with his neighbors because he "knew well how to recite to a stringed instrument [*psallendo promere*] the deeds of men of old and the battles of kings."[21] Since the cast of heroic poetry is royal and the subject strife, this description accords better with the heroic genre than any oral alternative in the eighth century. The most frequently cited and least ambiguous example comes from a monitory letter by Alcuin addressed to Bishop Higbald of Lindisfarne in 797.[22] Alcuin urges that in a religious community it is appropriate to listen to the lector and patristic writings, not to the harper or heathen songs. "What does Ingeld have to do with Christ?" With this question Alcuin supplies the contents of the heathen songs he objects to; they deal with such figures as Ingeld, known to us as a protagonist of heroic legend from *Beowulf* and Saxo Grammaticus' *Gesta Danorum* (Book 6). The recital of heroic poetry was therefore a popular entertainment in Alcuin's day.

Scarcely less famous is the reference to vernacular poetry in Einhard's *Life of Charlemagne* (Chap. 29). The biographer notes that Charlemagne recorded certain barbarian songs celebrating the deeds and wars of ancient kings: "Item barbara et antiquissima carmina, quibus veterum regum actus et bella canebantur, scripsit memoriaeque mandavit." [23] This passage has been taken to document a lost collection of German heroic poetry, all the more readily because the only German remnant of the genre, the *Hildebrandslied*, dates from the same period. An opposing view enunciated by Gerhard Meissburger holds that the reference applies not to heroic poetry but to lost poems celebrating Charlemagne's dynastic ancestors. [24] The difficulty with this theory is that there is no evidence of such historical panegyrics in the vernacular. On the other hand, Einhard's "veterum regum actus et bella" (deeds and wars of ancient kings) accord well with Altfrid's "antiquorum actus regumque certamina" (deeds of men of old and the battles of kings), which quite clearly do not refer to dynastic panegyrics.

A passage frequently connected with Charlemagne's collection comes from Theganus' biography of his son Louis the Pious (Chap. 19). [25] Theganus reports that Louis rejected the "carmina gentilia" he had learned in his youth, and refused to read, hear, or teach them. This phrasing could apply equally well to vernacular heroic poetry or to the Latin verse of the Roman poets. The sense of "carmina gentilia" is ambiguous. Alcuin refers to the heroic poems about Ingeld as "carmina gentilium," but Otfrid von Weissenburg (ca. 870) refers to the Roman poets Virgil, Lucan, and Ovid as "gentilium vates." [26] In the circumstances it seems best to make no use of Theganus' remark.

The harvest may appear meager: two clear references to heroic poems by Paul the Deacon and Alcuin, and two other references in Altfrid's *Vita Liudgeri* and Einhard's *Life of Charlemagne* that are destined to remain in some doubt. Disappointment may be tempered, however, by the realization that in the far richer legacy of Old Norse literature there is only one reference to the recital of native heroic poetry. [27] In the *Saga of St. Olaf*, Olaf asks his skald Þormóðr to recite something on the morning of the fateful battle of Stiklarstaðir (1030). Þormóðr chooses *Bjarkamál in fornu*, a heroic poem about the death of the Danish king Hrólfr kraki in a nighttime assault.[28] Snorri Sturluson sets down two stanzas of the original poem in his version of the story, but a sense of the whole poem emerges from Saxo Grammaticus' adaptation in Latin.[29] The dearth of performance reports in Scandinavia may reconcile us to the handful of references on the Continent. They are in any event enough to show that heroic poetry was known and recited throughout the Germanic world. The first decisive references are from the eighth century, but there can be little doubt that the practice was two or three centuries older. Exactly how old is again the question.

We have so far passed over the fullest and earliest record of oral recitation, which appears in the absorbing account of a mission to the court of Attila undertaken in 448 by the Greek historian Priscus.[30] Priscus describes in detail the evening entertainment that Attila provides for his guests (Bury, pp. 287–88): "When evening fell, torches were lit, and two barbarians coming forward in front of Attila sang songs they had composed, celebrating his victories and deeds of valour in war. And of the guests, as they looked at the singers, some were pleased with the verses, others reminded of wars were excited in their souls, while yet others, whose bodies were feeble with age and their spirits compelled to rest, shed tears." The subject of these songs is not "the deeds of men of old and the battles of kings" but the contemporary achievements of the living king Attila; it is panegyric poetry. On the other hand, the idea has frequently been entertained that the two singers were Gothic and their performance Germanic, this chiefly on the basis of indications that Gothic as well as Hunnish was spoken and understood at Attila's court (Bury, pp. 283 and 288).

Such a supposition cannot be disproved, but it seems more likely that the songs were performed in Attila's own tongue.[31] Priscus's report cannot therefore be used to document Germanic practice directly, but an analogy remains attractive. If Hunnish entertainment included warrior songs, the Germanic repertory of the same period, and presumably at the same kind of court, may not have been very different. Furthermore, the situation in Priscus's narrative is similar to what we find in *Beowulf*. Beowulf's victory over Grendel, like Attila's unspecified victories, is celebrated in song (vv. 853–97), and the evening entertainment in the king's hall includes a recitation of *The Fight at Finnsburg* (vv. 1,008–1,162).

If the argument by analogy is allowable, we may suppose that the recitation of heroic deeds, both contemporary and ancient, was customary in Germanic Migration Age courts. The mid-fifth century is about the earliest moment at which we can imagine the Germanic heroic lay in its classical form. Priscus's eyewitness account dates from seventy years after the death of Ermanaric. At that time the story of Hamðir and Sǫrli, which was full-blown a century later according to the testimony of Jordanes, may just have been attaining the shape we know.[32]

Before the fifth and sixth centuries there is no documentary evidence to guide us in determining the early literary developments. An absence of references to heroic poetry does not of course preclude its existence. On the other hand, literary traditions are not static. They are created, evolve, and decline with altering social conditions. If we survey the general conditions of the Germanic world in the early centuries of our era, we can make a case for believing that heroic poetry was plausible in the social framework of the Migration Age, but not before. Heroic poetry appears as a royal entertainment, for and about kings and their retainers, but Germanic kingship and the king's retinue were relatively late institutions. If they were the seedbed of heroic poetry, that poetry must also be late.

Pooling information from Caesar and Tacitus, E. A. Thompson tried to establish in broad outline the nature of Germanic life before the period of tribal irruptions across the Roman borders that marked the end of the Roman Empire.[33] The Germans were pastoralists depending chiefly on their herds and on hunting, while agriculture was relatively undeveloped. The Iron Age in northern Europe is dated from about 400 B.C., but this metal continued to be in short supply, and the bronze of an earlier age persisted in the manufacture of tools and weapons. There is no reason to believe that the Germans were literate in the early Iron Age, and it seems unlikely that the runic alphabet, the earliest examples of which date from the first or second century, had come into common use. Tacitus mentions some markings on wooden staves used for the purpose of augury, but these markings were presumably ideograms, not alphabetic characters.

If we try to form a picture of Germanic social organization, we may infer that differences in wealth were slight and that there was no private ownership of land. Each year the leading men, whom the Romans referred to as "magistrates," decided what part of the common land to till and allocated portions to the various clans. The allocated portions were not divided among individuals and the harvest was presumably made in common. As a result there must have been a fairly even distribution of resources and no monopolization on the part of the leaders. Caesar seems to suggest an absence of tensions that might accrue from an inequitable division. In his day there were no chieftains, only village elders, one of whose functions must have been to arbitrate disputes. In times of crisis a council assembled to make military decisions, but it is uncertain whether such a council was convened on any regular basis. There is in any case no evidence of strong personal authority or administrative coercion.

This situation changed as contact with the Roman south became more frequent and Germany began to adjust to the Roman impingement on her economy and institutions. The change is reflected in the differences between Caesar's earlier impressions and the report given by Tacitus in 98 A.D. At that time land was no longer distributed by clan but, says Tacitus, "according to social standing" (*Germania* 26). That is to say, in the intervening 150 years some latitude had developed for the individual to emerge from the community in terms of relative importance. Even in Caesar's time trade for luxuries had existed. This trade must have increased substantially with the presence of the Romans on the Rhine, leading to an increased concentration of wealth among the more powerful members of the community, wealth in the form of glass, bronze, textiles, ceramics, wine, weapons, coins, and so forth. These things could not have been owned communally and must have accumulated in the hands of individuals, with payment most likely rendered in cattle and slaves. It is also fair to assume that agriculture and handicrafts improved in Germany with the arrival of the Romans. Indeed, archeology shows that all the basic tools and implements of this age in northern Europe were of Roman design. The four centuries from the birth of Christ to 400 A.D. are hence termed the Roman Iron Age.

As material conditions changed, some of the older institutions evolved to keep pace. A tribal council was convened on a regular basis in peacetime as well as wartime. A military chieftainship was introduced, though as an elective office and still with no provision for coercion. The electors in this arrangement were probably the assembled warriors, but the decision-making process is unclear and it is difficult to establish whether the ultimate authority lay with the chieftain, the leading men, or the rank and file of the assembly; perhaps these classes were not yet so differentiated as to constitute contending parties.

A degree of differentiation was, however, introduced by the formation of military retinues. In Caesar's day there were only voluntary and spontaneous raiding parties, assembled on the spur of the moment and dissolved when the raid was over. But successful raids, along with expanded commerce, produced an increment of wealth that made possible the establishment of regular military forces. These were in existence by the time Tacitus wrote. A leader was now able to feed and supply his own band of warriors, although he did not yet have land on which to settle them, as became customary in the Middle Ages.[34] Consequently the leading men in Tacitus' day had already begun to detach themselves from the business of production to form a specialized warrior class and, in peacetime, a leisure class. As the military and political contacts with the Romans increased in scale, there was a tendency to concentrate power in the hands of individual chieftains, who were better able to cope directly with the new pressures than were the tribal institutions of the earlier period. It had become necessary to develop some decision-making process that was more centralized and efficient in handling the increasingly complicated negotiations with the Romans. This consolidation of power in Germany led eventually to the emergence of the great Germanic kings of the Migration Age.

Such considerations provide only the most general context for literary speculations, and Karl Heinz Ihlenburg has countered with sociohistorical arguments for the existence of heroic poetry before the Migration Age.[35] He adverts to the possibility of poems about Arminius and argues that the heroic mentality would have been present among the Germanic warriors of the raiding age, before the advent of the military retinue. Yet it seems unlikely that a type of poetry so definitely predicated on the court situation, on the bonds joining lord and retainer, and on the military profession should have originated in the communal society of early Germany. This poetry is more obviously connected with the life of the Migration Age, in which the military class had become organized and important, and in which the retinue was the focal institution. Given the growth of military culture and a class of warriors with separate status, it is only natural to suppose that this group also acquired its own literary form. Heroic poetry fills the slot nicely. Whether it evolved gradually out of an antecedent form, such as panegyric verse or heroic tales of a different stamp, or whether it was newly invented by one or more poets of special powers cannot be determined. However it came into being, the evidence suggests that it flourished between the fifth and eighth centuries and became a repository of stories on which the poets of the High Middle Ages continued to draw, just as they drew on the classical, Carolingian, and Arthurian traditions.

2. From Lay to Epic

Roughly speaking, the *Nibelungenlied* is twenty-five times the length of the corresponding Eddic poems, *Sigurðarkviða in forna* for Part I and *Atlakviða* for Part II. There has never been any question about the relative chronology of these texts; the Eddic lays represent an earlier stage, the *Nibelungenlied* a later development. The question is rather, How did such a radical expansion of the narrative come about? The issue was resolved in the nineteenth century in terms of the rhapsodic theory, that is, the view that epic arose from the concatenation of short lays attached end to end. Thus Karl Lachmann conceived of the *Nibelungenlied* as an amalgamation of twenty episodic poems arranged to form an epic.[1] In 1905 Andreas Heusler successfully dismantled Lachmann's theory and replaced it with the argument that epic tells the same story as the short lay but achieves new dimensions through even increments of detail throughout the narrative. New characters are added, more dialogue is introduced, interstices in action and motivation are filled in, and so forth.[2]

Heusler's view has not been explicitly revised, but it has been implicitly challenged by the rise of the oral-formulaic theory in Homeric studies.[3] Just as the rhapsodic theory was once transferred from Homeric studies to the *Nibelungenlied*, so the oral-formulaic theory of Homeric composition has been transferred to Germanic epic in more recent times. The oral-formulaic idea derives from the observation, originally made by Milman Parry and elaborated by Albert Lord, that Yugoslav epic is composed by methods of oral improvisation based on the singer's ability to internalize certain poetic patterns and vary them on the spur of the moment to fit any new context. This observation relieves us of the difficult supposition that an illiterate performer could memorize thousands of lines of verse and reproduce them on command. Instead we may suppose that he created the epic anew for each recitation by keeping the plot in mind and improvising the exact wording as the inspiration of the moment and a rich poetic experience dictated. The question has naturally arisen whether such a practice, which appears quite secure in the Yugoslav tradition and is hypothetically attractive in its application to Homer, provides a useful framework for understanding the development of medieval epic.[4]

In 1953 Francis P. Magoun, Jr., a Harvard colleague of Milman Parry and Albert Lord, extended the oral-formulaic theory to Anglo-Saxon verse.[5] He argued that *Beowulf* showed the same kind of repetitive ("formulaic") patterns that Parry observed in the language of Homer and the Yugoslav performers and that these patterns could be explained in the same way. That is, the poet had a ready stock of phrases with which to render the standard situations in his story. There has subsequently been a great deal of debate on whether the application of the oral-formulaic theory to Anglo-Saxon is appropriate. Are the type and density of "formulicity" in Old English really analogous to the Homeric evidence? How much "formulicity" is required to demonstrate oral composition? In 1966 Larry D. Benson showed that Old English poems manifestly translated or reworked from Latin exemplars (notably the *Meters of Boethius*) are just as formulaic as *Beowulf*.[6] If this is true, should we consider *Beowulf* to be less literary and more oral than the *Meters of Boethius*? Or should we not rather consider that they are both written in a stylized poetic mode peculiar to the Anglo-Saxons? In other words, should we not consider that "formulicity" can be a feature of literary style as well as oral style?

The peculiar difficulty in applying oral-formulaic theory to Germanic poetry lies in the irreconcilability of improvised composition with our information about the earliest history of that poetry. Vernacular epic has always stood in the shadow of classical philology and has therefore lent itself to hypotheses devised in the first instance for Homer, but Germanic poetry offers the literary historian definite advantages over Homer.[7] We have only the Homeric poems and nothing before them, no textual history against which to evaluate them. We do, however, have something approaching a history of Germanic poetry. There are the tantalizing remnants of and references to early poetry surveyed in the previous chapter. Most importantly, Jordanes, writing in 551, tells a story of Ermanaric that can be compared to later poems (notably the Eddic *Hamðismál*) and can be seen to incorporate a Germanic poem from the sixth century. This and all other early references (including those in *Beowulf*) presuppose short poems. Nowhere is there any reference to Germanic epic of the sort requiring oral-formulaic composition.

We have seen in the previous chapter that the form and characteristics of the common Germanic lay can be roughly identified on the basis of the earliest extant examples: *Fight at Finnsburg, Hildebrandslied, Atlakviða,*

Hamðismál, Brot af Sigurðarkviðu, and *Hlǫðskviða.* The evidence of these poems suggests that the prototype was short and dramatic, not epic. The only question is whether the short lay was orally improvised along the lines of the Parry-Lord hypothesis and then transmitted formulaically, or whether it was composed word by word by individual poets and transmitted memorially, subject of course to memorial lapses.

We observed in Chapter 1 that *The Fight at Finnsburg* and the *Hildebrandslied* share a phrase ("gyrde hine his swurde" / "gurtun sih iro suert ana"). This phrase could be taken to represent an oral formula and to signal oral-formulaic composition, but the corpus of old heroic poetry is far too small to allow for oral-formulaic analysis. Such analysis presupposes a corpus large enough to permit us to study statistically the density of formulas. Where an insufficient sample exists, we cannot distinguish between a literary commonplace and an oral formula. Furthermore, the theory of oral-formulaic composition was devised to explain a volume of poetry that would appear to defy memorization. In the Germanic lay of one or two hundred verses there is no necessity to invoke such a hypothesis. Memorization is the most natural vehicle. In favor of formulaic composition it could be argued, by analogy, that the Norse skalds were in the habit of improvising their verse. But this improvisation was confined to single stanzas, and we will see that when the skalds composed longer poems they required time to reflect and commit the composition to memory.

The fullest description of deliberate composition and memorization is found in *Egils saga Skalla-Grímssonar,* which was written at the best guess between 1220 and 1240. The saga relates how the skald Egill came to the court of Erik Bloodax in York despite a previous history of irreconcilable hostilities. Egill is in imminent danger of execution and is advised by his friend Arinbjǫrn to placate the offended king by composing a so-called "head-ransom" poem in his honor. Egill retires for the night to perform the task, but when Arinbjǫrn inquires about his progress, he complains that a swallow has been twittering at his window and distracting him. Arinbjǫrn accordingly spends the night with him to ensure quiet: "Arinbjǫrn sat there all night at the window until it dawned, and after Arinbjǫrn came, Egill composed the whole praise poem and fastened it in his mind so that he could recite it in the morning."[8] We learn from this passage that the composition of a longer poem (twenty stanzas) was assumed to require time, concentration, and an active effort at memorization.

Egill's poem is a skaldic composition and cannot be used uncritically to illuminate the conditions under which heroic poetry was created and passed on, but the only account of a heroic recitation in the Germanic world would appear to second *Egils saga* in arguing memorial transmis-

sion. When recounting how Þormóðr performed *Bjarkamál in fornu*, before the battle of Stiklarstaðir, Snorri Sturluson records only the first few
lines of the poem: "Ok er þetta upphaf," he writes, "and this is the beginning"—"Dagr es upp kominn / Dynja hana fjaðrar" (The sun has risen /
The cock beats his wings).[9] There is no doubt about how the poem continues because everybody knows it by heart. Snorri needs only to cite the
opening stanzas in order to recall the piece to memory. Fixed transmission
is further bespoken by Saxo Grammaticus' Latin rendering of *Bjarkamál*
in his Danish chronicle *Gesta Danorum* (ca. 1200).[10] Indeed, Saxo's very
role as translator presupposes a memorized heroic poem rather than the
formulaic re-creation of heroic stories on the Yugoslav model.

The only evidence of Germanic epic is therefore *Beowulf* itself. Magoun
tacitly assumed that the poem could be projected as a whole into the oral
stage, although he later broke it into smaller units on the ground that oral
singers do not compose cyclic poems.[11] Edward Haymes explicitly criticized Heusler for positing the short lay as the original form on the basis
of the *Poetic Edda* and substituted *Beowulf* as the touchstone of early
Germanic practice.[12] This criticism of Heusler misses the mark, because
Heusler based his supposition not just on the *Poetic Edda* but equally on
the *Hildebrandslied* and *Finnsburg*. His theory has the advantage of a
threefold documentation in German, English, and Icelandic, whereas
Haymes's theory depends on one poem in one branch of Germanic.

The postulate that there was such a thing as oral epic in Germanic has
haunted much of the work done by Anglo-Saxonists, whose purview has
not always included German and Norse materials. As a rule they have
failed to address the problem involved in making the anomalous *Beowulf*
a standard for judging Germanic poetry. The only scholar to face the issue
squarely is John D. Niles. He argues that, beginning in the late seventh
century, the economic well-being and increased availability of patronage
in England allowed for the development of a new and longer oral form of
poetry alongside the old memorial short form.[13] This new long form culminated in *Beowulf*, which Niles dates in the tenth century. In other
words, because of growing prosperity and a relatively early cultural preeminence in the Germanic world, England became a special case.

It is not impossible that England fostered a poetic innovation at the
oral level, but many scholars have found it easier to explain *Beowulf* as a
strictly literary, bookish development. The debate is made difficult by the
uncertain dates of almost all Anglo-Saxon poems. They are for the most
part preserved in tenth-century manuscripts, but the dates of composition
may fall in any period from the late seventh to the late tenth century.
Since the relative chronology is so insecure, it is hard to establish the literary context of *Beowulf* and to guess what models were available to the

poet. The comparable works fall into two groups: biblical poems (*Genesis A* and *B*, *Exodus*, *Daniel*, *Judith*), and hagiographic poems (*Andreas*, *Juliana*, *Elene*, *Guthlac*). Most of these texts are rather long, certainly longer than we allow for the Germanic heroic lay. *Genesis A* comprises 2,318 verses and is generally considered to be older than *Beowulf*. In addition, all these poems are translated or paraphrased from Latin models and are therefore a literary phenomenon quite comprehensible without reference to oral-formulaic theory. If *Genesis A* or any one of the other poems was written before *Beowulf*, the idea of writing a long poem would not have been strange to the *Beowulf* poet. The long form would have been a literary currency readily available to him.

But *Beowulf* is, in distinction to the other Old English poems, a secular epic. As such it should perhaps not be derived from biblical or hagiographic models. Those who believe in the literary provenance of *Beowulf* have therefore often located the epic inspiration in Virgil's *Aeneid*, a book that would have been available to an educated Anglo-Saxon. This hypothesis has, however, remained a matter of conviction and is no more susceptible of proof than the existence of an Anglo-Saxon oral epic composed by the oral-formulaic method.[14]

In considering the probabilities, the proponent of literary genesis may well begin by asking the oral-formulist how it came about that the Anglo-Saxons at the end of the seventh century invented a type of poetic diction that has no precedent in Germanic but bears a startling resemblance to Yugoslav and (hypothetically) Greek practice. The age of Bede in England already had a highly developed literature, and it seems unlikely that the poets of that age would have reinvented a preliterate form of diction. It would not have been a simple matter of transposing the conventional system of diction from the short lay to the longer epic, because the short lay was a memorial form. It was composed deliberatively, memorized by the composer and listener, and passed on from one generation to the next by memory. There is no latitude for oral-formulaic composition in this process. Indeed, wherever the oral-formulaic theory is applied to medieval European literature, proponents have failed to explain how this method of composition was newly invented or evolved out of the short form—how, in other words, a memorial culture became an oral-formulaic culture in a literate period.

Niles's assumption of oral-formulaic epic alongside the memorized lay therefore seems preferable to the assumption that oral-formulaic composition was the rule in short as well as long forms. But the question remains whether oral-formulaic composition is really a necessary premise in explaining the genesis of *Beowulf*. As a narrative text *Beowulf* does not in fact lend itself readily to the oral-formulaic surmise. It is not a unified, straightforward story like the Yugoslav epics. The composition is notoriously vexed—disjointed, discontinuous, and interrupted by digressions. Even the skeleton would be difficult to keep in mind for oral recreation. Such idiosyncrasies do not suggest the free flow of oral story or the likelihood of popular consumption. The plot includes three momentous fights between Beowulf and successive monsters; the last two are not only separated by fifty years and a national boundary but stand in no causal relationship to one another. The historical, genealogical, and literary allusions are recondite, the presentation rich in moral sentiment. *Beowulf* is not the performance we might expect from a singer of tales shortly after the invention of the long form.[15] It could of course be argued that the very complexities of the poem devolve from a practice not yet sufficiently refined, but there has never been any doubt among Anglo-Saxonists that the poetic power and vision of the *Beowulf* poet exceed anything else in Old English by a wide margin.

These considerations suggest that a literary derivation of *Beowulf* has advantages, if the case can be made. Whether we explain *Beowulf* from literary or oral antecedents, however, the underlying problem remains the same: bridging the gap between the original short form and the later long form. The following argument assumes that *Beowulf* was built up from the short form by literary means and tries to account for the procedure. Such an assumption posits no unknown quantities. Scholars have long recognized that *Beowulf* presupposes and subsumes the older short form. At the very least it is clear that the poet knew of classical heroic lays because he alludes to or partially retells several (Sigemund's dragon slaying, *The Fight at Finnsburg*, and the story of Ingeld). Joseph Harris has suggested that the poet programmatically recapitulated, in a sort of encyclopedic mosaic, all or most of the earlier short forms—genealogy, creation hymn, elegy, lament, heroic lay, praise poem, flyting, boast, and so forth.[16] This is a very bookish procedure indeed. But how, in detail, did the poet transmute short form into epic?

As the half-lines "gyrde hine his swurde" / "gurtun sih iro suert ana," cited from *Finnsburg* and *Hildebrandslied* in the previous chapter, constitute what the oral-formulaic analysts would call a formula, the larger context of arming and going into battle constitutes a theme.[17] Although the formula is not documented in Norse, the theme appears, for example, in *Atlamál* 42:

> Flycþuz þeir Atli   oc fóro í brynior,
> gengo svá gorvir,   at var garðr milli. . . .
>
> (Atli drew up his men and they donned their byrnies; they
> went fully armed where the stockade stood between them.)

When the theme is transferred from the short lay to epic, it appears in expanded form. Thus in *Waltharius* (vv. 537–41) the hero is awakened as the hostile Franks approach, arms himself, and practices with vigorous flourishes:

> Ipse oculos tersos somni glaucomate purgans
> Paulatim rigidos ferro vestiverat artus
> Atque gravem rursus parmam collegit et hastam
> Et saliens vacuas ferro transverberat auras
> Et celer ad pugnam telis prolusit amaram.
>
> (Wiping away the shades of sleep from his eyes, he deliberately encased his hardy limbs in armor and gathered up again his heavy shield and spear, and leaping up he whipped the empty air with steel and swiftly exercised his arms as a prelude to the bitter fight.)

Something in the style of the *Hildebrandslied* may have been in the German original of this passage, but it has been completely transformed by the fuller conventions of Virgilian epic.

Fuller still is Beowulf's arming as he sets out to do battle with Grendel's mother (*Beowulf*, vv. 1,441–72). The passage begins with the familiar formula:

> Gyrede hine Beowulf
> eorlgewædum,   nalles for ealdre mearn.
>
> (Beowulf girded himself with his armor; he feared not at all for his life.)

In the heroic lay this preparation would suffice, and the hero would proceed directly into battle, but the epic poet dwells on the scene. He specifies exactly that the armor is intended to protect his body against the "battle-grip" of an enemy in Grendel's mere (vv. 1,443–47). His helmet too is designed for the plunge, but its manufacture and ornamentation are also described at some leisure (vv. 1,448–54). The greatest praise, however, is reserved for the sword Hrunting that Unferth lends Beowulf for the enterprise (vv. 1,455–71). At the conclusion of the arming the poet then returns to the original formula (vv. 1,471–72):

> Ne wæs þæm oðrum swa,
> syðþan he hine to guðe   gegyred hæfde.
>
> (The other man [Beowulf] was not of this mind [scil. as cowardly as Unferth] when he had girded himself for battle.)

A traditional formula has thus been opened up to allow for the insertion of thirty lines of new detail. The poet shows how epic breadth can be achieved with the addition of information on the function of weapons, their manufacture, the circumstances in which they are acquired—in short, the history of the weapons. His procedure illustrates Heusler's idea of interstitial expansion.

Another important concept in the oral-formulaic arsenal is the type scene, a term used to describe a recurrent scene always elaborated with the same or similar poetic means.[18] By its very generic nature the Germanic heroic lay is a limited form with a circumscribed morphology and a stereotypical scenic inventory. A survey of the English, German, Norse, and Latin remnants reveals the following stock: (1) battle scenes in the open, (2) hall scenes of conviviality or celebration, (3) hall battles, (4) journeys in quest of heroic confrontation, (5) sentinel scenes, (6) welcoming scenes, (7) dispatching of messengers and intermediaries, (8) consultation of the hero with kings or queens, (9) incitations or flytings, and (10) leave-taking scenes. These ten scene types account for most of the action in the old heroic lay.[19] They also account for most of the action in *Beowulf*. One difference is that the *Beowulf* poet uses each type, which normally occurred just once in a heroic lay, repeatedly, thus enlarging the dimensions of the poem without expanding the scenic resources. His repertory is traditional; only the scope is new.

To some extent, then, the increased length of *Beowulf* accrues from repetition. But the added length also reflects an expansion of individual narrative units. In simplest terms the poem is a concatenation of battles between Beowulf and three successive opponents. Each battle is equivalent to the main action of the old heroic lay, represented in its most elementary form by the *Hildebrandslied*. But whereas the fragmentary *Hildebrandslied* runs to sixty-eight lines, and was not much longer as a whole, each battle sequence in *Beowulf* occupies roughly four hundred lines.

The armed encounter was a mainstay of Germanic poetry. That it existed as a standard narrative unit in England at an early stage is suggested not only by its recurrence in a number of poems but by its appearance in full-blown form in *Genesis A* (vv. 1,982–2,009).[20] This passage embodies the single most elaborate departure from the poet's biblical model and implies that he knew quite independently how to stage a battle description. From the barest indications in Genesis 14.8–11 (a campaign of four kings against the kings of Sodom and Gomorrah in the Valley of Siddim) he contrives to develop a regular battle narrative, including the rejoicing of the birds of prey, the clash of armies, the tumult of arms, the slaughter of comrades, the flight of the men of Sodom and Gomorrah, and the plundering by the victors. If the usual dating of *Genesis A* to around 700 is correct, this method of visualizing a battle was already established in the earliest period of recorded Old English poetry.

The description in *Genesis A* is only twenty-seven lines long, but the same sequence reappears at double that length in other Old English poems. We find the pattern embedded in *Elene* (vv. 99–150) and *Judith* (vv. 289–349) and developed independently in *The Battle of Brunan-burh* (73 verses). An even lengthier version, used in metaphorical terms, appears in *Exodus* (vv. 447–590). The 325 verses (perhaps four hundred in the original) of *The Battle of Maldon* evince the greatest elasticity of all. Here too the outline remains the same—marshalling of troops, birds of prey, battle action, slaughter, flight—but each section undergoes some form of elaboration. The poet expands the assembling and marshalling of troops to twenty-four lines largely by the device of singling out particular warriors for individual comment. The actual battle is delayed for some one hundred lines while the Vikings negotiate with the English. Casualties are itemized so that an account of the slaughter that requires only ten lines in *Brunanburh* occupies seventy-three lines in *Maldon*. Similarly, the poet identifies individual fugitives, and this additional information adds a hundred and twenty-four lines to the flight from the battlefield.

We may conclude then that battle description is a flexible narrative unit in Old English literature. While adhering to the same sequence of traditional motifs, it may be as short as twenty-seven lines in *Genesis A* or as long as the approximately four hundred lines of *Maldon*. In approaching *Beowulf*, we discover that the poet was master of both the short and the long form. His description of the battle of Ravenswood (vv. 2,922–98) echoes the language and approximates the length of the equivalent passages in *Elene*, *Judith*, and *Brunanburh*, which exemplify the short form. But in portraying Beowulf's three major combats, the poet broadens the form and attains the dimensions of *Maldon*. The fight with Grendel absorbs about 370 verses (702–1,070), the fight with Grendel's mother roughly four hundred verses (1,383–1,784), and the fight with the dragon another 380 verses (2,510–2,891), all in all some 1,150 verses, or more than a third of the whole poem.

Wrestling matches with monsters and a duel with a dragon are not strictly comparable with the clash of armies, but the *Beowulf* poet uses the standard description in an imaginative way, just as the *Exodus* poet capitalizes on this stock sequence in evoking the collision of the Red Sea with the Egyptian warriors. In *Beowulf* too each battle is thematized in terms of the traditional contrast between the enemy's flight and the triumph, even exultation, of the victor. Grendel struggles again and again to flee, and finally succeeds only at the cost of an arm, which remains behind as a trophy to focus Beowulf's triumph. The battle with the dragon, like *The Battle of Maldon*, is constructed on the contrasting behavior of the fugitive warriors and the faithful companion or companions. The dragon's hoard stands in for Grendel's arm and does service as the victor's plunder.

Seen as an elaboration on a traditional scenic repertory and flexible type scenes, *Beowulf* requires no presumption of a fully developed oral epic. The building blocks were available in the memorial lay and needed only to be expanded and multiplied in order to appear as something like epic. This literary procedure was adumbrated in Old English biblical and hagiographic epic and was applicable to secular poetry, as *Maldon* illustrates. We need not posit short and long forms at the oral stage, only the ability of the literate Anglo-Saxon poets to translate their experience of the Latin long forms (whether Bible or *Aeneid*) into equivalent native forms. That the English were the first Germanic people to carry out this project is not surprising, because they were the first to acquire medieval Latin culture.

If the English acquired an epic impulse through Latin learning, we might expect a similar development in the other two Germanic cultures, Germany and Scandinavia. The analogy holds true, at least for Germany. The revival of learning mediated by Latin literature occurred in Germany about a century later than in England, but it had a broadly similar impact. Instead of Old Testament epics based on Genesis, Exodus, and Daniel, Germany favored the New Testament and produced very substantial gospel harmonies: the Old Saxon *Heliand* (ca. 830) and Otfrid von Weissenburg's *Evangelienbuch* (ca. 870). But the Old Testament was not entirely neglected, as the fragmentary Old Saxon *Genesis* illustrates, supplemented by an Old English *Genesis B* translated from the Old Saxon. Biblical epic was thus quite as vital in Germany as in England. What we do not have in Germany is secular epic in the vernacular, but it should be borne in mind that the sum-total difference in the production of such epics in England and Germany is exactly one.

The idea of secular epic was in any event no less familiar in Carolingian Germany than in Anglo-Saxon England, although the German realizations of the idea were confined to Latin. Most nearly comparable to *Beowulf* are the 1,456 hexameters of *Waltharius*, a heroic poem most likely from the ninth century, and therefore contemporary with the *Heliand* and Otfrid's *Evangelienbuch*. Like *Beowulf*, *Waltharius* draws its fable from Germanic heroic legend (the same legend reflected in the Old English *Waldere* fragments), but, though quasi-epic in scope, it has never prompted the supposition of an underlying Germanic epic.[21] The language and epic devices mirror Virgil and Statius too clearly. *Waltharius* is therefore a counterpart to *Beowulf*; it shows that the short memorial lay of Germanic tradition acquires epic sweep not from an oral-formulaic long form but from Latin epic models.

The situation in Scandinavia is different by virtue of belatedness. Because Latin learning did not annex Scandinavia until the twelfth century, the old memorial lay survived longer in the North and remained the standard form throughout the twelfth century. When Icelandic poets began to experiment with longer forms at the end of that century, they drew their epic inspiration not from Latin or biblical narrative but from the growth of vernacular narrative in Germany. Here the short memorial lay of the Germanic age was developing into a longer written heroic poem. At the end of the twelfth century, knowledge of these longer German poems spread to Scandinavia, where many of the same heroic tales still circulated in the short form. Spurred to emulate the epic fashion, the Icelandic poets set about revising their shorter versions in accordance with the new standard. As a result, the short *Atlakviða* in forty-three stanzas was recast as the relatively long *Atlamál* in 105 stanzas. Similarly, a short poem on the death of Sigurd (*Sigurðarkviða in forna*) was first expanded into a poem of seventy-seven stanzas (*Sigurðarkviða in skamma*) and then into a poem of two hundred or more stanzas (*Sigurðarkviða in meiri*).[22] These Icelandic experiments never attained the dimensions of real epic, or even of short epic in the range of *Beowulf* or *Waltharius*, but they attest an epic consciousness, a sense that the long form was a new literary venture. They also show that the method for developing epic continued to be the same—expansion of the short memorial lay through the addition of new characters, new scenes, and new dialogue.

As long ago as 1896 W. P. Ker recognized the epic aspirations in *Atlamál*: "The significance of the *Atlamál* is considerable in the history of the Northern poetry. It may stand for the furthest mark in one particular direction; the epic poetry of the North never got further than this. If *Beowulf* or *Waldere* may perhaps represent the highest accomplishment of epic in Old English verse, the *Atlamál* has, at least, as good a claim in the other language."[23] The idea that *Atlamál* constitutes an attempt at epic is borne out by a comparison with *Atlakviða*.[24] The difference does not lie in an altered plot—both poems cover the same ground in the same order. *Atlamál* acquires its new dimensions through the mechanical insertion of new material: new characters, monitory dreams, and new dialogue chiefly between husbands and wives. In addition, the poet expands the departure of the Burgundians from one to seven stanzas and adds the killing of the messenger Vingi and a pitched battle between Huns and Burgundians. All of the new stanzas can be deleted without affecting the understanding of the poem. As in *Beowulf*, we are able to reconstruct the expansion procedure in some detail.

There is nothing mysterious about the evolution of epic in the Germanic world. It happens at different times in different parts of this world, in the eighth century in England, the ninth century in Germany, and the twelfth century in Iceland, but the rules remained the same. The point of departure was the short memorial lay. This form germinated when it came into contact with Latin narrative or, in Iceland, German vernacular narrative, but it never blossomed into full-fledged epic along Homeric or even Yugoslav lines. The products remained cramped and sporadic, as befits an artificial genre. To call the 3,182 lines of *Beowulf* "epic" testifies more to a wishful thought than to a generic reality. There is no magic number of lines to qualify for the epic class, but something closer to ten thousand might be a normal expectation. The resources of Germanic vernacular art fell far short of any such standard. The *Beowulf* poet encountered the same limitations of the older form that prevented the late Eddic poets from breaking through to real epic around 1200. It was reserved for the *Nibelungenlied* poet to overcome the last resistance of Germanic brevity, but he did not accomplish epic form in a single leap. Other poets had prepared the way for him.

His main source was the "Ältere Not," a lost short epic. As we will see in Chapter 6, the "Ältere Not" in turn grew out of a combination of a short heroic lay attested by Saxo Grammaticus (see pp. 252–55 below) with the first Dietrich epic, which supplied the figures of Rüdeger and Dietrich. We are thus in a position to observe the same gradual expansion that we observed in the Old English battle descriptions or the progressive growth of the Icelandic Sigurd poems.

But the elaboration of the "Ältere Not" into Part II of the *Nibelungenlied* did not exhaust the process of epic accrual. The final epic dimension was achieved with the addition of the Siegfried story in Part I, which was also elaborated from a short memorial form, this time with the aid of narrative insertions taken in large measure from Part II. The imitative procedure was clear even to the medieval caption writer of the so-called "Darmstädter Aventiurenverzeichnis," who noted that Kriemhild's banquet invitation in Part II duplicates Brünhild's similar invitation in Part I.[25] The poet drew liberally on the Fall of the Burgundians in creating epic fullness for Part I. He borrowed structural concepts such as the bridal-quest frame, scenic concepts such as the repeated messenger sequences, and many details of phraseology.

As in the Old English and Old Icelandic traditions, the narrative resources remained largely constant; only the narrative proportions underwent a significant expansion. Out of this disproportion between static resources and a dynamic growth in dimensions arises an art of repetition and variation that bears a curious resemblance to the idiom of South Slavic epic. Such formulicity need not, however, derive from oral performance. It may be explained from the gradual growth of the linguistically and scenically limited memorial lay into something approaching epic. The process was entirely literary and can be accounted for without recourse to the oral-formulaic hypothesis.

3. The Rise of German Epic

T HE FIRST ATTEMPTS to write extended narrative in Germany date back to the era of Charlemagne's cultural revival, the so-called Carolingian Renaissance. Most of these early epic experiments were in Latin, and the chief model was Virgil's *Aeneid*, as countless echoes of Virgilian phrasing reveal. But Germany, whose tribalism was only thinly masked by Charlemagne's conquests, had neither the literary nor the political potential for national epic. The poets of the period could apply Virgilian breadth only to more restricted topics: hagiography, contemporary history, and, in one isolated case, Germanic heroic legend.

The earliest experiment, *Karolus magnus et Leo papa*, acknowledged Charlemagne's cultural ambitions by commemorating his intercession on behalf of Pope Leo III in 799. The 536 hexameter lines of this perhaps incomplete poem were written immediately after the event. They are rich in pomp and circumstance, and the Virgilian resources are deployed in lavish disproportion to the episode described, but the anonymous poet succeeded at one stroke in establishing the epic manner in Germany.[1] Later poetic treatments of contemporary history in the ninth century clearly hark back to *Karolus magnus et Leo papa*, most obviously the panegyric in honor of Louis the Pious by Ermoldus Nigellus (*In honorem Hludowici*). This poem has been nominated as the first true epic in Germany, and with its four books, totaling 2,614 verses in distichs, it does approach epic volume.[2] But like *Karolus magnus* it is episodic, jumping from one event to the next in Louis's career and contriving a series of tableaux rather then a sustained narrative. Book 1 relates Louis's consecration as king in 781, his defeat of the Basques, and his siege of Barcelona in 801. Book 2 describes his coronation as emperor in 813, his first enactments and reforms, and the installation of Pope Stephen V in 816. Book 3 is given over to a campaign against the Bretons, and Book 4 centers on the conversion of the Danish king Harald Klak in 826. These events are bound together by turgid praise rather than an underlying idea.

The fragmentary surface of history, perceived only chronologically and not thematically, was in fact never conceptualized by the Carolingian poets. They either dealt with a single episode, without causal context, or a string of episodes, with no more interconnection than a series of annalistic entries. The first pattern is illustrated by Abbo of St.-Germain's account in 1,390 hexameters of the Viking attack on Paris in 888 (*Bella Parisiacae urbis*).[3] Abbo's narrative is a sometimes tedious record of siege operations, made more unpalatable by contrived diction. His only unifying idea is the moral commonplace that barbarian attacks are caused by the sinfulness of their victims—in this case pride, lust, and the love of fine clothes (2.596–612).

The alternative to such a single episode was a chronicling of events over time. This serialization of history is illustrated by a poetic version of the *Frankish Annals* and Einhard's *Life of Charlemagne*, composed about the same time as Abbo's poem by an anonymous Saxon poet referred to as Poeta Saxo (*Annales de gestis Caroli magni imperatoris*).[4] Five books totaling 2,691 hexameters and elegiacs recount the life of Charlemagne from 771 to 814. The poet takes a nostalgic view of a golden age from the perspective of Carolingian decline at the end of the ninth century, but he does not go beyond a recapitulation of his sources.

The idea of creating epic from German legend surfaced for the first time in *Waltharius*. In 1,456 hexameters it tells the story of the champion Walter of Aquitaine, who grows up as a hostage at the court of Attila the Hun, effects his escape with his betrothed Hiltgunt, single-handedly thwarts an attack by the Frankish king Guntharius (Gunther) and twelve retainers, is reconciled with his surviving attackers, and rules happily ever after with Hiltgunt in Spain.[5] Dating this poem is one of the perennial puzzles in early German literary study, with opinions ranging from the early ninth to the early tenth century. In manner *Waltharius* is closest to *Karolus magnus et Leo papa*, but it far exceeds any Carolingian narrative in liveliness, emotional variety, and humor. With about half the poem given over to heroic battle action, it capitalizes more easily on Virgilian and Statian models than do the epic counterfeits of contemporary history. Above and beyond the battle sequences, the poet also makes ingenious use of Virgilian scenic and atmospheric effects. He sometimes succeeds in providing the fuller rhythm, the narrative tension, and the alternation of dramatic action and authorial contemplation that characterize true epic. His poem could well have served as the point of departure for a transformation of the native heroic lay into epic, but the literary revival of the ninth century seems to have been tied to the political rise of the Carolingian dynasty, and when Carolingian fortunes waned at the end of the century the poetic impulse also ebbed. A conversion of heroic lay into epic was not undertaken again until the twelfth century, when the Carolingian precedent had been lost from view. By this time the literary preconditions were quite different.

The Carolingian experiment was not confined wholly to Latin. As we saw in the last chapter, the ninth century also produced two versifications of the New Testament in the vernacular, the Old Saxon *Heliand* (ca. 830) and Otfrid's *Evangelienbuch* in South Rhine Frankish (between 863 and 871).[6] The roughly six thousand verses of the *Heliand* and the more than seven thousand verses of Otfrid's *Evangelienbuch* make these works more than twice the length of the longest Latin poems of the era, those of Ermoldus and the Poeta Saxo. The *Heliand* is of particular interest because it adheres to the alliterative verse pattern of the native Germanic heroic lay and demonstrates the capacity of that form to accommodate epic themes. Although the versification differs in detail from Anglo-Saxon practice, we must assume that the Saxon poet's model was insular biblical poetry, perhaps the Old English *Genesis A* in particular. The relationship between Old English and Old Saxon verse was, however, symbiotic. There survive 337 lines of an Old Saxon *Genesis*, and this poem was adapted in an English version, of which the extant fragment is known as *Genesis B*.

Unlike the English poet who transferred the breadth of biblical narrative to native story in *Beowulf*, the German poets seem not to have attempted heroic epic in the vernacular. To some extent epic developments in both England and Saxony may have been hindered by political events. Saxon traditions succumbed to Frankish subjugation under Charlemagne, leading to the reduction of Saxony to a dependency. Frankish political aims surely welcomed, or even inspired, a book such as the *Heliand* as an element in Christian conversion policy, but there would have been no Frankish encouragement of Saxon heroic legend. In England fuller exploitation of Germanic themes was prevented by the Norman Conquest and the change in literary language and culture. In southern Germany native themes receded before the religious preoccupations of the Cluniac reform. This tide rose through the eleventh century and washed away the epic seeds of the Carolingian Renaissance.[7]

When poets again began to explore secular epic in the twelfth century, they duplicated Carolingian precedent by applying themselves to history and legend. In tracing this recovery of epic we may distinguish three types: regional history, legendary history, and heroic history. Regional history is exemplified by two bishops' lives: the anonymous life of Anno, bishop of Cologne, and Heinrich von Veldeke's life of Servatius, bishop of Tongeren and later of Maastricht. In addition we may assign the *Kaiserchronik* to this category. Although it aspires to something more like universal history, it has a strong regional focus in Bavaria and the town of Regensburg.

Legendary history in twelfth-century Germany includes the medieval life of Alexander (*Alexanderlied*), the legend of Charlemagne's nephew and paladin Roland (*Rolandslied*), and Heinrich von Veldeke's reworking of Virgil's *Aeneid*, the *Eneide*. Although these legends are of very different provenance, they have in common their derivation from French originals. The third and last category, heroic history, signals a renewed attempt, on a more ambitious scale than *Waltharius*, to create epic from the stuff of the Germanic heroic lay. Such lays continued to be recited in the twelfth century in some form, but were not recorded and are therefore available only by inference.[8] At the same time, there are indications that short written epics were composed about Dietrich von Bern and the Fall of the Burgundians around the middle of the twelfth century. These texts are lost, and the evidence from which their contents may be pieced together will be discussed in connection with the probable sources of the *Nibelungenlied*. The only extant heroic history is a compilation centering on Dietrich von Bern and probably written in the Westphalian town of Soest near the end of the century, but even this text is preserved only in a Norse translation, the so-called *Þiðreks saga*. It subsumes both the lost Dietrich epic and the lost epic on the Fall of the Burgundians and is therefore by far the most important key to our understanding of the *Nibelungenlied*.

REGIONAL HISTORY

If the *Annolied* were no more than a bishop's biography or saint's life, it would not qualify under such a heading as regional history.[9] But it is an anomalous example of hagiography. Of its forty-nine uneven stanzas (878 rhymed verses in all) only the last sixteen are concerned with Anno (d. 1075).[10] They relate his consecration in Cologne, his virtues and trials, his vision of a seat in paradise, his death, and the miracle of a man who blasphemes against him, loses his sight, and regains it when he prays to Anno for forgiveness. There is nothing remarkable in this portion, but it is prefaced by thirty-three stanzas of general and local history.

The historical orientation is motivated by a positive and a negative design. What the poet explicitly disclaims emerges from the first stanza, in which he states that his readers have heard stories of how heroes fought, how they conquered towns, how lovers parted, and how powerful kings perished, but that it is now time for them to think of their salvation. True history thus stands in opposition to popular fiction.[11] Exactly which fictions the poet has in mind is not clear. Heroes fight with equal abandon in classical epic and the vernacular lay, but the taking of towns is more likely to refer to the siege of Troy or Alexander's campaigns than to Germanic exploits.[12] The date of the *Annolied* is too early to allow us to think of the great medieval lovers such as Tristan and Isolde; perhaps the poet is referring to the endemic separations of Hellenistic romance. This genre was familiar at an early date in the tales of *Apollonius of Tyre* or the *Pseudo-Clementines*, which we will encounter in the *Kaiserchronik*. The deaths of powerful kings are again equally characteristic of classical tradition (the career of Alexander or the epics of Lucan and Statius) and Germanic poetry. Whatever referents are intended, it is clear that the poet is striving for a more edifying alternative, and in this he adheres to the tradition of the eleventh century.

The sacred context is established in stanzas 2–7 with an account of God's creation, the story of man's temptation, fall, and salvation, and the progress of conversion, culminating in Anno's consecration at Cologne. At this point the poet digresses into the foundation of the world's great cities, not least of all Cologne, and the importance of Germany. We learn that Caesar was sent to campaign in Germany and conquered successively the Swabians, Bavarians, and Saxons (stanzas 18–28). His conquest of the Franks is prefaced by the legend of the exiled Trojans who emigrated to Frankland and founded Xanten, a "little Troy" (v. 392), which will figure prominently in the *Nibelungenlied*.[13] When Caesar is subsequently not received at Rome, he appeals to his loyal Germans, who rally to his support in a great victory over Pompey. "Since then the Germans have been welcome and in high repute at Rome" (vv. 479–80). On his succession, Augustus gives his name to Augsburg, while Agrippa founds Cologne (Colonia Agrippinensis). The foundations at Worms, Speyer, Mainz, Metz, and Trier are recorded more briefly (stanza 30). The poet then reverts to the birth of Christ and tells how Saint Peter dispatched the three holy men Eucharius, Valerius, and Maternus to preach to the Franks. They preach in Trier first, then convert Cologne, where Maternus becomes the first of thirty-four bishops who preceded Anno on the episcopal throne of that city.

Regional and municipal patriotism quite overshadow the praise of Anno in this text. In some sense he serves only to focus the greatness of his heritage. The poet's real enthusiasm is reserved for Cologne, Frankland, and the eminence of the Germans, which he documents not only from the Trojan origin shared with the Romans but also with an ingeniously parochial understanding of Caesar's career. Ethnic consciousness is not new in German literature—Otfrid too began his poem with a somewhat plaintive defense of the Franks—but in the twelfth century this particularism was destined to have a much wider literary impact.

The *Annolied* or a related text served as a point of departure for the next monument of vernacular history in Germany, the *Kaiserchronik*, composed around 1150 (or compiled then from previously composed materials).[14] Caesar's German campaign and the foundation of German cities occupy verses 252–670, but the *Kaiserchronik*, which emanated from the Bavarian town of Regensburg, asserts its regional affiliation by supplementing the list of Rhenish cities in the *Annolied* and claiming that Emperor Tiberius founded Regensburg (vv. 683–89). Whereas the *Annolied* made mention of only two emperors, Caesar and Augustus, the *Kaiserchronik* harnesses the imperial succession as the theme and organizational principle of the book, recounting the lives of no fewer than thirty-three real or fictitious Roman emperors and adding briefer biographies of the Carolingian, Ottonian, and Salian monarchs from Charlemagne's father Pippin down to the dynastic struggles of the early twelfth century (the last event mentioned is from 1146). Of a total of 17,283 lines only the last three thousand or so are devoted to the German emperors. The disproportion between Roman and German coverage is caused by the inclusion of various legends and moral tales in the earlier portion. These tales make the *Kaiserchronik* the most significant repository of popular narrative in the first half of the twelfth century and the crucial text for our understanding of the renewal of German epic. It is not practical to summarize all the tales, but four of them may be singled out to illustrate the first stages of narrative art. Three of these will recur in connection with the discussion of later twelfth-century texts. Taken together they comprise something over five thousand lines of the total of around seventeen thousand.

Our first and longest story (vv. 1,219–4,082) originates in the fourth-century Christian romance *The Recognitions of Clement* and a ninth-century *Life of Clement* derived from it.[15] The events of the story are attached to the imperial succession by the expedient of making one of the principals, Faustinianus, a brother of Emperor Claudius. Faustinianus' wife Mechthild gives birth to twins, Faustinus and Faustus. Her brother-in-law Claudius subsequently attempts to seduce her, but she rebuffs him. A third child is born and named Clement. Mechthild insists that Faustinus and Faustus be sent abroad for their education, but they suffer a shipwreck that they alone survive. Rescued by a fisherman, they conceal their identities with the assumed names Niceta and Aquila. The fisherman puts them up for sale, and a worthy matron, who has lost a son of her own, purchases and raises them in her son's stead. In the meantime, Mechthild, setting out in search of her missing boys, also becomes the sole survivor of a shipwreck. Safe ashore, she earns her keep with a poor widow for thirteen years. Faustinianus sets out in turn, only to suffer the same fate. He makes his way by selling wicker.

We learn next of Saint Barnabas' mission in Rome and the conversion of the boy Clement, who follows Barnabas east to the Holy Land. At the same time Niceta and Aquila appear before Peter the Apostle and denounce the great sorcerer Simon Magus for killing a child and keeping the corpse under his bed for magical purposes. Peter and Simon engage in a great disputation (vv. 2,156–2,590), which ends with the revelation of the child's corpse and Simon's flight into the night.

Peter now encounters Mechthild, learns her story, and reunites her with her son Clement. When Niceta and Aquila also turn up, the scene is repeated. The following morning Faustinianus joins the group as well and enters into a protracted disputation on fate, in which he is opposed successively by Peter, Niceta, Aquila, and Clement (vv. 3,090–3,820). Peter promises to produce his lost family if only he will relinquish the idea of fate; Faustinianus agrees and all the recognitions, intellectual as well as personal, combine in a single moment. Simon Magus makes one last attempt by magically transferring his own appearance to Faustinianus, but Peter restores the natural state with the sign of the Cross. He then continues his missionary work in Rome while Simon pursues his deviltry on behalf of Claudius, until after thirteen years the emperor has become so unpopular that he is poisoned by his own followers.

Of similar proportions, when allowance is made for the forty percent of the Faustinianus story given over to disputations, is a version of the widespread tale of the long-suffering queen variously called Crescentia, Constance, or Genevieve.[16] English readers know the story best from Chaucer's "Man of Law's Tale." In the *Kaiserchronik* the story is connected with the fictitious emperor Narcissus and occupies verses 11,352–12,812.

Elizabeth, wife of Emperor Narcissus, gives birth to twins, both named Dietrich. On the death of mother and father the succession is disputed and the Senate decides to award the throne to that Dietrich whom the African paragon Crescentia chooses in marriage. One Dietrich is fair, the other ill-favored, but Crescentia chooses the latter. Her new husband is obliged to campaign abroad and leaves her in the care of his brother, who promptly makes an attempt on her virtue. She resorts to the device of bidding him first construct and provision a safe tower to protect them against the outrage of the Romans. When the tower is ready, she shows him in and locks the door behind him. On the news of her husband's homecoming, however, she releases the captive to receive his returning brother, and he avails himself of the opportunity to accuse her of infidelity. The credulous husband believes his story and leaves Crescentia in the hands of her accuser. He seeks to do away with her by plunging her into the Tiber, but she is rescued by a fisherman while God strikes both brothers with leprosy.

News of the rescued woman comes to the ears of a duke, whose service she enters as a nursemaid for his child. She leads an exemplary life, but becomes the object of the steward's attempts at seduction. To avenge her

rejection of his advances, he secretly enters her chamber at night and murders the duke's child, leaving the impression that she is the murderess.
Crescentia is once again plunged into the water, and God once again pun-
ishes her tormentors with leprosy.

On the third day she washes onto a sandbar, where Saint Peter appears
and leads her back across the waters to the duke's residence. Admitted to
his sickbed in an unrecognizable state, she hears his confession, which
includes contrition for her supposed drowning. He is healed forthwith.
The steward also confesses and reveals his murder of the duke's child,
clearing the way for his execution. Crescentia proceeds to Rome, where
she effects the same cure of her leprous husband and brother-in-law. Her
husband recognizes her by a mark between her shoulders, and husband
and wife withdraw to cloisters.

Both the Faustinianus and Crescentia tales are of an international type
not confined to a particular region, but the scenes of two other tales are
specifically German or Germanic. The first is the story of the Bavarian
duke Adelger (vv. 6,622–7,135), who, under the reign of Emperor Severus, is active against the Roman Empire. As a result he is summoned to
Rome and acquiesces to the summons on the advice of a venerable counselor. Severus threatens him with death, but the Senate appeals for clem-
ency and his punishment is commuted to symbolic humiliation: his tunic
is cut off at the knees and his forelock clipped. His trusted counselor finds
the remedy by advising that all his followers appear in the same manner,
thus neutralizing the disgrace. Emperor Severus is so impressed by this
ingenious stroke that he orders the counselor transferred to his own
service.

Adelger returns to Bavaria, but evil tongues at the Roman court bring
him into renewed disfavor and he is again summoned before the emperor.
Unsure of what course to take, he dispatches a messenger in secret to seek
once more the advice of his former counselor. The counselor, having
transferred his loyalty to the emperor, protests that he cannot comply. Instead, he bids the messenger listen carefully to a tale he will tell the emperor the following day. The tale is about a man with a prize garden,
which is invaded by a stag. He is able to drive the stag off temporarily
when he succeeds in cutting off an ear and a piece of tail, but as soon as
the stag recovers the incursions recommence. This time the man catches
the stag in nets and dispatches it with a spear. A vixen makes off with the
fallen beast's heart, and when the man discovers its absence, he reports in
some confusion to his wife. She explains that if the stag had had a heart
(i.e., intelligence), he would have known better than to visit the garden
again after losing ear and tail. The messenger listens to all of this uncom-
prehendingly, but faithfully reports the story to Adelger, who understands

perfectly that he should not risk another visit to Severus' garden. Learning of Adelger's refusal to appear before him, Severus gathers a mighty army and descends on Bavaria. Adelger dispatches divisions to hold Swabians, Bohemians, and Huns at bay, then confronts the Romans and defeats them. Severus falls in this battle after a reign of seven and a half years.

The last sample tale is connected with the cycle of the great Germanic hero Dietrich von Bern (vv. 13,825–14,193). Dietrich's historical prototype was Theodoric the Great, who was charged with the pacification of Italy by Emperor Zeno and ruled there until his death in 526. In the *Kaiserchronik* the matter is historical but the flavor legendary. Zeno leaves Rome in the hands of Aetius and withdraws to Constantinople. The champion Dietrich of Meran (not Merano in Tyrolia but roughly Bosnia) refuses to serve with Attila and takes refuge in Lombardy, where his son Dietmar is born. After the death of his father and Attila, Dietmar reclaims his land in Meran. Challenged by Attila's sons Plodel and Fritele, he defeats and kills them in battle. When his son Dietrich is born, he proclaims him heir to Rome, thus provoking a confrontation with the titular emperor Zeno. The conflict is resolved by sending the child, Dietrich, to Greece as Zeno's hostage.

Aetius now quarrels with the empress and makes Odoacer king of Italy. Zeno counters by putting Dietrich in command of his army. It comes to a great showdown at Ravenna, in which Dietrich defeats Aetius and Odoacer and clears the way for his own rise to power. When Boethius, Seneca (as the historical Symmachus is named in this text), and Pope John object to the presence of a heathen king (the historical Theodoric was in fact an Arian), Dietrich responds by seizing the pope and starving him in prison. Punishment is quick to follow. Devils carry off the sinner and plunge him into a volcano, where he will burn until the Last Judgment. The poet concludes with a historical protest against those who believe that this Dietrich was contemporary with Attila, because forty-three years elapsed between the death of Attila and Dietrich's birth.

With the stories assembled in the *Kaiserchronik* we have entered a region quite distinct from the contemporary or biblical landscapes of the Carolingian age or the pseudohistory of the *Annolied*. History, whether sacred or secular, is no longer the point, despite the poet's nicety about the chronology of Attila and Dietrich. The point is rather the moral or exemplary tale. History and fiction are equally subordinated to edification, and the studied symmetries of the first three tales in particular are deployed for maximum moral effect.

The tale of Faustinianus is structured in the tradition of the Hellenistic novel of separation and reunion, but it has become a parable of Christian understanding, not just the testing of young lovers repeatedly torn apart but always faithful to each other's memory. The novel of erotic danger becomes a novel of moral elevation. Material misfortune (menial labor for the wife, wicker peddling for Faustinianus) is the precondition for spiritual progress. The setting of the story in the era of Christian conversion is not a matter of historical color but an interpretive guide. The *recognitio* of the older novel becomes both the dramatic anagnorisis of the reunited family and the recognition of Christian truth preached in the disputations. Faustinianus regains his children only when they gain him for the apostolic mission. Reunion is not the contrived climax of infinitely multipliable adventures, as in the Hellenistic novel, but the celebration of heightened understanding.

The Crescentia story in its many manifestations is typically a triumph of personal fortitude and rewarded virtue. In the *Kaiserchronik*, however, the element of spiritual progress dominates once again; erotic anecdote reappears as penitential legend.[17] The seducer discountenanced by a woman's greater guile is the stuff of later medieval fabliaux, but Crescentia demonstrates at the outset that her intelligence is not mere cunning but superior vision when she chooses the deceptively ill-favored Dietrich over his fair-featured rival. Disappointingly, her Dietrich fails to match her intelligence and allows her to fall victim to her slanderers. Just as Faustinianus is brought to wisdom by his children, Dietrich achieves true understanding only through the intercession of his wife. The child Clement lectures Faustinianus on logic, and the woman Crescentia acts as Dietrich's priest in hearing his confession and healing his infected soul. God's ways are inscrutable and his instruments miraculous. Only submission to faith reveals the truth underlying the complexities of worldly life. When all is said and done, Crescentia and Dietrich retire to separate cloisters to devote themselves wholly to this truth.

The story of Adelger is also a parable of wisdom, this time on a secular and political plane. Despite the secularization, it remains a moral fable. Most immediately it is the story of a Bavarian triumph over Roman might, a story of David and Goliath.[18] Adelger is a hopeless underdog apparently trapped in the emperor's toils, but twice he is saved by the aged counselor's wits and his own quick understanding, contrasted to the messenger's obtuseness. Just as Faustinianus' children mediate his conversion and Dietrich's wife Crescentia mediates his salvation, here the aged counselor mediates the necessary political intelligence. The new twist is that he succeeds in a quandary of loyalties. Having been transferred to the emperor's service by virtue of his superior wisdom, he is barred from his prior duty to Adelger, but he surmounts the difficulty by making the situation, in fable form, equally clear to his former and his present masters. Emperor Severus fails to penetrate the ruse, but Adelger interprets it without hesitation. Like the two previous stories, this one marks out a path to understanding, but understanding is not enough without valor. Or rather, proper understanding makes the exercise of valor possible. Once he has grasped the situation, Adelger is able to neutralize his local enemies and overcome Emperor Severus by force of arms. His political salvation is no less a result of superior knowledge than the spiritual salvation of Faustinianus and Dietrich.

The story of Dietrich of Meran may be taken as a negative illustration of the same point. It too proceeds from the new German regionalism and centers on the most prominent figure of German heroic legend. But this figure, equally dominant in history and legend, is blind to the truth, an Arian in fact and a heathen in the *Kaiserchronik*. He can conquer Italy (Adelger can do no more than defend Bavaria), but he is doomed to burn. Unlike Adelger, who perceives the wisdom of his counselor, Dietrich does not share the wisdom of Boethius, Seneca, and Pope John. By condemning them he condemns himself. Since his military action is not predicated on understanding, as Adelger's was, it ultimately fails. In all these tales from the *Kaiserchronik* the medium is popular narrative, but the paradigm is intellectual.

Some twenty years later (ca. 1170) Heinrich von Veldeke begins his life of St. Servatius of Maastricht in much the same spirit.[19] The opening prayer, not found in the Latin *vita*, uses the metaphor of sleep to describe the indolent soul mired in sin. Veldeke prays that God may send his grace to awaken us so that the eye may perceive the inner heart and we may discover the path of truth that will lead us out of darkness into light (vv. 124–31). The saint's life stands thus not only as a model of the religious life but as an example to sharpen and guide our understanding.

Taken as hagiography the text is not of great interest. Despite its length of more than six thousand verses, there is not much to be told about Servatius. He is given a fabulous ancestry as a grandnephew of John the Baptist, becomes a priest, and receives a divine call to occupy the vacant see at Tongeren. Driven out by the citizenry, he takes refuge at Maastricht. Here God reveals to him that Gaul will be ravaged by the Huns, and he is accordingly dispatched to Rome to seek help. He prays at Saint Peter's grave and is witness to a vision in which the assembled saints turn a deaf ear to his plea. Saint Peter explains that the sinners, especially in Tongeren, must suffer their fate, but that Servatius will soon be saved. On his way home he encounters the Huns and actually converts Attila for a brief time until he relapses into paganism. In Metz he is approached by the penitent citizens of Tongeren but proclaims his intention to return to Maastricht, where he dies and is buried. The Huns subsequently rampage in the Rhenish and French towns; only Maastricht and Troyes are spared. Later kings and dukes venerate Servatius, and attempts to remove his relics or otherwise infringe his honor meet with divine punishment.

A quantity of miracles is interspersed throughout the text, but the narrative is thin and Servatius scarcely emerges as an imposing figure. It is of some interest that the first major vernacular saint's life singled out a relatively insignificant protagonist. Servatius serves in fact only as a figurehead for local history. Heinrich von Veldeke himself was born close to Maastricht, and, as he explains in an epilogue, was engaged under the patronage of a certain Countess Agnes of Loon, seconded by a Maastricht sacristan named Hessel, to write the book.[20] It is more about Maastricht and the surrounding cities than about the saint, whose role is to authenticate the claims of Maastricht against its neighbors, particularly Tongeren. History is enlisted in favor of patriotic sentiments, as was the case in the *Annolied* and the emphases on Bavaria and Regensburg in the *Kaiserchronik*.

This regional bias expresses itself in positive and negative tonalities. There are fine descriptions of the towns of Tongeren (vv. 843–72) and Maastricht (vv. 955–82), although the editors Frings and Schieb athetized the first on linguistic grounds.[21] There are frequent stops and visits in neighboring towns. When Servatius goes to Rome, he stops at Metz and Basel, and on his return he stops at Speyer, Worms, Metz, Cologne, and Trier. We are reminded of the ritual visits and receptions up and down the Danube in the *Nibelungenlied*. Every place must have its due. But Maastricht claims the greatest due, and much of the regionalism is manifestly competitive. Maastricht is a refuge from the sinfulness of Tongeren. Attila is not so much a common scourge as the instrument of divine retribution against Tongeren, which is destined to succumb while special grace rescues Maastricht. We know from the *Annolied* (stanza 32) that Bishop Maternus was active in Trier and Cologne, but Veldeke reminds us that he also built a church in Maastricht (vv. 1,020–22). It is no doubt with some satisfaction that he reports further how Servatius took a leading part in deposing the heretical bishop Effrata in rival Cologne (vv. 1,289–1,387). He lists the bishops of Maastricht and recapitulates the favor shown by various rulers, notably Charlemagne, Duke Henry of Lotharingia, and Emperor Henry II. But his particular interest attaches to the prerogatives of Maastricht. An attempt to remove the remains of Servatius to Quedlinburg is defeated by a group of loyalists who kidnap the relics in the dark of night and return them to Maastricht. Indeed, the zealous protection of privilege goes so far that a band of naughty children

is punished for plundering one of Servatius' vineyards; they are frozen to
the scene of their delinquency, where they remain until they are discovered. Local prerogatives brook no humor in this contentious account.

Such particularism may seem far removed from the concerns of the
Nibelungenlied, but we will see below in our discussion of *Þiðreks saga*
how closely local interests could be intertwined with the international
themes of Germanic heroic poetry. Before pursuing this thread further, we
must first explore another aspect of the *Nibelungenlied* poet's literary culture, the domestication of foreign heroic legend in Germany.

LEGENDARY HISTORY

The German literary scene in the second half of the twelfth century is
characterized by the import and adaptation of French secular narrative,
narratives of classical provenance (the stories of Alexander the Great and
the *Aeneid*) and narratives of native French origin (primarily the *Song of
Roland* and the Arthurian romances of Chrétien de Troyes). The first such
book in German was the cleric Lamprecht's reworking of an Alexander
romance by a certain Alberic de Pisançon. Of Alberic's work only 105
verses are extant. Nor do we have Lamprecht's original. Instead we have
three derivative versions from Vorau, Strasbourg (the manuscript was
burnt in 1870), and Basel.[22] It is judged that all three go back to a common prototype X from approximately 1160, which was in turn not identical with Lamprecht's work (customarily dated around 1150). Both the
Vorau and the destroyed Strasbourg manuscripts date from the late twelfth
century. The Vorau version contains 1,533 verses, the Strasbourg version
7,302 verses. The former recounts Alexander's life through his campaign
against the Persian Darius. The latter goes on to tell of further exploits,
including the fabulous tale of Alexander's attempt to storm Paradise.

Because of the complications of the manuscript transmission there has
been considerable debate about the original extent of the German *Alexanderlied*. Some scholars have argued that the Vorau version represents
Lamprecht's work in full, others that it is only a fragment of Lamprecht's
work, which may have gone on another thousand lines or so or may have
included the whole of Alexander's life as recorded in the Strasbourg
manuscript. Current opinion suggests that the Vorau text answers to
Lamprecht's original, except for the last thirteen verses, in which a later
scribe added references to Alberic and Lamprecht. The brevity of this account soon led to the longer redaction X, on which the Strasbourg and
Basel manuscripts were based.

Not only the extent but also the meaning of Lamprecht's book has been
disputed. Following Alberic, he begins with the words of Ecclesiastes 1.2

and 1.14 ("vanitas vanitatum"), and it has often been assumed that this is the moral underlying the titanic career and ultimate failure of Alexander. Wolfgang Fischer has, however, made a strong case for believing that Alberic was simply making use of a medieval topos with no larger implication.[23] His preface means only that he is undertaking a version of this ancient tale to alleviate his infirmity and to suggest that not everything is vanity. Fischer's interpretation has been well received and leads us to believe that Alberic had an entirely positive understanding of Alexander's career.[24] There is no evidence that Lamprecht departed substantially from this view.

The version underlying the Strasbourg and Basel manuscripts then broke new ground by making vanity the central idea of Alexander's life.[25] Darius' dying speech to Alexander sets the tone (vv. 3,839–48): "Consider, great King, who I was; who was ever born more powerful in subjects and fortified towns? What does it profit me now that I have come to this? Now I advise and admonish you—reflect earnestly on it—so that the same will not happen to you." Alexander does not pause to reflect, but pursues his campaign further east against the Indian king Porus. After defeating him, he approaches the land of the Occidracians, a people who live in philosophical destitution. Alexander proposes to grant them a boon, but when they ask for immortality, he responds angrily that he cannot fulfill their request, that even he must die. With real or feigned innocence the Occidracians ask him why, if he must die, he performs such frenetic deeds on earth; there is after all a measure in all things (vv. 4,864–72). Alexander answers that he acts under the compulsion of a higher power and that to do nothing is to deny life its meaning. But the question of vanity has clearly been posed.

It returns to bedevil Alexander in his adventure with Queen Candacis, whom he visits on the arrogant supposition that a disguised name will hide his identity. He is swiftly disabused. Having secured a portrait of him in advance, Candacis exposes him without difficulty and he finds himself in the power of a woman. Not content with her ruse, she delivers a moral lecture (vv. 6,165–86):

How does your strength profit you, and your victories over many lands? You have destroyed great Persia and wasted India and conquered Partos. Now a woman has defeated you without a fight. How do the many battles you have long been waging now profit you? Now you may correctly understand that no living being who exalts himself is exempt from the wrath of fortune, which turns and strikes down the great as readily as the humble. Of this I must warn you. And you have clearly perceived it if you will only own the truth.

But Alexander remains undeterred by such warnings. The German redactor underscores the point by turning to a new source, the *Iter ad Para-*

disum, the primary text for the medieval understanding of Alexander as an incarnation of blasphemous pride.[26] He proceeds from victory to victory, but nothing suffices (vv. 6,613–19): "All of this was not enough to satisfy him. His arrogance led him to seek the road to Paradise. He wished to subdue it and collect tribute from the angelic hosts." At the very walls of Paradise the angels sternly dismiss him. Given a magic stone, the virtue of which he is charged to discover, he makes his way back to Greece. Here an old Jew finally reveals the secret of the stone by placing it on the dish of a scale and demonstrating that no quantity of gold on the opposite dish will raise it. When, on the other hand, a feather and a speck of earth are placed on the counterbalance, they immediately plummet, showing that man's appetite for earthly riches is insatiable, but that his life is less substantial than a feather and the speck of earth from which life came and to which it returns. After twelve years Alexander succumbs to poison, like a number of tyrants in the *Kaiserchronik*, and is consigned to seven feet of earth, an example and a warning to all who might be tempted by the vain pursuit of glory.

This type of lesson is familiar enough from the Faustinianus and Crescentia stories in the *Kaiserchronik*, but the moralizing framework is more ambitious. We have passed beyond the stage of individual *exempla* incorporated in a longer collection. In the *Alexanderlied* a single long narrative is organized by a unified moral concept. The sermonizing spirit of the eleventh century and the nascent preoccupation with history in the early twelfth century fuse with the new secular literature from France to produce a work of pseudohistory that is both heroic and monitory. If the critics are right in their conclusion that the moral thrust was absent from Alberic de Pisançon's French version, which was more purely heroic, and that it originated in redaction X around 1160, then the ideology is peculiarly German. That the conceptualization of narrative was perhaps a characteristically German development is implied by another narrative taken over from the French about a decade later, Pfaffe Konrad's *Rolandslied*.

The dating of the *Rolandslied* was one of the great cruxes of medieval German literature for more than a century, with proposals clustering around 1130, 1150, and 1170, depending on the identity of the Duke Henry mentioned as patron in the epilogue. The debate was effectively concluded in 1965 when Dieter Kartschoke published a brilliant summation and refinement of the complex arguments.[27] He established Henry the Lion as the probable patron and set the date of composition around 1170. One of the traditional barriers to a late date had been the relatively primitive diction of the *Rolandslied*, but the reply is that prosodic skills do not develop in a smooth progression.[28] The same is true of narrative skills, for the poet of the *Rolandslied*, who names himself Pfaffe Konrad in the epilogue, is clearly inferior to the poet or poets of the *Kaiser-chronik*, who worked twenty or more years earlier. Because both texts originated in the Bavarian capital of Regensburg (mentioned in verse 1,602 of the *Rolandslied*), part or all of the anonymous *Kaiserchronik* has been attributed to Konrad, but it seems quite unlikely that such an ungifted storyteller should also have composed the pointed exemplary novellas of the *Kaiserchronik*.

The discrepancy is all the more palpable because Konrad had the advantage of working from one of the great classics of heroic literature, the *Song of Roland* from about 1100. His French precursor had an extraordinary command of lucid composition, dramatic tension, emotional portraiture, and scenic design. Most of this is lost in the German reworking. Gone is the careworn emperor Charlemagne, weighed down by the burden of office and endless warfare, hemmed in by the personal politics around him, and haunted by dire forebodings. Gone is Charlemagne's knowingly self-indulgent affection for his reckless but magnetic nephew Roland, gone too the special bond between Roland and his companion Olivier, and the unclear but grandly conceived psychopathy of the traitor Ganelon. The framed council scenes of Paynims and Franks, the vistas of Spain, and the serried hosts of warriors no longer emerge with the same panoramic splendor. Neither the common love of country nor the individual aristeia of each doomed warrior has the same high relief in Konrad's recasting.

What Konrad offers in lieu of personal and compositional profile is thematization in the tradition of *Kaiserchronik* and *Alexanderlied*. The theme is not true perception through faith or intellect, as in the *Kaiserchronik*, or the lesson of humility, as in the *Alexanderlied* (although *Rolandslied* vv. 3,509–10 echoes *Strassburger Alexanderlied* vv. 6,919–20), but the active defense of faith. Whereas the crusade spirit of the *Song of Roland* is never quite explicit and must be reasoned from historical circumstances, Pfaffe Konrad placed the crusade mentality at the center of his version.[29]

Unlike the French poet, who plunged directly into the action, Konrad begins his work with 272 verses of prefatory matter signaling that Charlemagne, who "is in the presence of God because, with God, he conquered many heathen lands" (vv. 12–14), is the hero of his tale. His expedition into Spain is a divine mission revealed in an angelic vision. The object is to convert the heathen. Charlemagne accordingly summons his twelve paladins and incites them to the service of God, reminding them that death on a crusade guarantees a place among the martyrs. Roland reinforces the idea and warriors are recruited throughout the land to take the cross. Charlemagne and Turpin harangue the assembled troops with denunciations of the pagans and promises of heavenly reward. In short, the text begins on a note of crusade propaganda.

This message is not inorganic, but recurs at frequent intervals throughout the *Rolandslied*. Konrad declares that the twenty thousand who join Roland in the rearguard to cover the emperor's departure from Spain "wished to be martyred for the sake of God" and desired to win nothing but the love of God (vv. 3,254–58). When they learn that the pagan multitude is sweeping down on them, they are filled with a yearning for God (vv. 3,407–25). By contrast, the pagans are described in a state of unutterable ignorance, plunged in darkness and arrogant superstition and disdaining their true Creator (vv. 3,465–88). The Oxford *Roland* also holds out the promise of martyrdom for the Franks (vv. 1,134–35), but there is no invidious diptych.[30]

The central scene in the Oxford *Roland*, in which Roland thrice refuses to sound his horn to summon aid (*laisses* 83–85), is similarly converted to religious use. In the French version Roland is solely concerned with his good name and the fear that a call for help would discredit him, his family, or his nation. Konrad's Roland resists because he is only too ready to die if God should deign to bestow a martyr's crown on him (vv. 3,880–90). Turpin reinforces the message with a miniature sermon (vv. 3,905–35) that contrasts sharply to the quick battlefield absolution he offers in the Oxford version (*laisse* 89). The opposition between the hero's preoccupation with honor in the French and with religious devotion in the German version is rendered with unaccustomed succinctness in Konrad's depiction of the battle between the French warrior Anseis and his pagan opponent Targis, a distinction in no way suggested by the original (vv. 4,719–22):

> Targis fought for honor,
> Anseis for his soul,
> Targis for this earth,
> Anseis for the kingdom of heaven.

These lines summarize in epigrammatic form the spiritual drift of early German epic and the pervasive adjustment of purely heroic themes. The opening stanza of the *Annolied* made the opposition between secular literature and religious commitment explicit, and the *Kaiserchronik*, *Alexanderlied*, *Servatius*, and *Rolandslied* continued to build on this religious foundation. A programmatic avowal of secular values in the epic does not surface until late in the century in Heinrich von Veldeke's reworking of Virgil's *Aeneid*, transmitted to him in a French version from the middle of the century.

The French *Roman d'Enéas* and Heinrich von Veldeke's *Eneide* are both landmarks in their respective literatures.[31] The *Roman d'Enéas* is the first full-scale tale of sentiment in France and heralds the works of Chrétien de Troyes, who was destined to mark out the course of romance for the rest of the Middle Ages. Veldeke's *Eneide* was recognized even by contemporaries (for example, Gottfried von Strassburg) as the crucial event in the emergence of German courtly literature around 1200. The liberating impact of this work is usually traced to a new fascination with love and its psychological complexities, explored for the first time with unalloyed delight and embellished with the rhetorical wit inherited from Ovid. The French poet gave scope to this new project by devising an amorous plot not found in Virgil's sober epic. According to Virgil the end of Aeneas' momentous trials and the final success of his foreordained but laborious conquest of Italy will be consummated by his marriage to Lavinia, the daughter of the native king Latinus. Thus the native dynasty will merge with the royal lineage of Troy and the epic mission will be accomplished. The persons who effect this unification are subordinate to the historical juncture. Hence we learn nothing of Lavinia beyond her identity, and nothing of the personal bond required by political ends.

The French poet adopted the opposite course. Not sharing Virgil's stake in Augustan Rome, he shed the historical framework, the Roman ideals, the quest of unity, and the pride born of tribulations.[32] His Enéas is the hero of a great adventure, and the culmination of adventure in romance is marriage. Marriage, not the foundation of a state, therefore becomes the focus of the narrative. Enéas escapes from his Roman model's adherence to duty, and Lavinie from a role of convenience. They become adolescent lovers, confounded and compelled by their passions. The climax of the epic is no longer the grand fulfillment of national destiny, somewhat tinged by the costs and sacrifices destiny requires, but a festive celebration of romantic love.

The medieval departures from Virgil's plan have been tabulated in detail and need not be rehearsed.[33] It is generally agreed that the French poet chose a simpler plot line, a more rational view of events, and a greater emphasis on realistic detail. He dispensed with Virgil's epic contrivances, the Olympian councils recycled from Homer, and some of the sequences that lend narrative scale and political purpose to the original, for example the content of *Aeneid* 3 and 5. For these matters he substituted additional description, extended dialogue, and ceremonial splendor. Veldeke's German reworking does not depart substantially from the French model, although he can moderate or accelerate the medieval drift on occasion, for example in the heightened grandeur of the marital finale.[34]

The essential difference between French original and German recasting is not in the text itself but in the literary context. Secular love literature was nothing new when the *Roman d'Enéas* was written. This composition was more or less contemporary with the first Tristan epic and was in any event read or heard by an audience familiar with Provençal love lyric. Erotic focus and psychological play were taken for granted. This is less true of Heinrich von Veldeke's Germany. When he carried out his adaptation in two stages before 1174 and during the 1180's, the courtly love lyric was in its first phase, and there is some dispute over whether Eilhart von Oberg's German version of the Tristan story was available.[35] Gottfried von Strassburg suggests in any case that it was Veldeke who took the decisive step to courtly literature. It seemed decisive because German literature was more conservative than French literature. "Conservative" in this case means more dominated by traditional didactic, exemplary, and historical emphases, and less open to the new secular themes.

Heinrich von Veldeke was the first German writer who did not deflect his narrative into the moralizing channels we have observed in the *Kaiserchronik*, *Alexanderlied*, and *Rolandslied*. If we consider the nature of his text, it is apparent that such a didactic course would not have been difficult of execution had the poet chosen it. Both the *Annolied* and the *Kaiserchronik* make much of the Trojan heritage in Germany, and Veldeke, with the Trojan prototype before him, could easily have capitalized on this tradition for patriotic purposes. Or, choosing a religious slant, he might have deplored Virgil's heathen apparatus, but there is none of the bigotry that defaces Pfaffe Konrad's view of pagans. Had Dido appeared in the *Kaiserchronik*, the poet's view of her would surely have been more Augustinian than Augustan, but Veldeke does not go beyond a certain grieved surprise that she should have killed herself for love (e.g., vv. 2,516–21), and he shows some decent defensiveness in explaining Eneas' role in her misfortune. In the light of earlier German narrative tradition he displays a remarkable agnosticism. He is regularly credited with a crucial advance in rhyme and diction, but the extent to which his intellectual neutrality prepared the way for the great secular epics of the next two decades may not have been sufficiently appreciated.

The significance of Veldeke's epic is broader than the customary emphasis on its erotic component suggests. We have seen that down to 1170 German narrative was guided by historical concerns in one form or another: national or parochial assertiveness in the *Annolied*, *Kaiserchronik*, and *Servatius*, exemplary pseudohistory in the *Alexanderlied*, and the great collision between Christianity and Islam in the *Rolandslied*. Veldeke's importance is not only that he legitimizes love but also that he dismisses history. Whereas the earlier trend was to isolate history in a literary text, whether in the form of chronological fussing in the legend of Dietrich von Bern or religious updating in the *Rolandslied*,[36] Veldeke reverses the trend, ignores the historical precedents, and accepts the belletrism of his French model. The *Roman d'Enéas* is a domestic novel, and Veldeke cooperates fully in the domestication.

It is in fact the element of domestication that has been lost from view in our critical concentration on romantic love. The medieval version restructures and reproportions the narrative to clear the way for the hero's progress toward domestic bliss. Much of Virgil's first six books is dropped entirely: the details of the fall of Troy, the long odyssey across the Mediterranean to the Tyrrhenian Sea, and the games in memory of Anchises. The result is not only that the first part of the epic is much shorter than in Virgil's text and that Eneas arrives in Italy when a little over a quarter of the story is told, but also that Dido's infatuation looms much larger than in the original. In the *Eneide* she dominates the scene for some seventeen hundred verses (vv. 805–2,528), and after her suicide the transition to Italy is more rapid.

Here the second romantic intrigue is engaged immediately. Eneas sends messengers to King Latinus, who promptly promises the newcomer his daughter and her realm against his wife's advocacy of the suitor Turnus. Although the king declares that he is obeying the dictates of the gods, these dictates do not figure prominently, and the story develops as a family dispute between a father and a mother promoting different marital candidates. This is not Virgil's concept. In the *Aeneid* father and mother are the instruments of higher destiny. Latinus has been informed by no uncertain portents that he is to wed his daughter to a designated foreigner and not to a Latin—in this version Turnus is only the most important of various suitors. Queen Amata's resistance is not a matter of personal allegiance to Turnus but a mania inspired by Allecto, whom Juno has dispatched in her relentless opposition to the Trojans. The domestic antagonism in Latium merely translates a divine contest onto the human plane. In the medieval version the human plane acquires a life of its own. Allecto disappears and Amata's objection to Eneas and advocacy of Turnus (vv. 4,150–70) are matters of family politics and personal preference.

The ensuing Italian war is an extension of the family conflict, not vice versa. This conflict originates at the moment of Eneas' arrival in Italy and controls the remainder of the narrative as Eneas and Turnus vie for Lavine's hand. Some thirty-six hundred lines (vv. 9,735–13,340), or more than a quarter of the whole narrative, are devoted to the actual love story, which was absent from Virgil's epic altogether. The suitors' rivalry activates the principals in an unprecedented way. Eneas declares that he will do battle for "the beautiful maiden" as well as the realm (vv. 11,076–81) and reflects that she has increased his courage tenfold (vv. 11,334–38). When Turnus falls, he laments that he has lost his life and honor for Lavine's sake (vv. 12,550–53). Marriage, not manifest destiny, has become the motivating force behind the strife.

This depoliticization of Virgil is pursued with greater energy by Heinrich von Veldeke than by his French predecessor. Whereas the *Roman d'Enéas* ends abruptly with a brief mention of the marriage, Veldeke enters into lavish detail, comparing the occasion with Frederick Barbarossa's great festival at Mainz in 1184. The family alliance between Trojans and Latins is cemented when the aged King Latinus adopts Eneas as his son and turns over the realm to him (vv. 13,287–91). Romantic love thus culminates in a marital idyll. Eneas lives magnificently forever after with his beloved and faithful wife, who founds with him the great Roman dynasty traced down as far as Augustus. It is not, however, the foundation of an imperial dynasty that preoccupies the poet but rather the family line happily established and successfully maintained. We will see in the following chapter to what extent this concept coincides with a dominant theme in twelfth-century romance.

The medieval story of Eneas has a curious resemblance to the modern middle-class novel. It depicts the life of a young male hero dominated by two women, one passionate and morally marginal, the other a paragon of proper naiveté. This pattern, destined for infinite variation in later fiction, was not suggested in Virgil's epic, but provides the underlying framework of the medieval book, especially in Heinrich von Veldeke's adaptation. Eneas takes Dido in an onrush of sexual desire (vv. 1,834–42) not described in the *Roman d'Enéas*, but he later reflects on these paltry feelings when he is inflamed with love for Lavine (vv. 11,180–86): "If I had known a tenth part of the love that I have now felt, I would never have left her." [37] Our hero is no longer an instrument of history, like Virgil's Aeneas or even Veldeke's own Servatius, but the protagonist of his own history. He is engaged in personal progress from desire to true love, which becomes a real and driving concept for the late twelfth century.

HEROIC HISTORY

The prologue to the *Annolied* noted that concern for the soul was preferable to the cultivation of heroic tales, but that preference presumably did not detract from the popularity of heroic recitations. Sometime in the middle of the twelfth century these recitations once again crossed the divide between oral performance and literary epic, as they had done earlier in *Beowulf* and *Waltharius*. The first fruits of the new attempt are not

extant, but in studying the sources of the *Nibelungenlied* we will see that
it absorbed at least two more modest heroic epics, one about the Fall of
the Burgundians, the other about Dietrich von Bern. When exactly these
lost epics were composed cannot be determined, but epic as such developed around the middle of the twelfth century, and it is unlikely that
Germanic heroic epic developed earlier. General considerations suggest
1150–70 as the likely period for such an innovation.

We possess only one heroic work that is, typologically at least, anterior
to the *Nibelungenlied*, but this work is not preserved in its original German form. It survives only in a Norse prose version known as *Þiðreks
saga af Bern* (The tale of Dietrich von Bern).[38] As the title indicates, the
central character is that Dietrich von Bern whose story was told in capsule
form in the *Kaiserchronik*. Like the *Kaiserchronik*, *Þiðreks saga* is a compilation of many stories. In addition to heroic stories it includes a number
of bridal-quest stories, to which we will return in the next chapter.

Because of its Norse disguise *Þiðreks saga* has never been integrated
into the study of twelfth-century German epic but has been left to the
Norsists. Over a century ago, in 1874, the Norwegian scholar Gustav
Storm surmised that the stories were collected by a Norwegian author
from the lips of German merchants in Bergen around 1250. All later
Scandinavian scholars have echoed this theory, and the lone voice of the
German scholar Heinrich Hempel, who argued in 1952 that *Þiðreks saga*
is simply the translation of a German book written in the Westphalian
town of Soest, has not been able to dispel the notion.

The historical premises on which Storm's supposition was based (Norwegian dealings with Russia and Lübeck around 1250) are not decisive,
and the gathering of folklore as a model for medieval literary composition is clearly anachronistic. It is more likely that a German book was
translated in Norway in the normal fashion. We know that there were
commercial relations between the Rhineland and Norway in the late
twelfth century and we can observe in the evolution of the Norse heroic
poems of the *Edda* how German influence in the literary sphere began
to exert itself during this period. We know too that the translation of foreign books became customary in Norway under the auspices of King
Hakon the Old (reigned 1217–63), whereas there is no evidence of oral
collecting.[39]

Exactly when the German original was composed and the Norse translation executed is a matter of reasoned speculation, but Hempel's location
of the work in Soest seems overwhelmingly likely. Soest is mentioned no
fewer than thirty-five times in *Þiðreks saga*, with special note taken of
local monuments associated with heroic events. This sort of local promo-
tion is unlikely to have survived an oral filter in Norway, but it is in keep-

ing with the regionalism we have observed in such German works as the *Annolied* and Veldeke's *Servatius* from neighboring Rhenish towns. The proximity of prosperous Cologne could well have incited emulation in Soest. We may recollect the unconcealed delight with which the Maastricht poet Heinrich von Veldeke reports how his hero Servatius deposed the heretical bishop Effrata of Cologne, or how the citizens of Maastricht retrieved Servatius' relics from Quedlinburg. Regional competition was in the air, and cultural ambitions may have been heightened in Soest when Philipp von Heinsberg, archbishop of Cologne and chancellor of Frederick Barbarossa, resided there in 1177–80.[40] This would have been an appropriate moment for a literary monument to the greater glory of Soest.

When the book came to Norway is not clear, but the route was well trafficked. In his praise of Maastricht Heinrich von Veldeke describes it (vv. 971–78): "It lies ideally situated on a common highway from England to Hungary by way of Cologne and Tongeren and similarly from Saxony to France and, by the ships that ply the route, to Denmark and to Norway." Soest lay squarely on the route from Saxony to Cologne, where river and sea passage to Norway was available. The customary date for the transfer of *Þiðreks saga* around 1250 has been repeated so often that it has almost mesmerizing force, but the German impact on Norse literature antedates the French fashion of King Hakon's reign and there is no reason why a manuscript of the book should not have been exported to Norway as early as 1200.

If we wish to integrate *Þiðreks saga* into the German literary scene, we must explore how it relates to other works of the same period. Like the *Kaiserchronik* it is a long and complex book, with a certain centrifugal effect bred by many subplots. It is, however, compositionally more ambitious. Whereas the author or authors of the *Kaiserchronik* discovered no organizational principle other than a progression of emperors, the author of *Þiðreks saga* sought to organize his narrative around the dominant figure of Dietrich von Bern, or Thidrek. He reviews Thidrek's ancestry briefly, just as the *Kaiserchronik* did, then makes Thidrek himself the focus of the action by attracting a series of more peripheral heroes to his court. Thidrek's central position is not unlike King Arthur's among the knights of the round table, or Charlemagne's among the twelve peers of France. The latter in particular would have been familiar from the *Rolandslied* (e.g., v. 67). Indeed, when the circle of heroes is complete, Thidrek celebrates a great feast with precisely twelve companions. The most important of these (in their Norse forms, Hildibrand, Heimir, Attila, Velent, Vidga, Sigurd, Gunnar, and Valtari) are well known from earlier and later German tradition. Each figure is introduced separately with information on his family background, rise to eminence, and the circumstances that lead to his service with Thidrek. After the festive banquet marks the creation of their fellowship, a series of romantic interludes accounts for the marriages of several of their number.

At this point the narrative addresses the Dietrich legend proper and the story turns tragic. Emperor Ermanaric drives Thidrek into exile, where he spends twenty years at Attila's court—the anachronism so vigorously disputed in the *Kaiserchronik*. The two of them join in a series of adventures, culminating in an attempt to reconquer Thidrek's realm at the great battle of Gronsport. The attempt fails and many of the leading heroes are killed, including Attila's sons. This is the signal for the disintegration of Thidrek's circle, as subsequent stories recount the fall of such figures as Sigurd (Siegfried in German), Gunnar (Gunther), Högni (Hagen), and Rodingeir (Rüdeger). Thidrek is finally able to repossess his realm after Ermanaric's death, but the remaining heroes succumb one after the other, and Thidrek himself disappears on a mysterious black horse.

The present chapter has touched on various types of twelfth-century history: dynastic history (whether episcopal in the *Annolied* and *Servatius* or imperial in the *Kaiserchronik*), regional history (*Annolied* and *Servatius*), exemplary history (*Kaiserchronik* and *Alexanderlied*), legendary history (*Alexanderlied* and *Rolandslied*), and family history (*Eneide*). *Þiðreks saga* shares some features with all these types. Although heroic tradition does not lend itself well to dynastic lines, the author develops as much ancestral history as possible, a full three generations for such heroes as Thidrek and Velent. In the context of regional history we have noted the special attachment to Soest, which figures as the scene of the momentous struggle between Huns and Burgundians.[41] The author specifies the layout of Soest and the location of particular events. He advises us that the wall at which Irung (Iring) fell and the snake tower in which Gunnar died can still be seen there. Elsewhere too the concern with localization is great. Each hero is attached to a particular region and his routes are traced in detail, although legendary distortion and perhaps the Norse translator's unfamiliarity with foreign geography obscured many points. Topography is an obvious preoccupation of the text and has been studied in considerable depth.[42]

It is somewhat more difficult to identify the role of exemplary history in *Þiðreks saga*. There may have been clues in the German original, but Norse saga writers were notoriously unreceptive to such moralizing as we find in the *Alexanderlied*, let alone the disputations of the Faustinianus story in the *Kaiserchronik*. Whatever authorial reflections may have been in the original would not have survived in the translation. Nevertheless, the very structure of the story suggests a particular understanding of history. The formation of a brilliant circle of heroes who celebrate their invincibility at a great banquet but are destined for exile and death conveys a bleak message. At the banquet Thidrek regales his companions with an exultant speech (1: 352–53):

An overwhelming force of valorous men has come together in one hall. What man would be so bold as to oppose them? Here thirteen men sit on a single bench, and if they arm themselves and mount their horses, I expect that they can ride unmolested throughout the world. Their equals can never be found, nor those who might dare to raise a spear against them. And if there should be men who are bold and enterprising and foolhardy enough not to fear our power and daring, our sharp swords and hard helmets and tough shields and strong byrnies and swift horses (we who kill like fearless beasts), they would condemn themselves to a quick death.

This speech is a piece of purest vainglory, and it predicts the opposite of what the future holds. Our heroes do not ride unmolested throughout the world, but after various hardships they are picked off in rapid succession. What they have in common is not invincibility but a tragic destiny. Thidrek's own destiny is the most tragic of all, twenty years in exile and the loss of all his men. The oral traditions available to the Soest compiler presumably differed from the fiery death in a volcano with which church legend in the *Kaiserchronik* punished the historical Theodoric's Arian heresy, but his disappearance on a black horse is no heroic end and does nothing to alleviate the melancholy tale. It may well be a concession to the negative reputation that clung to Theodoric in church tradition.[43] If so, Thidrek's great boast invites us to construe his end as a punishment for arrogance.

The most obvious model for such a moral is the story of Alexander. Cologne has frequently been mentioned as the location of the original *Alexanderlied*,[44] and we have seen the cultural proximity of Cologne and Soest in the person of Philipp von Heinsberg. There is in fact specific evidence that the author of *Þiðreks saga* knew the *Alexanderlied* and took a literary loan from it. One of the early episodes tells of the horse Bucephalus, which was so wild that no one could approach it for fear of his life, but which kneels submissively before Alexander. *Þiðreks saga* attaches this anecdote to Sigurd and his horse Grani.[45] The author may therefore have adhered to the broader concept of the *Alexanderlied* as well, predicating his book on the vanity of human ambition.

At the same time, *Þiðreks saga* may represent a reaction against the practice of foreign legendary history in earlier twelfth-century Germany. Both the *Alexanderlied* and the *Rolandslied* were French imports, and the time may have seemed ripe around 1180 to undertake a major German record of heroic deeds in competition with the French *Song of Roland*. Just as Otfrid von Weissenburg in the ninth century wished to rival his Latin predecessors with a Frankish version of the Gospels ("Cur scriptor hunc librum Theotisce dictaverit"), so the author of *Þiðreks saga* may have wished to assert the German claim in heroic history. Thidrek's twelve companions may be quite intentional rivals of the twelve peers of France.

The last strand in the web of twelfth-century vernacular epic is family history. Heinrich von Veldeke's *Eneide* may have been composed more or less simultaneously with the German original of *Þiðreks saga*, but family romance was already available in the Faustinianus and Crescentia stories of the *Kaiserchronik*. *Þiðreks saga* is scarcely conceivable without this background. The Germanic heroic lay is totally allusive on family relationships. By contrast *Þiðreks saga* is not only biographically constructed, pursuing each career through the stages of birth, youthful adventure, marriage, and death, but also much concerned with matters of ancestry and kinship. A whole section is set aside for marriages, in which no fewer than eleven weddings are celebrated. Several of them are preceded by romantic tales of courtship. This combination of romance and heroic epic is a significant innovation. As we will see in the next chapter, epic and romance traditions led separate existences until the end of the twelfth century. Their literary marriage in *Þiðreks saga* thus signals the birth of a new genre, and later German literature no longer allows for an easy distinction between epic and romance. Because of the scope assigned to romance in *Þiðreks saga*, about twenty percent of the whole, we may say that this first extensive recording of Germanic heroic epic already marks the end of the heroic genre in anything like a pure form.

4. The Rise of German Romance

THE APPEARANCE of romance in German medieval literature is routinely treated as a late phenomenon. Hermann Schneider's literary history suggested by its very title a sequence of events in which heroic literature came first and romance last.[1] This view is guided by a restrictive definition that equates romance with the courtly Arthurian variety that developed in the wake of Chrétien de Troyes. Most literary history accordingly dates German romance from Hartmann von Aue's *Erec* and *Iwein* in the 1180's and 1190's. The present chapter will advocate a broader definition of romance that includes the so-called minstrel or bridal-quest epics (*Spielmannsepen*) and their oral prototypes. In other words, it will admit all works centered on love and adventure. If such latitude is allowed, we are enabled to trace romance back in time almost as far as the Germanic heroic lay.

The first distinct example of a bridal-quest plot is associated with the figure of Clovis in the *Chronica Fredegarii* (ca. 660) and the *Liber historiae Francorum* (727).[2] These chronicles go beyond Gregory of Tours's *Historia Francorum* in supplying details on the marriage of Clovis to the Burgundian princess Clotilda (ca. 490). As told by Fredegar, and, with some variation, in the *Liber historiae*, the story can be summarized as follows:[3]

Clovis learns of Clotilda and dispatches a certain Aurilianus to woo her on his behalf. In the *Liber historiae* Aurilianus leaves his companions in a wood, then appears on a Sunday disguised as a beggar and sits down at the alms table outside the church where Clotilda attends mass. As she bestows a gold coin on him, he attracts her attention by kissing her hand and plucking her cloak. She subsequently has him summoned to her chamber, where he presents Clovis's suit and delivers his ring, remarking that other bridal gifts are outside in a sack. The sack has in the meantime disappeared, but Clotilda succeeds in recovering it. (In Fredegar's version a beggar steals the sack on the road home, but is caught and punished.) She deposits Clovis's ring in her uncle Gundobad's treasure chamber and instructs Aurilianus to convey her greetings with the message that a Christian woman may not marry a heathen, but that she is reconciled to God's will. (In Fredegar's version she urges haste because of a rival suitor, Aridius). The following year Clovis sends Aurilianus to woo Clotilda openly from King Gundobad. Gundobad refuses at first, but when Clovis's ring, identified by name and portrait, turns up in his treasure chamber, he acquiesces and gives the bride into the hands of the messengers to be taken to Soissons.

A similar story of surrogate wooing by the Langobard king Authari is recorded in Paul the Deacon's *Historia Langobardorum* (3.30) from the end of the eighth century: [4]

King Authari sends ambassadors to Bavaria to woo the daughter of King Garibald on his behalf. They succeed in their mission and report accordingly, but Authari is eager to see his bride for himself. He therefore presents himself before King Garibald in the guise of Authari's messenger, charged to view his master's betrothed. Theudelinda, produced for his inspection, immediately delights his heart, and he asks that she proffer him a cup of wine. When she accedes, he touches her hand with his finger. Theudelinda reports blushingly to her nurse, who surmises that the messenger can be none other than the suitor himself. Authari sets out for Italy, but as he takes leave of his Bavarian escort, he rises in his saddle and drives an ax deep into a tree with the words: "This is the kind of blow Authari strikes." By this gesture the Bavarians recognize his identity. Some time later, when the Franks have invaded Bavaria, Theudelinda takes refuge in Italy and marries Authari.

These chronicle synopses of wooing stories familiar among the Franks and Langobards in the seventh and eighth centuries illustrate the tale type that evolved into bridal-quest epic in twelfth-century Germany. The first such epic, *König Rother*, is in fact a much elaborated and transformed version of King Authari's wooing. At some point, then, the short, presumably oral, bridal-quest narrative crossed the literary frontier into written epic just as the Germanic heroic lay became Germanic epic. The scholar who formulated the clearest hypothesis on this transformation was Theodor Frings. [5] Frings based his hypothesis on a distinction between abduction stories, characterized by forcible seizure, and wooing stories, characterized by tricks and stratagems. He found the abduction stories concentrated in the North and classified them as Germanic. The wooing tales he assigned to the Mediterranean sphere, where they are akin to Hellenistic and Byzantine traditions and certain stories in the *Arabian Nights*. Northern abduction model and southern wooing model, he theorized, coalesced on the Rhine in the twelfth century, first in a proto-*Rother* of some two thousand verses. This new form then became the paradigm for the "Brünhildenlied" (the hypothetical source of Part I of the *Nibelungenlied*) and other "minstrel epics," which in turn infiltrated Scandinavia and exercised an influence on the wooing stories told in Saxo Grammaticus' *Gesta Danorum* and the late legendary sagas.

Frings's theory satisfies the evidence imperfectly. The only story that locates an abduction pattern in early Scandinavia is the legend of Hedin's
abduction of Hild (preliminary to the so-called *Hjaðningavíg*). It is secured for the ninth century by two stanzas of a skaldic poem, Bragi Boddason's *Ragnarsdrápa*, but we may doubt whether it involves forcible abduction of the kind Frings attributes to his Scandinavian prototype. In
Snorri Sturluson's account in *Skáldskaparmál* (ca. 1220), Hild offers no
resistance and later tries to reconcile her father Högni to the match. It
cannot therefore have been a story of forcible abduction. Elopement
might be a better term.[6]

Nor is it possible to isolate trickery as a southern paradigm. Frings is
able to do so only by referring to the Merovingian stories in Fredegar and
the *Liber historiae* as "Mediterranean" and ignoring the Langobardic
tale of King Authari's wooing. To label a seventh-century Frankish story
as Mediterranean rather than Germanic is arbitrary, and Paul the Deacon's bridal quest has all the earmarks of disguise and deception that
characterize the twelfth-century epics. But perhaps the most palpable
difficulty in a simple dichotomy between a northern abduction and a
southern wooing model is the existence of *Tristan*, which Frings also
omits from his discussion. *Tristan* is one long tale of trickery, and the further back we go in the evolution of the tale, the more evident the trickery
is.[7] Such guile is clearly not a Mediterranean superimposition. The Persian prototype, advocated most vigorously by Pierre Gallais, is remarkable for its failure to explain precisely this element.[8] On the evidence of
the Frankish and Langobardic stories, as well as *Tristan*, it therefore
seems certain that wooing strategems are indigenous in the literature of
northern Europe.

Frings, seconded by Max Braun and Friedmar Geissler, was more successful in establishing a descriptive morphology of bridal-quest narrative.[9] We may define this type as a story in which a king, often on the
advice of others, woos a distant princess with the aid of special envoys.
The difficulties to be overcome stem from the reluctance of the bride's father or the bride herself. Success is achieved to some extent through a
show of force, but often through trickery as well: disguise, impersonation, secret communications, magic rings or potions. Resistance is sometimes such as to require a second or even a third embassy. The stories conclude with a bridal journey, abduction, or elopement.

Reduced to simplest terms, the typical plot consists of three parts: identification of a bride, wooing, and marriage. The protagonist is almost
without exception a king (like Clovis and Authari), and the idea of marriage is often urged on him by his advisers, as in *Tristan*, Chrétien's

Cligès, or *König Rother*. Acceding to their advice, he dispatches an envoy, who is sometimes anonymous but more often a person of some importance (Aurilianus in the Frankish story of Clovis). Occasionally the king disguises himself and serves as his own envoy, as in the case of Authari. Circumstances may prevent the bride from being won on the first attempt so that a second embassy is required, a pattern again illustrated by the story of Clovis. The wooer, whether the king himself or an envoy, frequently appears in disguise as a beggar (Aurilianus), a messenger (Authari), a merchant (Tristan), an exile (Rother), or a pilgrim (Salman in *Salman und Morolf*).

The second phase of the tale recounts the wooing proper. No great detail is expended on the preparations, but one recurrent feature is the wooer's stationing of an armed contingent in a nearby forest. In the *Liber historiae* this is a blind motif, but in other stories, such as *Rother* and *Salman und Morolf*, the armed contingent later intervenes to assist the wooer. Having arrived at the foreign court, the wooer must sometimes overcome the handicap of his own disguise to make contact with the princess. Aurilianus poses as a beggar to intercept her at church. The wooer may choose to identify himself with a familiar gesture that is calculated to surprise and alert her. Aurilianus plucks Clotilda's cloak and Authari strokes Theudelinda's hand. In *Rother* the farce thickens when the king identifies himself to his future queen from beneath the banquet table. In the variant provided by *Þiðreks saga*, as well as in *Rother*, he first reveals his identity by setting her on his lap and fitting a slipper to her foot.

On occasion the surreptitious introduction of the wooer and the means of communication can be extravagant. Tristan gains access to Isolde by the tried and true device of killing a dragon. In one of the stories in *Þiðreks saga* the envoy reveals Attila's suit to his intended in full view of her hostile father and a rival suitor—but out of earshot. In a second story Thidrek's envoy Herburt releases two mice adorned with gold and silver to attract the bride's attention. In a third story Herborg communicates with her wooer Apollonius by means of messages secreted in an apple, and he gains access to her in the transvestite garb of the great whore Heppa. In a fourth story Iron smuggles a letter to Bolfriana through the good services of a minstrel.

The impediment to success may be the father's unwillingness, as in *Rother*, or the bride's own reluctance, as in *Salman und Morolf* and two of the stories in *Þiðreks saga*. In one of these, as well as in *Salman und Morolf*, her heart is softened by a love-inducing ring. A further complication may be present in the person of a rival suitor. Fredegar mentions a

certain Aridius as Clovis's rival. This part is played by the villainous seneschal in *Tristan* and a Saxon duke in *Cligès*. Whatever the difficulties, the
story culminates happily in a bridal journey ("Brünhildenlied"), abduction (*Rother*), or elopement (*Cligès*). In exceptional cases the surrogate
wooer himself makes off with the bride. This is true of Tristan, Herburt,
and in some sense Siegfried. In a few stories there is also a subsidiary
wedding that joins the surrogate wooer to a second lady. The double wedding in the *Nibelungenlied* is the most familiar case in point.

BRIDAL ROMANCE IN TWELFTH-CENTURY GERMANY

Bridal-quest narrative is at least as old as the seventh-century story of
Clovis's wooing. It is impossible to say in what form such stories circulated since we have no primary texts analogous to the heroic poems of the
Edda or the German *Hildebrandslied*, but the epics of the twelfth century
were surely preceded by shorter oral versions. These shorter versions appear to have undergone epic expansion in the same way and about the
same time as the short heroic lay developed into heroic epic around the
middle of the twelfth century. The short form of the bridal-quest narrative
is in fact still visible in *Þiðreks saga* alongside the longer quasi-epic form
of heroic narrative. The legend of the Fall of the Burgundians (Part II of
the *Nibelungenlied*) had already assumed epic proportions and existed as
a written text, which was incorporated into *Þiðreks saga* under the title
"Niflunga saga." "Niflunga saga" extends to fifty-three pages in Bertelsen's edition. At the same time the Soest compiler incorporated six
bridal-quest stories into his work. These stories average about thirteen
pages in Bertelsen's edition, or a quarter of the length of "Niflunga saga." [10]
They clearly reflect a short narrative form.

We are thus enabled to compare a pre-epic form of the bridal-quest tale
with the epic form that evolved in the second half of the twelfth century
and is preserved in the "minstrel epics" *König Rother, Salman und Morolf, Oswald*, and *Orendel*. Such a comparison is further facilitated by
the close correspondence between *König Rother* and one of the tales in
Þiðreks saga ("Osantrix and Oda"). A summary of the latter follows (according to Mb³ in Bertelsen, 2: 71–83; cf. 1: 49–56):

Osantrix dispatches six knights to woo Oda, daughter of King Milias of Hunland.
They are entrusted with a letter vowing war in the event of a refusal. Milias reads
the letter and rejects the suit, both because of the arrogant tone and because he
cannot part with Oda. The envoys are thrown in prison. Osantrix' nephews
Hertnid and Hirdir, aged eleven and ten, now come to his court. Osantrix makes
Hertnid an earl in his retinue and commissions him to renew the suit. Hertnid
accordingly woos Oda with gifts and fair words; when these are of no avail, he
delivers a stern letter and is thrown in prison with the previous messengers.

Osantrix himself assembles forces, including four giants, and appears before Milias under the pseudonym Thidrek and with the fiction that he has had a falling out with his lord Osantrix. He pleads to be taken into Milias' service, but Milias is reluctant. Outraged by his master's suppliant posture, the giant Vidolf protests loudly and Osantrix/Thidrek orders him chained to a wall. He then renews his plea. This time the giant Aspilian is so angered that he knocks Milias unconscious and calls aloud for Hertnid. Hearing him, Hertnid and his companions break out of prison, Vidolf snaps his fetters, and they join in a general slaughter. Milias flees.

Osantrix, still in the guise of Thidrek, visits Oda and declares his intention of bringing her to Osantrix. He puts her on his lap and tries first a silver, then a golden slipper on her foot. They fit perfectly, and she expresses her eagerness to have a place in Osantrix' high seat. Thidrek now reveals his identity, effects a reconciliation with Milias, and celebrates his marriage with Oda.

This story, which occupies twelve pages in Bertelsen's edition, was also converted into the epic *König Rother*, extending to 5,202 verses.[11] Severely reduced, the plot may be outlined in the following way.

King Rother in Bari is advised to woo the daughter of King Constantine and dispatches his envoy Lupolt with eleven followers to Constantinople. Lupolt and his retainers are thrown into a dungeon. Rother learns what has happened and is now advised to go to Greece in the guise of an exile. Adopting the name Dietrich, he sets sail with a band of men that includes a contingent of giants, notably Asprian and Widolt. He gains admission to the court with the fiction that he has been banished by Rother and wins favor with his generosity. Constantine's daughter hears of his liberality and persuades her father to organize a feast. Here she is smitten by Dietrich and has him brought to her quarters, where he fits silver and golden slippers on her feet and reveals his identity. She undertakes to free his envoys, but soon after their release they are returned to prison and she can do no more than provide for their comfort.

In the meantime the Egyptian king Ymelot mounts an attack against Constantine. Dietrich, stipulating the release of his prisoners, takes over the defense. He captures Ymelot, but creates consternation with a false report of defeat. In the ensuing confusion he abducts and marries the princess. A minstrel promises Constantine to recover her. He goes to Bari, sets up shop as a merchant, lures the queen aboard his ship with a stone that allegedly heals cripples, and abducts her back to Constantinople. Rother organizes a new campaign against Constantine. Leaving his army at a distance, he disguises himself as a pilgrim and learns that his wife is to be married to Ymelot's son. He penetrates the court and reveals his presence to his wife as he hides under the banquet table. Detected by the groom, he emerges and meekly agrees to be hanged in the forest. Here his companions come to his rescue and overwhelm the heathens. Ultimately reconciled with Constantine, Rother returns to Bari with his queen. From their union is descended the emperor Charlemagne. Rother ends his days as a monk.

The relationship between these two versions has been the subject of protracted and inconclusive debate. Initial difficulties are caused by doublets in the transmission of *Þiðreks saga*. The German original appears to have been translated twice independently and then inserted into *Þiðreks saga* in different locations by two different scribes designated as Mb² and Mb³. We must settle the relationship between these doublets before we can judge the relationship between *Þiðreks saga* and *König Rother*. It seems most likely that Mb² and Mb³ are not transcriptions of separate oral versions, as Jan de Vries once argued, but rather separate translations of one and the same German text, a case made by Friedrich Panzer.[12] Thus a single recording of a North German bridal-quest tale underlies both Norse versions.

Some scholars have considered this recording primary and *König Rother* secondary. Others have assigned the priority to *König Rother*.[13] This latter inclination has been fostered by an early date for *König Rother* in the middle of the twelfth century and the traditional late date for *Þiðreks saga* in the middle of the thirteenth century. But we have seen that the German original of *Þiðreks saga* may well date from about 1180, and, if we place *König Rother* in the period 1155–65,[14] there is no difficulty in supposing that they are independent versions of the same story, one in brief compass more or less faithful to the dimensions of the oral original, and one in greatly expanded form. The story itself may well be of Rhenish provenance. Though working in Bavaria, the poet of *Rother* betrays Rhenish and Low German connections,[15] and we have seen in the previous chapter that the Soest compiler of *Þiðreks saga* was the recipient of Rhenish impulses.

The epic expansion of *König Rother* is of two kinds. A comparison of the two synopses above shows that it is only the first part of *König Rother* (up to line 2,562) that corresponds exactly to the story in *Þiðreks saga*. To this core story the German poet added a whole new plot around the Egyptian king Ymelot and Ymelot's son, who is introduced as a rival suitor.[16] In some degree, then, the expansion is a matter of simple compounding, but the dimensions are also dilated by the customary epic addition of new detail, description, and dialogue throughout the plot. This is the same operation we observed in the transition from oral heroic lay to literary heroic epic, for example, in *Beowulf*.

The growth of epic in twelfth-century Germany accrued partly from an indigenous cultivation of historical narrative in such works as the *Kaiserchronik* and partly from the imitation of French epic in the *Alexanderlied*, *Rolandslied*, and *Eneide*. In dealing with the German literature of this period, we must as a matter of course inquire into French antecedents, all the more so when we observe that *König Rother* is exactly contemporary with the first German adaptations of French epic (ca. 1150–70). It is possible that the poet of *König Rother*, working in Bavaria, acquired his sense of narrative fullness from the *Kaiserchronik*, but it is also possible that, like the Bavarian Pfaffe Konrad who reworked the *Song of Roland* as the *Rolandslied*, he looked to French models.

BRIDAL ROMANCE IN TWELFTH-CENTURY FRANCE

France has no genre precisely equivalent to German bridal-quest romance, but did evolve analogous forms. By far the closest analogue is found in the little publicized romance *Florimont*, written in 1188 by Aimon de Varennes.[17] It is of interest to us not only in the general context of twelfth-century romance but also by virtue of special correspondences with the *Nibelungenlied*. We must therefore describe the action in some detail:

Philip of Macedonia inherits the kingdom of Greece and frees it from a marauding lion. Heeding his barons' advice to marry, he dispatches an embassy to King Meneÿs of Mautilion and Barbarie in Africa. Meneÿs grants him the hand of his daughter Amordyalé and the ambassadors return with her. The marriage is celebrated, and a daughter named Romadanaple is born. She becomes a miracle of learning and is sought after by suitors from many lands. To prevent her from falling in love with a man of unsuitable rank, Philip secludes her, offering those who wish to see her only the option of serving three years in return for a kiss. But King Camdiobras of Hungary sends an embassy with the haughty demand that she be given to him in marriage and that Philip submit. Philip's deceased father appears to him in a dream and urges him to resist in the expectation that a valiant man will turn up to avenge him against Camdiobras and win the hand of his daughter.

In the meantime a son named Florimont is born to the duke and duchess of Albania. At age fifteen he kills a flying dragon. A fairy from the invisible Ile Celee appears, solicits his secret love, and gives him a magic ring that will provide whatever he wants when he shows it to a stranger. In a second adventure he kills the giant Garganeüs. His tutor Floquart and the duchess now discover his secret love affair with the fairy and put an end to it, much to Florimont's dismay. (The fairy later becomes the mother of Alexander's tutor Netanabus.) After a bout with lovesickness he disguises himself as a poor knight with the eloquent name Povre Perdu and joins the following of a certain Risus, who is on his way to help Philip against Camdiobras.

Povre Perdu sends ahead his tutor Floquart, disguised as the old man Cacopedie, with his magic ring, to secure lodging and provisions from the wealthy merchant Delfin. On his arrival Povre Perdu sheds his ragged disguise and excites universal admiration. He offers his service to Philip, stipulating a meeting with Romadanaple, who, contrary to custom (but in analogy with the *Nibelungenlied*), is allowed to appear at a public banquet. Here the two young paragons exchange lovelorn glances. Povre Perdu subsequently distinguishes himself in a campaign against the Hungarians (analogous to Adventure 4 of the *Nibelungenlied*) and is granted a private interview with Romadanaple (Adventure 9 of the *Nibelungenlied*). Both suffer all the pangs of lovesickness. These pangs are diagnosed by their respective confidants, who contrive to satisfy their longing by smuggling Florimont into the chamber of Romadanaple (= Plena d'amor) in the guise of a tailor's apprentice.

Florimont's true name and identity are finally revealed amidst general jubilation, but news of a renewed Hungarian attack supervenes. Florimont's superior strategy and valor again win a glorious victory. Philip now agrees to the marriage of Romadanaple and Florimont, but first teases his daughter with the prospect of marrying the king of Crete, who has laid claim to her hand. Romadanaple swoons, the joke is quickly set aside, the king of Crete is reconciled, and the wedding is celebrated. A son called Philip, later father of Alexander the Great, is born to the couple. Florimont concludes his adventures by liberating his father from captivity in a perilous dungeon in Carthage.

Florimont elaborates a number of motifs from the Alexander romances, *Partonopeus de Blois,* and *Floire et Blancheflor,* but it also exhibits a striking community of motifs with German bridal-quest romance: a surrogate wooer, a much-sought-after princess, rival suitors, a reluctant father, contrived disguises and pseudonyms, a magic ring, and secret converse. The disguised foreigner who gains favor with a display of generosity is specifically reminiscent of *König Rother* (vv. 1,291–1,564), and the motif is further elaborated in the later German *Dukus Horant* (ca. 1250), in which the hero also takes lodging with a fabulously wealthy merchant.[18] Exactly how these texts are related to one another is not clear. *Florimont* is too late to serve as a model for *König Rother,* but it shows that the bridal-quest pattern was not unknown in France.

Indeed, the bridal quest emerged in France in its most celebrated form in the Tristan story around the middle of the twelfth century. We do not have the original French form, the so-called *version commune,* but in plot outline it may be assumed to correspond to what we find in the oldest German version (1160–70?) by Eilhart von Oberg.[19] The precise wording of this text is irretrievable because there are only fragments of early manuscripts from the end of the twelfth century, but the story is available in the recast wording of two fifteenth-century manuscripts. We may content ourselves with an outline of the bridal-quest portion:

Young Tristrant (as Eilhart spells the name) travels to Cornwall. Here the Cornish king Mark is threatened with single combat by the Irish champion Morholt unless he surrenders the tribute that has been withheld for fifteen years. Tristrant accepts the challenge on Mark's behalf and inflicts a fatal blow, but is himself stricken by a poisoned wound and elects to be set adrift. Driven to the coast of Ireland, he masquerades as a minstrel and merchant and is healed by medication that Isalde prescribes sight unseen. On the pretext of finding relief for an Irish famine he returns to Cornwall.

Mark now makes Tristrant his heir, but envious courtiers and counselors importune the king with advice to marry. He catches sight of a golden hair dropped by a swallow and, to escape the nagging of his courtiers, declares that he will marry the owner of the hair and no other. Tristrant undertakes the mission of finding her and sets out for Ireland, where he again poses as a merchant. After killing a ravaging dragon he falls into a faint that enables a wicked seneschal to claim the victory. Rescued by Isalde, he recognizes that she is the owner of the golden hair. She in turn recognizes that the notch on his sword matches the fragment found in Morholt's skull, but her lady in waiting, Brangene, dissuades her from killing him. Tristrant now produces the dragon's tongue as a trophy of his victory and the seneschal recants. The way is thus open for Tristrant to woo Isalde on Mark's behalf.

On the bridal voyage from Ireland to Cornwall Tristrant and Isalde mistakenly drink a love potion prepared by Isalde's mother, succumb to its magic, and become lovers. In Cornwall Isalde induces Brangene to take her place in the bridal bed and thus deceive Mark. There follows a long sequence of deceptions and adulterous adventures.

One way to understand this story is as a bridal quest gone awry. The motival repertory is familiar enough: king advised to woo, appointment of a delegate wooer, voyage abroad, wooer's disguise and pseudonym (Tantris), legitimation of wooer (here by valor rather than liberality), and the overcoming of a rival claim. But there is a novel twist. The delegate wooer, not the king for whom he acts, gets the bride. We will see that this is also the situation in the "Brünhildenlied," in which Siegfried becomes Gunther's delegate wooer and extends his service to the bridal bed.[20] Literary history was destined to show that this skewed bridal quest enjoyed far greater popularity than the straightforward variety. Whereas the German minstrel epics never transcended their twelfth-century form, the story of Tristan went on to become a massive success in the Middle Ages and beyond.[21] The obvious appeal lay in the creation of an erotic triangle with new latitude for psychological complexities.

The first to take advantage of this latitude was Chrétien de Troyes, who performed a series of witty variations on the theme in his *Cligès* (ca. 1176).[22] *Cligès*, like *Tristan*, is a two-part romance with a prefatory account of the hero's parents, the Greek prince Alexandre and the English princess Soredamors. We may pass over this generation and summarize the narrative from the point where the Greek throne is in the possession of Cligès's uncle Alis, who has agreed not to marry so that the throne will devolve on his nephew.

Alis keeps his promise for a time, then complies with the urging of his followers and woos the German princess Fénice in Regensburg. During the state visit Cligès and Fénice fall in love. Fénice's nurse Thessala diagnoses her love and brews a potion for Alis that will give him the illusion of making love to his wife while he is in reality asleep (a function transferred from a magic cushion in *Tristan*). With this safeguard the marriage is celebrated. A Saxon duke, to whom Fénice was formerly betrothed, now lays claim to her, but Cligès intervenes to rescue her from the interloper (Tristan rescues Isolde from an abductor in Thomas's version of the story). He then takes mournful leave of her and goes to Britain, where he distinguishes himself at a tournament by defeating Lancelot and Perceval and fighting Gawain to a draw. (Exile and foreign adventure are recurring features in *Tristan*). On his return to Greece he declares his love to Fénice and they arrange for her to counterfeit death with the aid of another of Thessala's potions. (The reader may equate these potions with the counterpart in *Tristan* in a variety of ways.[23]) The court physicians become suspicious and test her coma with molten lead, but she remains steadfast. Removed to a secret tower, she is finally free to cultivate her passion with Cligès, but one day a hunter loses a hawk, climbs over the garden wall, and discovers Cligès and Fénice asleep in each other's arms (just as Mark observes Tristan and Isolde in the cave of lovers). The hunter, having lost a leg in a narrow escape from the pursuing Cligès, reports his discovery to Alis (spies are ubiquitous in *Tristan*), but the lovers make good their escape to Britain with the aid of Thessala. When Alis dies of annoyance, they return to Constantinople to be crowned. Chrétien explains in a mock-didactic afterthought that from this time forward the Greek emperors were always suspicious of their wives and allowed no men in their presence other than eunuchs.

Most of the bridal-quest apparatus has disappeared from this story, notably the figure of the delegate wooer and the disguises and stratagems associated with him. Because the suitor-king has become a subsidiary character, part villain part victim, the focus has shifted from his ingenious ruses to the devices of the young lovers. The mature king is no longer the legitimate wooer. On the contrary, the rival suitor, who stands on the periphery of the standard bridal quest and may, as in *König Rother*, cut a hapless figure, has moved to center stage and now appears to exercise the more legitimate claim, the claim of youthful equality with the bride. Mark and Alis are the first incarnations of the fatuous old lover of fabliau and comedy. To what extent Tristan and Cligès are more legitimate in reality, or only by contrast, is open to question. Chrétien in particular is so equivocal that we cannot tell whether Cligès is a vindicated Tristan, a Tristan reduced to moral absurdity, or a burlesque conceived in perfect neutrality.

It is not happenstance that the focus shifted to young lovers in mid-century France. Two of the earliest narratives from this period are an Ovidian *Piramus et Tisbé* and a vernacular fragment of the Hellenistic romance of young lovers, *Apollonius of Tyre*.[24] The most famous example of the new fashion is *Aucassin et Nicolette*, a *chantefable* probably from half a century later, but of greatest impact on contemporary literature was the *roman idyllique* or Byzantine romance *Floire et Blancheflor* (ca. 1150–60).[25] The earlier or "aristocratic" version tells the following story:

A pagan king of Spain abducts the daughter of a French knight from Galicia and makes her a servant of his queen. They give birth on the same day, the pagan queen to a boy named Floire and the Christian captive to a girl named Blancheflor. The children grow up together as fast friends. Apprehensive about their affection, the king prepares to kill Blancheflor, but the queen persuades him instead to send Floire away so that he may forget his infatuation. The separation fails to achieve the desired end, and the queen now advises that Blancheflor be sold to a "Babylonian" (i.e., Egyptian) merchant, who in turn sells her to an emir in "Babylon" (i.e., Cairo).

In the meantime Floire's parents erect a false tomb and pretend that Blancheflor has died, but Floire, on the point of committing suicide, must finally be told the truth. He disguises himself as a merchant, receives a magic ring from his mother, and sets out to recover his beloved. With the aid of information gathered along the way he traces her to "Babylon," where she has been secluded in the emir's miraculous tower (*tour des pucelles*) in the midst of a no less miraculous garden. Floire's host informs him that she will soon be selected as the emir's wife for the period of one year and gives him advice on the best means of corrupting the guard. The strategy succeeds and the guard arranges to have him hoisted into the tower in a basket of flowers. Blancheflor's companion Clarisse discovers him in the basket, and the lovers are reunited.

One morning they sleep late, are discovered by the emir, and are condemned to death. Each presses the life-preserving magic ring on the other, and at the execution each struggles to submit to the sword first. The emir is finally touched by their love and pardons them. Floire marries Blancheflor and the emir marries Clarisse. After the death of his father Floire succeeds to the throne. For Blancheflor's sake he becomes a Christian and converts his kingdom.

The bridal quest appears here in a formulation that differs from its Germanic counterpart. Some of the motifs are similar—parental interference, a voyage overseas, disguise and deception, penetration into the bride's chamber, relegation of a rival suitor—but the theme of young love and perfect faith (from the Hellenistic romance) quite overshadows such plot accessories. What the author proposes is not the triumph of superior ingenuity but the triumph of superior sentiment. All obstacles yield to true love. Significantly, the ruse of the flower basket, which would have succeeded brilliantly in a German minstrel epic, eventually fails. It is only the emotional steadfastness of the lovers that bends the emir to compassion.

We must now return briefly to the *Roman d'Enéas* (ca. 1160), discussed at the end of the last chapter in the context of legendary narrative. It was evident that the French poet transformed Virgil's epic into romance, collapsing the central books of the *Aeneid* to hasten Enéas' wooing of Lavine and converting the political turmoil in Italy into a contest between rival suitors for the hand of the princess. The present chapter should confirm that the *Roman d'Enéas* is not only, or even primarily, a Roman legend, but a bridal quest in the medieval style. Like the poets of *Tristan* and *Floire et Blancheflor*, this poet too concentrated on a sentimental history: a portrayal of the lovers' emotions, their final union, and perfect bliss. It was first and foremost *Floire et Blancheflor* that set the pattern and established this specific narrative type, the story of separation and misfortune ultimately overcome. In the wake of *Floire* the pattern was exploited in such romances as *Aucassin et Nicolette, Guillaume de Palerne, Amadas et Ydoine*, and Jean Renart's *L'Escoufle*.[26] Peculiar to these stories is the childlike innocence of the lovers, the opposition of their parents because one or the other appears to be an unsuitable match, their passionate fidelity, their misadventures along the lines of Greek romance, and their final vindication. In place of the moral of triumphant guile promoted by German minstrel epic, the French *roman idyllique* promoted the more familiar moral of triumphant love.

Despite differences in emphasis, early French and German romances have obvious similarities. Both tell how the suitor wins the bride. In both the narrative action precedes the marriage; the wedding celebration itself merely serves to mark the conclusion. In either case the dramatic tension derives from parental opposition to the match, although this opposition is differently motivated. In the German minstrel epics opposition is an inherent factor. Folktale fathers and folktale brides have a built-in resistance to suitors. In French romance, on the other hand, the opposition is socially rationalized as an objection to a marriage partner of inferior status or convictions. Either way, a prejudice must be overcome so that the couple, predestined for one another, can be joined. In both types the drama is heightened by competition with a rival suitor, whether he be the Egyptian emir in *Floire et Blancheflor* or the Egyptian prince in *König Rother*.

The question posed at the beginning of this section remains unanswered: Was German bridal-quest epic an entirely indigenous development or did it stand in some literary debt to France, as did the German growth of legendary epic (*Alexanderlied, Rolandslied, Eneide*)? The chronology provides only the narrowest margin. If we date the *version commune* of *Tristan* around 1150, *Floire et Blancheflor* between 1150 and 1160, the *Roman d'Enéas* about 1160, and accept the estimate 1155–65 for *König Rother*, there is not much room for literary traffic. Furthermore, some immediate indebtedness to French prototypes should have left clearer traces. *König Rother* reveals no hint of the French predilection for passion but maintains the fascination with the machinery of courtship already evident in the stories of Clovis and Authari. On the whole it seems likely that *König Rother* antedates the fashion of French romance and that the poet acquired his sense of epic from the drift toward longer narrative that characterized mid-twelfth century German literature.[27]

MARITAL ROMANCE IN FRANCE AND GERMANY

Bridal romance in both France and Germany was soon displaced by another form of romance, which we may call marital romance because it dealt not with the problem of acquiring a bride but with the problem of preserving the marital state. This new form was inaugurated by Chrétien de Troyes in *Erec et Enide*, written before 1176 because it is mentioned in the list of "books by the same author" at the beginning of *Cligès*.[28] Hartmann von Aue adapted *Erec et Enide* in the 1180's, and this event transformed German letters no less radically than Chrétien had altered the course of French literature. The transformation was, however, not instantaneous. It involved a reaction against the old form as well as the creation of a new one. In both France and Germany the emergence of marital romance was accompanied by a continued cultivation and, at the same time, a decisive alteration of bridal romance. *Cligès* itself is such a reversion to the earlier form, albeit in corrosive terms. In Germany too there is a reaction against the vacuousness of the bridal adventure in its original form, with a moralization of the genre toward the end of the century.

The purest representative of the minstrel epic next to *Rother* is *Salman und Morolf.* It is extant only in late manuscripts from the fourteenth and fifteenth centuries and has been dated anywhere from 1160 to after 1190 because it refers to Acre, which fell to the crusaders on July 12, 1191, as a Christian city.[29] Even if this *terminus post quem* is correct, some version of the story was in prior circulation, because it clearly inspired the concluding portion of *König Rother.* The plot of *Salman und Morolf* differs from that of *König Rother* insofar as it dispenses with a clear buildup toward the culminating marriage. It develops the traditional disguise and deception motifs in an almost random manner, as the following summary may show.

King Salman in Jerusalem abducts the heathen princess Salme from India. Four years later the heathen king Fore summons a marriage council, and an aged adviser draws his attention to Salme. Abetted by her father Asprian, he determines to seize her. Great armies gather on both sides, but in a five-day battle Fore is defeated and captured. Salman's brother Morolf recommends execution, but Salman chooses to imprison Fore under Salme's supervision. Fore is able to gain Salme's love by the use of a magic ring and is set free. He returns later in the guise of a minstrel with an herb that plunges Salme into a deathlike trance. Morolf is suspicious and tests her by pouring molten gold into the palm of her hand, but the magic renders her insensible and the test fails. She is put in a coffin, then abducted by Fore in his minstrel disguise. Salman discovers the abduction and appeals to Morolf.

Morolf initiates his countermeasures by disguising himself in the skin of the Jew Berman. He arrives at Fore's court after seven years and occupies a forbidden seat, much to Fore's amusement. He then presents himself to Salme at church and gives news of her own abduction. A duchess notices chain mail under his cloak and informs Salme. The next day he plays chess with her to win the most beautiful maid in her retinue, contriving to distract her with a golden ring on which a mechanical nightingale sings. He too sings, and declares that he used to be a minstrel. With this hint she guesses his identity. Placed under the guard of twelve knights, he lulls them with a sleeping potion and returns to Salme disguised as one of her captors. Resorting once more to the potion, he substitutes a chaplain in the king's bed and another in the queen's. Morolf eludes the subsequent pursuit by submerging himself and breathing through a straw, then returns to Jerusalem and advises Salman to gather an army.

Disguised this time as a pilgrim and equipped with a horn that will summon the army to his aid, Morolf smuggles Salman into Fore's castle. Salman is recognized and condemned to be hanged the next day in the forest. As the execution is about to take place, he blows his horn and the army rallies to his rescue. Fore is hanged instead and Salman recovers his wife. He then defeats King Isolt in another engagement. Fore's sister is baptized and given the new name Affer.

Salme stays with Salman for seven years, but King Princian hears of her beauty, arrives in pilgrim's guise, charms her by dropping a ring in her cup, and abducts her. Morolf responds by making his way to Princian's court disguised as a cripple. He asks for, and is given, Princian's ring, and then departs. Salme guesses the cripple's identity, but Morolf again eludes pursuit, this time in successive disguises as a pilgrim, minstrel, butcher, and merchant. He returns to Jerusalem, mounts another expedition, and captures Salme and Princian with the aid of a mermaid niece. He first releases Princian, then beats off a relief force, then challenges Princian to single combat and beheads him. Once more in Jerusalem, he kills Salme in her bath and marries Salman to Fore's Christian sister Affer.

Salman und Morolf resembles bridal-quest narrative in its repertory of incident, not its structure. It lacks the underlying unity of the wooing theme and fragments into a loose succession of similar episodes that fade into sameness when recalled. The wholesale draft on bridal-quest motifs obscures the plot; one disguise becomes indistinguishable from another. Nor does the story have the grace of young love that we find in French romance. Salme, like Kriemhild in the *Nibelungenlied*, has become a rather timeworn lover when her final suitor, Princian, eventually arrives on the scene; at least eighteen years have passed since her first marriage. Equally absent are the passionate attachments of Greek romance resurrected in the *romans idylliques* and explicitly introduced to the French literary scene in Chrétien's *Cligès*. Far from being a tale of true love, *Salman und Morolf* is a story of endemic faithlessness. Salme is equally susceptible to each new charm. At the same time, the poet fails to capitalize on the literary possibilities of infidelity. The poem is not redeemed by the heightened emotions or the moral quandaries of a *Tristan*. The text might best be considered as an epic fabliau, a genre in which the sport of deception *is* the plot, but in which that sport can nonetheless be cruelly punished. Like the fabliaux, *Salman und Morolf* transpires in a moral twilight, in which the reader has difficulty distinguishing between fun and censure.

The two remaining bridal-quest epics, *Oswald* and *Orendel* (dated in the later part of the twelfth century), depart no less radically from the older paradigm, but in the opposite direction. Both place the bridal-quest pattern in the service of edifying legends. In *Oswald* the hero's quest for a bride (Pamige) in the heathen land of Aron becomes an opportunity for the miraculous conversion of thirty thousand pagans, after which he lives in chaste wedlock for two years and is transported to heaven. Even more artificial is the quest frame in *Orendel*, where it serves to motivate ceaseless campaigns against the heathen both in Jerusalem and at the hero's home in Trier. When all is said and done, the couple is informed by an angel that they are not to sleep together and have only six months and two days to live. They retire to monastic seclusion and are in due course taken off to their reward by a heavenly host. Michael Curschmann has shown how *Oswald* in particular occupies a midpoint on the ideological curve that leads from early bridal quest to the marital idealism of Wolfram von Eschenbach.[30]

It should be apparent from this survey that no sooner had bridal-quest narrative acquired epic form in *König Rother* than this form was diverted to other uses, profane or devout. If our experience of bridal-quest epic in a strict sense is reduced to *König Rother*, we may properly ask whether the category exists at all; a single work is not sufficient to constitute a genre. It therefore becomes necessary to revert once more to *Þiðreks saga*, which provides several examples (translated on pp. 214–51). As explained in the previous chapter, the Norse form of *Þiðreks saga* has clouded its German origin and its place in German literature, with the result that the standard research reports omit mention of the bridal-quest material in it except in dealing with the analogy of "Osantrix and Oda" to *König Rother*.[31] Aside from this analogue, there are three other bridal-quest stories that conform to the morphology of *König Rother*.

The best example of the type is "Attila and Erka." Like the story of "Osantrix and Oda" it exists in two redactions set down by the scribes Mb² and Mb³. In outline the story is so similar to the account of Clovis's wooing in the Frankish chronicles that this account was once taken to be the immediate literary source.[32] The analogies are, however, only generic. Characteristic features are the reluctant father, the delegate wooer, the outmaneuvered rival suitor, the armed contingent in a nearby forest, the abduction, and the marriage celebration. A second example, "Herburt and Hild," varies the pattern. Thidrek (Dietrich) himself, having heard of the fabled beauty of King Arthur's daughter Hild, dispatches his nephew Herburt to woo her on his behalf, but Herburt draws a terrifying portrait of his uncle on the wall and Hild bids him speak for himself. The two make their escape and become lovers.

That this variation was suggested by the story of Tristan and Isolde seems likely. Not only is the triangle of betrayed uncle, intrusive nephew, and pilfered bride identical, but the compiler of *Þiðreks saga* demonstrates his knowledge of the characters, and presumably the story, by naming Thidrek's sister Isolde and her son Tistram.[33] Whereas the Bavarian *König Rother* from 1155–65 shows no detectable sign of French influence, the Westphalian who compiled *Þiðreks saga*, perhaps around 1180, seems clearly to be the recipient of impulses from across the Rhine. His openness to French influence is borne out only slightly less clearly in the third bridal-quest story, "Apollonius and Herborg." The Apollonius in question is earl of Tiri and thereby validates his descent from that Apollonius of Tyre whose story was recast in French in the middle of the twelfth century. Not much, however, is left of the Hellenistic romance except a delicate hint of the incest theme when the reluctant father refuses Apollonius' suit on the grounds that he "loves her so much that he will not marry her to anyone."[34]

Despite marginal concessions to French literature, at least four bridal-quest stories in *Þiðreks saga* maintain the standard plot found in the Frankish chronicles, Paul the Deacon's *Historia Langobardorum*, and *König Rother*. They thus secure this narrative type as a characteristic form in twelfth-century German literature. But at the very moment that the Soest compiler was rescuing the bridal quest from the slow extinction of oral transmission, it was joined, and in some measure superseded, by the adoption of marital romance.

Whereas the older bridal-quest stories focused on the difficulty of winning a bride, the new form focused on the difficulty of maintaining a marriage once contracted. This latter type is more familiar to the modern reader because it strikes us as more ambitious and thoughtful, and because Chrétien and Hartmann stamped it in classical form from the outset. But innovation depends on continuity, and Chrétien wrote against the background of a romance form that was already fully developed. Since the dating of many romance texts is difficult, it is hard to judge exactly which ones he knew, but among them were at least some form of *Tristan* and *Floire et Blancheflor*. He therefore had the bridal-quest form well in mind. Starting from this literary premise, he transferred the emphasis from the vicissitudes of unmarried lovers to the vicissitudes of husband and wife, a profound change in perspective.

The shift may have capitalized on existing tradition, depending on the dating of Gautier d'Arras's *Eracle* and *Ille et Galeron*, to which we will return. It also depends on the dating and authorship of *Guillaume d'Angleterre*, written by a certain Chrétien who may or may not be identical with the master of Troyes.[35] If *Guillaume d'Angleterre* was written by Chrétien de Troyes, it was written after *Cligès*, where it goes unmentioned in the bibliographical preface, but the alternative possibility, that it was not written by our master and antedates *Erec et Enide*, is also tempting.

The latter thought is tempting because *Guillaume d'Angleterre* is the ideal bridge from bridal romance to marital romance. In structure it is a prototypical bridal romance after the Greek manner, except that the protagonists are a well-established marital couple. It is therefore a story not of lovers but of spouses, separated, variously assailed, and finally reunited.

Instead of the perfect faith of betrothed adolescents, it tells the story of perfect marital fidelity in a couple married for five years and sedately advancing toward middle life. The suffering is not inflicted by brutal buccaneers, authoritarian officers, or lecherous women in a position to have their way, as in Greek romance. It is purely mental anguish occasioned by the loss of spouse and children, as in the *Pseudo-Clementine Recognitions*. The poet focuses not on the sentimental dreams we found in *Floire et Blancheflor* but on the reintegration of the family.

Indicative of this reorientation is the new use to which the omnipresent ring of romance is put. In bridal-quest narrative the ring appears again and again as the magic talisman that gives access to the bride. Its magic potency is equally symptomatic of the German bridal epic and the sentimental romance in France. Both types are preoccupied with the magic of love and the magic by which love triumphs. In *Guillaume d'Angleterre* the equivalent ring is not magical. It is a perfectly ordinary ring with no special properties. We are not sure whether it is a wedding ring or just a keepsake that Guillaume wears in memory of his wife, but in either case it epitomizes the marital bond. Guillaume describes it as valueless although it is clearly not valueless to him. It is ordinary only because the symbolic focus has shifted from the magic fantasies of premarital love to the ordinary, real-life institution of marriage.

If *Guillaume d'Angleterre* does predate *Erec* and *Yvain*, it marks the birth of marital romance. If it postdates Chrétien's romances, it goes beyond them in celebrating marriage. *Erec* and *Yvain* still move in the world of faerie, from Arthur's court to the adventures of Joie de la Cour or Brocéliande. The ring that makes Yvain invisible in Laudine's castle is still the magic ring of bridal romance, and the hero's opponents are still dwarves, bandit knights, and giants. In *Guillaume d'Angleterre* there is something down-to-earth about king and queen, despite the poet's insistence on noble blood and his derogation of mere merchants. With due allowance made for the miraculous abduction of the princes, their fostering in the wilderness, and the artificial engines of separation and reunion, this romance exchanges flights of fancy for solid values. The solidity is guaranteed by divine decree. God commands the couple to be separated both from a privileged life of royal habit and from each other, so that they can be reconfirmed in their bond when the time comes. There is an explicit religious foundation for the story, lacking in the more secular *Erec* and *Yvain*. In the latter the separations are a matter of personal pique (*Erec*) or unexplained dilatoriness (*Yvain*); these romances are more about the dawning awareness of the marital state than they are a confirmation of that state.

It is hard to say just where Gautier d'Arras belongs in this colloquium on marriage.[36] Both his *Eracle* and his *Ille et Galeron* are marriage romances in the simple sense that marriage occurs early rather than late, but both confront the reader with more confusing indices than *Guillaume d'Angleterre*. *Eracle* is perhaps the less ambiguous of the two and has a number of correspondences to *Guillaume*. Eracle's parents Miriados and Casine are more than a little reminiscent of Guillaume and Gratienne, the perfect loving couple blessed with offspring after some years of marriage and ready to sacrifice all earthly possessions to satisfy God. But the focal marriage is that of the emperor and Athanais. At one level the story of this marriage is nothing more than an instructive fabliau.[37] Athanais cuckolds her pathologically jealous husband, contrives a meeting with her young lover through the services of a go-between, and wins her point. At another level the story is a mirror image of *Guillaume d'Angleterre*. *Guillaume* celebrates marital fidelity with a powerful positive example. *Eracle* celebrates fidelity with an extreme negative example. The moral of the story may be that the emperor and Athanais would have lived happily forever after if only the emperor had trusted her fidelity. His loss of the perfect wife is perhaps what he deserves, because he himself lacks faith. Her winning of a young lover is what she deserves because she does have faith, a faith that merits reciprocity.

More difficult to fathom is the position of *Ille et Galeron*. Gautier reverts to the narrative premise of sentimental romance, that is, the theme of social inequality, in this case the love of a young knight for a duke's daughter. But the customary impediment of parental disapproval vanishes when the duke freely proposes the match. The barrier is instead the knight's own concern with his social inferiority, which causes him to abandon his wife when a disfiguring wound undermines his confidence even further. This too is a failure of faith, contrasting sharply to Galeron's assurances of abiding loyalty. Ille, although he has a psychological pretext, nonetheless answers to the emperor of *Eracle* while Galeron fills the role of Athanais, with the crucial difference that she is perfectly long-suffering and not remotely inclined to emulate her husband's failure. The consequences of their conduct are, however, oddly shuffled. Whereas the emperor of *Eracle* is punished for his failure, Ille is rewarded with a new wife, while the steadfast Galeron is relegated to a convent. What are we to make of this incongruous resolution? Does it reflect some point of church doctrine that makes religious houses the ultimate refuge of wronged wives and allows inconstant husbands to remarry as long as the first wife is properly immured?[38]

The second half of the twelfth century saw the emergence of a dialogue between two competing types of romance that we may term bridal and marital. Literary histories usually draw the distinctions differently. French literary history distinguishes between *roman d'aventure* and *roman courtois*. German literary history distinguishes between *vorhöfische Epik*, *frühhöfische Epik*, and *hochhöfische Epik*, and assigns *Spielmannsepik* to none of these categories. The terms *courtois* and *höfisch* have been much debated and found by many scholars to be less than useful in describing narrative forms.[39] The only romances that are strictly "courtly," concerned, that is, with the elevation of extramarital relationships, are *Tristan*, *Cligès*, and *Lancelot*. In the larger picture extramarital love is decidedly underrepresented. Much more evident is the concern with stable marriage, either the contracting or maintenance of it. The key to our understanding of narrative in this period is not a doctrine of adultery but the institution of marriage.

In 1977, at Johns Hopkins University, Georges Duby gave a series of lectures on twelfth-century marriage, later published under the title *Medieval Marriage*. In 1981 he expanded his findings in a second book.[40] These books distinguished between two models of marriage in twelfth-century France: a lay model vigorously defended by the upper aristocracy and an ecclesiastical model vigorously pressed by the church. The aristocratic model was determined by the economic exigencies peculiar to this class, which wished to perpetuate itself and its wealth undiminished. The wealth of the great families was chiefly hereditary, and preservation of the inheritance encouraged strict observance of primogeniture. As a result, younger sons were at a distinct economic disadvantage. Each family made every effort to marry the eldest son and to forestall the marriage of the other sons, who were destined to live as bachelors. Duby traces the social strains imposed by such a practice, the unsettled existence of the bachelors (or *iuvenes*) consigned to a life of compensatory adventure, their resentment of the more comfortably settled *seniores*, and their mixture of envy and hostility toward the institution of marriage. Duby described their state of mind in his first book in the following terms: "These bachelors were abductors by their very nature, for they were always tempted to take by force from another household the wife that would make them, at last, into elders (*seniores*)."[41]

This situation contains the sort of social ferment that must have encouraged the composition of *romans d'aventure* and bridal-quest narratives. In France the visions of happy marriage despite parental opposition found in the *romans idylliques* look very much like the fantasies of the disadvantaged *iuvenes* described by Duby. The questing bachelors of German minstrel epic resemble nothing quite so much as Duby's wishful abductors. Erich Köhler views the key text for both countries, the *Roman d'Enéas*, in the same light: "Virgil's hero evolves in the *Roman d'Enéas* into an incarnation of the fantasy of the *iuvenes*, those landless have-nots of the knightly class, to wit, adventure abroad, trial of arms, conquest of a realm, marriage with a princess, and foundation of an illustrious lineage. Later romances repeat this narrative pattern by the dozens, a pattern calculated to enact the dream career of the valiant young knight in multiple variations."[42]

This was, however, only one aspect of the marriage debate; the church promoted a system quite different from the aristocratic model. While the aristocrats defended the economic integrity of the family, the ecclesiastics sought to extend the authority of the church, which emphasized the union of hearts and the consent of partners as opposed to purely dynastic criteria. Throughout the twelfth century the conflict between these two models centered on the issues of exogamy, monogamy, and adultery, on the authority of parents to marry their sons and daughters, on the repudiation of wives, and the marriage of cousins. But as time went on, the church was obliged to rank its priorities. It gradually entertained a degree of flexibility with respect to adultery and incest (marriage within certain degrees of consanguinity) and chose to concentrate on the paramount issue of the indissolubility of marriage. Thus we find that Eleanor of Aquitaine's claims of consanguinity in her marriage to Louis VII were treated as a shallow pretext for divorce and that more importance was attached to the indissolubility of her marriage. And we find the church stubbornly disallowing Philip Augustus' efforts to claim a similar excuse for divorcing his wife Ingeborg.

Ecclesiastical priorities underlie much of the thinking in marital romance. *Guillaume d'Angleterre* is a hymn to the indissolubility of marriage whatever trials and tribulations the partners may undergo. Gautier d'Arras deals with two cases in which divorce does become possible, once because faith and the perfect union of hearts have broken down (*Eracle*), and once because the first wife elects to enter a convent (*Ille et Galeron*). The latter case is illustrated historically by the wistful hope in Philip Augustus' circle that Ingeborg might facilitate his divorce by entering a convent.[43] Finally, Chrétien de Troyes deals with two cases of near divorce, that is, the threat of dissolution, which must be overcome by reflection and greater understanding, so as to restore the permanent union of hearts.

The marriage debate was carried on largely in France, but traces of it are evident in Germany as well. It may, for example, be significant that the bridal-quest epic in Germany hardly survived its inception around 1150 and was already a dead letter around 1200. Aside from the farcical improvisations in *Salman und Morolf*, the genre had no second growth. Instead, the secular ambitions of young knights bent on high adventure were converted into struggles for the rewards of heaven. This is the gist of both *Oswald* and *Orendel*, which are no longer true bridal quests but are well on the way toward the Grail quests of the thirteenth century. The heroes' brides are not the objects of yearning but fellow questers; Pamige in *Oswald* is a secret believer among the heathen and Bride in *Orendel* the guardian of the Holy Sepulchre in Jerusalem. Sexual and family fulfillment is renounced in favor of chaste marriages conceived of as the final requirement for entry into the Kingdom of God. Within fifty years spiritual purification replaced the secular dream as the determining feature of epic. It may also be significant that when French courtly romance entered Germany, Hartmann von Aue chose to use not the premarital and extramarital tales of *Cligès* and *Lancelot* but the marital romances of *Erec* and *Yvain*. Chrétien's view of his own creations in *Cligès* and *Lancelot* is notoriously opaque, but Hartmann avoided the issue altogether, as if there was no question in his mind that the preservation of marriage was the proper study of romance.[44]

Most significant of all in the marriage debate is Wolfram von Eschenbach's statement in *Parzival*, a book that is so intertwined with the *Nibelungenlied* that it is difficult to know which was written first or whether they were written simultaneously.[45] Wolfram proceeded beyond *Oswald* and *Orendel* on the path to the Grail, but he did more than make a meaningful advance; he included a historical commentary on the succession and relative merits of bridal quest and Grail quest.

Following the structural precedent in *Tristan*, he prefaced the story of his hero Parzival with the adventures of his hero's father Gahmuret. Gahmuret is a prior incarnation of Georges Duby's *iuvenis*. Wolfram explains in detail the practice of primogeniture in Anjou and the economic circumstances that compel a younger son to set out on distant adventures in the East. Gahmuret's longing to settle is conveyed by the anchor he adopts as his heraldic device, but he is condemned to an anchorless existence in the service of others. Wolfram, like Duby, explores the psychological consequences of this existence. Gahmuret is not only the great adventurer but also the great lover, though in a naive and almost unwitting way. In whatever fabulous realm he finds himself, he becomes implicated in a great passion, always in the form of the fantasy that the most splendid woman finds him irresistible and requires him only to acquiesce. Each courtship is a burlesque, and each marriage ends with the call to renewed adventure and Gahmuret's departure.

Wolfram's treatment of Gahmuret is parodistic; he is the humorous foil for the ultimately serious hero Parzival. Indeed, Wolfram loses no opportunity in his romance to mock the absurdity of wooing conventions, in the form of Gahmuret's easy conquests, Parzival's simplicity, the flirtations of the teenagers Obie and Obilot, the travestied courtesies of Gawan, the appetites of Antikonie, or the cruelties of Gawan's ladylove with the telling name Orgeluse. Wolfram dispels any doubt we might have that writers around 1200 were conscious of an opposition between imaginary bridal quests and true marriage validated by spiritual progress. Parzival marries only when his religious initiation is complete, and, unlike his father, he will not marry a second time.

II The 'Nibelungenlied'

5. The Literary Context

THE PREVIOUS two chapters have outlined the development of epic and romance in twelfth-century Germany. All critics agree that these two traditions merged in the *Nibelungenlied*, which thus constitutes a new hybrid form. The task of the present chapter is to analyze this generic experiment and set out the ways in which the *Nibelungenlied* absorbed the literary revolution that took place in the period 1150–1200. Proceeding hysteron proteron, we may begin with romance, which had become, in its Arthurian manifestation, the dominant narrative form in the two decades before the composition of the *Nibelungenlied*. When scholarly interest shifted from the paleology of heroic legend to the location of the *Nibelungenlied* in the contemporary literary scene, it was logical that Arthurian romance was the first focus of attention. Thus Hartmann, Wolfram, and Gottfried were the chief standard for Nelly Dürrenmatt's comparisons.[1] The focus should be widened, however, to include bridal-quest romance in the overall picture of twelfth-century narrative. Dürrenmatt referred only to *König Rother*, and tended to relegate it on the ground that it was too unrefined. But bridal-quest narrative is more important to our understanding of the form of the *Nibelungenlied* than Arthurian romance. As we will see in the next two chapters, the primary source underlying the *Nibelungenlied* was a no-longer-extant poem cast in the bridal-quest mold. Our poet elaborated this structure in Part II of his epic and transferred it to Part I as well. In simplest terms, then, the *Nibelungenlied* is a compounding of two bridal-quest plots, just as the later *Kudrun* is a compounding of four such plots.[2]

THE INFLUENCE OF ROMANCE

Of the two originally separate plots in the *Nibelungenlied*, we are more clearly informed on the prehistory of Part II, the tale of Etzel's invitation of his in-laws to a feast in Hunland on Kriemhild's instigation and of the outbreak of fighting that results in the extermination of the Burgundians. At the end of Chapter 2 we saw how the earliest known version of this story, the Norse lay *Atlakviða*, was expanded into a somewhat longer account in *Atlamál*. In these versions the marriage of Atli and Gudrun (Etzel and Kriemhild) has already taken place, but neither version served as a model for the *Nibelungenlied*.[3] The German poet worked from a still fuller version, a written epic estimated at several thousand lines, which can be approximately reconstituted by comparing the *Nibelungenlied* with "Niflunga saga" in *Þiðreks saga* (translated on pp. 186–208 below). This comparison shows that the underlying epic began not with Etzel's invitation to a banquet but with his wooing of Kriemhild, a topic foreign to the Norse versions.

According to the older epic, Etzel loses his wife Helche and learns that after Siegfried's death Kriemhild has become an eligible widow. He therefore dispatches his vassal Rüdeger in state to woo Kriemhild on his behalf. Rüdeger is received at Worms and given a favorable hearing, but no decision is reached until Gunther convenes a council to discuss the matter. During the council Hagen warns of Kriemhild's vengefulness but is obliged to acquiesce. Kriemhild herself is moved to accept when she considers Etzel's power and the prospect of revenge that such power offers. After Hagen seeks to curb Kriemhild's power to do harm by seizing the treasure that is her legacy from Siegfried, she sets out with Rüdeger and proceeds down the Danube. If the *Nibelungenlied* is faithful to the source, we may infer that she is met by Etzel at Tulln and that the marriage is celebrated at Vienna.

This sequence is modeled on the bridal-quest stereotype: report of a distant and eligible princess, dispatching of a delegate wooer, the overcoming of resistance, a bridal journey and marriage. So much at least was provided by the source, perhaps more. But it is certain that the *Nibelungenlied* poet elaborated the stereotype even further. He added the advice of "friends," who urge Etzel's remarriage and identify a partner in stanzas 1,143–46. These "friends" are the almost ubiquitous marriage councillors of bridal-quest narrative. The *Nibelungenlied* poet, like the poet of *Rother*, makes a special point of the wooer's magnificence (stanzas 1,171–74). Rüdeger, one of the chief characters in the epic, more than fulfills the conventional requirement of a distinguished delegate wooer; he goes as far as to assume the total cost of the expedition (stanza 1,153).

It is unclear to what extent there was any resistance to the suit in the epic source, but the *Nibelungenlied* poet makes such resistance the dramatic focus of Adventure 20. It is not, however, the traditional hostility of a guardian father or the pride of a virgin princess that stands in the way. Our poet finds new and more interesting motifs. Hagen voices determined resistance because he surmises the uses to which Kriemhild will put a new marriage. Kriemhild herself begins with seemly modesty (1,218) when approached by her brothers, protests her permanent state of grief (1,233 and 1,238) in her first interview with Rüdeger, and adverts in her own mind to the disgrace of marrying a heathen (1,248). The barriers are piled one on the other because it is the traditional task of the delegate wooer to overcome substantial objections with an extraordinary display of guile, boldness, or perspicacity.

In its most primitive form this task entails no more than the exercise of magic (a potion or ring), but some earlier stories had already moved in the direction of psychological manipulation. Rother, disguised as Dietrich, captivates his bride with an irresistible display of magnificence. In the story of Attila and Erka in *Þiðreks saga* (translated on pp. 225–40) Rodolf, disguised as Sigurd, exploits Erka's secret desire to marry Attila in carrying out his hazardous mission. We find that all such representations progress from public declarations to secret interviews; the object of the wooer or delegate wooer is to penetrate the princess's private chamber so as to reveal his true intention. So it is in the *Nibelungenlied*, in which Kriemhild goes through a series of official interviews until Rüdeger can finally speak to her "in heimlîche" (in secret, 1,255). What he offers is unconditional loyalty, and she suddenly perceives (1,259–60) the potential of such loyalty, together with Etzel's wealth, in facilitating the revenge for Siegfried that she has harbored in her mind for thirteen years.

The poet's special exploitation of bridal-quest patterns lies partly in greater psychological penetration (Kriemhild's interior monologues) and partly in a new dramatic concept. He duplicates the standard narrative only to reverse the usual point, that point being a demonstration of the delegate wooer's superior guile. Rüdeger is the diametric opposite of the customary trickster; he is open, honest, loyal, and totally earnest. Rather than exercising guile, he succumbs to it. By swearing with all his men an oath of perfect loyalty (1,258) he is trapped in Kriemhild's toils and condemned to be an instrument in her maniacal schemes for revenge. The consummate trickster of bridal-quest narrative, embodied most clearly in Morolf, becomes the helpless victim of a moral quandary, and low comedy is transformed, with the agile twist of a literary commonplace, into high tragedy.

In Part II the *Nibelungenlied* poet thus converted bridal-quest comedy to serious uses, but the alteration does not stem from a failure to appreciate the comic mode. This mode is amply displayed in Part I, in which, far from suppressing bridal-quest humor, the poet exploits it almost to the point of absurdity. He does so to a great extent on his own initiative. Whereas the bridal stereotype was already present in the epic source of

Part II, it was less obvious in the source of Part I. Again anticipating the results of the next chapter, we may briefly summarize this lost source as follows:

Siegfried grows up in the wilds, kills a dragon, wins a treasure, and woos Brünhild with a show of force. After his betrothal to her he rides to Burgundy and undertakes further adventures with the Burgundian brothers. Setting aside his betrothal to Brünhild, he wins her hand for Gunther and marries Gunther's sister Kriemhild. Brünhild resists her husband during the bridal night, and Siegfried, disguised as Gunther, is called on to tame her and take her virginity. Brünhild, married to the lesser man, grieves over her lot. She becomes embroiled in a quarrel with Kriemhild over a matter of precedence, and in the course of the quarrel Kriemhild reveals that it was Siegfried who subdued her. Mortified by the revelation, Brünhild incites Gunther and Hagen to kill Siegfried for his betrayal of the secret. The murder is carried out during a hunt.

This condensed plot shows that the *Nibelungenlied* poet had before him not a bridal-quest story but a tale of erotic betrayal and jealousy. Unlike Rüdeger, Siegfried does not play the part of a delegate wooer; he merely accompanies Gunther on the expedition, speaks in his support, and tries to reconcile Brünhild to the new match. There is no evidence of trickery at this point.

If the story as it was transformed in the *Nibelungenlied* has taken on the appearance of bridal-quest narrative, this appearance is almost entirely the result of the poet's elaborations. In the first place he reformed the plot of his source in terms of a double bridal quest, Siegfried's quest for Kriemhild and Gunther's quest for Brünhild. Put another way, Part I is a bridal quest within a bridal quest because the success of Siegfried's suit for Kriemhild's hand is made contingent on his assistance in winning Brünhild. Siegfried is at one and the same time his own wooer and Gunther's delegate wooer. These interlocking actions are both construed along traditional lines.

Although Siegfried grew up in the wilderness as a homeless waif in the source, he becomes the scion of a royal house at Xanten in the *Nibelungenlied*. The protagonist of bridal-quest narrative must, almost by definition, be of royal extraction. As a prince, Siegfried must also necessarily think of a suitable marriage, and his counselors advise him accordingly (stanza 48). We have already learned that Kriemhild's beauty is known far and wide (stanza 45—the hearsay motif).[4] Siegfried promptly chooses her. His parents betoken a somewhat mysterious dismay (50–51), but their concern is comprehensible if we remember that in literary tradition the bridal quest is a dangerous business, resulting as often as not in a dungeon sentence. This tradition may also explain why Siegfried, an eminently qualified suitor, is prepared from the outset (55) for armed confrontation.[5] Despite his anticipation of hostilities he declines his father's offer of an armed contingent and determines to set out with eleven companions (59). Here too the tradition is a decisive factor; it dictates that the wooer (or delegate wooer) be alone and reliant on his own devices. The only preparation for Siegfried's journey is his mother's and father's provision of magnificent attire (63–66), a motif developed most lavishly in *König Rother*. Some of these narrative elements make only moderate sense in the economy of the *Nibelungenlied*, but they are commonplace requirements of the bridal-quest tale as such. Once the poet decided on this model, he made full use of every facet.

Kriemhild is also recruited into the stereotype. She is a reluctant bride because that is the traditional bridal role. From the very outset (15 and 18) she resists the idea of love or wooers, and in two somewhat gratuitous stanzas (45–46) we learn that her arrogance ("hôhgemüete" here in the negative sense) attracts to Worms a series of suitors who are destined to be rejected. She is very much the inaccessible princess whose disinclination must be overcome by the extraordinary prince.[6] But just as the poet lent additional depth to Kriemhild's reluctance to remarry in Part II, so he provides a psychological explanation of her reluctance in Part I by recycling (14–17) the love colloquy between Lavine and her mother in Heinrich von Veldeke's *Eneide*; Kriemhild simply has a young adolescent's native suspicion of love.[7]

The poet's adoption of the bridal-quest frame, including the endangered suitor and the inaccessible bride, forces him into the most awkwardly motivated part of his narrative, the notorious Adventure 3, in which Siegfried and the Burgundians play out a sham conflict staged without apparent reason and set aside as awkwardly as it began.[8] Again, the story type simply requires a brazen suitor and a hostile response from the bride's family. Once these requirements are satisfied, the cordial relationship between Siegfried and the Burgundian brothers that obtained in the source is restored. Putting behind him the brash wooer of older romance, Siegfried enters the lover's service of later romance and performs miracles of valor in a defensive war against the Danes and Saxons. This service earns him his first reward in the form of a celebratory banquet at which the ladies are allowed to appear (273–75).[9] Here Siegfried has his first opportunity to see Kriemhild, a moment for which he has secretly longed (136 and 260). But before the suit can progress further, he must perform a second service and lend his assistance in winning Brünhild for Gunther. In his own wooing of Kriemhild service is substituted for the trickery of bridal-quest tradition, but in his secondary wooing on Gunther's behalf trickery reasserts itself in ebullient form.

Gunther's quest follows many of the standard procedures we have observed in Siegfried's case. He learns of the distant princess Brünhild on

Islant and determines to woo her (325–28). Like Kriemhild, Brünhild is a reluctant bride, but strictly in terms of popular convention; she subjects each prospective husband to three athletic contests, the loss of any of which will cost him his life. Siegfried naturally enough counsels against the adventure, but Hagen proposes that it may be accomplished with the help of Siegfried's prior knowledge. He agrees in exchange for Kriemhild's hand. At this point he changes character. Instead of the alternately belligerent and devoted wooer we have seen thus far, he becomes the master of wooing stratagems in the mold of Rother/Dietrich and Morolf. The key item in his undertaking is a "tarnkappe" (97), a magic cloak that lends him both invisibility and the strength of twelve men (336–38). In addition, the participants in the expedition are fitted out with even greater ostentation (350–70) than Siegfried or Rüdeger on their journeys to Worms. As in his first wooing expedition Siegfried turns down an offer of thirty thousand men and elects to set out with three companions (341). This time, in keeping with the minstrel epics, the journey is by sea and takes twelve days.

Siegfried practices a dual deception. Before landing, he instructs his companions to maintain the fiction that he is Gunther's vassal (386). Once on Islant, he dons his magic cloak and guides Gunther's hand in the required contests. Throughout the enterprise his "list" (guile) is emphasized (426, 452, 455, 464, and 471). All of this is familiar matter. The magic cloak is reminiscent of the rings and herbs of *Salman und Morolf*, but also of the ring that confers invisibility in *Iwein*. The theme of *list* echoes both *Rother* and *Salman und Morolf*; in the latter Morolf is referred to every few stanzas as "der listige man" (the phrase applies to Siegfried in stanza 471 of the *Nibelungenlied*).

Most intriguing is the vassal fiction, which has been the focus of much discussion because it does not seem strictly necessary in terms of the plot. It is of course part of the deception that mortifies Brünhild and animates her revenge, but in view of the athletic deception and the later substitution in her bridal bed it scarcely seems essential to add a third offense. In the context of bridal-quest structure, however, this fiction is just another commonplace; wooers and delegate wooers assume fictitious identities as a matter of course. Thus Rother, before landing in Constantinople, instructs his men to call him Dietrich so that no one will penetrate his mission (*Rother*, vv. 810–15). He then presents himself to Constantine claiming to be Rother's exile (vv. 909–33). Such false identities are also to be found in *Tristan* and the story of Attila and Erka in *Þiðreks saga*.

Perhaps most puzzling of all is Adventure 8, in which Siegfried puts his command of the situation in question by suddenly sailing off to Nibelungenland for a reinforcement of a thousand men. The adventure provides an opportunity for a farcical interlude in which Siegfried, again disguising his identity, fights mock battles with his steward Alberich and a guardian giant. Only when he has secured his reinforcement and returned to Islant is Brünhild's betrothal to Gunther finalized. In this sequence Siegfried seems to have become totally enamored of identity games, hardly less so than Morolf. But Adventure 8 also corresponds to a particular slot in the traditional bridal-quest story. As early as the *Liber historiae* we saw the delegate wooer leave an armed contingent in a nearby forest, and as late as *Rother* this contingent sallied forth to rescue the hero. Siegfried's faithful Nibelungs seem to play the part of this emergency reserve force, but in the hands of the *Nibelungenlied* poet the motif takes on the exaggerated dimensions of parody.

No less parodistic is Adventure 9, in which Siegfried again cultivates confused identities as envoy and wooer. Hagen suggests that messengers be sent ahead to Worms to announce the success of the bridal quest, and he nominates Siegfried for the mission. Reluctance gives way to readiness when Gunther pleads with Siegfried on Kriemhild's behalf. Having played the part of delegate wooer on Islant, Siegfried now sets out on his own wooing journey under the guise of a messenger, like Rother in the guise of Dietrich. But in this case the disguise is an open joke in which everyone participates, not least of all the poet, who assures us that "there couldn't have been a better messenger in the whole world" (541). In his much-coveted interview with Kriemhild, Siegfried plays his part to the hilt by insisting on the messenger's traditional reward. Kriemhild, politely acknowledging the joke, demurs because his station and wealth forbid, but Siegfried treasures his joke and gleefully persists until Kriemhild delivers twenty gold rings, which he promptly bestows on the nearest retainers. In the meantime the poet colludes by referring to him not as Siegfried but as "the messenger"—"she proceeded to thank the messenger for the report" (555), or "she asked the messenger to take a seat" (556). As in Adventure 8, Siegfried takes an almost childlike delight in make-believe. Seen in literary terms, however, all his impostures play off the traditions of bridal-quest narrative. He avails himself of this familiar form to act out a little series of dramatic charades for his own amusement and to regale his audience. It seems clear that the contemporary reader or listener would have appreciated not only the antics but also the parody of underlying literary forms.

With the conclusion of Adventure 9, however, the fun is at an end, and the confusion of identities becomes earnest. When Brünhild resists Gunther during the bridal night, he again calls on Siegfried for assistance. Siegfried impersonates him in bed and subdues the recalcitrant bride. In the source he actually took her virginity, but that motif was too crude for the later poet, who allows him only to exhaust her resistance. Some rollicking humor persists in the account of how Brünhild hung her ardent husband on a peg, but the bed substitution goes beyond the limits of innocent sport, especially since Siegfried absconds with her belt and ring as trophies of his conquest.

This is the crucial break, and the poet is at a loss to explain it (680): "I don't know whether he did it because of his arrogance" (or "high spirits"?—"durh sînen hôhen muot"). In entering Brünhild's bed Siegfried indulges himself in a final impersonation, but here his make-believe crosses an invisible border into reality. Although he does not become her husband technically, he comes much too close. As in *Tristan*, the delegate wooer becomes the actual wooer, or very nearly so; the degree of intimacy is enough to create doubt and occasion Siegfried's murder. He thus falls victim to his own mania for misidentification. The theme of disguise, so prevalent in bridal-quest narrative, is pressed beyond epic commonplace and into a psychological realm. The consequences of a confusion between actual wooer and delegate wooer had of course already been probed in Eilhart's *Tristan*, but the *Nibelungenlied* poet was the first to develop the problem of false identity as a major theme. Just as he converted the comic delegate wooer into a moral quester in the figure of Rüdeger, so he converted the resourceful impersonator into a tragic victim in the person of Siegfried. Disguise was the secret of success in the minstrel epic, but it becomes the mainspring of disaster in the *Nibelungenlied*.

The wealth of bridal-quest allusion in the *Nibelungenlied* makes it certain that the poet was familiar with the form as such, but a separate question is whether he knew specific bridal-quest texts. The clearest model is *König Rother*, the poet's knowledge of which has sometimes been affirmed and sometimes denied.[10] This is not the place to decide such technical issues, but possible echoes of *König Rother* in the *Nibelungenlied* are numerous: the formulaic anticipations of woe (*Rother*, vv. 49, 179); the suitor's mortal jeopardy (*Rother*, vv. 82–83, 336–37); the bridal expedition of twelve men (*Rother*, vv. 124–29; *Nibelungenlied*, stanza 59) or "in recken wîse" ("as an unaccompanied warrior" or "loner," *Rother*, vv. 554, 583, 714; *Nibelungenlied*, 341); the emphasis on splendid clothing (*Rother*, vv. 130–33, 156–57, 218–33, 245–49, 280–87, 1,337–40, 1,500–7, 1,833–60); giant vassals (Rother's giant retainers Asprian, Widolt, and Grimme, and Siegfried's unnamed porter in stanza 487); the wooer's announcement of a false identity to his crew before landing (*Rother*, vv. 805–19; *Nibelungenlied*, 386–87), specifically the fiction that the wooer is the delegate's superior (*Rother*, vv. 911–33); the possession of a treasure requiring transport in twelve wagons for seven nights (*Rother*, vv. 1,026–30) or too large to transport in a hundred wagons

(*Nibelungenlied*, 92); a royal antagonist whose feebleness is exposed in the banquet hall (Constantine and Etzel); the special appearance of ladies at a banquet (*Rother*, vv. 1,804–32; *Nibelungenlied*, 273–75); the athletic events of jumping and heaving a huge stone (*Rother*, vv. 2,163–65); the conveying of a real or false campaign report to the ladies of the court (*Rother*, vv. 2,841–62); repeated distributions of wealth, sometimes by the shieldful (*Rother*, vv. 3,045–51; *Nibelungenlied*, 2,025); and the use of a minstrel as envoy (*Rother*, vv. 3,055–82; *Nibelungenlied*, 1,407). These parallels may not be absolutely conclusive, but they suggest strongly that the *Nibelungenlied* poet was parodying not only a tradition but also a particular text.

König Rother was open to parody because it was an antiquated piece, some forty years old at the time the *Nibelungenlied* was written. It no longer belonged to contemporary literary culture, having been superseded by a more modern form of romance, the marital romance discussed in the last chapter. But before turning to this context, we must cast a glance backward at Heinrich von Veldeke, whose *Eneide* is the only earlier text that all critics agree served as a source for the *Nibelungenlied* poet; he availed himself of the long dialogue on love between mother and daughter in the *Eneide* in forming the conversation between Uote and Kriemhild in his stanzas 14–17. These four stanzas are a negligible sidelight in a poem of 2,379 stanzas, but it is possible to find in the *Eneide* a more fundamental influence on the thinking of the *Nibelungenlied* poet.

We have already observed that Veldeke went beyond his French predecessor in transforming Virgil's political legend into a family drama culminating in the bridal-quest denouement of marriage and dynastic foundation. In a real sense Veldeke's *Eneide* is the last and most elaborate of the bridal romances. It recounts the adventures of an exiled prince, celebrates his triumph, and rewards him with the right princess. After the marriage is concluded and progeny assured, there is nothing more to tell. The *Nibelungenlied* poet made elaborate drafts on this simple plot paradigm, but we may wonder why he should resort to such an outdated narrative form. The answer may be that the wooing adventure had acquired new life in Veldeke's elegant and successful poem. At this late date, however, bridal quest was artistically feasible only in some magnified framework, either in Veldeke's grand account of the founding of Rome, that twin star in the German political firmament and the special focus of Barbarossa's imperial ambitions, or in the hardly less grandiose but more immediately German legend of the Nibelungs.

In either case the bridal quest was subsidiary to a greater historical design and was surely colored by historical events. The *Eneide* was completed at the height of Barbarossa's Italian success after the Treaty of Venice (1177). The *Nibelungenlied*, on the other hand, seems to have been written at the nadir of civil disorder after the failure of the Italian policy in 1197. One epic is animated by the grandeur of the renovated Roman Empire, the other by political and dynastic collapse. In the *Eneide* family alliance is solid and valid for foreseeable history. In the *Nibelungenlied* the family alliances are undermined by passion, greed, and treachery. Heinrich von Veldeke could adopt the bridal-quest model piously, but for the *Nibelungenlied* poet family and political alliances had gone sour. There was no happy denouement in sight. He therefore reverted ironically to the outdated model of bridal quest, illustrated by *König Rother*, that had preceded Veldeke's work, and riddled it with parody and captious implications about real identity, false appearances, and the ultimate fate of true love.

Unlike the *Eneide*, the *Nibelungenlied* does not conclude the action with marriage. Gunther and Siegfried marry Brünhild and Kriemhild in Adventure 10, halfway through Part I. Etzel marries Kriemhild three adventures into Part II. These marriages are not joyous finales but harbingers of doom. The structure of Part I is particularly symmetrical. The first ten adventures are full of fun and mirth, grand schemes, easy success, and seemingly harmless deviltry, but the last nine adventures are dark with deceit and murder. Adventure 16, in which the murder actually takes place, duplicates this structure in miniature by prefacing Siegfried's death with his antic hunting exploits, a last glimpse of the happy-go-lucky adventurer who fails to see beyond his frolics. Both the larger pattern in Part I and the smaller pattern in Adventure 16 make comedy the vehicle of tragedy; festive occasions and festive spirits are preludes to disaster and suggest that the traditional optimism of bridal romance is a delusion.

Part II has none of the ebullience of Part I because the reader is no longer under any misapprehension. The false premises of Kriemhild's second marriage are clearly stated: she marries only for revenge. Her invitation to a reunion in Hunland is therefore transparent, and the remaining adventures are a serial revelation of her treachery. But the poet reserves one final irony for Adventure 27, in which Rüdeger's daughter is betrothed to Giselher. We are given to understand that this is the marriage that might have worked, but the betrothal turns out to be just another deceptive prelude because Giselher is destined to fall in Hunland. Here the *Nibelungenlied* seems to play off the tradition of Greek romance (or *roman idyllique*), in which the lovers, hardly more than children, are betrothed only to be separated immediately. The crucial difference is that whereas romance disdains no improbability in reuniting the lovers, the *Nibelungenlied* poet contrives to block this happy outcome with the death of both groom and father-in-law. (His source was even more unrelenting and arranged for Giselher to kill Rüdeger.) Despite the drafts on bridal romance, then, the *Nibelungenlied* appears more in the light of an anti-romance, subverting as it does the optimism of this tradition.

Bridal-quest romance culminated in marriage but was not about marriage. A preoccupation with marriage as a problematical institution, not just an epic resolution, was reserved for Arthurian romance in the last quarter of the twelfth century. This new type of romance was the most immediate context for the *Nibelungenlied*, but our first impression is that it left very little trace in the poet's thinking. To be sure, he lavishes great detail on the marriage ceremonies, but this instinct was inherited from Heinrich von Veldeke and ran counter to marital romance. Hartmann von Aue depreciates his description of Enite's wedding finery with a concluding emphasis on her good character (v. 1,578), and Wolfram von Eschenbach has no tolerance at all for pomp and circumstance. By contrast, the *Nibelungenlied* seems almost exclusively attached to outward manifestations and has little or nothing to say about marital dealings. Gunther and Brünhild speak only about matters of status, and Siegfried's private communications with Kriemhild are one of the abiding mysteries of the text; we never learn how or under what circumstances Brünhild's belt and ring pass into Kriemhild's possession. That phase of her married relations with Siegfried is unaccounted for and constitutes a crucial lacuna in both our understanding of their marriage and our grasp of the plot.

But if the *Nibelungenlied* is reticent on marital relations, it is contrastingly expansive on family politics. We may recall the possibility that marital romance began as family narrative (*Guillaume d'Angleterre*) and the ample space assigned to family fictions in the Faustinianus and Crescentia stories of the *Kaiserchronik*. The larger family unit subsequently receded in both bridal quest and marital romance, one predicated on the establishment of the lineage and the other on the contract of the spouses. But the focus expands greatly in the *Nibelungenlied*, which displays equal interest in the formation and dissolution of alliances among great families and the microtensions within the immediate family. All the royal protagonists appear in group portraits. Kriemhild is the darling of her mother and three brothers. Siegfried, although he was an orphan in the source, is the apple of his parents' eyes and the object of universal admiration as he comes of age in Xanten. Even the independent princess Brünhild on her imaginary island summons a family council. Etzel is not the covetous Hun of *Atlakviða* but a grieved widower lamenting the death of Helche, and an indulgent husband to his new wife Kriemhild. The unkindness of Rüdeger's fate is heightened by the fondness of his family. Initially, at least, domestic relations in the *Nibelungenlied* appear in the same warm glow that suffuses *Guillaume d'Angleterre* and the Faustinianus story.

Such intimacy, however, turns out to be as deceptive as the bright optimism of bridal romance. All the marriages are undermined by fraud, not just the rectifiable misunderstandings of Hartmann's couples but intentional deceit. The very foundations of marriage are flawed. Both Kriemhild and Brünhild are deceived about the status of their husbands, and Etzel, who thinks he is acquiring a loving wife, must learn that he has been duped to serve as an instrument in her private vengeance. The story is a fabric of domestic lies, and when the truth comes out, the domestic structures crumble. Kriemhild's brothers are portrayed as her protectors at the very outset (stanza 4), but they murder her husband, while she, originally the focus of so much solicitude, becomes the diabolical engineer of their demise. One of the most palpable themes binding the poem together is treachery, specifically domestic treachery. The narration of Siegfried's death is governed by the words "lüge" (lie, 877), "valsch" (falseness, 887, 964, 966), "untriuwe" (faithlessness, 887, 915, 916, 971, 988), "mein" (perfidy, 970), and Siegfried's dying words lament the fate of a son who must live with the reproach of murderous kinsmen (995). The subsequent outcries against Kriemhild's perfidy are even shriller.[11]

Whereas marital romance in general probes the interaction of spouses and ignores larger family concerns, the *Nibelungenlied* is silent on marital relations and voluble on kinship. The Burgundian clan is introduced in perfect harmony four stanzas from the beginning and is destroyed four stanzas from the end with Hildebrand's execution of Kriemhild. It has been argued that Kriemhild herself is the narrative thread, but the story is not so much biography as family drama.[12] It analyzes the mechanisms of family disintegration, how Kriemhild is married in the family interest of acquiring a formidable vassal, how she is pitilessly widowed when the vassal becomes more of a liability than a support, how she is then deprived of the means to reassert herself (Siegfried's treasure), and how she is finally married off again in the hope of removing her from the scene and limiting her capacity for creating dissension. Family politics are consistently the determining factor in this sequence of events.

Kriemhild is repeatedly the object of family representations urging her to accommodate their larger interests. This is especially true of the veritable siege laid to her in an effort to overcome her objections to a heathen mate in Hunland. At the center of the epic the poet adds two new adventures (18 and 19) not prefigured in the source and designed to explain in detail the relations between Kriemhild and her family after Siegfried's death, the hostility between her advocates Giselher and Gernot and her mortal enemy Hagen over the seizure of her treasure, and her reluctant reconciliation with Gunther. The operations of kinship are obviously a matter of some fascination for the poet, but his interest also attaches to the family in a larger, feudal sense. Hagen's ascendancy at Worms and Rüdeger's special position in Etzel's circle illustrate the broader concept, as do the bonds of friendship joining Hagen and Volker or Hagen and Dietrich.

These relationships were once understood as a throwback to Germanic clan feelings, but they are now more readily transparent as a reflection of the poet's aristocratic outlook, as described by Karl Heinz Ihlenburg.[13] In terms of twelfth-century romance, the *Nibelungenlied* may be viewed as a battleground on which the competing ideals of family were contested. The aristocratic model, which dictated the arrangement of marriages to maintain central authority, undiminished wealth, and powerful family alliances, explains Kriemhild's history, whereas the ecclesiastical doctrine of the indissolubility of marriage explains her uncompromising devotion to Siegfried. She is caught between the demands of clan loyalty and marital fidelity. It might be argued that a conservative poet is here retreating to an aristocratic ideology that, in literary terms, predates Chrétien de Troyes, Gautier d'Arras, and Hartmann von Aue, but in light of the disastrous consequences that appear to flow from that ideology, it might also be argued that aristocratic self-interest has become, in the poet's mind, a model to be shunned.

Instead, the new ideal of marital fidelity has invaded his poetic world and transformed Kriemhild. She may originally have had no role in the death of her brothers, as the Norse versions suggest, but when she first surfaces in German tradition reported in the pages of Saxo Grammaticus (see pp. 252–55 below), she is quintessentially the fratricidal sister and her deed is described simply as "erga fratres perfidia." As we will see in the next chapter, she continued to figure in the epic source of Part II as a cold-hearted and remorseless avenger. By the time the *Nibelungenlied* poet wrote his book, however, the spiritual horizons had changed. Harsh heroism had been tempered by the literary cult of women and the ecclesiastical cult of marriage. Kriemhild is still a diabolical avenger, but a large measure of sympathy has been injected into the idyll at Worms and her unshakeable devotion to the memory of her husband. That these were indeed mitigating features for the contemporary audience is shown by the consistent efforts of redactor C to develop them still further.[14] In the popular mind Kriemhild may well have lived on as a devil incarnate, but in her greatest literary portrait she is a figure awkwardly suspended between clan values and marital ideals.

HISTORICAL BACKGROUNDS

Chapter 3 traced the development of historical narrative in Germany beginning with three works roughly classified as "regional history" (*Annolied, Kaiserchronik, Servatius*). In several senses the *Nibelungenlied* also qualifies as regional history. It follows the Rhenish-Bavarian axis so much in evidence elsewhere in twelfth-century German literature. The Rhenish *Annolied* was amalgamated into the Bavarian *Kaiserchronik*; the Rhenish *Alexanderlied* came to be preserved primarily in the Austrian Vorau manuscript; Heinrich von Veldeke's local activity on behalf of his native Maastricht expanded into Middle German Thuringia; the Bavarian *König Rother* betrays a Lower Rhenish poet who gave epic scope to an oral tale preserved in more original brevity in *Þiðreks saga*. In all these works there is a consistent drift from West to East, a drift that also appears to underlie the Austro-Bavarian *Nibelungenlied*.

The first reference to the Nibelung tale in Germany is Saxo Grammaticus' account of "the well-known perfidy of Grimhild against her brothers" (see pp. 252–55 below). Saxo assigns his version to the year 1131, although the exact shape of the tale he had in mind may belong to his own period around 1200. There is little doubt, however, that such a tale did exist in early twelfth-century Germany and could have been recited by a Saxon singer in the way Saxo describes. As we will see in the next chapter, such a North German or Saxon version was known to the Soest compiler of *Þiðreks saga*, and the rough outline of the plot can be retrieved from his composite story. Whether similar versions existed at the same time in western and southern Germany cannot be determined with the same precision, but the Rhenish elements in the *Nibelungenlied*, notably the Rhenish origins of Siegfried, Hagen, and the Burgundians, are so manifest that the tradition must have been alive in this region too. Heusler thought he could detect traces of a Bavarian version of the eighth century.[15] It is in any case clear that the story, probably of Rhenish origin, was elaborated in an Austro-Bavarian epic sometime after the middle of the twelfth century, very much in the same way that an oral Rhenish tale developed into the ultimately Bavarian *König Rother* about the same time. In the course of the Nibelung transmission, however, the Austro-Bavarian proto-epic found its way back to the West and was combined with the older oral version in the Soest compilation underlying *Þiðreks saga*. The literary traffic did not move in only one direction.

The three ascertainable locations of Nibelung tradition, North, West, and Southeast, correspond to the three dominant political regions of twelfth-century Germany—Saxony, Swabia, and Bavaria. The political rivalries among these regions are reflected in the *Nibelungenlied*, as an outline of the historical situation will clarify.

The political scene in twelfth-century Germany was determined by the competing claims of the Swabian Hohenstaufens and the Bavarian (and later Saxon) Welfs. These two dominant families entered a power vacuum when the last Salian emperor, Henry V, died in 1125. At this point Henry's designee was passed over and Lothar of Supplinburg, duke of Saxony, was elected, but he was subsequently obliged to struggle against the Hohenstaufen contender Konrad (later Konrad III) for a full ten years. One of Lothar's remedies during this period was to ally himself with the Welf duke of Bavaria, Henry the Proud. The alliance was a natural one inasmuch as the Welfs had gained a foothold in Saxony as early as 1106, and the connection was strengthened in 1127 when Henry the Proud married Lothar's daughter Gertrude. On Lothar's death in 1137 Henry was the natural heir to the imperial title, but the centrifugal policies of the German princes led to the election of the Hohenstaufen candidate Konrad III.

Konrad had in turn to contend with Welf opposition and sought to curb it by forcing the son of Henry the Proud, Henry the Lion, to relinquish Bavaria in 1143 and by transferring this duchy to a new ally, the Babenberg Henry Jasomirgott of Austria. But Henry the Lion reasserted his claim as early as 1147, and when the next Hohenstaufen monarch, Frederick I Barbarossa, acceded to the throne in 1152, he found Welf opposition undiminished. He met it with a policy of accommodation, restoring Bavaria to Henry the Lion in 1156 and creating a new duchy of Austria for Henry Jasomirgott with a special grant of privileges, the so-called *privilegium minus*. Accommodation was successful for a period of twenty years, but when Henry declined Frederick's request for military support in Italy in the year 1175, relations deteriorated.[16] The final break came when Frederick, with the consent of the princes, stripped Henry of his fief in 1180 and exiled him in 1182.

In the meantime, however, Henry had pursued a vigorous policy of expansion in the East, often in league with Valdemar the Great of Denmark. Valdemar held his throne technically in fief from Frederick Barbarossa, and after the fall of Henry the Lion the feudal bond was reaffirmed (1181), but Frederick's far-flung politics kept him at a distance from the Baltic arena, and Valdemar's son, Cnut VI, did not find it necessary to acknowledge the emperor's suzerainty. Cnut's heir, Valdemar the Victorious, who followed in 1202 at the height of a German war of succession between Philip of Swabia and Otto of Brunswick, was under even less constraint and ushered in a period of Danish supremacy in the Baltic, often at German expense. These events are tabulated in the chronology on p. 97.

It is clear that the importance of Worms, where Barbarossa spent more time than in any other city,[17] and of Austria, Bavaria, Saxony, and Denmark in a poem from the end of the twelfth century is not out of keeping with contemporary events. Furthermore, the poet's political sympathies are readily apparent. He embroiders broadly on his source by describing a gratuitous Dano-Saxon attack on the Burgundians in Adventure 4 and by delighting in the characterization of the Bavarians as highway robbers (stanzas 1,174, 1,302, 1,429, 1,494).[18] These antipathies seem sufficient to establish him outside the Welf domain. On the other hand, his considerable familiarity with Austrian topography[19] and his elaboration of the Austrian margrave Rüdeger even beyond the high status this figure enjoyed in the source suggest clear-cut Austrian sympathies. The betrothal of Rüdeger's daughter to the West German Giselher implies further an interest in fostering the Austrian-Hohenstaufen alliance. This feature was fully developed in the source and led Heusler to surmise that the older epic may have been composed under the Austrian patronage of Henry Jasomirgott (d. 1177).[20] The Nibelungenlied clearly remained in the same political orbit.

These political connections have been remarked on frequently and have been reinforced, by analogy, in recent work on the Bavarian König Rother. Uwe Meves refocuses the diplomatic contacts between the Hohenstaufens and the Byzantine emperor Manuel I Comnenus (1143–80) as the background for Rother's dealings with the fictitious Greek emperor Constantine.[21] Ferdinand Urbanek concentrates more on the allusions in König Rother to internal German politics, especially the manifestly significant references to the counts of Tengelingen.[22] Urbanek makes a surprisingly convincing case for equating certain characters in Rother with contemporary figures: Wolfrat with Count Konrad I of Peilstein and Hall (the hypothetical chief patron of the poem), Lupolt with Count Liutpold of Plaien (a secondary patron), Berker with Count Gebhard I of Burghausen, and Rother himself with Barbarossa. In addition, he finds evidence of uncertain and divided allegiance along the border newly established in 1156 between Welf Bavaria and Babenberg Austria.[23] These findings make the political undercurrents in the Nibelungenlied (and the older epic), especially the anti-Bavarian barbs, more meaningful. It appears that by 1176 the hostility between the Bavarian duke Henry the Lion and the Austrian duke Henry Jasomirgott had been resolved, but local frictions may have persisted.[24] It is in any case clear that a sense of Austrian autonomy distinct from, or in opposition to, Bavaria was only possible after Frederick Barbarossa's partition of 1156. Whether more

Family Politics in the Holy Roman Empire, 1106–1214

1106	The Bavarian Welfs gain a foothold in Saxony.
1115	Lothar of Saxony defeats Henry V at Welfesholz and puts an end to Salian control in Saxony.
1125	Lothar succeeds Henry V on the imperial throne.
1127	Henry the Proud of Bavaria marries Lothar's daughter Gertrude.
1135	Lothar prevails over the Hohenstaufen Konrad.
1137	Lothar dies and Henry the Proud becomes the dominant figure in Germany.
1138	Konrad III is crowned in Aachen. He strips Henry the Proud of Bavaria and transfers it to the Babenberg Leopold IV of Austria, thus initiating the alliance between Hohenstaufens and Babenbergs.
1139	Henry the Proud dies.
1143	Henry the Lion, son of Henry the Proud and Gertrude, relinquishes his claim on Bavaria and Konrad III invests the Babenberg Henry Jasomirgott.
1147	At a diet in Frankfurt Henry the Lion reasserts his claim to Bavaria.
1152	Frederick of Hohenstaufen becomes emperor and gives Denmark in fief to Svend.
1154	King Svend of Denmark is obliged to flee his kingdom and take refuge with Henry the Lion in Saxony.
1156	Frederick Barbarossa restores Bavaria to Henry the Lion and creates the duchy of Austria for Henry Jasomirgott.
1157	Valdemar wins the Danish throne from Svend.
1160	Valdemar and Henry the Lion cooperate in a campaign against the Obodrites.
1162	Valdemar receives Denmark in fief from Frederick Barbarossa.
1164	Valdemar and Henry the Lion again make common cause.
1166	Valdemar and Henry join forces against Pomerania.
1168	Henry is unable to join Valdemar's operations on Rügen and conflicting claims cause dissensions between Saxons and Danes.
1171	Henry and Valdemar set aside their differences.
1175	Henry fails to support Frederick in his Italian campaigns.
1777	Henry and Valdemar again campaign in the East.
1180	Frederick strips Henry of his fief.
1181	Frederick forms an alliance with Valdemar.
1182	Henry the Lion goes into exile in England. Valdemar's son, Cnut VI, does not renew his feudal obligation to Frederick.
1189	Frederick dies.
1195	Henry the Lion dies.
1197	Frederick's successor, Henry VI, dies.
1198	Henry VI is succeeded by Philip of Swabia and a decade of conflict between Philip and Otto of Brunswick ensues.
1202	Valdemar the Victorious follows Cnut on the Danish throne and expands Danish power in the Baltic.
1214	Frederick II confirms the Danish gains.

exact political correlations may be drawn between the *Nibelungenlied* and contemporary history, analogous to those isolated by Urbanek, is doubtful, because it will never be possible to distinguish adequately between the older epic (1160–70?) and the *Nibelungenlied* in political terms. A political orientation in the first may have been ignored, altered, or elaborated in the second, so that the final indices are hopelessly jumbled.

Although the poet's sympathies are clearly anti-Welf and are therefore almost by definition pro-Hohenstaufen, they are not necessarily royalist or imperial. In a broad political assessment of the poem Karl Heinz Ihlenburg argues that the *Nibelungenlied* reflects the problematical nature of feudal structures at the end of the twelfth century, especially the political crisis precipitated by the death of Barbarossa's son Henry VI in 1197 and the ensuing contest between the Hohenstaufen candidate Philip of Swabia and the Welf candidate Otto of Brunswick.[25] Ihlenburg points out that the twelfth century was marked by the rise of the feudal aristocracy and their attempt to make good their claims against imperial authority. Frederick Barbarossa had held them in check, but the conflict after 1197 brought these frictions to the surface once more. The same struggle is played out in the *Nibelungenlied*, in which the conflict involves feeble kings (Gunther and Etzel) and powerful vassals (Hagen and Rüdeger). Ihlenburg interprets Part I in terms of Gunther's display of weakness in meeting Siegfried's challenge, confronting the Dano-Saxon threat, wooing Brünhild, and dealing with the consequences of the queens' quarrel. A fateful discrepancy develops between the king's illusion of power and the real power of Siegfried. At the same time, Hagen enters the power vacuum left by a helpless king, first as a faithful servant of the court but later as a relentless vindicator of his own personal honor. His counterpart, Rüdeger, though occupying higher moral ground, also concedes the binding force of feudal obligation and succumbs in the constricting political web. Only Dietrich rises above the system and points the way beyond the flawed feudal institutions depicted by the poet.

Ihlenburg's analysis is conducted with skill but encounters no fewer difficulties than previous attempts at a comprehensive interpretation. In the first place, it remains to be shown that poetic characters in the twelfth century were assigned such symbolic values. In addition, the interpretive model, both in historical and literary terms, may be too general. Barbarossa had effectively curbed the assertiveness of the German aristocracy, and restiveness after 1197 was surely of too recent date to affect the outlook of the *Nibelungenlied* so pervasively and so systematically. Such an outlook would have been more appropriate around 1150 after a long period of imperial weakness and aristocratic ambition. The contest between monarchy and aristocracy was endemic and would serve as an effective interpretive instrument only at moments of particularly severe strain.

The features Ihlenburg observes may finally be more literary than historical. The contrast between heroic vassal and passive king is indeed a commonplace of epic patterning from the *Iliad* to *Waltharius* to the *Song of Roland* and the *Chanson de Guillaume*.[26] However this may be, Ihlenburg's book serves to remind us of certain issues to which the audience of the *Nibelungenlied* would have been alive. Surely the text struck more

than a few political chords, but literary echoes would not have gone un-
detected either, not echoes of those peaks in the epic progression familiar
to the modern reader but of the forgotten epics of the German twelfth
century. Chapter 3 divided these works into regional history, legendary
history, and heroic history. We may now pursue the links between this earlier historical writing and the *Nibelungenlied.*

THE INFLUENCE OF HISTORICAL NARRATIVE

The *Annolied* reports the founding of Siegfried's native town of Xanten
by the fictive and eponymous Trojan ancestor Franko (vv. 389–95):

> Franko settled with his men
> Very far downstream by the Rhine.
> There they joyfully built
> A little Troy.
> They called the brook Xanten
> After the river in their land;
> They thought the Rhine was the sea.

This curious account is inherited from the learned legend of the Franks'
descent from the Trojans, the name of Xanten being associated with the
river Xanthus on the Trojan plain. Xanten thus enjoys a special historical
distinction, which it may owe to the importance of its church, second
only to the mother cathedral in Cologne. Friedrich Panzer pointed out
that when Xanten is introduced in stanza 20 of the *Nibelungenlied*, the
location "nidene bî dem Rîne" (downstream by the Rhine) echoes the
"nidir bî Rîni" of the *Annolied*, and he surmised an influence.[27] Whether
the *Annolied* is the immediate source of the location or not, Siegfried is
associated with Xanten in no other text. Indeed, in other versions, the
Eddic poems and *Þiðreks saga*, he has no specified birthplace and grows
up in the wilds. Heir to a tradition of regional history, the poet of the *Nibelungenlied* (or the interpolator responsible for stanza 20) was not satisfied
with such vagueness and gave Siegfried a home on a par with Worms, Passau, Pöchlarn, Vienna, and the other identifiable locations of the poem.
Beyond that, he placed him in the context of political legend. Siegfried is
a specifically Frankish name, and it is scarcely happenstance that the poet
locates the greatest Frankish hero in the city of the founding father
Franko.[28] By so doing he adheres not only to a tradition of regional spe-
cificity but also to a tradition of historical continuity. This sense of continuity was a legacy from the *Annolied* and the *Kaiserchronik.*

Continuity and validation in terms of universal history (the legend of
Trojan origins) are, however, no longer the dominant concern of late
twelfth-century narrative. The classical heritage still loomed large in the

mid-century *Kaiserchronik*, but other priorities had supervened. Literary hegemony had shifted to France, and Rome was now equated increasingly with the papacy, a focus of national antagonism, especially for the Hohenstaufen party after almost forty years of struggle between papal and imperial interests during the reign of Frederick Barbarossa. The colors of this antagonism during the crisis after 1197 are brilliantly displayed in the political verse of Walther von der Vogelweide. But even in the *Kaiserchronik* the voice of German particularism is raised. The story of how Duke Adelger of Bavaria and his sage counselor overcome Emperor Severus is not just a moral exemplum but an expression of German assertiveness that marks a stage in the rise of German (especially Bavarian) self-esteem. It illustrates that the Germans have surpassed the Romans both in wisdom and force of arms. This claim is echoed in the anti-Byzantine humor of the Bavarian *König Rother* just a few years later, and it is surely no coincidence that indigenous heroic epic emerged about the same time in the Nibelung proto-epic. Succeeding decades between 1160 and the *Nibelungenlied* did nothing to shake such budding confidence—quite the contrary. The intervening reign of Frederick Barbarossa could only serve to reinforce German self-reliance. As a result, although the stories of Adelger and *König Rother* still speak the language of contentious assertiveness, the *Nibelungenlied* is free of invidious rhetoric. German legend now contains its own justification and shows no obvious signs of derivation from or emulation of Roman models.

On the other hand, the *Nibelungenlied* clearly demonstrates that an absence of overt national chauvinism does not imply the surrender of regional pride. Such pride was an almost universal feature of twelfth-century narrative. Heinrich von Veldeke's elevation of Maastricht especially at the expense of Tongeren is the most egregious example, but the special mention of Regensburg in the *Kaiserchronik* and the *Rolandslied* and the centrality of Soest still obvious in the Norse translation of *Þiðreks saga* illustrate the same point. Like Veldeke's *Servatius*, the *Nibelungenlied* parades us through the cities of a particular region, but the question that has preoccupied scholars is whether any one of these cities commands the poet's special affiliation.

Many have felt that Passau meets the requirements. It receives a good deal of apparently unmotivated attention; every traveller makes a point of stopping there to visit with a certain Bishop Pilgerin or Pilgrim: Kriemhild on her bridal journey (stanzas 1,296 and 1,298), Wärbel and Swemmel on their diplomatic mission (stanzas 1,427 and 1,495), and the Burgundians on their expedition to Hunland (stanzas 1,627 and 1,629).[29] Oddly enough, Pilgrim, who is identified as the uncle of Kriemhild and her brothers, has no role other than to receive these visits. His purely ceremonial presence has suggested to critics that he may be a stand-in for the patron of the poem, specifically for Wolfger of Erla, bishop of Passau. The indices were gathered in particular by Dietrich Kralik in a lecture of 1954.[30]

Kralik believed that the poet probably had dual sponsorship from Duke Leopold VI of Austria and Bishop Wolfger. Of the two, however, Wolfger was the more important. Whereas Leopold is acknowledged in the figure of Rüdeger, who was already present in the older epic,[31] Pilgrim is almost certainly a new creation introduced for no other purpose than to honor Wolfger. Furthermore, the poet seems more at home in Passau than in Leopold's Vienna. He confuses the towns of Zeiselmauer and Traismauer near Vienna, but describes vividly in stanza 1,295 how the strong current of the river Inn washes into the Danube at Passau, the kind of impression available only to an eyewitness. This local color is equivalent to Veldeke's praise of Maastricht or the references to the historical monuments of Soest in *Þiðreks saga*. Although Wolfger was bishop in Bavarian Passau, he belonged to an Austrian family and would, at least privately, have shared the poet's Austrian allegiance. We know too that he was a patron of literature, because a contemporary document notes that he made Walther von der Vogelweide a gift of money for the purchase of a fur cloak.

But why the name Pilgrim? Kralik believed that the name was borrowed from a famous predecessor of Wolfger's, a Bishop Pilgrim of Passau from the tenth century. This Bishop Pilgrim was a current topic because miracles were reported around his tomb in the Passau cathedral in 1181. An association between Pilgrim and Wolfger would have been promoted by Wolfger's consecration as bishop in 1191, exactly two hundred years after Pilgrim's death in 991. Furthermore, Wolfger became patriarch of Aquileia in 1204 as successor to a certain Peregrinus (Latin for "pilgrim"). We may suppose that if the *Nibelungenlied* was not finished before 1204, the name Pilgrim would have served to celebrate Wolfger's elevation to the patriarchate. If it was finished earlier, the name would have functioned as a forecast and a recommendation. Pilgrim would in fact have been a particularly appropriate name for Wolfger because the word could be used to mean crusader, and Wolfger participated in the crusade of 1197–98. All these connections would have been clear to the contemporary audience.

Against this background Kralik went on to evaluate a curious testimony in an appendix to the *Nibelungenlied* known as the *Klage*. According to the *Klage* Etzel's minstrel messenger Swemmel reported to Bishop Pilgrim on the tragic events in Hunland, and Pilgrim had a certain Meister Konrad set down the account in Latin. Kralik agreed with most other critics that this is an evident fiction, but he thought it a fiction with a purpose. The purpose is to reveal, in historical code, the poet of the *Nibelungenlied*, whom Kralik identified as a "magister Chunradus de Patavia (Passau)" active as scribe and notary in Passau from at least 1207, and probably from 1196 to 1224. Kralik's identification may not be exactly right,[32] but some such correlation is certainly suggested by the evidence and has gained greatly in credibility by virtue of Urbanek's inquiry into the analogous topical references in *König Rother*. It seems clear that, despite the objective traditions of heroic poetry, the poet of the *Nibelungenlied* participated in the regionalism that characterizes much of twelfth-century narrative. In this respect too he proves to be a conservative writer reaching back beyond the supraregional Arthurian literature of the 1180's and 1190's to the historical frames of 1150 to 1180.

A distinct category in the literature of this period was the legendary epic inspired by French models: *Alexanderlied, Rolandslied,* and *Eneide*. The impact of these works on the *Nibelungenlied* is not so immediate as the obvious influence of bridal-quest romance, but together they develop certain narrative practices without which the *Nibelungenlied* might have turned out differently.[33] Perhaps the most obvious of these is the biographical mode. The *Alexanderlied* was the first heroic biography in Germany, relating the protagonist's career from birth to death. The older epic that served as the *Nibelungenlied* poet's primary model was not biographical; it began with Etzel's wooing of the widowed Kriemhild. A point of departure in mid-career is one of the generic markers of Germanic heroic poetry, and in this respect the older epic simply adhered to a long-standing tradition.[34]

The *Nibelungenlied* poet, aside from the Soest compiler of *Þiðreks saga*, was the first to depart from it and adopt the biographical frame. A frequent view of his poem, beginning in the medieval period with the manuscript heading "daz buoch Kriemhilden," takes it as a biography of Kriemhild because it begins with her childhood and ends, somewhat abruptly, with her death.[35] Part I is, in addition, constructed as a biography of Siegfried, a pattern that does not hold true for the Eddic Sigurd poems. The epic as a whole is thus a male biography within a female biography. There is some evidence that the author of *Þiðreks saga* may have known the *Alexanderlied* and modeled his epic conception on it.[36] The same may be true of the *Nibelungenlied* poet. It is in any event certain that he did not derive his biographical instincts from Hartmann's Arthurian romance, which introduces its knights full-grown. Eilhart's *Tristan,* Chrétien's *Cligès,* and, depending on relative dating, Wolfram's *Parzival* or Ulrich von Zatzikhoven's *Lanzelet* could have provided models for the hero's *enfance,* but only the *Alexanderlied* carries the reader full course to the hero's death.

Another feature that the *Nibelungenlied* poet would not have found in Arthurian romance, focused as it is on individual deeds, is the succession of full-scale military campaigns with mass movements of troops in both the Dano-Saxon campaign and the march to Hunland. Such military maneuvers are more immediately reminiscent of Alexander's campaign in the East, the Spanish crusade of the *Rolandslied*, and the war between Trojans and Latins in the *Eneide*. Part and parcel of these movements are the council and recruitment scenes, both of which are characteristic of the *Nibelungenlied*. Marianne Ott-Meimberg has connected the council scenes of the *Rolandslied* with German political institutions, and the *Nibelungenlied* poet may be heir to both the actual practice and the literary reflex.[37] His almost cloying taste for lavish festivals has, once again, relatively little precedent in Arthurian romance and may owe more to the great marriage finale of Veldeke's *Eneide*.

The *Eneide* is palpably a model by virtue of the borrowed love debate between Uote and Kriemhild in Adventure 1 of the *Nibelungenlied*, but this model, like the model of bridal-quest romance, is inverted. Lavine's protests against love and marriage have no larger significance since she is destined to marry and live happily ever after. Her protests are tantamount to the disclaimers of youths in Greek romance, for example Clitophon or Habrocomes, who proclaim that they are proof against love just before they succumb hopelessly to the turmoil of a temporarily thwarted but ultimately fulfilled passion. But Kriemhild has more in common with Hippolytus. Her resistance to love, which begins happily but ends in calamity, turns out to be amply justified. Her protests have real meaning in the outcome—they are not just the hollow echo of a commonplace. This reversal of a motif is symptomatic of the larger plot reversal. The *Nibelungenlied* poet converts the dynastic comedy of the *Eneide* into a dynastic tragedy. One poem culminates in a glittering marriage festival to celebrate the founding of the perpetual Roman Empire; the other ends in a treacherous banquet at which the Burgundian dynasty is extinguished.

Central to all the French legendary works was some form of hero worship: a Greek hero in Alexander, a Roman hero in Aeneas, and a French hero in Roland. Chrétien went on to point out explicitly in *Cligès* that chivalry and learning had passed from Greece to Rome and then to France.[38] To what extent the poet of the *Song of Roland* was already aware of this *translatio* and intent on providing a French symbol of it is uncertain, but we have seen the rising tide of German confidence in the twelfth century and it seems not unlikely that the poet of the *Nibelungenlied* was in search of a German figure to match the heroes of France, Rome, and Greece. He created such a figure in Siegfried, who looms far larger in the *Nibelungenlied* than in any other Germanic text. In *Þiðreks saga* Siegfried moves in Dietrich's orbit, and in the Eddic poems he is subordinate to Brünhild. Only in the *Nibelungenlied* does he grow into a central character dominating all others with his strength and prowess. Just how great a hero can be fashioned from mere strength and prowess is a question that bothers modern readers, but we must remember that the French Roland is similarly shallow. Siegfried's elevation to a new status is made particularly obvious by the removal of the ruffian pranks in the forest that were present in the source and the provision of a dignified ancestry at Xanten, with its resonance of Trojan ancestry and an implied supplanting of Roman power.

What the historical and legendary works of the earlier twelfth century do not entirely prepare us for is the tragic culmination of both Part I and Part II. These somber conclusions were of course carried over from the sources, but the loving construction of pathos and calamity that we encounter in Adventure 16 and the whole of Part II is the most obvious signature of the last poet. Catastrophe was his particular forte. The only possible source for such drama is the Soest compilation underlying *Þiðreks saga*. This text not only merged romance and heroic epic for the first time but also projected a sense of gathering doom leading up to total destruction. The central figure, Thidrek, like Siegfried and all the Burgundians in the *Nibelungenlied*, is ordained for disaster.

Despite the easy literary movements between the Rhenish cities and Austro-Bavarian territory, it seems unlikely that the *Nibelungenlied* poet knew the Soest compilation as such because he used sources anterior to it: a relatively short poem about Siegfried, a quasi-epic about the Fall of the Burgundians, and a Dietrich epic. Before we can explore the tragic dimensions bequeathed to the *Nibelungenlied* by these poems, we must review what they contained and how the poet used them.

6. The Sources

W E K N O W both too much and too little about the prototypes of the *Nibelungenlied*. The evidence is sufficient to have tempted a generation of scholars after 1900 into an effort to reconstruct the lost sources on the basis of our extant texts. This project is associated in particular with the name of the Swiss scholar Andreas Heusler, but the labor was shared by others who are now less frequently mentioned, chief among them Léon Polak, Gustav Neckel, Heinrich Hempel, Hermann Schneider, Helmut de Boor, Per Wieselgren, and Dietrich Kralik.[1] Heusler's first important study dates from 1902, and Kralik's unfinished attempt at a radically different reconstruction dates from 1941.[2]

After World War II the project was largely abandoned and replaced by literary studies of the *Nibelungenlied* without reference to putative sources. It was abandoned because scholars decided that the previous generation had been lured into an enterprise that was doomed to failure by inadequate evidence. But the underlying reasons for this decision may have less to do with the nature of the evidence itself than with certain historical factors: the political reaction against a preoccupation with Germanic antiquities after the demise of the National Socialists, the advent of descriptive modes of criticism, the fragmentation of Germanic philology as a field after the war, and even such purely cosmetic matters as Heusler's lapidary mannerisms of style.[3]

The generation after 1945 was ready for a new beginning, and scholarly developments acquiesced. Kralik's massive study of Part I in 1941 would, in an earlier era, have been rejected as an implausible interpretation of the evidence, but in 1945 scholars were only too happy to regard it as a *reductio ad absurdum* that cancelled not only itself but all previous efforts as well. It was assumed that evidence leading to such irreconcilable interpretations was very weak evidence indeed, and it was lost from sight that earlier studies by Heusler, Polak, Neckel, Hempel, Schneider, and de Boor had achieved a good measure of consensus that was easier to ignore than to overturn.

The central article in the consensus reached before 1940 was the positing of an earlier epic that served as a model for Part II of the *Nibelungenlied*. The deduction was based on the close similarity between the narrative of the *Nibelungenlied* and "Niflunga saga" in *Þiðreks saga*. Since it
seemed equally difficult to derive the *Nibelungenlied* from "Niflunga
saga" or "Niflunga saga" from the *Nibelungenlied*, all scholars, at least
since Wilhelm Wilmanns, agreed on the third hypothesis, namely that
both texts drew on a lost written epic or quasi epic and elaborated it in
different ways.[4] In 1945 Friedrich Panzer upset this consensus by arguing
that the *Nibelungenlied* was the immediate source of "Niflunga saga."[5]
Scholarly opinion was ripe for revolution and assumed either that Panzer
was right or that there was simply no telling. Schneider, however, rejected
Panzer's argument in 1950, as did Lohse in 1959, and in 1961 Roswitha
Wisniewski published a dense and tightly argued book restoring the old
consensus, but the new day in *Nibelungenlied* studies had been welcomed
with such enthusiasm that her arguments were passed over in silence.[6]
Scholars preferred to believe Panzer's unlikely proposition that the author
of "Niflunga saga" reworked the *Nibelungenlied* while omitting such
crucial themes as Rüdeger's dilemma, thus crediting a Norse translator
with an anomalous degree of independence.

One of the difficulties in postwar criticism was a new separation of do-
mains. Until 1940 it was a matter of course that Germanists concerned
with the *Nibelungenlied* were familiar with Norse literature. After the
war, partly because of the political reaction but partly too because of in-
creasing specialization, German scholars no longer automatically combined Old Norse with Middle High German studies and were content to
believe that the Norse material did not have the importance once attributed to it. In the meantime, however, the trend has been reversed, and
German, Norse, and Anglo-Saxon studies are once more being integrated
into a single endeavor. In what must now be considered the standard introduction to the *Nibelungenlied*, Werner Hoffmann devotes thirty pages
to the interrelationship of the Nibelung texts and explicitly discounts
Panzer's thesis.[7] We are therefore in the process of reestablishing the traditional view.

THE SOURCES OF PART II

The present chapter identifies the extant Nibelung texts and explains
how they are used in reconstructing the sources of the *Nibelungenlied*.
The object is not to carry out the reconstruction in detail, a task performed elsewhere, but only to clarify the procedure. We may begin with
Part II because the history of the Fall of the Burgundians is somewhat

clearer than the story of Siegfried's death in Part I. First and foremost, the historical events on which the Burgundian legend is founded are more palpable. The early medieval chronicler Prosper of Aquitaine reports that shortly after 435 the Huns destroyed the Burgundian king Gundicharius with his whole people.[8] We assume that Gundicharius is the historical prototype of the legendary Gunther and that his death at the hands of the Huns is the historical event that gave rise to (or redefined) the legend. We learn further from the *Laws of the Burgundians*, set down around 500, that men and women who were free under the kings Gibica, Gundomar, Gislaharius, and Gundaharius shall retain their freedom.[9] This list adds three names to the already familiar Gundaharius. Gislaharius appears to be the prototype for Giselher, but the other two names do not have transparent counterparts in the *Nibelungenlied*. Here the Norse analogues come to our assistance. Gibica produces, by regular phonological development, the name Giúci or Gjúki in Old Norse, and that is the name assigned to the father of the Burgundian brothers in *Atlakviða*.[10] Gundomar has a little more similarity to the name of the third Norse brother, Gotþormr, than to that of the third brother Gernot in the *Nibelungenlied*.

Finally, a number of sources, notably Jordanes' *Getica*, written in 551, tell us about Attila's death from a hemorrhage as he lay by his new bride Ildico after the marriage feast in the year 454. Later accounts embroider the event to the effect that the bride slew her husband to avenge her father.[11] Attila, again by normal phonological development, is identical with Etzel in the *Nibelungenlied*. In this poem Etzel does not die by his wife's hand, surely in part because he had also acquired a crucial role in the legend of Dietrich and according to the legendary chronology had to survive his encounter with the Burgundians in order to help Dietrich recover his realm. But it will be recalled that Atli does die by the hand of his wife Gudrun in *Atlakviða*, so that in this version the historical events of 435 and 454 are coalesced into a single sequence.

Atlakviða was touched on in Chapter 1 and at the end of Chapter 2, but we must now return to it because it provides the point of departure for any study of the legend. It is considered to be an early Eddic poem, perhaps the earliest of all, but, though the chiefly stylistic arguments used to support this early dating are more persuasive than average, we must bear in mind that the dating of all Eddic poems is exceedingly tenuous.[12] The late ninth-century date proposed by scholars for *Atlakviða* may be right, but it is safer to agree simply that this poem is relatively early.[13] "Relatively" means that it is typologically early by comparison to the known German versions. Several of the Eddic poems we will have occasion to discuss below show the influence of German versions from the twelfth century, but *Atlakviða* appears to antedate this wave of Continental influence. As the Rhenish location betrays, the poem must derive ultimately from a German source, but this source subscribed to an earlier form than we find in the twelfth century.

It is difficult to say how many of the differences derive from the German original and how many represent Norse innovations, but *Atlakviða* is narratively quite independent of the *Nibelungenlied*. The main differences are these:

1. Atli, not Gudrun (equivalent to Kriemhild), initiates the invitation to Hunland.

2. The invitation is not motivated by Gudrun's wish for revenge but by Atli's greed for the Niflung gold.

3. Gudrun tries to warn her brothers.

4. Gunnar, not Hǫgni (Hagen), is the chief focus of the heroic action.

5. Gudrun avenges her brothers by feeding Atli his own sons and murdering him in bed.

6. Having taken revenge, she commits suicide in the flaming hall.

It will be evident that the fundamental discrepancy is in the role of Kriemhild/Gudrun and centers on the question whether she makes use of her husband to compass her revenge for Siegfried's death (*Nibelungenlied*) or joins with her brothers against the perfidy of her husband (*Atlakviða*). It is probably futile to speculate which form of the story is closer to the Continental original; logical arguments can be produced on both sides of the issue. With its forty-three stanzas *Atlakviða* does, however, represent the earlier dimensions of the heroic lay before it made the transition to epic in the twelfth century. To this extent it is closer to the original.

Atlamál, on the other hand, is typical of the later Eddic poems that emulated, on a modest scale, the German movement toward epic. We saw at the end of Chapter 2 how the poet of *Atlamál* went about expanding the dimensions of *Atlakviða*, chiefly with the addition of monitory dreams and fuller dialogue, thus extending the narrative by some sixty stanzas. We may surmise that this expansion was inspired by German models because the story is somewhat altered to conform with the plot of the extant German versions.[14] There are two particularly obvious concessions to German tradition. The journey of the Burgundians to Hunland is not overland, as in *Atlakviða*, but takes them over a body of water, as in the *Nibelungenlied*, though in this case they cross the Limfjord in northern Jutland rather than the Danube. In the second place, the focus of the action is transferred from Gunnar to Hǫgni, in accordance with Hagen's preeminence in the German texts.

If the poet of *Atlamál* knew and was influenced by a German variant of the story, presumably in the second half of the twelfth century, we may ask what the form of that variant was. It was not the form known to us from the *Nibelungenlied*, or even Heusler's "Ältere Not," because these versions had already combined the Fall of the Burgundians with the story of Dietrich's exile, thus adding the important figures of Rüdeger and Dietrich himself. There is no trace of either in *Atlamál*. The poet of *Atlamál* therefore knew a more primitive form.

The evidence of such a form comes from the Fall of the Burgundians as it is told in *Þiðreks saga* ("Niflunga saga"). This text is very close to the *Nibelungenlied*, so close that both texts can be derived from a lost written epic, the "Ältere Not." But whereas the *Nibelungenlied* poet used only this version (supplementing it with a scene from an older Dietrich epic and four episodes of his own creation), the Soest compiler of *Þiðreks saga* combined the "Ältere Not" with another, shorter form of the story, presumably known to him from some local source.

The combination is carried out in such an obvious way that it is possible to pick out the elements foreign to the "Ältere Not" and assemble them into an approximate narrative embodying the compiler's second source.[15] The content was as follows:

Grimhild seeks vengeance for the death of Siegfried at the hands of her brothers and dispatches a letter in Attila's name to lure them to Hunland. They accept the invitation and set out, crossing a river in a boat rowed by Hagen. He rows so hard that the oarlocks break, the boat capsizes, and the company arrives at Attila's court with drenched clothing. As they dry themselves around a fire, Grimhild sees the armor under their cloaks and realizes that they are prepared for hostilities. She tries unsuccessfully to remove their weapons, then prepares a banquet for them in an orchard. To prevent their escape from the orchard she spreads raw oxhides before the gates, on which they will lose their footing and become easy prey. The Huns now set upon the trapped Nibelungs. Gunther is cast into a snake pit and only Hagen survives for one night to beget an avenger.

The two most striking features that separate *Atlamál* from *Atlakviða* and associate it more nearly with twelfth-century German tradition—the boat crossing and Hagen's conspicuous role—are present in this presumably oral version used by the Soest compiler. That such a North German variant did exist and could be recited to a Scandinavian audience is confirmed, by sheer coincidence, in an episode related in Saxo Grammaticus' *Gesta Danorum*.[16] In reporting the murder of Cnut Lavard by his cousin Magnus in 1131, Saxo tells us that Magnus dispatched a Saxon singer to summon Cnut to the treacherous meeting. This singer is in the same position as Adelger's counselor in the story from the *Kaiserchronik* recounted in Chapter 3; he wishes to warn Cnut but is restrained by his loyalty to Magnus. He therefore resorts to code and recites to Cnut the story of "Grimhild's well-known perfidy toward her brothers," hoping that Cnut will interpret this parable of familial treachery correctly and make his escape before it is too late. Cnut misses the point and the singer tries to make it more explicit by disclosing a fringe of armor beneath his cloak, a gesture that clearly associates his version with the Soest compiler's second source, in which Grimhild is forewarned of her brothers' preparedness when she sees the armor beneath the cloaks they are drying at the fire. Cnut again fails to make the connection, and succumbs. If the story is true, it tells us exactly how the Norse poet of *Atlamál* could have become familiar with an oral North German variant of the tale. Saxo's lay of Grimhild's treachery, the Soest compiler's second source, and the *Atlamál* poet's German source may have been more or less one and the same version.

This version was older than the "Ältere Not" and may in some sense have been the oral source for the "Not" poet. But the latter poet enriched the tale and lent it epic proportions by combining it with a Dietrich epic, which is also lost. The reconstruction of this Dietrich epic is even more vexed and controversial than our Nibelung reconstructions. It is also more peripheral to our task and may therefore be dealt with more briefly. The reconstruction attempts are based on the comparison of a section of *Þiðreks saga* with twin German tales from the latter half of the thirteenth century, *Dietrichs Flucht* (Dietrich's flight) and *Rabenschlacht* (the battle of Ravenna). Discussions differ not only on details of the reconstruction but also on the question whether there was one early Dietrich text or two, and whether, if there were two, they were both of epic dimensions.

The fullest analyses are by Hermann Schneider, W. E. D. Stephens, and Georges Zink.[17] The most recent of these scholars, Georges Zink, argues for a lost epic on the battle of Ravenna and a lost narrative lay on Dietrich's flight from Verona, but he believes that the account of Dietrich's final homecoming, as we have it in *Þiðreks saga* and the *Klage*, was a later accretion. Hermann Schneider, with the general support of W. E. D. Stephens, argued for a single Dietrich epic that included his flight from Verona, the battle of Ravenna, and his final homecoming. Schneider's arguments seem somewhat stronger. Adhering to them, with only one minor deviation, we may postulate that the lost Dietrich epic had the following outline:[18]

Dietrich abandons his throne in Verona (Bern) under the threat of an attack by Ermanaric. After a successful action against a detachment of Ermanaric's army he makes his way over the Alps to Pöchlarn, where he is graciously received by Margrave Rüdeger and his wife. Rüdeger accompanies him to Attila's court, where he is again given a cordial reception and where he settles down for a protracted period of exile. He marries Herrad, the niece of Attila's wife Helche. After twenty years Dietrich yearns to reconquer his realm. Observing his grief, Helche promises to help him. He is accordingly provided with a body of two thousand men under Rüdeger's command and is also accompanied by Attila's young sons

Erp and Ort. During the ensuing campaign around Ravenna (but under circumstances that are not altogether clear) Erp and Ort are slain by Witege. Learning of their death, Dietrich engages in an epic pursuit of Witege on horseback, but the fugitive eludes him by riding into the sea. Thus drawn off and deprived of victory, he laments the death of Erp and Ort and refuses to present himself again before Attila, but Rüdeger pleads his case and a reconciliation is brought about.

Twelve years later Dietrich learns that Ermanaric has fallen ill and takes his leave of Attila to attempt the recovery of his realm once more. He departs with his wife Herrad and Hildebrand. They stop at Pöchlarn and lament the death of Rüdeger, who in the meantime has fallen during the great battle between Huns and Burgundians. As they ride on, they are attacked by Else and Amelung; Dietrich kills the former, but makes peace with Amelung. Approaching Verona, Hildebrand has an encounter with his son Alibrand, who refuses to identify himself, but the conflict is happily resolved. In the meantime Ermanaric has succumbed to his illness, and Dietrich is welcomed joyfully by his subjects.

This story explains the presence in Part II of the *Nibelungenlied* of certain persons who are not strictly required by the conflict between Burgundians and Huns—Dietrich, Hildebrand, and Rüdeger. Dietrich is present because the battle between Burgundians and Huns is understood to have taken place during Dietrich's exile in Hunland. Hildebrand is present in his capacity as Dietrich's companion and fellow exile. Rüdeger is taken over from the Dietrich epic in his role as Etzel's faithful retainer and benefactor of distinguished visitors. It is particularly in this latter role that Rüdeger excels in the Dietrich epic; he introduces Dietrich at the Hunnish court, joins him in his first attempt to reconquer Verona, and intercedes for him after the death of Erp and Ort. Pöchlarn is the way station for honored travellers, and Rüdeger is their spokesman at the Hunnish court. This is precisely the role assigned him in the *Nibelungenlied*, in which a new affiliation with the Burgundians is added to his prior affiliation with Dietrich.

This new affiliation was already present in the "Ältere Not," as a comparison of the *Nibelungenlied* with *Þiðreks saga* instructs us. The Dietrich epic is therefore anterior to the "Ältere Not." No precise dates can be assigned, but the general drift of epic development in the twelfth century suggests that 1150 is the very earliest moment at which a German heroic epic is imaginable. Perhaps if we place the Dietrich epic around 1150–60 and the "Ältere Not" around 1160–70, we will not be too far off the mark. Looking back at the ascertainable forms of the legend thus far, we may stipulate the following stages.

1. An early form most nearly reflected by the Norse *Atlakviða*. Because we have no other texts from this period, we do not know how closely *Atlakviða* adheres to the German version from which it must derive.

2. A North German lay of Grimhild's perfidy from the mid-twelfth cen-

tury. This version was recited to Cnut Lavard, if Saxo Grammaticus' account is true; it influenced the poet of *Atlamál* when he recast *Atlakviða*, and was conflated with the "Ältere Not" by the Soest compiler of *Þiðreks saga*. It did not include the figures of Dietrich, Hildebrand, and Rüdeger.

3. The first Dietrich epic from around 1150–60. This story supplied Dietrich, Hildebrand, and Rüdeger, as well as certain lesser figures in the cast of the *Nibelungenlied*.

4. The "Ältere Not" from about 1160–70. This version combined the North German lay (or the South German equivalent) with the Dietrich epic.

Compared to the previous versions, the "Ältere Not" is relatively easy to reconstruct by noting the common features in "Niflunga saga" and the *Nibelungenlied*. These common features are extensive and allow the recovery of certain details as well as the main outline of the epic. The ascertainable narrative, printed on pages 210–13, is an approximation of the story that the *Nibelungenlied* poet had before him when he composed Part II. The use to which he put it will be surveyed in Chapter 7.

THE SOURCES OF PART I

Reconstructing the sources of Part I is a complex undertaking. We do not have an independent Eddic poem, such as *Atlakviða*, antedating the German form of the legend in the twelfth century. Instead, we have a series of Eddic poems, or parts of Eddic poems, all of which appear to have undergone late German influence to a greater or lesser extent. Pictorial carvings and skaldic references suggest that Sigurd was known in Scandinavia at least as early as the year 1000, but they provide limited hints about the form of the story at that stage.[19] The Eddic poems differ from the *Nibelungenlied* by virtue of focusing primarily on Brynhild rather than Sigurd and Gudrun (Kriemhild). Brynhild's central position in Scandinavian tradition may indicate that she was also more central in German tradition before the twelfth century, but her importance may also be a peculiarly Scandinavian innovation. We cannot be sure.

Despite the complications attendant on the dating and analysis of the relevant Eddic poems, these poems remain the only key to the evolution of the story told in Part I of the *Nibelungenlied*. What follows is one possible explanation of the evolution, but it does not preclude others.[20] It is based primarily on three Eddic poems about Sigurd and Brynhild: *Sigurðarkviða in forna* (the old lay of Sigurd), *Sigurðarkviða in skamma* (the short lay of Sigurd), and *Sigurðarkviða in meiri* (the long lay of Sigurd). Even the listing of these poems is misleading, because only *Skamma* survives in complete form. All of *Meiri*, of which *Vǫlsunga saga* quotes at least one and perhaps as many as five stanzas, and about half of

Forna are missing in a substantial lacuna in the chief manuscript of the *Poetic Edda*. We have some idea of what these poems contained only because they were incorporated into a prose version of the legend, *Vǫlsunga saga*, before they were lost.[21] Unfortunately, the author of *Vǫlsunga saga* did not summarize the poems one at a time, but combined and interwove them into a harmonized narrative. We can tell exactly how he used *Skamma* because we have the full text of that poem for comparison, but it is very difficult to calculate exactly what he derived from *Meiri* and the lost portion of *Forna*.[22]

Despite the obvious difficulties, scholars agree in a general way on the content of the lost poems. They also agree that *Forna*, as the title Heusler gave it indicates,[23] is the oldest of the poems and most representative of the prototypical form. Heusler's surmise about the content of *Forna* is as follows:[24]

Sigurd comes to the court of the Gjukungs (Gunnar, Hǫgni, and Gotþorm), swears blood brotherhood with Gunnar and Hǫgni, and marries their sister Gudrun. He then accompanies Gunnar on an expedition to woo Brynhild, an independent warrior princess residing in her flame-encircled hall. Gunnar's mount balks at leaping the flames and he borrows Sigurd's horse Grani. When Grani too stays rooted to the spot, Sigurd and Gunnar exchange shapes and Sigurd clears the flames. He presents himself as Gunnar Gjukason and lays claim to Brynhild's hand. She adduces her warlike proclivities and urges him to refrain from his suit unless he is the foremost of men and prepared to slay her wooers. He reminds her of her promise (not previously mentioned) to marry the man who crosses the wall of flame, and she acquiesces. The couple then spends three nights together, but Sigurd places his sword Gram between them, explaining that it is ordained that he should marry in this way or else die. On departing he takes a ring from Brynhild, rides off, and resumes his natural shape.

The two couples, Sigurd and Gudrun and Gunnar and Brynhild, now live in temporary concord at Gunnar's court, but one day trouble erupts when Brynhild takes precedence as the two queens bathe in the Rhine. She justifies her privilege by claiming that her husband has performed many bold deeds while Sigurd was a thrall (a reference to his childhood as a smith's apprentice in the forest). Gudrun disputes the contention and points out that Brynhild is scarcely the right person to vilify Sigurd, since he was her first lover. To verify the accusation she exhibits the ring that Sigurd took from Brynhild when he shared her bed as Gunnar's proxy. Brynhild recognizes the ring, turns pale as death, and lapses into silence.

That evening Gunnar inquires into her grief and she replies that she no longer wishes to live because Sigurd betrayed them both when Gunnar caused him to enter her bed: "I do not wish to have two husbands in the same hall, and this will be the death of Sigurd, or your death, or mine, for he has told Gudrun everything and she abuses me." Gunnar accedes to her urging and takes counsel with Hǫgni, who warns of Brynhild's envy but is unable to deter Gunnar. A magic brew is concocted to fortify the courage of their brother Gotþorm; then the three of them kill Sigurd (presumably in the forest because a raven calls prophetically from a tree). On their return Gudrun questions them and Hǫgni proclaims the deed. Brynhild exults and Gudrun laments.

That night Gunnar stays awake musing on the raven's prophecy that the Hunnish king Atli will murder them. Brynhild awakens a little before day and at last gives free rein to her sorrow. She mourns Sigurd and describes an ominous dream in which she saw Gunnar riding fettered in the midst of his enemies. She reminds the brothers of their broken oaths of blood brotherhood and reveals that Sigurd was faithful to his oath when he placed a sword between them during the proxy nuptials.

This poem is about Brynhild, her avenging of Sigurd's deception, and her conflicting passions. We will see that her emotional conflict is rooted in the German version of the twelfth century, in which Siegfried betroths himself to Brünhild, then marries Kriemhild, thus provoking jealous revenge (a motif referred to as the "prior betrothal").[25] *Forna* hints strongly at jealousy. Brynhild emerges as an ambiguous figure; she both longs for revenge and grieves profoundly over Sigurd's death. Indeed, it seems possible that what she wants is not so much revenge for Sigurd's impersonation of Gunnar as revenge against Gudrun for having the man she wants and was destined to marry. These psychological complications suggest a late stage, and de Vries has pointed out that *Forna* has much in common with the introspective Eddic poetry of the late twelfth century.[26] *Forna* may in fact presuppose knowledge of the prior betrothal.

On the other hand, the poet's failure to acknowledge the prior betrothal explicitly suggests that he adheres in some respects to an earlier stage of poetic development. If so, this earlier stage was characterized by several identifiable features: an absence of prefatory matter either depicting Sigurd's youth or prior betrothal, the delegate wooing of Brynhild behind a wall of flame, the quarrel of the rival queens in a river, and Brynhild's accusation of faithlessness against Sigurd in order to motivate his murder. As in the case of *Atlakviða*, we cannot tell which of these motifs reflect the Continental original and which are Norse innovations. We can only say that they do not derive from the known German variant of the twelfth century.

Skamma elaborates *Forna* in a variety of ways, but is similarly inscrutable on the matter of the prior betrothal. It is not until we come to *Meiri* (ca. 1200?) that we find the prior betrothal fully acknowledged.[27] As retold in *Vǫlsunga saga*, *Meiri* narrates how Sigurd once goes out hunting with hawks and hounds. One of the hawks alights by a window in Brynhild's tower, and as Sigurd climbs up to retrieve it, he sees her through the window. Made pensive by her beauty, he inquires into her identity and learns that she is a warrior princess with no interest in men. Sigurd woos her nonetheless, but she insists on her martial priorities and declares that he is fated to marry Gudrun, the daughter of Gjuki. He continues to press his suit, she finally agrees, and they swear mutual oaths before he departs. The story goes on to tell how Sigurd comes to Gjuki's court, is given a potion of forgetfulness that makes him oblivious of his first betrothal and hence willing to marry Gudrun, and how he clears Brynhild's wall of flame in order to win her for Gunnar. In this version the queens quarrel in the hall rather than at the bath. Attempts are made to console Brynhild, and Sigurd even offers to relinquish Gudrun for her sake, but she is immovable. The poem appears to have concluded along the same lines as *Skamma*: Brynhild incites Gunnar with a false accusation of Sigurd, and the younger brother Gotþorm is delegated to murder him in bed. Brynhild grieves and commits suicide.

There are two crucial departures in this version: the prior betrothal and the queens' quarrel in the hall. Both of these features associate *Meiri* more closely with the twelfth-century German story. This story can be established in the same way as the "Ältere Not," by comparing the *Nibelungenlied* with the Sigurd story in *Þiðreks saga* (pp. 169–87 below). We will again pass over the mechanics of the reconstruction and merely summarize the likely content of the common source, noting that this version is prefaced by an account of Siegfried's childhood, which is not found in the Eddic Sigurd poems just reviewed but is paralleled in other Eddic poems (notably *Reginsmál* and *Fáfnismál*) and in the late German poem *Das Lied vom Hürnen Seyfrid*.[28]

Grimhild has an ominous dream in which her falcon (or hawk) is killed; the bird is interpreted to represent her future husband. Siegfried grows up under the tutelage of the smith Mimir, but behaves outrageously by abusing his apprentices and demolishing his anvil. In reprisal Mimir arranges to have him killed by a serpent. The plan fails when Siegfried clubs the serpent to death with a tree and acquires an invulnerable skin by bathing in its blood. He subsequently wins the Nibelung treasure. In his next adventure he breaks into Brünhild's residence and betroths himself to her. Undeterred by this commitment, he later woos Gunther's sister Grimhild, then urges Gunther to woo Brünhild, offering to act on his behalf because he knows the way to her residence. He succeeds in arranging the match and the weddings are celebrated, but Brünhild hangs her ardent husband on a nail for three consecutive nights. In desperation Gunther appeals to Siegfried, who exchanges clothes with him, takes his place in bed, and deflowers Brünhild. She and Grimhild later quarrel over precedence in seating, and during the heated exchange Grimhild reveals the deception practiced on her rival. Brünhild responds by inciting Gunther to avenge her. Hagen accordingly arranges a hunt with salt food and an absence of drink, thus obliging Siegfried to slake his thirst at a fountain. As he does so, Hagen avails himself of a vulnerable spot on his otherwise impenetrable skin and kills him. When they return from the hunt with the corpse, Brünhild directs them to deposit it in Grimhild's bed. Grimhild infers from the undamaged shield that he has been murdered, but Hagen attributes the killing to a boar. Brünhild rejoices while Grimhild prepares the body for burial.

In reconstructing the "Ältere Not" we are guided by close verbal similarities between the *Nibelungenlied* and "Niflunga saga." Their shared phrasing is so extensive that the relationship of these texts can only be explained from a common written source, not from the necessarily unstable shapes of oral transmission.[29] With respect to the "Brünhilden-lied," the reconstructed source of Part I, we are less certain. In the first place, it was obviously shorter than the epic source of Part II and could have been a memorial lay of the same type as the Saxon lay of Grimhild's perfidy recited to Cnut Lavard.[30] In the second place, the verbal correspondences between *Nibelungenlied* and *Þiðreks saga* are less pervasive. As a consequence, Andreas Heusler assumed that the common source was oral.[31] It may have been, but there are two verbal correspondences in particular that give pause. The first comes from Kriemhild's lament for Siegfried (*Nibelungenlied*, stanza 1,012, and *Þiðreks saga*, 2: 267.25–268.1); the similarity is especially striking if the German verse and the prose of *Þiðreks saga* are compared:

> du lîst ermorderôt.
> wesse ich wer iz het getân,   ich riet' im immer sînen tôt.

> (You lie murdered. If I knew who had done it, I would surely bring about his death.)

> Þú munt vera myrðr.
> Vissi ek hverr þat hefði gǫrt,   þá mætti þat vera hans gjald.

> (You must have been murdered. If I knew who had done it, I would repay him.)

As Heusler pointed out, the correspondence suggests that the common source was in rhyming long lines,[32] but it is also close enough to suggest that both texts derive from an identical written text rather than variant oral versions. Such a supposition is reinforced by another correspondence, this time extending to three relevant texts. It occurs when Siegfried promises to woo Brünhild for Gunther because he knows the way. This idea recurs in the *Nibelungenlied* (stanza 378), *Þiðreks saga* (2: 38.14), and *Skamma* (stanzas 2–3):

> die rehten wazzerstrâzen   die sint mir wol bekant.

> (I am quite familiar with the right sea routes.)

> Þessa konu skyldir þú fá til eiginkonu, ok má ek því
> þar til stoða, fyrir því at ek veit þangat allar leiðir.

> (You shall have this woman as your wife, and I am able to help because I know all the routes thither.)

> drucco oc dœmðo   dœgr mart saman,
> Sigurðr ungi   oc synir Giúca.

Unz þeir Brynhildar   biðia fóro,
svá at þeim Sigurðr   reið í sinni,
Vǫlsungr ungi,   oc vega kunni.

(Young Sigurd and the sons of Gjuki drank and conversed together for many a day until they went to woo Brynhild with
Sigurd riding in their company, the young Volsung—he knew
the ways.)[33]

In the second case the verbal correspondence is less striking than the
motival correspondence, but it may nonetheless suggest the sort of sta-
bility perhaps more easily associated with written versions than with oral
variants. Whichever mode we choose, it seems clear that the underlying
story was known to the Soest compiler and the poet of the *Nibelungenlied* in a fully defined form. There is evidence that this form was also familiar to the late Eddic poets who composed *Skamma* and *Meiri*, perhaps
even to the earlier poet of *Forna*.[34] Of the antecedent form, which shows
through in *Forna* by virtue of the specifically Norse wall of flame, the
quarrel at the river, and the absence of the prior betrothal, we can say
very little.

In summary, then, we may posit the following stages:

1. A relatively old but undatable version, certain features of which appear to survive in *Forna*: Siegfried's proxy wooing of Brünhild behind
a wall of flame, the quarrel of the queens in the bath, and the absence
of a prior betrothal between Siegfried and Brünhild. As in the case of
Atlakviða, we cannot be certain which of these features derive from a
Continental original and which are Norse innovations.[35]

2. A twelfth-century German version (the "Brünhildenlied") ascertainable through a comparison of the *Nibelungenlied* with *Þiðreks saga*.
This version was characterized by prefatory matter on Siegfried's childhood and his prior betrothal to Brünhild. It located the quarrel of the
queens in a hall and Siegfried's murder in the forest. It also made Hagen
the sole instrument of Siegfried's murder.

3. A late Scandinavian version that conflated *Forna* with the German
version of the twelfth century. This stage is represented chiefly by *Meiri*,
which was incorporated into *Vǫlsunga saga*. It added the prior betrothal
and the hall quarrel from the German tale, but not Hagen's murder of
Siegfried in the forest.

These, then, are the lineaments of the story that the poet of the *Nibelungenlied* set about transforming into a large-scale heroic romance
about the year 1200. The methods he used to effect such a transformation are the subject we must turn to next.

7. Originality

T H E *Nibelungenlied* is a long poem, and the compositional permutations are inexhaustible. It cannot be the critic's object to argue any full constellation of features, but only to subject some of the larger narrative procedures to scrutiny.[1] The discovery of further niceties in the text remains the privilege of the observant reader.

Our poet's most substantial source, as well as his obvious point of departure, was the "Ältere Not." It told the same story as Part II with similar dimensions. There was no need to create a plot or devise an overall strategy; this task had fallen to the poet's predecessor. What remained to do was to modernize the old text after a lapse of thirty or forty years and bring it into line with the higher formal and psychological expectations that had evolved, especially since the writing of Heinrich von Veldeke's *Eneide*. There had been a real revolution of taste during these years. The audience that had read or listened to Veldeke and Hartmann, Reinmar von Hagenau and Walther von der Vogelweide, had, we may assume, outgrown the "Ältere Not." On the other hand, the "Ältere Not" must have made a sufficient impression to warrant continued attention. It qualified for perpetuation because it had established itself as a classic of the precourtly period.

THE REVISIONS OF PART II

The content of the "Ältere Not" was briefly this:

Etzel becomes a widower and charges Rüdeger to woo Kriemhild on his behalf. Despite Hagen's misgivings the match is arranged, but before Kriemhild's departure Hagen seizes her gold. Married in Hunland, Kriemhild continues to mourn the loss of Siegfried. She gives birth to a son, Ortlieb, but after seven years she continues to reflect on Siegfried's death and the loss of her treasure. Accordingly she persuades Etzel to allow her to invite her kinsmen to a feast and dispatches two minstrels to Worms for the purpose. Hagen opposes the invitation, but is shamed into acquiescence with slurs on his ancestry and charges of cowardice.

The Nibelungs march to the Danube, where Hagen, holding watch at night, encounters mermaids bathing in a pond. They prophesy that only the chaplain will return from Hunland. Hagen kills the mermaids, secures passage across the Danube (killing the ferryman to boot), and tries to drown the chaplain, who, however, survives to seal the prophecy. The next night Hagen encounters the border guard Eckewart, who warns him of hostility in Hunland and directs him to Rüdeger in Pöchlarn. Here the Nibelungs are splendidly feted, and Giselher is betrothed to Rüdeger's daughter. Rüdeger joins the procession to Hunland. Learning of their approach, Dietrich rides out to welcome them and warn them that Kriemhild still mourns for Siegfried. She greets Giselher with a kiss, but demands her treasure from Hagen, thus revealing her antagonism for all to see. That night Etzel entertains his guests sumptuously, and they retire to their sleeping quarters.

The following day the Nibelungs appear armed for the worst, and while a banquet is prepared, Kriemhild recruits allies for her vengeance. Dietrich refuses her request, but Blœdelin finally agrees and is charged with killing the Nibelung attendants. In the meantime, the banquet commences. Here Kriemhild bids her seven-year-old son Ortliep strike Hagen in the face. Hagen responds by beheading both the child and his tutor, and general fighting breaks out. Dietrich withdraws, but Kriemhild urges the Hunnish warriors on with offers of gold. When Blœdelin falls before Gernot, Rüdeger is so infuriated at the news that he too plunges into the fray. Kriemhild incites Iring with her gold, but after some initial success he falls before Hagen. Kriemhild now orders the hall set ablaze, and the Nibelungs pass the night in terrible straits.

In the morning the engagement recommences. Rüdeger leads the Hunnish attack and is killed by Giselher, who would have become his son-in-law. Gernot and Giselher counterattack, and Dietrich, seeing that Rüdeger is dead, orders his men into battle. He himself kills Volker, while Hildebrand kills Gernot and turns to face Giselher. Hagen asks that Giselher, a child at the time of Siegfried's death, be spared, but Giselher disdains mercy and falls, leaving Hildebrand to confront Hagen while Dietrich does battle with Gunther. Hildebrand is wounded and Gunther subdued, leaving only Hagen and Dietrich in battle trim. Dietrich overcomes Hagen and delivers him bound to Kriemhild. She demands her treasure once more, but he replies that his lips are sealed as long as any of his lords is alive. Kriemhild responds by bringing him Gunther's head, and he now exults in the certainty that the location of the gold will never be revealed. Kriemhild strikes off his head and falls in turn to Dietrich's avenging sword.

This is the approximate outline of the older poem, many details of which are subject to debate and will never be beyond doubt. Whatever the precise form of the story, it is certain that the *Nibelungenlied* poet introduced countless changes. These changes serve as a guide to his view of the legend. What he found before him was a poem with emphases open to revision. Looking at the summary above, we can tabulate a few of his changes:

1. The *Nibelungenlied* poet allows a lapse of thirteen years, instead of seven, before the Burgundians are invited to Hunland.

2. He transfers the dispatching of messengers from Kriemhild to Etzel.

3. He eliminates a slur on Hagen's birth during the Burgundians' discussion of the invitation.

4. He reschedules Hagen's meeting with the mermaids during daylight hours and suppresses his killing of them.

5. He adds a nocturnal encounter between Burgundians and Bavarians.

6. He shifts the meeting with Eckewart from nighttime to daylight hours.

7. On the arrival in Hunland he adds a scene in which Hagen and Volker refuse to acknowledge Kriemhild by standing as she approaches.

8. During the first night in Hunland he adds an episode in which Hagen and Volker stand guard over the sleeping Burgundians and repel a detachment of Huns.

9. At the banquet he suppresses Kriemhild's use of her son Ortliep to provoke Hagen and precipitate the fighting.

10. Instead he introduces Dankwart's report of the slain attendants to ignite the conflict.

11. He introduces an extended analysis of Rüdeger's dilemma in deciding between his fealty to Etzel and his kinship with the Burgundians.

12. He effects an elaborate redistribution of single combats. In the "Ältere Not" the probable sequence was: Gernot/Blœdelin, Hagen/Iring, Giselher/Rüdeger, Volker/Dietrich, Gernot/Hildebrand, Giselher/Hildebrand, Hagen/Hildebrand, Gunther/Dietrich, Hagen/Dietrich. In the *Nibelungenlied* the sequence is: Dankwart/Blœdelin, Hagen/Iring, Gernot/Rüdeger (both succumb), Volker/Hildebrand, Giselher/Wolfhart (both succumb), Hagen/Dietrich, Gunther/Dietrich.

13. He transfers Kriemhild's execution from Dietrich to Hildebrand.

These are some of the more palpable changes, but each affected episode can be broken down into smaller components, in which innumerable details are also changed. It is pointless to pursue such alterations beyond a certain level; the smaller the changes, the less certain we are of establishing them securely. Even if we had the lost source before us and could make a precise comparison, an accumulation of minor deviations would become ever less meaningful. Some changes are hardly more than curiosities, for example the extension of seven years to thirteen before the invitation is issued to the Burgundians. We may simply observe that the *Nibelungenlied* raises numbers and stretches the chronological frame, without attaching particular significance to this practice. Other changes appear to stem from hierarchical propriety or respect for court ritual, for example Etzel's prerogative to issue an official invitation. Still other changes reflect heightened decorum, for example the elimination of the slur on Hagen's ancestry (he was fathered by an elf in the "Ältere Not"). A new standard of civilization shows through when Hagen is not permitted to kill the prophetic mermaids, or when the poet balks at the idea that Giselher should kill his prospective father-in-law Rüdeger, or refuses to have Kriemhild sacrifice her son in her provocation of Hagen. Some deviations are adjustments required by larger changes, as when certain nocturnal actions are relocated during the day because the night hours have been preempted by new episodes. These are, however, not the changes that will figure prominently in our efforts to penetrate the mind of the *Nibelungenlied* poet. The minor changes are peripheral to the concept, matters of taste or tone, probably as symptomatic of a new age as of a new poet.

More likely to interest us are the larger innovations, changes that hint at some fundamental reconceptualization of the story. Gauging the idea of the *Nibelungenlied* is naturally a problematical undertaking because we have no direct access to the idea of the "Ältere Not." Werner Hoffmann has warned us about the futility of trying to recapture the literary quality of the older poem,[2] but *Þiðreks saga* provides a close approximation. The general line of the plot is reasonably clear, and it is this line that we must try to understand.

Because the "Ältere Not" was not prefaced by an account of Siegfried's death, it was obliged to fill in the background by exposition. This was the task of the opening scenes, in which Etzel sues for the hand of Siegfried's widow, and Gunther convenes a council to consider the proposal. Here the theme of the poem is revealed in Hagen's foreboding; Siegfried's murder is unatoned and Kriemhild will bring his murderers to grief if she has the power (*Nibelungenlied*, stanzas 1,210 and 1,212). Hagen's fears are borne out when Kriemhild accepts the suit, overtly out of deference to Etzel's distinction, secretly because of the power and wealth that her marriage will put at the disposal of her vengeance. The marriage sequence ends as ominously as it began, with Kriemhild bewailing the loss of Siegfried; there is clearly no wavering in her designs. Thus the exposition focuses on the two antagonists. Hagen sees clearly, but his warnings go unheeded. Kriemhild emerges as both inconsolable and cunning in her passion for revenge.

The next section of the poem picks up the theme of gnawing vengefulness after seven years in Hunland; we are given to understand that Kriemhild has scarcely let a day go by without pondering her secret intentions, and we surmise that she has wasted no time in accumulating the necessary power and influence. Her calculations surface when she approaches Etzel in bed, feigning a longing to see her brothers. Etzel, whose role throughout is to be his wife's dupe, agrees to the desired invitation and compounds his witlessness by leaving the arrangements to Kriemhild. Upon receipt of her letter, Gunther, whom seven years have made as oblivious as they have made Kriemhild unswerving, reconvenes his council. Time has not obscured Hagen's vision, but in a threefold exchange of mounting rancor he is baited into an angry acceptance of the invitation. The first phases of the poem thus stage a contest of wills between Hagen and Kriemhild, an exercise in which Kriemhild, preying on the credulity of Etzel and her brothers, gains the initial advantage. This sequence, like the first, ends on an ominous note, as Hagen, now absorbed in his own anger, rejects Uote's monitory dreams, Giselher refuses to be detained, and the Nibelungs depart, leaving behind many fair women whom they will never see again.

What follows is the book of Hagen's wrath; he has been outmaneuvered but is terrible in his fury. Meeting the mermaids, he cuts down the unoffending soothsayers. He would happily make an end of the chaplain as well. Finally, he destroys the ferryboat, presumably to forestall any thought of return.[3] Thus the journey is focused through the magnification of Hagen's anger; it is not the itinerary that preoccupies the poet but Hagen's pent-up resolve and the restless energy with which he directs the march.

This energy is conveyed most forcefully by Hagen's two night watches after full days on the road. By the second night his wrath gives way to a courtly exchange with Eckewart. The generous words and polite gestures of this interview contradict his relationship to the Nibelungs, temporarily darkened by insult and frustration. The new tone also ushers in the peaceful interlude at Pöchlarn. Whereas the preceding passages of the poem are given over to anger and misunderstanding, this one is characterized by bright intimacy and hope, sealed by Giselher's betrothal and the giving of gifts. But even in this idyllic setting the foreboding persists. Gotelind wonders whether Giselher will live to marry her daughter, and her parting with Rüdeger reenacts the wistful parting of the Nibelungs from many fair women at Worms.

The foreboding becomes more explicit when Dietrich warns the Nibelungs of Kriemhild's mood, but Hagen is committed to the encounter and shrugs off the warning. He advances amidst the admiration of the Huns, secure not only in his conspicuous stature but also in the strength of his determination. This is the moment for the first direct confrontation. Kriemhild demonstratively kisses only Giselher while Hagen, with a wry gesture, tightens his helmet. Kriemhild responds to the goad and mockingly inquires whether Hagen has brought her treasure. Hagen replies in kind: his weapons were all he could manage on the trip! The mention of weapons suggests to Kriemhild that she can disarm her enemies by the simple device of storing their weapons outside the banquet hall, but when Hagen refuses, she drops her sarcasm and angrily exclaims that the

Nibelungs are forewarned. Dietrich promptly assumes responsibility for the warning and Kriemhild must depart in smoldering silence, leaving Hagen in command of the verbal battlefield. This is the compensatory pattern of heroic poetry; Hagen is already a doomed man, but he is given the satisfaction of a verbal and moral victory before succumbing. When the confrontation has been resolved in this sense, Etzel emerges to issue a guileless welcome, and there is another intermission in the drama while the Nibelungs banquet and retire for their last sleep.

The following morning their last rest is followed by their last church service. As preparations are made to renew the banquet, Kriemhild begins to work her will behind the scenes in earnest. She fails to enlist Dietrich's support, but prevails on Blœdelin and dispatches him to kill the Nibelung retinue, thus precluding relief from outside the banquet hall. Within the hall she gives the quintessential proof of her ruthlessness by prodding her son to strike Hagen full in the face. Hagen understands the finality of her resolve and responds by striking off the child's head, perhaps not so much out of anger as a sense of inevitability and a realization that there is no point in buying a little time. Whereas Hagen initiates the combat with full awareness, Etzel, seeing the death of his son, orders his warriors into battle without ever suspecting that he is a victim of his wife's manipulations. Only Hagen and Kriemhild stand above the action in the full knowledge of what is happening.

The fighting itself is without psychological interest. The most obvious narrative pattern is symmetrical doubling. Etzel orders an initial attack within the hall, then a second attack from without. Kriemhild first incites the Hunnish warriors with a general offer of gold, then applies specifically to Iring with an individual offer. Rüdeger is activated by Blœdelin's fall, Dietrich in turn by Rüdeger's fall. The first combats hint at a Nibelung victory as the chief Hunnish warriors, Blœdelin, Iring, and Rüdeger, fall successively before Gernot, Hagen, and Giselher. Then the tide turns when Dietrich enters the battle and kills Volker. The chief Nibelungs now succumb one after the other, and following a final confrontation between Hagen and Kriemhild the action concludes with the execution of Gunther, Hagen, and Kriemhild.

This outline suggests that the older poem was characterized by clarity of construction and motivation. Kriemhild's revenge is the theme. She raises the issue of her treasure in the first instance as a mockery, but in the final confrontation the mockery becomes earnest. She baits Hagen with one last demand for her gold, and he baits her in return by stipulating Gunther's death. As if to prove her utter abandon and her disregard of everything but her ties to Siegfried, she takes him at his word and delivers Gunther's head, thus leading him, once more mockingly, to exult in his secret, which is now inviolable. At this point the game is played out, and Kriemhild concludes her revenge. Her last exchange with Hagen enables him to even the score before succumbing; the gold is not a real issue, but it allows him a momentary victory, however hollow, to counterbalance Kriemhild's triumph.[4] The scene preserves intact the dramatic line of the poem, which maintains the contest between Hagen and Kriemhild on center stage and on even terms. Symptomatic of the deadlock is the final symmetry of the bloodletting, capping a conflict between two inflexible antagonists, who, after a lengthy prelude of equalized attrition, end in a standoff. The chief excellence of the old poem was the sharpness with which it focused this contest. There is of course no way to calculate the poetic qualities of the text, but the dramatic power must have been considerable.

The poet of the *Nibelungenlied* adhered closely to the plan of the "Ältere Not." His version appears to be coterminous with the original. He also maintains the central conflict between Hagen and Kriemhild, and seems to have retained all the episodes of the older epic, to the extent they can be ascertained. On the other hand, he made major additions. Many of these additions are incidental in nature, ceremonial or merely amplificatory, but others are fundamental and to some degree reformulate the plot. A comparison of the *Nibelungenlied* with "Niflunga saga" leads us to believe that the former added five substantial new episodes beyond what could be found in the "Ältere Not." These episodes provide an insight into the poet's originality and inventiveness. They also offer welcome relief from constant comparison with the analogues and the uncertainties of reconstruction; in reading them, we may hope for more immediate access to the poet's literary predilections. Taken together, they provide the best index to his achievement.

The first of the episodes in question is a night encounter between the Burgundian rear guard and a contingent of Bavarians (Adventure 26). The cause of this clash is Hagen's killing of the ferryman, whose lord, Count Else, joined by Count Gelpfrat, learns of the killing and gathers forces for a pursuit. They meet in the darkness with somewhat surprising consequences; in the first encounter Gelpfrat unhorses Hagen, who must call on his brother Dankwart for aid. Dankwart comes to his rescue and kills Gelpfrat. Else is wounded and the Bavarians are put to flight with substantial losses.

As we have seen, this episode is not pure invention but a borrowing from the lost Dietrich epic, in which Dietrich and Hildebrand, on their way to Verona after the fall of the Burgundians, are attacked by Else and Amelung. What prompted the poet to press the scene into service in a new context? Conceptually it is at least implicit in the "Ältere Not," to the extent that it reflects Hagen's transition from unnatural fury to a more normal state of mind. This transition was marked in the source by the following episode, Hagen's courteous meeting with Eckewart. The *Nibelungenlied* poet simply anticipates the normalization.

The general theme that he is bent on elaborating is Hagen's companionability, a theme suggested in the earlier poem not only by his cordialities with Eckewart but later by his warm relations with Dietrich, with whom he walks arm in arm in the Hunnish camp, a scene recorded explicitly in both "Niflunga saga" (2: 299.22–25) and the *Nibelungenlied* (1,750). In the encounter with the Bavarians the theme is deepened to suggest not only sociability but also vulnerability; Hagen is in real jeopardy and must be saved. His savior is a character not found in the "Ältere Not," his younger brother Dankwart. Dankwart's presence gives Hagen a new context, kinship. In the older poem he was only half human—half brother to the Burgundians, but fathered by an elf. There was something isolated and diabolical about him, a quality that may have explained his inhuman rampage against the mermaids, the ferryman, and the chaplain. The *Nibelungenlied* poet, on the other hand, is at pains to naturalize him, to give him a real family and real personal sympathies. The chief function of Adventure 26 is to establish a fraternal relationship and a special indebtedness on Hagen's part.

A second notable feature of the episode is vivid action. The Burgundians hear the clatter of pursuing hooves behind them (1,601) and see the gleam of shields in the darkness (1,602). Hagen is overthrown, nearly killed, and rescued in the nick of time. The clash of metal echoes as the Burgundians pursue the Bavarians into the night (1,616). Under the half illumination of the moon emerging from behind the clouds Hagen urges his men not to report the action to their commanders until the next morning (1,620), when the dawn reveals their armor bloodied by the night's battle (1,624). Such night action is unexampled in earlier German literature.[5] A particularly striking counterexample is that Heinrich von Veldeke, when referring to the fall of Troy, a haunting nocturnal scene of destruction in Virgil, fails even to mention that the action took place at night. The effects achieved by the *Nibelungenlied* poet are rudimentary by Virgilian standards, but they are strikingly innovative in the German context.

The second major revision occurs as the Nibelungs are about to be entertained by Etzel on the first evening (Adventure 29). Hagen seeks out Volker and sits down with him on a bench opposite Kriemhild's hall, where she observes them, once again remembers her sorrow, and bursts into tears. As Hagen had once responded to Brünhild's tears (864), the Hunnish warriors now respond to Kriemhild's and promise vengeance.

Sixty of them arm, but Kriemhild warns them that Volker is even more to be feared than Hagen, and four hundred more arm themselves. Before they attack, Kriemhild wishes to confront her enemies alone and extract the truth about Hagen's murder of Siegfried. In the meantime Volker observes the hostile dispositions and questions Hagen; Hagen is in no doubt about the Huns' intentions and asks whether Volker will stand by him. Volker's reply is that he will not retreat so much as a foot before Etzel or his whole army. He does, however, propose to rise respectfully as Kriemhild approaches, but Hagen in rekindled anger refuses, lest the gesture betray some trace of fear. He contemptuously lays Siegfried's sword across his knees, and Kriemhild again weeps at the thought of her grief.[6] She demands to know who invited him, and he replies that the invitation was extended to his three lords, to whom he is obligated as a vassal and whom he is not accustomed to abandon. She then charges him with Siegfried's murder, which he readily admits but justifies as vengeance for her abuse of Brünhild. She appeals finally to her Hunnish followers, who recall Hagen's miracles of valor when he was a hostage at Etzel's court in his youth, then look at one another in a state of paralysis, decide on prudence, and retreat. The scene concludes with one of the poet's rare reflections, in the words of Volker (1,801):

> Wie dicke ein man durch vorhte   manigiu dinc verlât,
> swâ sô friunt bî friunde   friuntlîchen stât;
> und hât er guote sinne,   daz erz nine tuot,
> schade vil maniges mannes   wirt von sinnen wol behuot.

> (How often a man leaves many a thing undone because of fear when friend stands by friend in friendship; if such a man is prudent and refrains from action, many an injury is prevented by prudence.)[7]

This episode reveals the same sense of vivid staging and gesture found in the encounter with the Bavarians, a sense revealed in the precise location of the parties, the preparatory discussions on both sides, the narrowing focus of the confrontation, the demonstrative symbolism of seating and sword, and the humiliation of Kriemhild brought about in contrasting but equal measure by the shrinking spirit of the Huns and the determination of Hagen and Volker. Also in evidence is the poet's intensification of emotion, especially Kriemhild's recurrent grief and Hagen's granite temper. But beyond the visual and emotional effects, the episode suggests certain capital themes.

Although centered on the conflict between Hagen and Kriemhild, the traditional focus of the poem, Adventure 29 is almost equally concerned with the special bond between Hagen and Volker and their loyal support of each other. We may speculate, perhaps extravagantly, that had the scene been a part of the "Ältere Not," it would have focused exclusively on

Hagen and Kriemhild in line with that poem's more concentrated dynamics. The *Nibelungenlied* poet, however, was interested not only in bitter antagonism but also in an ideal of partnership. Adventure 26 established mutual trust and dependence between Hagen and Dankwart; Adventure 29 extends the concept to Hagen and Volker, but more insistently. Hagen's request for support and Volker's absolute commitment are verbalized in detail.

A second theme is decorum, which preoccupies the poet in ways large and small at almost every turn. In devising the ultimate insult, calculated to make the conflict irrevocable, he characteristically relies on a breach of court etiquette, the failure of Hagen and Volker to rise before a queen. Nelly Dürrenmatt's *Das Nibelungenlied im Kreis der höfischen Dichtung*, the signal for a new approach to the *Nibelungenlied* in contemporary terms, associated the poet's sense of ritual with the other courtly epics of the period. But, she concluded, he is even more deeply committed to propriety than his contemporaries.[8] Hartmann is more interested in meaning than surface, Wolfram has little patience with courtly niceties, and Gottfried has an amused and almost academic perspective on ritual (for example, Tristan's hunting pedantries). It may be recalled that rising before a queen is also an issue in the first scene of Hartmann's *Iwein*, as Kalogreant leaps to his feet at the entry of Guinevere only to suffer the taunts of Sir Kay for his wanton display of good breeding. For Hartmann (and Chrétien) etiquette is a debatable matter, but for the *Nibelungenlied* poet it has more absolute value.

A third capital theme is candor and loyalty. Kriemhild approaches Hagen with the avowed intention of forcing him to confess the murder of Siegfried (1,771: "I know he is so proud that he will not deny it"). Hagen is indeed only too ready to admit and justify the deed.[9] His justification is that Kriemhild insulted his queen (an insult that he now reciprocates). That justification is in line with his reply when Kriemhild challenges his very presence in Hunland: he is there, he says, as the loyal vassal of his lords. In his short exchange with Kriemhild he thus manages to establish himself as the faithful servant of both his masters and his mistress. Such fidelity is the underlying sense of the newly formed alliance between Hagen and Volker as well. The gist of Volker's summary maxim is that loyal friends standing together in perfect solidarity can overcome all odds, with the implied warning that friends who fail one another will succumb. This sentiment is of course controverted by the outcome of the poem, but it is confirmed for the moment by the retreat of the Huns. In any event, it demonstrates the poet's ability not only to plot dramatic action but also to crystallize a theme.

The third new episode follows directly and occupies the brief Adventure 30. After the evening banquet the Burgundians retire to their night quarters, but in the process are jostled by the Huns. Volker bids them make way, while managing to impugn their valor at the same time (1,821: "They all call themselves warriors but don't have equal measures of courage," or perhaps, "don't have the courage that would justify the name"). Hagen chimes in and tells them to come back in the morning if they have anything in mind. The magnificence of their quarters is then described in three stanzas. Giselher expresses apprehension, and Hagen volunteers to hold the watch. When Volker immediately offers to join him, Hagen responds with warm thanks (1,831): "May God in heaven reward you, dear Volker. I desire no remedy for all my cares but you alone, if I should be in jeopardy." They take up their posts and Volker lulls the Burgundians to sleep with the sweet tones of his fiddle. In the middle of the night he sees the shining helmet of an approaching Hun, and he and Hagen bide their time quietly. But when one of the Huns observes Volker on guard, the others panic and retreat fearfully. Volker is inclined to pursue them, but Hagen warns against exposing the sleeping Burgundians by abandoning the door. Volker therefore confines himself to denouncing the treachery and cowardice of the Huns in scathing words.

There is no hint that this episode existed in the "Ältere Not." The *Nibelungenlied* poet found room for it in his time frame by using the otherwise unexploited night hours between the first and second days in Hunland; the Bavarian attack in Adventure 26 gave precedent for the elaboration of night action, and Hagen's night watches in the "Ältere Not" predestined him for the new roles. Having dropped those two night watches, the meetings with the mermaids and Eckewart, the poet found that he could recoup the idea in a new form. Adventure 30 simply extends the partnership between Hagen and Volker formed in the preceding adventure.

Somewhat dissonant, on the other hand, is the digression on magnificent furnishings; the poet seems quite unable to contain his predilection for ornament and hospitable etiquette. No more than in the case of courtly ritual (rising before a queen) is this a straightforward transfer from contemporary romance. Indeed, Hartmann, independently of Chrétien, goes out of his way to deride such amenities when, during Erec's stay with the impoverished knight Koralus, he tabulates an impressive inventory of furnishings only to conclude (*Erec*, vv. 380–81):

> diu wâren bî dem viure
> des âbendes vil tiure.
>
> (They [scil. such furnishings] were notable for their absence by
> the fireside that evening.)

This is Hartmann's way of disparaging finery, a point on which the *Nibelungenlied* poet would have disagreed emphatically.

Luxury is, however, only a literary hobby in this passage, which otherwise continues to develop more fundamental ideas. One such idea is the discomfiture of the Huns, who have already been faced down in the previous adventure and must now retreat in confusion once more with Volker's mockery ringing in their ears. This denigration of the Huns belongs to the context of heroic compensation that we have noted before. Because the Burgundians are fated to succumb to their enemies, it is vital to establish that they are superior in courage and that the Huns will emerge victorious only by virtue of overwhelming numbers. Spiritual quality is limited to the losers, who are thus transformed into moral victors.

Passing beyond this invidious comparison, the adventure consolidates the special relationship between Volker and Hagen. It would be interesting to know why the poet took such an exceptional interest in Volker, for whom he created two new roles in Adventures 29 and 30. Thinking in terms of patronage, analyzed in detail for *König Rother* by Ferdinand Urbanek, we might speculate that he is honoring an unknown sponsor or benefactor. Aside from Rüdeger, Volker is the beneficiary of greater elevation than any other figure in the poem. In fact, he is twice exalted above Hagen; in Adventure 29 (1,768) Kriemhild notes that he is even stronger than Hagen, and in Adventure 30 (1,840) it is first and foremost Volker's presence that frightens off the Huns. In Volker, Hagen has not only a fast friend but a rival in arms.

The underlying theme of the episode, as in the previous one, is loyalty. We could imagine a situation in which Hagen appoints Volker to the watch, just as Siegfried appoints his three companions for the voyage to Islant (342), but instead Volker volunteers. Personal esteem brings the two together, and they address each other in correspondingly warm terms. It is truly a case of "friend standing by friend." This theme of individual loyalty merges into the larger theme of group loyalty; inspired by Giselher's apprehension, they stand guard over the whole army. Once more Hagen plays the part of the faithful retainer by doing the bidding of his lord. His fidelity stands in stark contrast to the faithlessness of the Huns, who not only mount a treacherous night assault but have so little regard for their obligation to their queen that they fall back at the first sign of danger. In the previous adventure a Hunnish warrior did not blush to make his desertion public (1,794): "Then one of the warriors spoke: 'Why are you looking at me? I propose to go back on my promise and not lose my life for anybody's reward.'" Hagen and Volker value faith and have only contempt for life. They would happily plunge into the Hunnish army, and refrain from doing so only because they risk exposing the companions to whose protection they are dedicated.

A fourth original episode pursues the idea of Burgundian solidarity further, but reverts to the bond between Dankwart and Hagen developed in their encounter with the Bavarians. In Adventure 32 Dankwart has a new office; he is charged with the supervision of nine thousand Burgundian pages in a separate lodging. Unable to make headway in her direct assaults on Hagen, Kriemhild now chooses an oblique approach and dispatches a thousand Huns under Blœdelin to attack the pages. Dankwart performs miracles of valor and kills Blœdelin, while the pages defend themselves with benches and footrests. So vigorous is the defense that they kill five hundred Huns and drive off the rest, but the Huns return to the attack with a reinforcement of two thousand. They slaughter all the pages and twelve of Dankwart's knights. Dankwart is himself the sole survivor and reflects on Hagen as his last resort (1,941): "'Would to God,' spoke Dankwart, 'that I had a messenger who would inform my brother Hagen that I stand in such peril among these warriors! He would help me get away or suffer death with me.'" The Huns jeer that his corpse will be the messenger, but with a supreme effort he breaks through his attackers, beats off the stewards who bar his way to the main banquet hall, and appears dripping with blood in the doorway to apprise Hagen of what has happened. Hagen bids him guard the doorway to prevent any Huns from exiting, then precipitates the melee by striking off Ortliep's head.

The themes of guardianship, kinship, and friendship merge in this sequence. Dankwart is charged with the protection of the pages and is vulnerable only because he is separated from his brother Hagen. Once they are rejoined, one guarding the exit, the other playing havoc within, they are, for the moment at least, invincible. Hunnish treachery is restated and serves to exonerate Hagen's action. His beheading of Ortliep, precipitated by no more than a slap in the face in the "Ältere Not," is now justified by the perfidious attack on his brother and the helpless pages. It may be of some importance that Hagen draws blood in Etzel's family only after his own family has suffered an unprovoked attack first. The *Nibelungenlied* poet once more strengthens Hagen's moral position by arguing the obligations of solidarity and loyalty. We are invited to understand that his violent reaction to Dankwart's news stems from his resentment at not being present to assist his brother in his need. Thus the final outbreak of fighting builds on a series of episodes in which the Burgundians increasingly draw together in the face of the impending catastrophe.

The poet's final and fullest improvisation is the most celebrated episode of the *Nibelungenlied*, Adventure 37, in which Rüdeger is trapped between his conflicting loyalties to Huns and Burgundians. This episode succeeds paradoxically in conveying the fateful break in solidarity that leads to the downfall of the Burgundians and, at the same time, in transcending the disaster with the unexpected creation of a new and overarching solidarity. The Adventure comprises exactly one hundred stanzas and falls into three sections of roughly equivalent length. In the first section (thirty-five stanzas) Rüdeger debates his quandary among the Huns and finally accedes to the compelling force of his feudal obligation to Etzel. He and his men arm and advance on the Burgundians, who are still penned in the banquet hall. The following section (thirty-five stanzas) describes in rending detail the exchanges between the Burgundians, who seek to dissuade Rüdeger from his course of action, and Rüdeger, who does not justify his action but only laments the compulsion under which he stands. In the final section battle is renewed, Rüdeger and Gernot succumb under each other's blows, and both sides mourn the loss of Rüdeger. This last section is subdivided about evenly between fighting (fifteen stanzas) and mourning (fourteen stanzas). In more specific detail the narrative runs as follows:

Rüdeger sends for Dietrich in an effort to find some way to halt the bloodshed, but Dietrich offers no hope in the light of Etzel's irreconcilability. A Hunnish warrior chides Rüdeger for standing aside, and Rüdeger avenges the imputation of cowardice by killing him with a blow of his fist. He protests that he cannot fight against the Burgundians because he acted as their guide. Etzel protests the slaying of his warrior, but Rüdeger replies that he was forced to defend his honor. Kriemhild now reminds Rüdeger of his oath to be always in her service (referring to stanzas 1,256–58, when he first overcame her reluctance to marry Etzel). Rüdeger replies that he swore to risk honor and life in her service, but did not swear his soul away. Kriemhild renews her appeal and, together with Etzel, throws herself at his feet. Rüdeger is in an extremity of despair and offers to restore his fief, but Etzel only escalates the pressure by offering joint rule. Rüdeger pleads the hospitality and gifts bestowed on the Burgundians and the betrothal of his daughter to Giselher, but under Kriemhild's continued urging he must resign himself to his fate and to death. He commends wife, children, and retinue to his lord.

Giselher watches Rüdeger approach with his men under arms and naively assumes that he is coming to their aid; Volker must disabuse him. Rüdeger now declares that he must withdraw his allegiance. Gunther scarcely credits his ears, but Rüdeger can only protest the wish that he were free to do otherwise. Gernot repeats Gunther's plea, dwelling particularly on Rüdeger's gift of a sword, but to no avail. Giselher in turn remonstrates on the grounds of his betrothal to Rüdeger's daughter. Rüdeger asks that his daughter not suffer the consequences of his action, but Giselher declares that the death of his kinsmen will cancel all bonds. Rüdeger calls on God's mercy and prepares for battle, but at this moment Hagen intervenes with the request that Rüdeger make him a gift of his shield because his own shield, a gift from Gotelind, has been hewn apart. Rüdeger agrees, and the gesture is acknowledged by the tears of the bystanders. Hagen vows not to attack Rüdeger even if he should slay every last Burgundian, and Volker joins the compact.

As the battle recommences, Hagen and Volker hold aloof according to their vow, as does Giselher, but Gernot, seeing the decimation of his men, challenges Rüdeger. They fall together. In the meantime all of Rüdeger's men have succumbed as well. The chief Burgundians mourn. Kriemhild, aware that stillness has fallen on the scene, believes that Rüdeger has entered into negotiations with the enemy, but Volker informs her of the true situation. Rüdeger's corpse is brought to the Huns. Seeing it, both Etzel and Kriemhild break into loud lamentations.

This adventure, with its gripping impasse and intense emotions, has been the subject of much commentary, the most brilliant being a study published by Peter Wapnewski in 1960.[10] Wapnewski analyzed Rüdeger's choice against the background of the law governing feudal obligations, thus anticipating later attempts to see medieval literature in more historical terms. He also argued that Hagen, not Rüdeger, is the true hero of the adventure. Rüdeger must act as he does, and the Burgundians must understand his plight, but Giselher, in his inexperience, declares himself free of obligations, thus breaking faith with Rüdeger and signaling a combat without redemption. At this moment of moral default Hagen steps forward with his request for Rüdeger's shield, a gesture that gives Rüdeger a reprieve and restores the bond of affection that is about to be severed: "Hagen has done the impossible—accepted battle and maintained the faith of friendship."[11] But Hagen goes even further by vowing to spare Rüdeger in battle. As Wapnewski points out, Rüdeger, the quintessential friend, must abide by his fate as vassal, whereas Hagen, the quintessential vassal, places the value of friendship, just this once, above his feudal obligations.

Heusler, basing himself on the Danish ballad *Kremolds hævn* (Kriemhild's revenge), believed that Rüdeger's dilemma was inherited from the "Ältere Not," although it does not appear in "Niflunga saga."[12] Wapnewski, on the other hand, found it unlikely that the episode would have been so totally deleted from *Þiðreks saga* had it been present in the older epic. He therefore credited it to the *Nibelungenlied* poet. At the same time he argued for primitive Germanic sensibilities in the scene more vigorously than contemporary scholars are likely to approve. He doubted that the underlying dilemma originated at the end of the twelfth century, but we have seen in Saxo's account of "Grimhild's perfidy against her brothers" and in the Adelger story of the *Kaiserchronik* that the reconciliation of loyalties was indeed a twelfth-century theme. We may even surmise that it was suggested to the *Nibelungenlied* poet by the lost Dietrich epic, in which Rüdeger found himself in the dilemma of mediating between his friend Dietrich and his lord Etzel after the death of Etzel's sons at the battle of Ravenna.

But nowhere in earlier literature are the emotional dimensions of the conflict delineated with such intensity as in the *Nibelungenlied*. In the *Kaiserchronik* the reconciliation of loyalties is hardly more than a casuistic exercise, but in the *Nibelungenlied* it is high drama that puts the inner life of the leading characters on trial. Wapnewski is therefore surely right in his most sweeping and liberating generalization to the effect that Rüdeger's dilemma reflects the individual concerns of romance as well as the harsh demands of heroic action. He is, in Wapnewski's words, an "Individuum mit präindividuellem Auftrag" (a romance individual with an epic role).[13]

We may place Wapnewski's analysis in an expanded context by connecting it with the other episodes that appear to be the original work of the *Nibelungenlied* poet. It turns out that they have important features in common. If Wapnewski is right in believing that Hagen is the true hero of Adventure 37, we may observe in the first place that Hagen is the beneficiary of all five new episodes. He benefits each time in very much the same sense; in each new episode he is drawn into a closer personal relationship with another figure, twice Dankwart, twice Volker, and finally Rüdeger. Hagen's social reintegration is therefore the dominant theme of the poet's original efforts. The warrior who was most isolated in Part I becomes the major focus of human companionship in Part II. Because of his treacherous killing of Siegfried and his seizure of Kriemhild's treasure he had developed a strained relationship with Gernot and Giselher; his clear-sighted objections to Kriemhild's marriage and her subsequent invitation had only intensified this dissension. In Part II he not only repairs his relations with the Burgundians but preserves their bond with Rüdeger. Abandoning the narrow vassal loyalty that led to Siegfried's death and divided the court at Worms, he espouses a more generous humanity that heals divisions. If, following Wapnewski, we try to relate this pattern to romance, we may note a broad resemblance to the two most immediate romance precursors of the *Nibelungenlied*, Hartmann von Aue's *Erec* and *Iwein*. These too are works in which human relations that seem at first deficient are ultimately adjusted and vindicated. In Hartmann's romances the hero must balance the demands of marriage and knighthood; in the *Nibelungenlied* Hagen must balance the demands of feudal obligation and friendship. In both cases it is a question of reconciling public and private spheres. The *Nibelungenlied* is thus structurally and thematically analogous to its romance counterparts. What is generally not appreciated, however, is that the *Nibelungenlied* far exceeds contemporary romance in the intensity with which it depicts human relations, especially in Adventure 37. Hartmann, Wolfram, and Gottfried have nothing in their amorous or domestic crises to compare with the high moments of loyalty and friendship in the *Nibelungenlied*.

We may judge from what has been said so far that the poet was not without conceptual horizons, but many critics have noted that his execution in detail is not always equal to his ambition. Two examples among many may serve to illustrate the perils of elaboration. The first comes from the scene in which Kriemhild persuades Etzel to invite her kinsmen to the banquet, a passage in which the shape of the source emerges from "Niflunga saga" with unusual clarity. In the source Kriemhild proposed the invitation to Etzel at night, he agreed, and sometime later she summoned messengers and dispatched them to Worms. The *Nibelungenlied* poet retains the nighttime consultation in bed, but shifts the authority for the dispatching of the messengers to Etzel (stanzas 1,400–8) and extends the discussion considerably. By the time the discussion is over, the poet has forgotten that the couple are in bed and has mentally transferred the scene to the council chamber in which the king might be expected to transact official business. As a result Etzel summons the messengers immediately (1,408): "They hastened immediately to where the king sat (!) next to the queen."[14] The poet thus short-circuits his own narrative innovation.

A second difficulty is connected with Dietrich's role in the last two adventures. In Adventure 37 (stanza 2,137) Rüdeger had sent for Dietrich to explore the possibility of conciliation, but at the conclusion of the extended action surrounding Rüdeger's death the poet has forgotten about Dietrich's presence and imagines him at some distance from the scene. He does this for good reason, to preserve Dietrich's Olympian perspective on the action until the last moment, but he has omitted to account for his departure. In the source it appears that Dietrich simply plunged into the fray when he saw Rüdeger fall, just as Rüdeger's entry into battle was motivated by Blœdelin's fall. The *Nibelungenlied* poet, however, contrives a long preface of some fifty stanzas, in which Dietrich dispatches messengers to learn what has happened. These embassies result in a new clash leading to the fall of all of Dietrich's men except Hildebrand, who is wounded, and all the remaining Burgundians except Hagen and Gunther.

This is the situation when Dietrich reenters the scene. It produces a new anomaly. In the "Ältere Not" the pattern of the final combats was an elimination series in which all participants were active simultaneously. In the final combats Hildebrand overcame Hagen while Dietrich overcame Gunther, but the *Nibelungenlied* poet has magnified Hagen too much to allow him to succumb to a secondary figure; only Dietrich himself is imaginable in the role of victor. Accordingly, he allows Hagen to disable Hildebrand, thus destroying the symmetry of the finale, and leaves Dietrich confronting Hagen and Gunther at the same time. Dietrich must therefore defeat and bind one after the other. The oddity of this arrangement is that Gunther stands idly by while Dietrich overcomes his only surviving companion.[15] Again, the poet has not quite managed the narrative mechanics required by his altered concept. In Part II the difficulties are minor; in the second instance a couple of narrative imperfections are a small price to pay for the ennobled portrait of Dietrich. But in Part I we will see that narrative flaws can, in the worst case, compromise an elevated concept severely.

THE REVISIONS OF PART I

The reason for reversing the sequential order and studying Part II of the *Nibelungenlied* first is that Part I is in some sense a secondary accretion. Its composition is predicated on and determined by what follows. It did not already exist in a fully elaborated form as did the epic precursor of Part II. Heusler calculated the Siegfried source, the "Brünhildenlied," to have been an oral poem in about five hundred long lines.[16] We have seen that this poem may have been a written composition, but it had not attained epic proportions. It lies rather in the range of the *Annolied*, in other words, the length that might be contemplated before the great epic surge of the mid-twelfth century. The *Nibelungenlied* poet did not therefore conjoin twin epics but prefaced an epic with a story that serves to explain the background more fully.

In this process the preface grew until it became an epic counterpoise. Why the poet was so determined to bring Part I up to an epic standard is not a question that has been much explored. Perhaps it was his aim to rival the poet of the "Ältere Not," who had shown the way by converting a relatively short heroic poem into epic, thus leaving his successor relatively little opportunity for original creation in that portion of the undertaking. Given a restricted role in Part II, the poet perhaps sought to make his epic mark in Part I, where he did not have to contend with the work of a significant precursor. Whatever the motivation, it seems clear that the great model for his literary ambition was the poet of the "Ältere Not," whose precedent is visible in many of the procedures used to enlarge the tale of Siegfried. It is conceivable that he learned his art by first revising the "Ältere Not" and then adding Part I in matching compass, but he may also have begun at the beginning, with the requirements and the methods of the older poet in mind. Then, having completed Part I, he could have turned to a revision of the "Ältere Not" based on his new Siegfried epic.[17]

In either of these hypothetical sequences the "Ältere Not" is the underlying model. We saw in Chapter 5 how the *Nibelungenlied* poet exploited the bridal-quest pattern in describing Rüdeger's delegate wooing of Kriemhild for Etzel, and how he then transferred this pattern to Part I. The original form of Siegfried's story was not a bridal quest, but in the revision it became a double quest; Siegfried's wooing of Kriemhild is contingent on his fulfilling of the delegate role in Gunther's wooing of Brünhild. Both suits are depicted as arduous conquests of reluctant brides in foreign lands. The surmounting of the difficulties is crowned by the double wedding in Worms. The whole narrative concept of Adventures 1–10 is therefore indebted to the "Ältere Not."

There is further evidence of restructuring on the model of the "Ältere Not" in the narrative following the weddings (Adventures 12–16). Just as the poet of the "Ältere Not" prepared the way for the fall of the Burgundians with a banquet invitation to Hunland, so the *Nibelungenlied* poet prepared the way for Siegfried's death with a banquet invitation to Worms. Helmut de Boor pointed out that this parallel was already apparent to the medieval redactor of the so-called "Darmstädter Aventiurenverzeichnis." [18] This redactor provides his version of Adventure 27 with the heading: "Abinture wie daz kriemelt warp daz ir brudir kam zün hunē also det brunhilt vor daz siferit kam zün burgundin" (adventure telling how Kriemhild caused her brother[s] to come to the Huns as Brünhild previously caused Siegfried to come to the Burgundians). In setting the stage for Siegfried's murder, the poet thus resorted to the same use of a woman's devious invitation that was central in the "Ältere Not." The duplicity in Brünhild's case is that, while alleging hospitality, she covets the feudal service to which she believes herself entitled because Siegfried falsely declared himself to be Gunther's vassal in Islant.

The parallelism goes beyond a general similarity in outline and extends to the level of motif and wording. [19] In both sequences the queen proposing the invitation reflects in her own mind on the real reasons (724–25 = 1,391–99), but openly professes a longing to see her guests (726, 729–30 = 1,393, 1,397, 1,403); Brünhild claims a desire to see Kriemhild, Kriemhild a desire to see her brothers. In both cases the king protests that the distance is too great (727.3 = 1,404.2), but he declares that there are no guests he would rather see (731.2 = 1,406.2–3). The queen's urging results in the dispatching of messengers (732–57 = 1,407–49), and the receipt of the invitation is considered in a council scene (757–62 = 1,457–72) with the outcome that the king is advised to take a retinue of a thousand men (760 = 1,472).

Nowhere else is the dependence on the "Ältere Not" (or the remodeled version in Part II) quite so pervasive, but there are many signs of incidental borrowing:

1. Siegfried's first meeting with Kriemhild (291–97) is modeled on Etzel's first meeting with Kriemhild (1,347–58).

2. The departure for Islant (373–76) is modeled on the departure for Hunland (1,517–22).

3. Brünhild's observation of Siegfried's arrival in Islant (394–96) is modeled on Kriemhild's observation of the Burgundians' arrival in Hunland (1,716–17).

4. The requirement that visitors disarm themselves in Islant (406–7) is modeled on Kriemhild's attempt to disarm the Burgundians in Hunland (1,745–46).

5. The identification of the strangers arriving in Islant (409–15) is modeled on the identification of Hagen arriving in Hunland (1,752–57).

6. The dispatching of Siegfried as a messenger to announce the success of the bridal mission in Islant (529–41) is modeled on Rüdeger's dispatching of messengers to announce the arrival of the Burgundians in Hunland (1,713–15).

7. After the marriage of Siegfried and Kriemhild and their return to Xanten, the ensuing death of Queen Sigelind (717) may have been suggested by Queen Helche's death (1,143), and the birth of sons to both Kriemhild and Brünhild after ten years of marriage (715, 718) may have been suggested by the birth of Ortlieb after Kriemhild's seven years of marriage in Hunland (1,387).

8. The farewell scene before the fateful hunt, and in particular the monitory dreams (918–25), are modeled on the departure of the Burgundians for Hunland (1,509–10).

A glance at these borrowings shows that almost all pertain to departure and arrival sequences, as indeed do the major bridal-quest and banquet innovations previously discussed. These are the ornamental increments largely responsible for giving Part I a disproportionately ceremonial cast in comparison to the conflict drama of Part II. There is a constant coming and going of messengers, a procession of announcements, declarations, invitations, and receptions, all undertaken with a sense of style and sartorial elegance that has traditionally struck readers as particularly tedious. Even where the poet does attempt a dramatic confrontation, the results are trivial. Siegfried's challenge of the Burgundians at Worms in Adventure 3 has no point and dissolves awkwardly. The Dano-Saxon war degenerates into a display of courtly niceties. The conquest of Brünhild in a series of martial games in Adventure 7 is farcical, as is Siegfried's summoning of reinforcements in Adventure 8. The final reduction of Brünhild in her bedchamber in Adventure 10 achieves nothing more than a fusion of low comedy and poor taste.[20]

Whereas we found a series of new adventures in Part II characterized by dramatic energy and conceptual focus, the new adventures of Part I are inspired by a fascination with protocol. Adventure 5 is a platform for Siegfried's first meeting with Kriemhild under magnificent and festive circumstances inspired by the victory celebration after the Dano-Saxon war. Adventure 9 enlists Siegfried as messenger so that he can convey the news of the bridal mission in Islant to Kriemhild, with a mixture of official etiquette and arch banter. Adventure 11 records the journey of the newlyweds Siegfried and Kriemhild to Xanten and their festive reception. Adventure 12 relates the invitation to a banquet at Worms, and Adventure 13 describes their reception and the circumstances of still another magnificent feast. Adventure 15 recounts the alleged declaration of war by Saxons and Danes and provides the pretext for Kriemhild's revelation of the vulnerable spot on Siegfried's back in the awkward hope that Hagen will somehow be able to protect it. All of these original episodes are oddly devoid of real content; they provide volume without weight, and betray none of the talent for emotional intensification displayed by the poet in Part II.

This does not mean, however, that he has made only insubstantial alterations in the story. There are in fact important differences between the probable content of the source and what we find in Part I of the *Nibelungenlied*. Siegfried is no longer an orphan fostered in the wilds but a prince in the Netherlands, with every advantage in lineage and upbringing. He is not compromised by a previous betrothal to Brünhild that he must break to marry Kriemhild, although mysterious hints of this earlier liaison persist. The Dano-Saxon war is developed far beyond whatever suggestion of joint military campaigns the source may have contained, and it is placed exclusively in Siegfried's hands. The martial games with Brünhild appear to be entirely original to the *Nibelungenlied*. Finally, Siegfried's sexual conquest of Brünhild in the source has been suppressed in favor of a victory at wrestling, so that Gunther can consummate the marriage.

These are the most substantial changes. It will be readily apparent that, in one way or another, they redound to Siegfried's credit, physical or moral. His princely youth in Xanten is simply a matter of social rectification, but the Dano-Saxon war and the martial games in Islant document his surpassing strength and prowess, while the suppression of his prior betrothal and sexual infringement rehabilitate his character. There can be no doubt that the poet had a transcendent interest in Siegfried. Just as he devoted his innovations in Part II to the elevation of Hagen, so in Part I he intervenes to glorify Siegfried. This was not the only possible option, as the Norse poets clearly show. *Forna, Skamma,* and *Meiri* all betoken a far greater interest in Brynhild than in Sigurd, who never emerged as an important dramatic figure in Scandinavia. But the *Nibelungenlied* moves in a male world. Siegfried is omnipresent, whereas Brünhild is a somewhat distant and shadowy character, who disappears almost entirely after the quarrel of the queens in Adventure 14.

A reformulation of Siegfried's role was the poet's chief preoccupation, but also his chief source of narrative difficulty. In the source Siegfried was a headstrong adventurer, who plighted his troth to Brünhild, abandoned her, took her forcibly for Gunther while promising to be discreet, then revealed the secret to his wife Kriemhild. This was perhaps the stuff of legend, but it was not an image to the liking of the *Nibelungenlied* poet or, presumably, the sophisticated audience to which he aspired. The new Siegfried, although retaining a good deal of the elemental vitality of tradition, was required to be a courtly gentleman. Accordingly, the poet began by eliminating the prior betrothal, but not altogether successfully; traces of the earlier acquaintanceship persist, especially in Siegfried's and Brünhild's knowing comments about each other.[21] The real difficulties begin when the poet attempts to minimize Siegfried's invasion of Gunther's and Brünhild's marriage.

The problem is that he eliminates the sexual act without eliminating the sexual accusation. Kriemhild confronts Brünhild with the charge that Siegfried, not Gunther, took her virginity (840). Brünhild therefore complains to Gunther of the accusation that she has slept with Siegfried (853). Gunther then deflects the accusation by requiring that Siegfried swear, not that he is not guilty, but only that he has not boasted of possessing Brünhild (855). After all, Gunther was present at the time and knows that Siegfried is not actually guilty of sleeping with Brünhild; the only question in his mind is whether Siegfried may have made such a claim. He therefore proposes an oath to validate that Siegfried is innocent of the claim (857–58), but at the last moment he exonerates Siegfried apparently without the oath.

The confusion in this passage arises because the poet has dropped the old motivation of Siegfried's murder (the revelation of his sexual conquest to his wife) and retained the old accusation of sexual transgression. At the same time he is eager to exculpate his hero publicly as well as in fact; hence the oath. But he realizes that if the exculpation is complete there will be no further reason to proceed against Siegfried and no justification for his murder. He therefore aborts the oath in order to leave the impression, at least in the minds of Brünhild and her faithful vassal Hagen, that Siegfried may indeed have made the boast.[22] For the reader the sequence of events becomes obscure. We do not know whether Siegfried actually made the boast to Kriemhild (why would he fabricate such a lie?), whether Kriemhild assumed sexual relations on the basis of the belt and ring (why would she not seek clarification?), or whether Kriemhild simply made a reckless accusation in anger (why did she not then correct the record in order to unburden her husband?). These unanswered questions are crucial because Siegfried's death is the central event of Part I and the central motivation of Part II. The fact that we do not understand either the circumstances leading up to his death or the distribution of guilt casts the whole plot in a penumbra of moral uncertainty.

The failure to explain Siegfried's murder persuasively is the chief blemish in the work. This failure has fed persistent doubts about the poet's intellectual command of the story and has fostered a disinclination to admit him as a full partner to the company of his contemporaries Hartmann, Wolfram, and Gottfried. The reader is faced with a disturbing contradiction between a brilliantly transparent Rüdeger in Part II and a hopelessly opaque Siegfried in Part I. How could the creator of one so badly mismanage the other? The roles are not dissimilar. Rüdeger too is trapped in guilt by special circumstances, but he understands the guilt and gives a full account of it. Siegfried seems unaware of the moral twilight gathering around him; he enters into no reflections of his own, speaks to no one, and makes no formal declarations. There is no hint that he appreciates the complexities of the deceits he is involved in, either the fiction of vassalage with which he misleads Brünhild or his impersonation of Gunther on two occasions. Rüdeger undertakes a commitment to Kriemhild that turns into a moral trap. Siegfried's situation could have been construed in the same way, a commitment to Gunther that entailed a betrayal of Brünhild, but no such dilemma is established.

The question thrust on the critic is whether the poet could actually perform at two apparently irreconcilable levels of skill in the two parts of the epic, or whether there is a method in his depiction of Siegfried's blindness. If we make the latter assumption, we must decide whether his blindness is attributable to guilt or guilelessness. Because it seems critically unsatisfactory to posit two radically different levels of competence in the same poem, and because it seems implausible that the poet should lavish such loving detail on Siegfried with the intention of implying that he is guilt-ridden and deserving of his fate, we must probably accommodate ourselves to the third option: Siegfried's naiveté is real and intended by the poet. He originates in a world of innocence, enters a world of intrigue, and succumbs to it without quite realizing what is afoot. The moral problem lies in his new sphere of action at the Burgundian court.

The best evidence for such a view is perhaps the natural ebullience with which the poet endows Siegfried. This feature was to some extent carried over from the wild boy and dragon slayer of tradition, but his traditional characteristics are emphasized to an almost burlesque degree in the *Nibelungenlied*. Although the acquisition of treasure and the dragon slaying are themselves reported only retrospectively, Siegfried acquires new adventures of legendary proportions: the martial games in Islant, the wanton struggle with his own retainers in Nibelungenland, and the hunting feats in the Vosges (or the Odenwald in redaction C). These adventures are characterized by broad humor and a sense of fun for its own sake. Siegfried's last prank, loosing a bear among the hunters in camp and running it down on foot, is as much in character as it is outrageous. Siegfried is a perpetual child.

As such he lives on the margins of the real world, beyond which he constantly ventures in search of new amusements. He joins the equally child-like and innocent Kriemhild in a curtain-raising comedy of love and laughter, a happy and illusory prelude to the twofold disaster of his own murder and the cataclysm in Hunland. To this extent Siegfried is not so much a participant in the tragic action of the poem as a foil to it. His death marks the end of innocence and the onset of disaster. The contrast has something in common with the oppositions between the reckless quester Gahmuret, the youthful ingénu Parzival, and the maturity of the morally instructed Parzival. Indeed, growth from innocence is a feature of all the major courtly romances, those of Hartmann and Gottfried as well as Wolfram. In the *Nibelungenlied* the transition is effected not in the development of a single individual but in the superseding of the artless Siegfried by the clairvoyant Hagen.

Once Siegfried is dead and buried, the serious consequences set in. Kriemhild is filled with an unquenchable hatred for her husband's slayers, but this situation confronts the poet with certain psychological problems. How can she remain in the company of the murderers? How can they allow her to escape their surveillance and establish an independent power base in Hunland? These problems were not so pressing as long as the two stories existed separately, but when they were brought together in a single epic, the poet was obliged to resolve the awkward questions through the addition of Adventures 18 and 19. He did so in a way that is more reminiscent of his successes in Part II than the disparities of Part I, but one that continues to show signs of faltering narrative logic.

He deals squarely with the problem of Kriemhild's continued residence at Worms. Her father-in-law Sigemund cordially invites her to return to Xanten with him, but her younger brother Giselher, seconded by Gernot and Uote, pleads with her to remain in the midst of her kinsmen. Giselher in particular commits himself to her protection just as Rüdeger will do later. The poet has carefully prepared the intercession of her younger brothers with the information that they did not participate in the fateful hunt (926); in contrast to the Norse sources, the *Nibelungenlied* poet burdens Gernot and Giselher with no guilt for Siegfried's death and they are in a position to treat with Kriemhild. Gernot specifically protests his ignorance of the circumstances (1,097), but here the poet nods again because stanza 865 shows Gernot at the murder council.

For four and a half years Kriemhild lives in isolation, comforted only by Uote and her retinue. Then Hagen, inspired by an interest in the Nibelung treasure that she received from Siegfried as a bride price, urges Gunther to effect a reconciliation. Acceding to the pleas of Gernot and Giselher, she makes peace with Gunther, but not with Hagen. Her brothers are thus enabled to retrieve her treasure from Nibelungenland, but when she proceeds to make lavish distributions, Hagen suspects that she has designs against them. He therefore seizes the treasure. Kriemhild appeals to Gernot and Giselher, who promise to recover the treasure after their return from an impending journey, but while they are away Hagen sinks the treasure in the Rhine. At the last moment this rather elaborate contrivance unravels when the poet tells us in retrospect (1,140) that before Hagen sank the treasure he and his lords swore oaths not to reveal its location as long as more than one remained alive. The contradictions in this account are too unfathomable to enter into; Gernot and Giselher vow to restore Kriemhild's treasure but are at the same time implicated in a conspiracy against her. Once more the poet failed to reconcile a traditional theme (the sunken treasure) with a new psychological perception of the action.[23]

His thinking is nonetheless clear. Kriemhild would remain in Worms only if there were some residue of congeniality. This is provided by her special relationship to Gernot and Giselher. The development of such a relationship also lends a certain plausibility to her later claim that she longs to see her brothers. Etzel must know that she has at least a fondness for two of them and will therefore be inclined to credit her pretext. Her formal reconciliation with Gunther further strengthens her credibility. It also explains why Gunther is disposed to accept the idea of her marriage in Hunland, and the subsequent invitation, and why Hagen's opposition is entirely isolated. But there is a price in terms of psychological consistency; the more we believe that Kriemhild has a genuine affection for Gernot and Giselher, the more difficult it is to accept her callous sacrifice of them along with all the other Burgundians in Part II. As long as her animosity was equally directed against all her brothers, her relentless vengeance was more understandable.

In coming to terms with the poet's concept, we must again think not only of the narrative mechanics but also of the thematic concerns. In Adventures 18 and 19 the poet motivates the action of Part II; he also reaffirms his dominant interest in personal and family relationships. Part I is the tale of family fragmentation and broken relationships, the destruction of Kriemhild's marriage, the disaffection in the Burgundian family, and the isolation of Hagen. Part II is, paradoxically, a tale of reintegration within the framework of total destruction, the reparation for Siegfried, the drawing together of Hagen and his kinsmen and companions, and the common cause of all the Burgundians. As Adventure 37 illustrates best, the poet is fascinated by personal bonds subjected to maximum pressure. This interest dictates the focus of the transitional Adventures 18 and 19, in which the attitudes of Kriemhild, her brothers, and Hagen with respect to each other are defined in preparation for the final confrontation.

At the beginning of Chapter 5, we observed that the *Nibelungenlied* represents a merging of two traditions, epic and romance. The older heroic tradition survives in an emphasis on military prowess and steadfastness, and in the tragic denouement. At the same time, the episodic focus of the heroic lay, described in Chapter 1 and still alive in oral performances of the twelfth century, has given way to the fuller biographic frame created in twelfth-century epic, notably in the *Alexanderlied* and the German prototype of *Þiðreks saga*. The theme is no longer the hero's dilemma, as in the older lay, but the life and death of heroes, notably Siegfried and Hagen.

Equally evident is the heritage of romance. Siegfried, like Erec and Iwein, enters the enchanted realm of love and marriage, but like his romance counterparts he is destined to be disenchanted. Hagen too is in some sense a romance hero and is subjected to the characteristic double sequence of parallel events that reveal his deficiencies in Part I but allow him to rise to greater insight in Part II. As in Hartmann's romances, important social values are lost at first only to be recovered in the sequel. In Hagen's case the values are not the Arthurian concepts of knighthood and marriage but vassalage, kinship, and loyalty. Nor are these values vindicated under the festive auspices of Arthur's court. Instead they are retrieved from the flames of the cataclysm in the Hunnish banquet hall and from the dark pessimism of heroic tragedy.

The *Nibelungenlied* poet has traditionally been viewed as an unthinking recipient of the new literature of romance, but he may also be viewed as a critic of the current fashion. By subsuming romance within the compass of heroic epic, he questioned its offer of an optimistic alternative (especially with the parodistic frivolities of Part I) and deepened the search for social values by setting the artificialities of romance against the tragic outcome of Part II. Our poet thus succeeds both in tempering the naiveté of romance by placing it in a tragic context, and in tempering the pessimism of epic by allowing scope for the romance quest of greater understanding. To appreciate this raised perspective, we must grasp the *Nibelungenlied* poet not only in terms of the rise of romance, as has been urged since 1945, but also in terms of his reformulation of heroic epic, as Heusler argued in the preceding period.

8. Interpretations

Two PUBLICATIONS by Nelly Dürrenmatt and Friedrich Panzer in 1945 marked a turning point in the analysis of the *Nibelungenlied* and ushered in a period of postwar criticism that differed distinctly from the work done during the forty years before the war.[1] These earlier years were dominated by Andreas Heusler, whose pertinent studies appeared from 1902 to 1941.[2] Heusler's project was to comprehend the *Nibelungenlied* against the background of the earlier forms of the legend. Much of his work was therefore devoted to a reconstruction of these forms through a painstaking comparison of the surviving versions. After the war scholars came to believe that his approach was too backward-looking, and strenuous efforts were made to find a new method that would integrate the *Nibelungenlied* more decisively into the literary scene around 1200. This was the underlying rationale in both Dürrenmatt's and Panzer's books.

Panzer proceeded from the observation that German literature in the second half of the twelfth century was revolutionized by French impulses. He set out to show that French literature was no less crucial for the *Nibelungenlied* than for courtly romance and sought to demonstrate a series of borrowings from the *chansons de geste*, notably *Daurel et Beton*, *Renaus de Montauban*, and the *Song of Roland*. In addition, he believed that he could isolate occasional Virgilian echoes and derive certain scenes in the *Nibelungenlied* from contemporary political events. For example, he associated the idyll at Pöchlarn in Adventure 27 with Frederick Barbarossa's visit to the court of King Bela of Hungary in 1189, during which the emperor betrothed his youngest son to Bela's daughter. In other words, Panzer argued both a more elevated literary culture for the poet and a greater freedom in devising new episodes. Occasionally his derivation of the narrative from French sources or current events ran counter to Heusler's location of the same episodes in the native "Brünhildenlied" or the "Ältere Not." In order to argue that the idyll at Pöchlarn originated in the state visit of 1189 he was obliged, for example, to demonstrate that the poet did not find the episode in the "Ältere Not," as Heusler assumed. This constraint led to a long chapter in which he argued that the "Ältere Not" in fact never existed. Instead, Panzer reasoned, the relationship between the *Nibelungenlied* and *Þiðreks saga* should be explained not from a common source but from the Norwegian compiler's extensive reworking of the *Nibelungenlied* itself.

Panzer's book is a curious example of the wrong solution put forward at the right historical moment. His new source proposals have enjoyed little favor, and the direct derivation of the account in *Þiðreks saga* from the *Nibelungenlied* has never been credited by the scholars most competent to judge the issue.[3] Nevertheless, his book had a liberating effect because it offered release from Heusler's constructions. Scholars who had not performed the source operations themselves were inclined to believe Panzer, at least to the extent that Heusler's system now appeared to be more fragile than they had previously imagined. Even where Panzer's book is not directly mentioned in the critical literature, the reader senses that it lies beneath a new skepticism toward source study and a new eagerness to evaluate the *Nibelungenlied* on its own terms, as an autonomous creation comparable to the works of Hartmann, Wolfram, and Gottfried.

Whereas Panzer's book followed tradition by dealing almost exclusively with source questions, Nelly Dürrenmatt broke more clearly with the past. She made a considerably juster estimate of Heusler's achievements than Panzer but argued that he had isolated the *Nibelungenlied* too programmatically from courtly epic.[4] She therefore set herself the task of identifying the courtly elements. This labor is carried out in the form of a somewhat mechanical comparison of ritual scenes: reception and leave-taking formalities, forms of hospitality, gift-giving, festive arrangements, mourning practices, knighting and marriage ceremonies. Her conclusion is that the *Nibelungenlied* poet is in fact more interested and prodigal in these ritual matters than the writers of precourtly or courtly epic. He therefore emerges as an almost hypercourtly figure rather than a nostalgic re-creator of heroic antiquity.

Like Panzer's book, Dürrenmatt's had an impact not quite commensurate with its real accomplishment. The ceremonial elements she singles out are not a characteristic feature of German courtly epic, so that the comparison does not so much establish an analogy as point up a difference. Moreover, in the second section of the book, on some of the more important characters in the poem, she distinguishes carefully between those features already present in the sources as posited by Heusler and new features not anticipated by the sources. She does not therefore disallow Heusler's findings but merely tries to focus the extant redaction

more clearly. In the heat of a new critical day, however, her book lent itself
to a more far-reaching interpretation. It was read as a reorientation of the
Nibelungenlied away from earlier literature and into closer apposition
with the latest fashions. Though still grounded in Heusler's work, it offered
an alternative context that encouraged the abandonment of Heusler's
system.

One of the criticisms leveled at Heusler, especially by Panzer, was the
origin of his science in Germanic or even Scandinavian studies. Not only
Heusler but also the other important Nibelung scholars of the 1920's and
1930's (Neckel, Schneider, de Boor, Hempel) belonged to this tradition.
Dürrenmatt's shift of focus to classical Middle High German literature
allowed scholars in this latter field to turn their attention to the *Nibelungenlied* less hesitantly than before. Wolfram and Gottfried scholars
figured prominently in the new generation (Mergell, W. J. Schröder,
W. Schröder, Weber, Wapnewski, Bumke). The *Nibelungenlied* had now
been recruited for their literature, and they were free to approach it
unencumbered by the legendary apparatus that Panzer had declared
irrelevant.

This trend was of course promoted in no small measure by the New
Critical methods that prevailed in German literary studies just after
World War II. Close reading was the order of the day, and Panzer's abolition
of legendary history extended this critical license to the *Nibelungenlied*.
The first result was a series of intense interpretations of the poem without
regard to possible sources.

TEXTUAL INTERPRETATIONS (1950–65)

Three studies by Bodo Mergell, Walter Johannes Schröder, and Werner
Schröder, the last two of monograph size, may serve as samples of the new
approach. They appeared in 1950, 1955, and 1960 and have in common
a concern with the structure of the poem and the capacity of that structure to communicate the poet's intention. They assume that the structure
is coherent and meaningful, thus departing from an earlier view that the
poet recast an inherited story, making piecemeal modifications without
strict regard for the overall plan of the poem and without necessarily im-
puting a consistent meaning to the whole.

Mergell attaches his study explicitly to Dürrenmatt's precedent, but is
more interested in the governing idea of the poem than in the outer trap-
pings.[5] He discovers a set of counterbalancing tensions. Siegfried stands
in significant opposition to the court at Worms, in which he represents a
new dynamic vitality in the context of an older petrified culture. The relationship is dialectical because Gunther needs the primitive strength of a

Siegfried for his bridal quest, and Siegfried needs the courtly polish of a Gunther for his wooing. Mergell sees Siegfried's entry into the life at Worms as analogous to Parzival's entry into the world in search of renewal. Kriemhild and Hagen form a similar polarity; she is gradually reduced from loving wife and grieving widow to avenging demon, while Hagen experiences a countervalent rise from traitor to triumphant guardian. This contrast dominates the poem as a whole and describes a religious arc culminating in a final confrontation with God. Hagen, however, stands alone with God in his victorious preservation of the hidden gold,[6] whereas Kriemhild is condemned as a "vâlandinne" (she-devil). Mergell compares this structural chiasmus to the rise of the Grail hero and the counterbalancing fall of the neutral angels in *Parzival.*

A second preoccupation of Mergell's article is the formal patterning of the poem as a whole. He divides it into eight pentads, each comprising five adventures, with the centerpiece (Adventure 20) doing service in both the fourth and fifth pentad. More interestingly, he notes that the *Nibelungenlied* shares its two-part structure with courtly romance. As in courtly romance, the bipartition is not arbitrary or meaningless but a contrastive design revealing different degrees of religious awareness.

W. J. Schröder's analysis is also structural in nature, but it attempts a more encompassing interpretation.[7] He takes note of Heusler's caution against the imposition of a didactic principle on heroic stories, but advocates a search not so much for a didactic principle as for a coherent plot.[8] He begins with an analysis of the characters, urging that they are not to be confused with real people, whose actions are motivated by individual responses to a given situation. Heroic poetry does not motivate action psychologically but through the manipulation of motifs. The characters are comparable to chess pieces, each limited to a particular type of move. Thus a queen will make only moves that are inherent in her nature as a queen. The drastic changes in such characters as Kriemhild and Siegfried (maiden becomes maenad, aggressor becomes ally) would appear to contradict this principle, but the changes are only apparent. Kriemhild merely becomes what she already is; she realizes her latent queenliness. Siegfried, on the other hand, merely takes on the deceptive appearance of a different being. Corresponding to these split-level characters is a split-level stage: a courtly contemporary scene (Worms) and a mythic past (Nibelungenland, Islant, Hunland).

Within this divided realm each man seeks out the matching woman. Siegfried (strength) woos Kriemhild (beauty), while Gunther (king) woos Brünhild (queen). They achieve their goals not by virtue of what they are but by assuming opposite characteristics. Siegfried becomes a courtier, and Gunther borrows Siegfried's strength. Reality is traded for appearance. Thus the ground is laid for deceived expectations. Kriemhild, who desires the strongest man, must be reassured that it was actually Siegfried, not Gunther, who subdued Brünhild, but Brünhild, who desires to be a queen, must be reassured that Siegfried is in truth a vassal. Their insistence precipitates the revelations of the queens' quarrel and makes Siegfried's presence in Worms a threat to the status quo.

The underlying problem in the poem is the survival of the court at Worms. It stands in jeopardy because Kriemhild and her brothers represent two different spheres; she is a creature of nature, but the outlook of her brothers is determined by their social milieu. It is the function of the plot to bring this latent conflict to the surface. Siegfried is the catalyst. He lays claim to Worms by virtue of his inherent strength. Gunther, on the other hand, maintains his claim by virtue of his legitimacy. The strain is further exacerbated by the subsequent marriages, which aim at joining compatible partners. These partners achieve their ends, however, only by resorting to a mode of existence contradictory to their inherent mode. Siegfried, the quintessence of natural strength, must subordinate himself to the artificial demands of society and become dependent on it. Gunther, the quintessential king, must put himself under Siegfried's tutelage. Thus, when the contract is fulfilled, both discover that in the process they have betrayed themselves and compromised their very existence.

The upshot of the inherent differences between Kriemhild's nature and that of her brothers is a deadly conflict. First the men, Gunther and Siegfried, act to set the conflict aside, but then the women, Kriemhild and Brünhild, act to ensure that it will assert itself with full force. Gunther triumphs at the end of Part I and Kriemhild at the end of Part II, but both triumph only in appearance, because both are powerless without the outsider Siegfried. Society, in the person of Gunther, enlists nature (Siegfried's strength) in Part I, while nature (Kriemhild) enlists the festive forms of society in Part II. Nature succumbs in Part I, society in Part II. In this drama the strong characters (Siegfried and Brünhild) play the secondary roles, while the weak characters (Gunther and Kriemhild) play the lead roles. The implication is that catastrophe ensues from weakness.

Not content with these largely structural and functional collocations, Schröder goes on to speculate on the historical theme of the *Nibelungenlied*, that is, the extent to which it transposes the past into the present. Reversing Heusler's dictum that heroic poetry is personalized history, Schröder proposes to penetrate the historical layer by depersonalizing and thereby repoliticizing the action of the *Nibelungenlied*. Gunther's personal weakness is tantamount to political incompetence; the courtly culture of Worms is no more than an empty form. Siegfried's strength is therefore a prerequisite for political security. In this way the poet plays off "old" strength against "new" culture, nature against society. In the process Siegfried and Brünhild are modernized at Worms, while Kriemhild and Gunther are transported back into mythic time in Nibelungenland and Islant. Schröder suggests that this pattern reflects the discrepancy between real power and nominal rule that led to the downfall of the Merovingian dynasty. Seen in this way, the primitive narrative material of the *Nibelungenlied*, generally taken to betray the poet's inability to adjust the old story to his new purposes, becomes meaningful. The poet's intention was to redramatize the basic thought of the old story, the incongruence of political power and political rule.

Like Mergell, Schröder comes to the study of the *Nibelungenlied* from Wolfram's *Parzival*. Unlike Mergell, he is intent on drawing a distinction. After reviewing the broad similarities and dissimilarities between the *Nibelungenlied* and *Parzival*, he concludes that they pose the same question but provide different answers. They ask how the weak individual can assume power. The *Nibelungenlied* judges that he cannot. Wolfram judges that he can if he undergoes a transformation. Parzival obeys an ethical imperative to seek the truth. The figures in the *Nibelungenlied* follow no such imperative and are trapped in a static existence. The two-part narrative structures contrast correspondingly; in the first part of each the king establishes himself, but in the second part Gunther loses his life whereas Parzival is guided *volens nolens* by God. In other words, *Parzival* is predicated on the model of salvation, but death in the *Nibelungenlied* is unredeemed. Where Wolfram constructs teleologically, the *Nibelungenlied* merely observes the human state.

In a final section Schröder urges the importance of the *Klage* as the first interpretation of the *Nibelungenlied* and a key to the contemporary understanding of the work. It exculpates Kriemhild but condemns Hagen and Gunther, attributing the catastrophe to their arrogance (vv. 3,434–38). By implication their guilt lies in an excessive self-reliance without regard for a higher truth. This critique bears out Schröder's comparison between the *Nibelungenlied* and *Parzival*.

Although Werner Schröder places his study under the auspices of the title "Das Buoch Chreimhilden" found in MS Munich 341 (D), just as Heusler had done forty years earlier, he begins with the rejection of Heusler's method that had by now become a new exordial topic.[9] He held that Heusler's approach was not so different from Lachmann's; Heusler merely made his slices vertically rather than horizontally, assigning much of the flavor to the bottom layers of the cake. According to Schröder any concession of literary qualities to the earlier forms of the story necessarily detracted from the final confection. Another part of the exordial topic, this one borrowed from Panzer, is the overestimation of a book by the

French scholar Ernest Tonnelat, which German scholars espoused after the war because it adhered faithfully to the text of the *Nibelungenlied* without undertaking excursions into textual prehistory.[10]

W. Schröder too was intent on a precise understanding of the text as it stands, but on the basis of a much more cautious reading than the one put forward by W. J. Schröder, with whom he takes strong issue, particularly on the symbolic interpretation of characters. As a consequence, much of the study is devoted to lexical tallies and the gauging of shades of meaning, particularly in the word *leit* (sorrow, injury, etc.), which Friedrich Maurer had placed at the center of his interpretation.[11] Whereas W. J. Schröder probably made the *Nibelungenlied* more interesting than it really is, W. Schröder's recapitulations make it decidedly less interesting than it is.

Schröder's aim is not only to vindicate Kriemhild's place at the center of the poet's design but also to rehabilitate her, to rescue her on the one hand from symbolic reductionism (p. 93) and on the other hand from the suspicion of mixed motives. Maurer had interpreted her desire for the Nibelung treasure as a real desire for reparation of the wrong committed against her and a symbolic restoration of her honor.[12] Schröder argues repeatedly that the treasure is not a real issue.[13] The poet would not have lavished so much attention on the love relationship if that were not the sole motive for her revenge. Kriemhild thus grieves only for her husband, not for the power or prestige that he conferred. When she demands the treasure from Hagen, her wish is only to triumph over her husband's killer. Her interest in the treasure only masks her longing for Siegfried. Like W. J. Schröder, W. Schröder concludes with an appeal to the *Klage* (and redaction C), which authenticate his reading by emphasizing Kriemhild's fidelity and guiltlessness.

The rethinking of the *Nibelungenlied* apparent in these German studies was echoed in a group of articles by three British scholars in 1960 and 1961. J. K. Bostock's contribution was temperamentally in line with Werner Schröder's close reading.[14] It interprets the poem in terms of church teaching and attributes the final catastrophe to moral flaws, notably *übermuot*, or arrogance, a sin of which virtually everyone in the poem is convicted.[15] The strength of the article is that it locates a unified moral principle supported by the frequent occurrence of a particular word. The weakness is that it reads rather like a critical penitential, in which the sins of the various characters are tallied up and penance duly prescribed.

D. G. Mowatt's article is more in keeping with W. J. Schröder's symbolical reading, but it is theoretically uncompromising.[16] Mowatt categorically declares the principles of New Criticism applicable to medieval literature in general and the *Nibelungenlied* in particular, decrying only the tendency of German scholars to make occasional concessions to his-

torical thinking. He finds it unnecessary to invoke different narrative
layers in explaining apparent contradictions. With W. J. Schröder he locates a meaningful design in the fateful bringing together of dissimilar na-
tures (Brünhild/Gunther, Kriemhild/Siegfried), and uses the Goethean
analogy of elective affinities. The incompatibility of social and individu-
alistic instincts is the theme of the *Nibelungenlied*, just as it is of other
courtly epics.

Hugh Sacker credits the poet not only with thematic structures but with
ironic and symbolic effects as well.[17] He resists the idea that epithets are
merely stereotypical and urges cases in which adjectives such as *übermüete*
(bold) or *minneclîch* (lovely) signal quite the opposite. Indeed, he finds
the first twelve stanzas of the poem thoroughly shot through with irony.
In the area of symbolism he offers not only the sexually significant ring
and belt taken from Brünhild and a plausible analogy between the wild
falcon of Kriemhild's dream and the wild suitor who materializes at
Worms, but also some rather unexpected sexual symbolism in Siegfried's
death scene. Such imputations represent a real leap in our estimate of the
poet, since they imply his ability both to create intricate meanings and to
undermine them at the same time. If true, Sacker's observations would
not so much clarify as complicate our understanding of the poem.[18]

The postwar attempts to come to terms with the *Nibelungenlied* in
more text-oriented studies culminated in a series of books published
between 1955 and 1965. The first was Friedrich Panzer's volume of almost five hundred pages.[19] Those sections devoted to the form of the
Nibelungenlied remain an indispensable compendium of tabulations relating to such matters as metrics, style, vocabulary, formulas, rhetorical
devices, numerical predilections, ceremonial effects, descriptive modes,
sentential expressions, inner chronology, contradictions, and so forth.
The long chapter of 165 pages on sources is flawed, however, by Panzer's
misconstruction of the textual relationships. It is symptomatic that he
cites approvingly the work on French heroic epic by Joseph Bédier, whose
inventionism was swept away just four years later by Ramón Menéndez
Pidal.[20] Panzer conceded Heusler's "Brünhildenlied" but abolished the
"Ältere Not," emphasizing instead the role of French borrowings and
contemporary history. All these pages must now be read with a grain of
salt. Panzer does not offer an interpretation as such, only a brief chapter
of general assessment (pp. 454–69), which serves as a summation of the
poetic qualities of the *Nibelungenlied* and its position between heroic poetry and chivalric literature. A concluding comparison with Homer notes
the great distance between the parochialism of the German poem and
Homer's Hellenic panorama, but suggests that the *Nibelungenlied* offers
some compensation in making the inner life of its characters transparent.

Whereas Panzer's book attempts to consolidate the revolution against traditional source studies, Burghart Wachinger's sober monograph both participates in and tempers the revolution.[21] His book consists of discrete sections on anticipations, structure, and motivation. The first two in particular reflect the preoccupations of the postwar descriptivists, but Wachinger refrains from the temptation to impose ideal proportions in his calculation of the structural divisions. He sees the macrostructure in terms of the major temporal intervals at the end of Adventure 11 (eleven years), the beginning and end of Adventure 19 (three and a half and nine years), and the beginning of Adventure 23 (twelve years), thus singling out an objective criterion for his divisions. The most interesting section of the book is the last, which is an exercise in ascertaining whether the motivations of the action may be grasped without reference to underlying versions that the *Nibelungenlied* poet failed to integrate convincingly into his final elaboration. In the course of this examination three cruxes are subjected to careful analysis: the motivation of Siegfried's death, the reconciliation of Kriemhild with her brothers at the end of Adventure 19, and her demand for the treasure at the end of the poem. Siegfried's tragedy is interpreted as a result of his subordination to the service of love and hence to Gunther, a sham service with dire consequences. Wachinger thus proposes ill-fated love as the cause of Siegfried's death, but confesses that the motivation is overgrown by other issues to the point of mystification.

The peculiarity that in Adventure 19 the seizure of Kriemhild's treasure comes directly on the heels of her reconciliation is explained by the rigors of the story, which required that the reconciliation take place in order to make Kriemhild's new marriage and the subsequent invitation possible, while at the same time allowing scope for the unresolved hostilities. Kriemhild's loss of her treasure effectively, though not ostensibly, cancels the reconciliation, thus allowing the antagonism to persist unabated below the surface of the action. The difficulties involved in a clear reading of the passage are illustrated by a particularly massive intervention of the C redactor at this point in the story. Finally, Wachinger turns to Kriemhild's last-minute demand for the restoration of her treasure, the motif that so preoccupied Werner Schröder in the same year. Wachinger suggests that she commits herself not to kill Hagen when Dietrich delivers him bound and helpless into her hands. She at first honors the commitment by demanding only satisfaction, but Hagen seizes the opportunity by contriving Gunther's death. Kriemhild now goes back on her commitment, kills Hagen, and thereby justifies her own death.

Unlike other more impetuous apologists, Wachinger formulates his explanations with great caution. In a concluding statement (pp. 139–45) he warns against the dangers of positive overinterpretation along either psychological or symbolical lines (in the manner of W. J. Schröder). At the same time, a reduction of the *Nibelungenlied* to mere dramatic vitality seems to him less than adequate. He suggests that the interest of the poem may finally lie in the unresolved tension between the parts and the whole, between psychological portrayal and the unintegrated narrative facts. His book is admirable in its reserve, but it offers the student relatively little encouragement. It confirms that the *Nibelungenlied* is indeed very difficult to explain and hints that its charm may lie in its very uninterpretability.

Other critics were not ready for Wachinger's resignation. In 1963 Gottfried Weber published a general interpretation as ambitious in scope as W. J. Schröder's.[22] It pursues the reaction against Heusler (and the compensatory elevation of Tonnelat) in decisive terms, arguing that "attention to the sources perforce obscures the clear recognition of the literary work" (p. 2). Accordingly, about half the book is devoted to a step-by-step retracing of the roles played by the major characters. In the process the heroic figures emerge in the same questionable light that Bostock's brief essay had thrown on them. Siegfried is judged to have succumbed to hubris and a misguided subservience to love. He is flawed by the split between outward courtliness and inner arrogance. Hagen betrays his own better vision when, in vain concern for his honor, he agrees to the journey to Hunland though he knows it is fatal. The Burgundian and Hunnish kings are feeble enough to suggest that the poet had had some unedifying experience of kingship (p. 83). Rüdeger too is a victim of his own chivalric ambition and lack of internalized Christianity.

In all these figures Weber detects a deep-seated pride, which breeds hate, which in turn breeds vengeance and deception. They have in common an inability to transcend their egocentric interests. As a result the formal requirements of chivalry are transformed into a demonic preoccupation with honor, unmitigated by religious faith. The unfulfilled knights of the *Nibelungenlied* are driven to take refuge in heroic action. In terms of intellectual history, the poet was suspended between heroic nostalgia and the false optimism of chivalric culture. He portrayed a disillusionment with the latter and a reversion to the former. He thus associated himself with the more conservative and less intellectual impulses of Austro-Bavarian writers in opposition to the cultivation of chivalric and courtly values in the West.[23]

Bert Nagel's contributions to the study of the *Nibelungenlied* span more than twenty-five years from 1953 to 1979. One of the earliest and perhaps the best dates from 1954 and is remarkable for its delicate application of textual analysis and keen aesthetic observations.[24] Whereas other critics urged a reformulation of doctrine, Nagel was more eager to promote a greater appreciation of the poetic qualities, not least of all the particular effects of the *Nibelungenlied* stanza. His comments are therefore difficult to summarize. Fundamentally he is concerned with the poet's difficult position between old and new literary conventions, and the skill with which he navigates the shoals. He suggests how the poet mediates between the "old lore" of the Nibelung legend and the new biographical incorporation of Kriemhild, how Kriemhild and Hagen function both as exemplary victims of dark drama and individual personalities, how the dissonant intimations of doom merge with scenes of courtly splendor from the outset to unify the poem as a whole, how the obvious difficulty of maintaining a clear epic flow is offset by dramatic scenes, how the archaic bridal-quest pattern is modernized in terms of courtly love, and how the poet capitalizes on the discrepancy between traditional energy and new refinement to create a feeling of "realism" and vitality in a figure such as Siegfried.

Nagel does not dispute the importance of earlier versions and the residue of discrepancies, but he believes that the poet's Janus position could be an opportunity as well as a dilemma. This does not mean that characters speak and act according to a perfectly consistent idea of their personalities. They can speak "out of character," as the poet's mouthpiece, for example when Hagen urges church attendance on his companions (stanzas 1,855–56). Nor does it mean that the poem is faultlessly composed, but Nagel asks us to bear in mind that it was intended to be read aloud in installments and that under these circumstances the power of individual scenes would have overshadowed defects in the narrative as a whole.

The undeniable contradictions in the text lend themselves to an analysis in terms of active renovation as well as passive reception. Kriemhild is in some sense two persons, but in the poet's new design she also grows organically from courtly maiden to demonic avenger. In the invitation sequence Nagel accepts the confusing indices of her real longing to see her brothers and her mania for revenge as psychologically comprehensible (stanzas 1,391–1,405). Even the notorious chronological difficulties that enable Kriemhild to give birth to Ortlieb in her fifties can be justified to the extent that they convey the timelessness of the vengeance imperative. Similarly, Siegfried's knowledge of Brünhild and his familiarity with Isenstein may be understood symbolically as evidence of an inner affinity. Hence Siegfried's tragedy grows out of his failure to realize his natural destiny with Brünhild and his formation of an unnatural bond with Kriemhild. Brünhild, correspondingly deprived of her destiny, sheds tears in stanza 618, alleging the injustice done Kriemhild in marrying her to a vassal, but this allegation is a pretext designed at once to mask and reveal her own bitter disappointment.

The early phase in Nagel's work culminated in his book of 1965.[25]

Where the early monograph succeeds in its suggestive impressionism, the book fails because it attempts, but does not attain, comprehensiveness. It is the true heir of the period between 1950 and 1965 in its emphasis on formal criteria. The first section, on history, is half the length of the following sections on *Form* and *Ethos*, and "history" turns out to mean only contemporary history, not the literary history of the poem. Like Panzer's book, Nagel's tends to become a repertory of rhetorical features, for example structural schemes, parallelisms, and motival repetitions.[26] No summation or theory emerges from these pages, which offer something more like a running commentary. Nagel's book marked the end of a period. Formal analysis was for the moment exhausted in Germany and gave way to other trends. Only in England and the United States did it survive as a brief aftermath.[27]

BETWEEN THE TRENDS (1960–75)

Even before 1960 there was an uneasy stirring that may be understood as a reaction against the freewheeling surface interpretations of the postwar years. Klaus von See published two traditional source studies in 1957 and 1958, proposing a legal-historical background for Siegfried's role as delegate wooer.[28] Joachim Bumke published three source studies in 1958 and 1960, one constructing a source for Adventure 8, one exploring the relationship between the *Nibelungenlied* and *Daurel et Beton*, and one outlining dual sources for Part I of the *Nibelungenlied*.[29] As we saw in the previous chapter, Wapnewski's article of 1960 set Rüdeger's dilemma in a legal-historical context and took conscientious account of the source problems.[30] In 1959 Gerhart Lohse returned to the relationship between the *Nibelungenlied* and *Þiðreks saga*, and in 1961 Roswitha Wisniewski published an elaborate study of the sources of Part II, vindicating Heusler's "Ältere Not" despite the persistent doubts of the previous decade.[31] That the field was not yet ready for such a reaction is indicated by the unbroken silence surrounding Lohse's study and the belated acceptance of Wisniewski's conclusions by Werner Hoffmann in 1982.[32] An analogous English reaction against descriptivism was expressed by K. C. King in 1962; he too reclaimed a role for source study.[33]

The intermediate period between text interpretation and historical interpretation also saw the appearance of two books by Friedrich Neumann (1967) and Walter Falk (1974). One looks backward in time, the other forward. Neumann's volume is not a unified study but a reprinting and refurbishing of earlier articles.[34] The collection is of interest because it shows a scholar of the older school coming to grips with the formalist revolution. His first article originally appeared in 1924.[35] It analyzes various characters with attention to the discrepancy between traditional roles in earlier versions of the legend and the more refined manners of the *Nibelungenlied*: Siegfried's old role as uncouth interloper at Worms and his new role as courtly prince, Brünhild's old role as powerful princess and her new role as comic amazon, Kriemhild's old role as merciless avenger and her new role as courtly lady. According to Neumann such characters were not conceived as living individuals but as exemplary figures embodying particular functions. When ideals and social functions changed, the characters remained suspended between two times. The poet failed to modernize in consistent detail. Neumann agrees with Heusler that the refrain on "love and sorrow" is not adequate to thematize the epic, and he is content to see the poet's achievement in his presentation of dramatic events and colorful scenes.[36] By prefacing his book with this essay, Neumann clearly declares his skepticism toward attempts to interpret the poem from a purely contemporary stance and without reference to the residue of older layers.

His chief essay nonetheless makes a real effort to absorb the descriptivist approach by rehearsing the action in painstaking detail, not once but twice.[37] These summaries are followed by a critique of Mergell, Maurer, Beyschlag, W. Schröder, and Weber. Mergell receives particularly harsh criticism for remaining on the surface of the text, ignoring problems, and arriving at an interpretation on the basis of a few passages randomly selected and arbitrarily connected. Neumann's criticism achieves its effect through an appeal to sound common sense, but it is not sophisticated and fails to do much damage to the descriptivist hypothesis. The interpretation of all epic depends, after all, on the selection and combination of significant moments. Neumann does not show why the *Nibelungenlied* should constitute a special exception to this procedure and why disharmonies caused by the retention of old motifs in a new context should be disabling for the interpreter who seeks to establish an ideological framework.

To assign as recent a book as Walter Falk's to the intermediate period is stretching a point, but the author explains in his preface that the central Chapters 5–9 go back to 1961–63, that is, to what we might call the high interpretive period.[38] Falk espouses two fundamental doctrines of this period, the "crime and punishment hypothesis" most clearly formulated by Bostock, and the "two-world hypothesis," which we have encountered in the work of Mergell, W. J. Schröder, Weber, and, in subdued form, Wachinger.[39] The "crime and punishment hypothesis" observes that the poem culminates in disaster and posits moral guilt to explain it; the attractiveness of such an interpretation to the postwar generation is obvious. The "two-world hypothesis" holds that two incongruent spheres are brought together with disastrous consequences (e.g., Siegfried or Brünhild in the courtly world of Worms), or that natural affinities (most commonly the bond between Siegfried and Brünhild) are ignored to the detriment of all.

Falk's book has perhaps most in common with Weber's because it advances a religious interpretation. The point of departure is Walther von der Vogelweide's "Ich saz ûf eime steine" and the idea that "guot und weltlîch êre" (wealth and worldly honor) cannot be reconciled with "gotes hulde" (God's grace). Falk explains Walther's view as the result of an inner crisis precipitated by a disillusionment with *Minnedienst* (love service), and suggests that the characters in the *Nibelungenlied* also strive for *guot* and *êre* without being able to reconcile them with *gotes hulde*. Siegfried belongs by nature to an "inner world," but he enters the artificial world of Worms and therefore finds himself straddling two opposed existences. Because he belongs to the same world as Brünhild, he is able to win her for the "world of honor" in Worms. In so doing, he tricks Gunther by drawing him out of the "world of honor," thus realizing his boast to conquer Worms.

At the same time, however, Siegfried succumbs to the "world of honor" for the sake of love. By winning Kriemhild with *Minnedienst* he transforms himself from a servant of love into its master; *Minnedienst* is revealed in its true light as an instrument for achieving power. As a result of his *Minnedienst* Siegfried makes the transition from challenger and conqueror to a new existence as representative and defender of the "world of honor," but Kriemhild, out of arrogance, wishes to free him from this restrictive existence. Hence the quarrel of the queens. But ultimately she too is trapped; in appealing to Hagen to protect Siegfried, she submits to the prime representative of the "world of honor." We are led to understand that an allegiance to courtly love has also undermined her natural principles. Love is thus the root cause of Siegfried's death, but he is love's accomplice; having fulfilled his boast to subdue the Burgundians, he has become a threat to them and thus motivates his own death. As in Walther's "Ich saz ûf eime steine," *untriuwe* and *gewalt* (faithlessness and violence) lurk in the *Nibelungenlied*, which is an epic counterpart to Walther's lyric.

HISTORICAL INTERPRETATIONS (1965–80)

Falk's structural principles look back to the analytical methods of the 1960's, but his attempt to locate the *Nibelungenlied* in the political crisis that inspired Walther belongs to the following period of historical interpretations. The latter preoccupation is perhaps already implicit in

Panzer's emphasis on contemporary events underlying certain episodes in the *Nibelungenlied*, but the first explicitly political interpretation was put forward in an essay of 1952 by Siegfried Beyschlag.[40]

Beyschlag begins by pointing out a passage in *Þiðreks saga* (2:262.17–26) suggesting that Sigurd's presence challenges Gunnar's status as king and that Grimhild poses a similar threat to Brynhild. The same threat is hinted at in the *Nibelungenlied* when Kriemhild blandly states that the whole realm should be subject to Siegfried (stanza 815) and then demands precedence before the court. Beyschlag assembles indications of a court party in opposition to Siegfried and in favor of his elimination, concluding that political issues are a significant factor in the motivation of his death. According to Beyschlag, it could scarcely be coincidental that such a theme surfaced in a literary work during the interregnum years after 1197, and he anticipates Falk with a reference to Walther's political poetry.

Wapnewski's essay of 1960 also made use of political facts to illumine Rüdeger's options in Adventure 37, but the period of systematic historical interpretations was ushered in with a brief article by Josef Szövérffy in 1965.[41] Szövérffy points out that the disaster of Part I is conditioned by Siegfried's quasi-feudal subordination to Gunther in the hope of winning Kriemhild, and that the disaster of Part II is predicated on Rüdeger's similarly quasi-feudal oath to support Kriemhild in Hunland. Feudal allegiances of a questionable nature are therefore the motor of tragedy, and Szövérffy suggests that such skepticism must have been a feature of the years following the quarrel between pope and emperor over the investiture of bishops; the excommunication of emperors and the release of vassals from feudal bonds during these years had destabilized the system of obligations. Szövérffy's proposal is too general to have much explanatory force, but it was the first to establish itself as a clear alternative to legendary analysis in Heusler's tradition or to the more recent textual interpretations.

As we saw in Chapter 5, Karl Heinz Ihlenburg also adduced the problematical character of feudal structures in a full-scale study from 1969.[42] He projected the *Nibelungenlied* against the background of the troubled political scene after the death of Henry VI in 1197, but more broadly against the efforts of the aristocracy to assert itself against imperial authority in the twelfth century. The pattern of weak kings (Gunther and Etzel) and powerful vassals (Hagen and Rüdeger) suggested to him the inherent frailty of political institutions.

In an important article from 1974, Jan-Dirk Müller focuses the social forces in a somewhat different light, as a contest not between royalty and aristocracy but between competing elements within the aristocracy.[43] Departing from earlier efforts to thematize the action of the *Nibelungenlied* allegorically, Müller undertakes only to identify certain tensions in the text that mirror contemporary social conditions.

Müller begins with Siegfried's brash claim at Worms, which cannot succeed because it is a challenge to legitimate authority. In the context of political realities such a demonstration of knightly prowess is illusory. Gunther, contrary to Ihlenburg's view, is not to be seen as a weak king but as the bearer of royal authority, charged with the maintenance of peace and able to contain Siegfried's challenge. Siegfried becomes socialized when he relinquishes the idea of individual combat and enters the world of service, love service for Kriemhild's hand and political service on Gunther's behalf. But the idea of service is ambiguous because it is associated both with the voluntary service undertaken by the free hereditary nobility and the obligatory service performed by the unfree *eigenman* or *ministerialis*. In Islant, where, in distinction to Worms, strength and status are the same thing, Siegfried must impersonate an *eigenman* and feign social inferiority not to be mistaken for the suitor himself. Brünhild is therefore confronted with confusing indices, and her confusion determines the sequel.

This confusion is the substance of the queens' quarrel, which is designed to clarify whether Siegfried is Gunther's "genôz" (equal—stanza 819) or his "man" (stanza 821). The word *man* can mean free vassal, but it can also mean unfree *ministerialis*, and this is the sense in which Brünhild understands it. The semantic ambiguity reflects a historical development in which unfree *ministeriales* were rising into positions previously reserved for free nobles, and in which these nobles were themselves losing traditional prerogatives. Class friction ensued, and the question whether a particular man in royal service was a *man* (free vassal) or *eigenholt* (*ministerialis*) was socially crucial. The calamity of Part I thus grows out of Brünhild's misconstruction of Siegfried's voluntary service as obligatory service. Müller points out that the class tension between old and new nobility seems to have been prevalent in southeastern Germany, where the hereditary nobility lost ground in the last third of the twelfth century but in some cases vigorously resisted the trend. This situation may have been particularly pronounced around Passau, where the *Nibelungenlied* is most likely to have been written.

Two rather more impressionistic historical studies appeared in a volume of essays on medieval Austrian literature published in 1977. Helmut Birkhan concentrates on the broader literary and political context and suggests that the *Nibelungenlied* may have represented a compromise between the historically oriented Welf literature of the East and the courtly Hohenstaufen literature of the West.[44] Passau, with its Hohenstaufen sympathies but Welf location in Bavaria, would have been conducive to this double vision, and the period after Henry the Lion's fall in 1180 and the submission of his Danish ally Valdemar in 1181 would have been the right moment for the poet's barbs against the Bavarian and Saxon targets of Hohenstaufen animosity. Birkhan doubts that Rüdeger was conceived as a fictional reflection of a Babenberg duke, such as Leopold VI, because a duke would scarcely have been flattered to see himself counterfeited as a count. Birkhan suggests instead that Rüdeger may have been intended as an idealized antitype to Barbarossa's faithless vassal Henry the Lion.

In the same volume Sylvia Konecny draws attention to King Sigemund's abdication in Siegfried's favor (stanza 713) and explains it on the basis of a Frankish practice that precluded an uncrowned prince from having a binding marriage or legitimate heirs.[45] Sigemund's abdication may there-fore be understood as an effort to maximize Siegfried's value as a mar-riage partner for Kriemhild. Of particular interest in this line of argument is Konecny's further assumption of a hypothetical earlier version of the tale incorporating the abdication motif. Thus the old practice of basing interpretations on genetic deductions is reversed, and historical con-siderations lead to the positing of new sources. In more general terms Konecny urges the thematic contrast between a weak monarchy at Worms, where Gunther allows himself to become Hagen's instrument, and a strong monarchy at Xanten, where there is no visible sign of aristocratic encroachment.

A contrast between Xanten and Worms is also the point of departure for Peter Czerwinski, who understands the former as a primitive culture predicated on force and the latter as a more advanced bureaucratic cul-ture.[46] Siegfried, the exponent of primitive culture, must validate himself by an exercise of strength at Worms, but the challenge is averted and his energy is translated into formal service in the new hierarchy. The relations between Siegfried and Gunther are regulated by subordinating one to the other. Siegfried then takes over the Saxon campaign because Gunther can maintain his position only as long as he is exempt from the exercise of force. Love also works to socialize natural impulses, and Kriemhild's beauty is placed in the service of the court's larger interests.

The upshot of the wooing on Islant dramatizes the conflict between a primitive and a more advanced form of culture. When representatives of the primitive culture (Siegfried and Brünhild) are installed at Worms, they incite violence and jeopardize the hierarchical structure. Hagen's contra-dictory role in this situation is that he is technically a vassal in the hierar-chical model, but refuses to subordinate himself and acts on his own ini-tiative. The catastrophe in Hunland also proceeds from a disintegration of the new order in the face of uncontrolled violence. What Czerwinski proposes is another version of the "two-world hypothesis," but despite his references to twelfth-century territorialization, his reading is more in keeping with W. J. Schröder's symbolical interpretation than with the more recent historical interpretations.

A summary by Gert Kaiser may serve as the final example in this group.[47] It combines sociohistorical and reception analysis by seeking to identify a socially distinct readership. Following Jan-Dirk Müller, Kaiser argues that the trouble arises because Brünhild misunderstands Siegfried's service as that of an unfree *ministerialis*, but he goes on to suggest that the view of service in the *Nibelungenlied* stands in direct opposition to the approval of service in Arthurian epic and the *romans d'antiquité*. The *Nibelungenlied* poet rejects the idea of service precisely because it is tainted by association with the class of *ministeriales*. Part II is in effect a conservative celebration of voluntary loyalty in opposition to obligatory service, but the ideological message is esthetically rescued by Hagen's private pact with Rüdeger in defiance of strict feudal loyalty. Kaiser thus goes a step further than Müller, who suggested only involuntary echoes of social tensions. Kaiser assigns these tensions to the thematic fabric of the poem.

CONCLUSION

The status of *Nibelungenlied* research at the end of our period is conveniently represented by fourteen articles from a conference held in Hohenems in September of 1979 and published the following year.[48] These papers are remarkable for the lack of continuity they display. None pursues the text-interpretive model prevalent in the period 1950–65, and only one attaches to the sociohistorical tradition of 1965–80. Significantly, the one exception, an important essay by Ursula Hennig, levels some telling criticism at such proponents of historical interpretation as Szövérffy, Ihlenburg, and Jan-Dirk Müller.[49] Against Müller she argues that *eigenholt* does not mean *ministerialis* but rather 'bondsman'. Brünhild's description of Siegfried as *eigenholt* in stanzas 620 and 803 does not therefore constitute a subtle misunderstanding of feudal distinctions; it is a deliberately exaggerated provocation. Hennig denies that feudal concepts have motivating force in the *Nibelungenlied* and reasserts the importance of literary comprehension. By virtue of its exclusions, then, the Hohenems conference would seem to mark the end of an era.

Equally remarkable is the conference's thematic consistency in another area. No fewer than six of the fourteen contributions are connected in some way with oral-formulaic composition.[50] Some make positive use of the theory, but others are cautious about it. In a paper independent of similar suggestions made a year earlier by Michael Curschmann, Norbert Voorwinden arrives at the conclusion that the *Klage* was composed chiefly on the basis of a preliterary transmission of the Nibelung story.[51] Burghart Wachinger, this time with explicit reference to Curschmann, comes to the opposite conclusion, that the *Klage* is based on a definite text of the *Nibelungenlied*, although it may in turn have contributed to the final shape of that epic as we know it.[52] Both agree that the transmission of these texts was more open to oral alteration than has traditionally been assumed. Achim Masser solidifies the evidence for oral transmission by identifying oral doublets inserted at different points in the written text of the *Nibelungenlied*.[53] Peter K. Stein, on the other hand, reduces the significance of oral-formulaic analysis by showing that the formulism in a text of *Orendel* is literary in nature.[54]

The period of oral-formulaic analysis as applied to the *Nibelungenlied* corresponds roughly to the period of sociohistorical analysis; Franz Bäuml's first relevant study appeared in 1967 and his latest in the Hohenems volume of 1980.[55] On the other hand, the theory as it pertains to Germanic belongs more generally speaking to the preceding period of textual study, which began with the *Beowulf* article by Francis P. Magoun, Jr., in 1953.[56] Oral-formulaic analysis occupies an ambiguous position in both periods. It is both textual and nontextual, historical and nonhistorical. It is textual because it adheres closely to the phrasing of the poem and seeks to account precisely for that phrasing, but it is nontextual because it causes the reader to retreat quickly into the obscurity of textlessness. It is historical because it provides a genetic explanation of the poem and probes the context of literacy, but it is nonhistorical because it posits earlier versions that are not readily distinguishable from the extant ones. It does not, for example, provide an instrument for measuring the differences between the *Nibelungenlied* of 1200, the "Ältere Not" of 1160–70, and Saxo's *carmen* of Grimhild's perfidy from 1131. It is in any event noninterpretive because the art of preliterary criticism has yet to be evolved. That nearly half the contributions in the Hohenems volume grow out of the oral-formulaic debate in itself signals a retreat from the interpretive efforts of the previous decades.

Subtracting a study by Stefan Sonderegger on conversational language in the *Nibelungenlied* and a plenary address by Werner Schröder, we are left with five papers on various topics. Werner Hoffmann provides a helpful review of discussions in the literary histories from Gervinus to Bertau.[57] Walter Haug, in the tradition of Kurt Wais, undertakes a comparison with a bridal-quest story in the *Mabinogion*.[58] Alois Wolf revives Panzer's problem of French sources and suggests motival and scenic similarities, especially to the cycle of Guillaume d'Orange.[59] Uwe Meves returns to the

Passau archives and suggests that the literary patronage of *König Rother* may underlie the acknowledgment of Wolfger's patronage in the *Nibelungenlied*.[60] Otfrid Ehrismann adopts a psychological angle in contrasting Parts I and II and locating the superior appeal of the latter in its therapeutic exorcism of death.[61] What these contributions have in common is an attempt to extract new perspectives from traditional approaches. A reading of the volume as a whole suggests a temporary lack of consensus on the direction *Nibelungenlied* studies should take and hence an open prospect.

This sense of equilibrium, in contrast to the decisive critical initiatives of 1950–65 and 1965–80, also emerges from the most important recent contribution to *Nibelungenlied* studies, Werner Hoffmann's fifth revised edition of the Metzler volume *Das Nibelungenlied* (1982), originally published in collaboration with Gottfried Weber in 1961.[62] In its latest form this book has undergone not only a great development in coverage, which makes it the indispensable guide, but also a shift in emphasis. The first edition, presumably under Weber's influence, largely accepted Friedrich Panzer's revolution (e.g., pp. 13–16) and participated in the ensuing descriptivist redefinition of the task (e.g., pp. 63–64). Hoffmann's revision of 1982 rejects Panzer's philological conclusions (pp. 53–54), provides an ample review of the Norse texts and the relevant source questions (pp. 47–56), and allows cautiously for the usefulness of diachronic study in the interpretive project (p. 61).[63]

It is not the task of this chapter to propose yet another interpretation of the *Nibelungenlied* but rather to suggest a strategy and outline the parameters of interpretation. Clearly a close reading of the text is as fundamental now as it was in 1950, and the sociohistorical studies of 1965–80 have just as clearly widened our perspective on the text. But both these approaches, which undertook to root the *Nibelungenlied* more firmly in the contemporary scene, have failed to fulfill that promise. The literary readings of 1950–65 limited the context too exclusively to courtly romance, particularly to *Parzival*, all or large parts of which were written later. The sociohistorical analyses disregarded the literary context altogether. The *Nibelungenlied* has therefore remained in the isolation about which Dürrenmatt, Panzer, and later critics complained.

The strategy proposed in Chapters 5–7 aims to anchor the poem not only in contemporary Arthurian epic but also in the more general context of German literature during the period 1150–1200, including the immediate sources, the "Ältere Not" and the "Brünhildenlied." These poems were also a part of twelfth-century German literature and contributed to the literary framework in which the author of the *Nibelungenlied* worked. Just as the historical critics have taught us to hear institutional echoes in the text, so too we should learn to identify literary echoes. Perhaps most neglected in its formative role is the minstrel epic, especially *König Rother*. A glance at this tradition reveals a series of literary ironies. We may see in Rüdeger the subverted delegate wooer, the trickster tricked, the comic figure of tradition recast in a tragic role. Similarly, Siegfried inherits both the roles of wooer and of delegate wooer from bridal-quest romance. The conventions of this form shed light on a number of traditionally difficult scenes: the puzzling apprehension of Siegfried's parents when he declares his intention to woo Kriemhild, the obsession with finery, his journey "in recken wîse," Kriemhild's reluctance, the discordant hostility between the suitor and the bride's family in the notorious confrontation of Adventure 3, the magic cloak and extravagant trickery in Islant, Siegfried's fictitious identity as Gunther's vassal, his rescue force from Nibelungenland, and the comic doubling of his role as both suitor and delegate in Adventure 9. When the listeners around 1200 heard these scenes, they recognized the literary background, and when the happy-go-lucky wooer was transformed into the tragic victim of Adventure 16, they appreciated the discrepancy between the old convention and the new creation.

More than a few listeners would have been familiar with Heinrich von Veldeke's *Eneide* and would have pondered the distance between marital comedy and marital tragedy. They would have been acquainted with the new idealization of marriage, if not in *Guillaume d'Angleterre*, at least in Hartmann's epics. In some form they would have known the Hellenistic tradition of family fidelity and domestic reintegration, for example the stories of Faustinianus and Crescentia in the *Kaiserchronik*. The family disintegrations of the *Nibelungenlied* would have echoed harshly against this happier legacy.

More learned listeners would have known something of the tradition of universal history reflected in the *Annolied* and *Kaiserchronik*. If they knew of Franko's foundation at Xanten, they were in a position to connect Siegfried's preeminence with the idea of national emergence. The anti-Roman story of Adelger in the *Kaiserchronik* and the anti-Byzantine barbs in *König Rother* would have promoted such an understanding. Franco-German competition was no less a part of the political scene than the disparagement of Rome and Constantinople. The elevation of Siegfried could very well have been perceived as an epic counterthrust to the French Roland, well known from the *Rolandslied*, as well as to the Greek Alexander and the Roman Aeneas. Regional politics was also a factor in contemporary literature, as the *Annolied*, Heinrich von Veldeke's *Servatius*, and the Soest claim to the Nibelung catastrophe illustrate. Regionalism clarifies the Austro-Hohenstaufen bias against Bavarians and

Saxons, as well as Passau's counterclaim to possession of the true transmission of the legend.

These general considerations can be further refined by measuring the *Nibelungenlied* against the immediate sources. Part II in particular lends itself to such comparison and permits us to isolate the poet's concerns. He rehabilitates Hagen in no fewer than five new adventures designed to vindicate his standing among the Burgundians. Breeding, candor, loyalty, kinship, and friendship are the values the poet espouses. Ferdinand Urbanek produced interesting evidence for advocacy of family loyalty and fast friendship, connected with contemporary Austro-Bavarian tensions, underlying *König Rother*, and some analogous political background might be surmised for the *Nibelungenlied*.[64] Rüdeger's dilemma in Adventure 37 could be making an immediate political point. In any event, the resurrection of Hagen from his treachery in Part I and the reintegration of kith and kin in Part II are evident when our knowledge of the "Ältere Not" is brought to bear.

Siegfried is also promoted from a lesser role in the "Brünhildenlied" to more heroic dimensions in the *Nibelungenlied*. In his case as well as Hagen's, a study of the text's development from earlier versions produces evidence against the descriptivist hypotheses. These hypotheses (e.g., W. J. Schröder, Weber, Falk) have suggested a pattern of weakness, falseness, and prevarication subtending the catastrophe of the *Nibelungenlied*. They subscribe to what I have called the "crime and punishment" interpretation, the idea that Siegfried, Hagen, and the others contract a guilt that they must ultimately expiate. A historical reading against the sources suggests rather that they are heroic figures caught in the traditional impasse of heroic action. They must die, for that is the generic law of heroic literature, but they transcend their fate with a display of personal qualities. They do so in different ways. Siegfried's display is limited to an exhibition of matchless strength; he has the surplus vitality but also the unconsciousness of youth. Hagen is older, more experienced, more vulnerable, but completely aware of the world around him. His heroism is the triumph of consciousness. In this sense, perhaps, the *Nibelungenlied* fits into the structure of contemporary Arthurian romance, in which the two-part structure cultivated by both Hartmann and Wolfram marks out a growth from innocence to knowledge. In the Arthurian epics the trajectory is constructive and optimistic. In the *Nibelungenlied* it is tragic, but not necessarily pessimistic. The moral qualities displayed in Part II are no less triumphant for being ill-fated.

Kriemhild too appears in a somewhat different light if she is viewed in the mirror of the sources. Critics have frequently remarked on her rehabilitation in redaction C and the *Klage*, compared to the standard redaction B, and have argued a difference in interpretation. But if we in turn compare the Kriemhild of B to her ancestor in the "Ältere Not," we may find reasons to moderate our judgment. The poets of the "Ältere Not" and the *Nibelungenlied* were both heir to the idea of Kriemhild's unequivocal "perfidy against her brothers." The poet of the "Ältere Not" does not appear to have deviated from this image. Kriemhild cajoles Etzel into the treacherous invitation of her relatives and personally dispatches a letter with false promises. She confronts Hagen directly on his arrival, then undertakes machinations behind Etzel's back to instigate an attack on the guests. When all else fails, she incites her young son to strike Hagen in the face in order to precipitate the fray. Without a preface telling of Siegfried's death, these actions appear in a clearly negative light.

But the *Nibelungenlied* poet altered the portrait completely by adding Kriemhild's youthful love story, her betrayal by Hagen and her brothers, her four and a half years of widowed grief cut off from her family in Worms, and the seizure of her bride price. In this version her action is amply motivated. It is no longer a question of perfidy but of marital fidelity of the sort encouraged by ecclesiastical emphasis on the permanent union of hearts and by such models of marital faith as Hartmann's Enîte or Wolfram's Sigûne. A historical perspective on Kriemhild suggests not that the B and C poets had substantially different views of her character but that there was a consistent and linear unburdening of her, undertaken first by the B poet and then pursued logically by the C poet.

After a prolonged period of reaction against source criticism and literary-historical analysis the time may be ripe to experiment once again with these traditional approaches. The *Nibelungenlied* should indeed be integrated more decisively into the period in which it was written, but this procedure stands to profit no less from the study of contemporary literature than from the study of contemporary history. Only a small part of that literature has been touched on here. The rest remains to be explored.

Sources and Analogues

The Story of Sigurd in 'Þiðreks saga'

The following story is translated from *Þiðreks saga*, ed. Bertelsen, 1:282–318, and 2:37–43, 258–68. On the breaking up of the narrative into three non-sequential sections see Klein, "Zur Þiðreks saga," and Andersson, "An Interpretation of *Þiðreks saga*." Since the Norse name forms are of no particular interest in an originally German text, they have been simplified throughout: hence Thidrek for Þiðrekr, Sigurd for Sigurðr, Nidung for Niðungr, and so forth. The translation is as faithful to the original as possible. It does not, for example, consistently normalize the mixture of past and present tense characteristic of Norse prose or suppress the repetitive narrative particle "now."

Concerning King Sigmund

There was a king named Sigmund, who ruled over the land called Tarlungaland. His father's name was Sifjan. He was a powerful man and a great chieftain. And when he had inherited the realm from his father, he sent word west to Spain to King Nidung and his son Ortvangis, asking whether King Nidung would give him his daughter Sisibe in marriage. She was to his knowledge the most beautiful of all women and the most courteous in all respects. King Nidung and his son accord a good reception to King Sigmund's messengers and grant them great honor and great gifts in gold and such valuables as are rare in their own country. But he responded to their message from King Sigmund by saying that he did not want to send his daughter to a foreign country "with men who are unknown both to her and to me. But your king has the reputation of being a distinguished man, and that reputation reached us long before you did. Now I do not want to refuse to marry my daughter to him since you have sought me out for her sake."

And with this King Nidung and his son Ortvangis send costly gifts to King Sigmund and the messengers return with nothing more accomplished. And when they come home, they give a full account to King Sigmund of how magnificently King Nidung received them. It was not long before King Sigmund made ready his journey and desired to ride from his realm to Spain on this business. And he had four hundred knights with him, all well equipped. Now he set out with great splendor and magnificence and did not stop until he arrived west in Spain in the realm of King Nidung. Now King Nidung learns of King Sigmund's expedition and provides markets and hospitality wherever he goes until they meet. King Nidung receives King Sigmund honorably and prepares great feasts with all marks of honor and esteem. Now King Sigmund declares his business, saying that he wishes to woo King Nidung's daughter, just as it has been related above that King Nidung had given this proposal a good reception. Now King Nidung replies that it shall be just as they had indicated to the messengers. "And now you may well make this match since you have come yourself." And before the conversation was over, King Nidung betrothed his daughter to King Sigmund.

King Sigmund's wedding

Now the wedding was held at great expense because King Nidung gave his daughter and son-in-law great towns and strong castles and almost half his realm. And what was left over he gave to his son Ortvangis and gave him the title of king because King Nidung was by that time feeble with age. This great feast was held with all manner of good cheer and distinction both with respect to the provision of the feast and tableware and hall decor and the attendance of the greatest chieftains in all of Spain and all types of entertainment and song and great gifts and such a multitude that no such magnificence had been displayed in all of Spain. And when this feast had lasted five days, King Sigmund rode away with his knights, and with him his wife Sisibe. And now he journeyed with great honor until he came home to his realm.

Concerning King Sigmund's military campaign

Now when he had been at home for seven days, two messengers came from King Drasolf and went before Sigmund and showed him letters and seals and told him their business. These messengers state: "King Drasolf and your sister send you greetings and let you know that he has now readied his whole army with all his dukes and counts, and that he will now campaign in Poland. And he sends you word with proper identification that you should come to his aid with all your men, as many as you can assemble." Now King Sigmund answers: "It is not amiss if my brother-in-law and sister think they need my aid and that I should give them assistance and support, and so it shall be." And the same day he had letters and seals prepared for his vassals as far as his realm extends. And he ordered that within four days each man should come to him who wished to give assistance and could hold a shield and ride a horse and dared to fight; and he should set out prepared not to return home for twelve months. Now when this army was all assembled, he set out headlong from his realm.

But before King Sigmund departed, he called his counselors Artvin and Hermann to him. They were counts in Swabia and great chieftains and very handsome men and great warriors. And now he assigned these two warriors to guard his wife and kingdom and all his possessions because he had every confidence in them. But it has often happened that a man who trusts another man is betrayed by him. And these two chieftains rode out with the king and he told them in detail how they should manage things while he was away. And above all he bade them do everything Sisibe said, and they promised that it should be so. And now when King Sigmund and his brother-in-law met, Drasolf had no fewer than three thousand knights, and in all no fewer than seven thousand knights. And King Sigmund had no fewer than his brother-in-law when they met, and now they set out with their whole army and harried in Poland and performed many great deeds.

Concerning the counts and Queen Sisibe

Now when these counts had ruled the realm for a long time, it happened one day that Artvin went to his mistress Sisibe and said to her: "This realm and all the treasures and your person are now in my safekeeping, and I will tell you what I have in mind; I intend to make you my lover and wife, and at the same time I intend that we shall share this realm that I have received. It is uncertain that King Sigmund will return from this campaign. And even if he does come back, he will not get it back from me, or either of us, if your wish is the same as mine. I am no less a knight than King Sigmund, and perhaps a bit better." Now Sisibe replies: "You shall not address me in this fashion. I will await my lord King Sigmund and take no man before he comes home. But even if you have spoken in this way, I may well conceal it for the time being. But if you bring it up again, I will tell my lord of your designs when he comes home, and you will be promptly hanged."

Now he speaks: "Lady, you should not speak as you have because you are well aware that in my country I am no less powerful than King Sigmund in his country." Now she replies: "Even if you were so powerful that you ruled the greater part of the world and King Sigmund was a retainer, still I wish to have him and not you. And you should not say another word about this if you value your life." Now Artvin departs and they break off their conversation. Now Artvin tells his companion everything that has transpired between him and the queen and asks for advice on how to work his will. Now Hermann replies: "Good friend, I wish to discourage you as best I can from doing this. But whatever you determine to do, I am obligated to support you with counsel or otherwise." Now Artvin replies: "I can make no secret of my eagerness to succeed as I wish, or else to lose my life; the third option is for her to die." Now Hermann replies: "If you are so eager in this matter, it may still come to pass as we both wish."

Now when some time had passed, Hermann goes to speak with his mistress, and she receives him well, and they speak of many things. Finally Hermann brought up the matter with which Artvin had charged him. But she replies in the same way and is greatly angered. Now Hermann goes away with nothing further accomplished and tells his companion of their conversation. Now time passes and Artvin often seeks out his mistress and can never get what he asks for. At the same time, King Sigmund and his brother-in-law Drasolf harry far and wide in Poland and do great damage to their antagonists in slaughter, wasting of the land, and plundering. And they often do battle with the natives, sometimes winning and sometimes losing. And when they return home, they have lost great numbers of their men, but return unscathed themselves.

The death of Queen Sisibe

Now King Sigmund comes to the frontier of his realm. His stewards Artvin and Hermann learn of this and take counsel. Artvin said to his companion: "I expect that when King Sigmund comes home, Queen Sisibe will reveal all our conversations to him, considering the reluctant and discourteous response she has given to all our representations. And the king will reproach us greatly when he learns the truth. Now let us be no slower in taking measures, and there is great need if they are to be effective." And before they part, they settle their plan of action. Now they go before the queen and declare their intention to ride out to meet the king and learn the news of him. She expressed her satisfaction and bids them ride as fast as they can, and so they do.

But when they meet King Sigmund, he welcomes them, and they ask him for a private conference. And when the three were alone, Artvin spoke: "Lord, I have ill tidings to communicate, and yet they are true. And I ask you not to hold it against me though I tell you, because I cannot deceive you when you have left all your possessions in my hands and those of my companion. As soon as you left home, your wife Sisibe chose an evil and dishonorable course. She took one of your thralls, with a handsome countenance, into her bed. And when the two of us wished to prevent her from doing it, she vowed to slander us when you returned, and she said that you would have us killed if she so desired. And that same thrall has slept with her every night in her embrace, and she is now pregnant. And we dared not have you return home, lord, without knowing this first."

Now the king replies: "You may know as a certainty that if you lie about her with a single word, that will be the death of you." Now Hermann replies and swears that "all that I have said to you is true." Now the king said: "Good friends, what shall I do with this woman now that such a villainy has taken place?" Now Artvin answers: "That is up to you, sire; we will do whatever you wish." The king spoke again: "She might be hanged, or she might be blinded, or she might have her feet severed and be returned thus to her father." Now Artvin replies: "Another possibility is to send her into the Swabian Forest [Black Forest?]—it is not a thoroughfare and no one has been there for ten years—and cut out her tongue there and let her live as long as God wishes." The king is well satisfied with this plan.

Now the counts ride off homeward. One day the queen stands on the ramparts and sees dust raised by the hooves of horses, and then she sees men riding and recognizes by their weapons [armorial bearings?] that it is the counts who have returned home with their men. And as soon as she can expect them to hear, she calls out: "May God grant that I hear good tidings of King Sigmund. What do you tell of him? Tell the truth now and do not lie." Now Artvin answers: "King Sigmund is in good health and has fared well. He is now in the Swabian Forest with his army. He sends word that you should join him there, and he wishes to meet you. We may well accompany you there on his orders." Now the queen replies: "I will not delay in setting out to meet him, but what woman will accompany me?" Now Hermann answers: "It is of no importance what woman accompanies you, and it is not a long way for you to travel." Then she replies: "Now I am ready."

And now they proceed until they come to a valley in the forest, where no man had previously come, and here they alight from their horses. And now the queen spoke in great wrath: "Where are you now, King Sigmund, and why did you bid these men bring me here? Now I know for a certainty that I am betrayed, and you have not betrayed me alone but also your child." And she wept sorely. Now Count Artvin said: "Now we will do as we have been told and as the king commanded, and you are to die here." Now Hermann spoke: "This woman is blameless, and let us adopt another plan. Let us take one of the dogs we have along and cut out its tongue and take it to the king." Now Artvin replies: "She shall now pay for having rejected us so often, and our intention shall be carried out to the full extent." Now Hermann answers: "So help me God, you shall never harm her if I can prevent it," and he draws his sword. And at this moment the queen gives birth and bears a well-formed child. And then she took from her mead cask, which she had brought along, a glass vessel, and when she had wrapped the child in cloth, she put him in the glass vessel and closed it carefully and placed it next to her.

And now they begin to fight, and it is a very stout encounter, and finally Artvin falls just where the queen is lying. Artvin kicks the glass vessel with his foot so that it topples out into the river. At that moment Hermann brings his sword down on Artvin's neck with both hands so that the head flew off. And now when the queen sees what has happened to the child, what with her previous infirmity, a swoon comes over her and she dies. Now Hermann takes her corpse and attends to it as seems to him most fitting. Then he takes his horse, mounts, and rides until he meets up with King Sigmund. Now the king asks: "Where is your companion Artvin?" Hermann says: "We had a falling out because he wanted to kill or mutilate the woman, and I thought it pitiable when I saw what was intended, and I wanted to help her. And we quarreled about our difference until we fought, and I killed him before it was over. And the woman gave birth to a boy, and a very fair one, and Artvin killed him before he died himself." Then King Sigmund asks whether the queen had declared the king or the thrall father to the child, "and have you lied?" Then Hermann answers: "It is no lie, lord, that it is possible for a man to commit a great crime and then realize it and repent, and then be a worthy man forever after." Now the king spoke angrily: "Get out of my sight. I do not wish to have your service any longer for you are a traitor." Now Hermann goes to his horse and rides away with all his men and is glad to escape with his life. And King Sigmund now remains in his realm.

Concerning Young Sigurd

This same glass vessel [A: It is now told that the glass vessel] floats down the river to the sea. And that is not very far, and now it is low tide and the vessel is stranded on a sandbar. Now the tide goes down so that the vessel is left high and dry. At this point the boy has grown a bit and when the vessel hits the sandbar, it breaks apart and the child begins to cry. Now a hind comes along and takes the child in her mouth and takes it back to her lair where she has two fawns. There she puts the boy down and lets him drink, and there she raises him like her own offspring. And he stays with the hind for twelve months, and now he is as big and strong as other children at the age of four.

Concerning Mimir and Regin

There was a man named Mimir. He is such a famous and skillful smith that he has hardly any equal in this art, and he has many apprentices with him who serve him. He has a wife, and during the nine years after they married they were unable to have children. That grieves him greatly. He has a brother named Regin. He was a powerful man and very evil, and for that he got his just deserts because he worked such magic and wonders that he was turned into a serpent. And he became the greatest and most villainous of serpents and wanted to kill everyone, except that he was well-disposed toward his brother. And now he surpasses all in strength, and no man knows the location of his den except his brother Mimir.

Concerning Mimir and Young Sigurd

Now it happens one day that Mimir is minded to go to the forest and burn charcoal and intends to be there for three days. And when he goes to the forest, they build great fires and as he is standing alone by a fire, a boy comes up to him. He was fair, and came running up to him. He asks the boy who he is, but the boy cannot speak. But Mimir takes him and puts him on his lap and puts clothes on him because he had no clothes before. And then a hind comes running up and approaches Mimir's knees and licks the child's face and head. From this Mimir guessed that the hind had fostered the child, and for this reason he does not wish to harm the hind. He takes the boy in his keeping and brings him home and intends to raise him as a son and gives him a name and calls him Siegfried [the German form of the name is used in the first five occurrences, then the Norse form Sigurd]. The boy now grows up until he reaches the age of nine and is so big and strong that no one had seen his equal. He is so difficult to deal with that he beats and maims Mimir's apprentices so that it is almost intolerable to be near him.

Concerning Sigurd and Ekkihard

One of the apprentices was named Ekkihard. He was the leader of the twelve apprentices. Now it happens one day that Siegfried comes to the smithy where Ekkihard was working. Now Ekkihard hits Siegfried by the ear with his tongs. Now Siegfried seizes the apprentice by the hair with his left hand so firmly that he falls to the ground immediately, and now all the apprentice smiths run at him and want to help Ekkihard, but Siegfried dodges quickly to the door, and out the door, and drags Ekkihard after him by the hair. In this way they come to Mimir, and now Mimir said to Sigurd: "You do wrong to beat up little boys who want to do something useful, whereas you do nothing but mischief. And now you are strong enough and can work no less than one of them, and now I will make you do it and like it, or else I will beat you so that you will be only too glad to work instead." And he takes him by the hand and leads him to the smithy. Now Mimir sits down by the hearth and takes a great piece of

iron and puts it in the fire and grasps the heaviest hammer and gives it to
Sigurd. And when the iron was hot, he took it out of the fire and put it on
the anvil and told Sigurd to hammer it. Sigurd strikes the first blow so
firmly that the anvil base split and the anvil sank in flush with the base.
And the ingot flew off and the tongs break, and the hammer shaft, and
they land far off. And now Mimir says: "I have never seen a more mon-
strous or a clumsier blow than this. And whatever becomes of you, you
can't be used for this handiwork." Now Sigurd goes to the women's room
and sits down by his foster mother and tells no one whether he takes this
well or badly.

How Sigurd kills Regin

Now Mimir takes counsel with himself and realizes that this boy is
going to cause him a lot of ill fortune, and he decides to do away with
him. Now he goes into the forest where there is a great serpent and says
that he will give him a boy and bids him kill him. Now Mimir goes home.
And the next day Mimir asks his foster son Sigurd if he wants to go to the
forest to burn charcoal for him. Then Sigurd answers: "If you are as good
to me from now on as you have been hitherto, then I will go and do whatever you wish." Now Mimir equips him for the trip and gives him wine
and food for the nine days he is to be away. And he gives him a woods-
man's ax, and now he goes and shows him the way to the forest, to the
place he has in mind.

Now Sigurd goes to the forest and makes ready, and cuts down big trees
and builds a great fire and lays the big trees he has felled over it. Then it is
time for early lunch and he sits down to eat, and he eats until all his food
is gone, and he doesn't leave a drop of wine from the ration that Mimir
thought would suffice for nine days. And now he says to himself: "I don't
expect there is any man I wouldn't fight if he came against me now. And I
doubt that one man's combat would be beyond my strength." And when
he has said this, a great serpent comes toward him. And again he spoke:
"Now it may be that I will quickly have the chance to test myself as I
wished." And he jumps up and to the fire and seizes the largest tree that
was on the flaming fire and rushes at the serpent and strikes him on the
head and levels him with the blow. And he strikes the serpent a second
time on the head and now the serpent collapses on the ground. And now
he strikes one blow after the other until the serpent is dead. And now he
takes his ax and cuts off the head of the serpent. And now he sits down
and has become very tired.

And the day is now far advanced and he knows that he will not get
home that evening. And he does not know what to use for food, but it
occurs to him to cook the serpent and provide himself with the evening

meal. And he takes his kettle and fills it with water and hangs it over the fire. Now he takes his ax and cuts off rather big pieces until his kettle is full. And now he is eager for his food, and when he thinks it is done, he puts his hand in the kettle, and since it was boiling in the kettle he burned his hands and fingers. Now he sticks them in his mouth and cools them in this way. And when the broth dripped on his tongue and down his throat, he heard that two birds were sitting in a tree and twittering to each other, and now he heard what one of them said: "It would be better if this man knew what we know. Then he would go home and kill his foster father Mimir for having planned his death if things had turned out as he intended. And this serpent was Mimir's brother. And if he doesn't want to kill Mimir, he will avenge his brother and kill the boy." Now he takes the serpent's blood and rubs it on himself and his hands and everywhere he could reach, and afterward it is hard as horn. Now he takes off his clothes and rubs blood all over himself as far as he can reach, but he cannot reach between his shoulders. Now he gets into his clothes and then goes home and carries the serpent's head in his hands.

How Sigurd kills his foster father Mimir

Now Ekkihard is outside and sees Sigurd approaching and goes to his master and says: "Master, here comes Sigurd home and he has the serpent's head in his hand, and it looks as though he has killed him, and now there is nothing to do but for everyone to save himself because even though there are twelve of us, and even if we were far more numerous, he is so angry now that he would kill us all." And now they run to the woods and hide. But Mimir goes alone to meet Sigurd and bids him welcome. Now Sigurd replies: "None of you will be welcome for you shall gnaw this head like a dog." Now Mimir replies: "Don't do what you are now saying. I would rather give compensation for what I have done to you. I will give you a helmet, a shield, and a byrnie. These weapons I have made for Hertnid in Russia and they are excellent weapons. And I will give you a horse named Grani, which is in Brynhild's stud, and a sword named Gram, which is an excellent sword." Now Sigurd replies: "This I will agree to if you fulfill what you promise." And now they both go home together. Now Mimir takes a pair of greaves and gives them to him, and he arms himself with them, and then a byrnie, and pulls it down over his head. Then he gives him a helmet that he sets on his head. And now he gives him a shield, and all these weapons are so excellent that one could scarcely find others of equal quality. Now he gives him a sword, and as Sigurd takes the sword, he draws it, and it seems to him to be an excellent weapon. And now he swings the sword as hard as he can and strikes Mimir his death blow.

How Young Sigurd acquires Grani

Now Sigurd departs and travels along the road on which he is directed to Brynhild's castle. And when he comes to the castle gate, he finds an iron door, and no one is there to open for him. Now he gives the door such a push that the iron bars that hold it closed burst apart, and now he goes into the castle. Then seven guards who were supposed to guard the castle gate came toward him and are ill-pleased that he has broken open the gate. And for this reason they want to kill him, but now Sigurd draws his sword and doesn't stop until he has killed all these servants. And now the knights become aware of what is happening and run for their weapons and attack him, but he defends himself well and stoutly. Brynhild learns these tidings as she sits in her chamber and says: "Sigurd, the son of Sigmund, must have arrived, and even if he had killed seven of my knights instead of seven of my thralls, he would still be welcome."

And now she goes out to where they are fighting and bids them stop. Now she asks what man it is who has come, and he names himself and says that his name is Sigurd. She asks from what family he is descended, but he says that he is unable to tell her. Then Brynhild says: "If you can't tell me, then I can tell you that you are Sigurd the son of King Sigmund and Sisibe, and you are welcome here. But where does your path lead?" Now Sigurd answers: "I have made you the object of my trip because my foster father Mimir directed me here for a horse you have, named Grani. Now I would like to have him as a gift if you will grant him." "You may have a horse from me if you wish, and more if you so desire. And my hospitality is at your disposal if you wish it."

Now she gets men to capture the horse, and they spend the whole day at it, but are unable to capture it and go home in the evening with nothing accomplished. And that night Sigurd is entertained well. And in the morning she picks twelve men and he goes himself as the thirteenth. And now those twelve approach and pursue the horse for a long time and fail to capture it. And before it is over, Sigurd asks for the bridle and goes up to the horse and the horse comes to him and he takes the horse and puts the bridle on and mounts it. Now Sigurd rides away and gives Brynhild warm thanks for her hospitality. Now he never spends two nights in the same place.

[Here a long section on his adventures in Bertangaland (Brittany) is omitted.]

The marriages of Sigurd and Gunnar

Now King Thidrek and all his remaining champions ride home with King Gunnar to the land of the Niflungs, and now that marriage takes place that has since become very famous, to wit the marriage in which Sigurd weds Grimhild, the sister of King Gunnar and Högni, and receives with her half of King Gunnar's realm. And now a great banquet is prepared and the most distinguished men are invited and those who are noblest in the land. And this banquet lasts five days and is very magnificent in every way. And now as they sit together, King Thidrek and King Gunnar and Young Sigurd, Young Sigurd said to his brother-in-law Gunnar: "I know a woman who exceeds all women in the world in beauty and all courtly demeanor. And in addition she exceeds all other women in wisdom and courtliness and insight and high-mindedness and enterprise, and her name is Brynhild. She rules a castle called Sægard. You should win this woman as your wife and I can be of assistance because I know the way there."

Now Gunnar replies and says that he is very eager for this marriage. Now King Thidrek and King Gunnar and Högni and Young Sigurd and all their companions depart from the banquet and travel a long way and do not stop until they come to Brynhild's castle. And when they arrive there, she gives a good reception to King Thidrek and King Gunnar, but a rather bad one to Young Sigurd, because she now knows that he is married. The previous time they had met he had sworn oaths to her that he would have no woman except her and she likewise to marry no other man. And now Young Sigurd takes counsel with Brynhild and tells her their proposal, and bids her marry King Gunnar. And she replies in this way: "I have truly learned how ill you have kept your word to me, and the vows we took that even if I could choose among all men in the world, I would choose you as my husband." And now Young Sigurd replies: "It must now be as it has been arranged, and because you are the noblest and most distinguished woman I know, and our relationship may not be as was intended, I have urged King Gunnar because he is the greatest man and a most excellent gentleman and a powerful king. And you and he seem to me a good match. And I married his sister rather than you because you have no brother. And he and I have sworn that he shall be my brother, and I his." Now Brynhild answers: "I see now that I cannot possess you, but I will take your good advice and that of King Thidrek."

Now King Thidrek and King Gunnar join the discussion and do not drop it until it was determined that King Gunnar shall marry Brynhild. And now a great banquet is arranged, and when it is ready and a great multitude of noble men is assembled, King Gunnar is to celebrate his wedding with Brynhild. And the first evening King Gunnar is to sleep with Brynhild in his bed, and no third person is to sleep in the house, and the guards are to hold guard outside. And now when the two of them are alone, the king wishes to have intercourse with his wife, but she does not wish that at all, and they dispute this matter between them until she takes her belt and his and ties his hands and feet and hangs him up on a nail by his hands and feet, and there he stays until close to daybreak. And when day approaches, she releases him and he goes to bed and lies there until his men come and he is to get up. And the drinking is to start, and he tells no one of this, nor does she.

And the second night the same thing happens, and the third night as well. And now King Gunnar is very cheerless and has no idea how to conduct himself in this matter. And now it comes to his mind that his brother-in-law Sigurd has sworn to be in his brother's stead in every way, and [AB: he knows] that he is such a wise man that he can trust him in this matter, and let him know and ask his advice on what to do. And now he seeks him out in private and tells him the truth, and now Sigurd replies: "I will tell you what causes this to happen. Her nature is such that as long as she retains her virginity, there will scarcely be any man who can rival her in strength. But as soon as that is changed, she will be no stronger than other women." Now Gunnar replies: "Because of our friendship and marriage kinship I trust no other man as well as you, since it is of the greatest importance that the matter be held in secret. And I know that you are a man strong enough to take her virginity, if such a man exists in the world. And I would rather trust you never to reveal this to anyone if it is done in this way." Now Sigurd replied and said he would do as he wished. And now this is settled.

And now when the evening comes and Gunnar is to go to bed, and does so first, it is arranged so that Young Sigurd goes to bed and Gunnar leaves in Sigurd's clothes and everyone thinks that it is Young Sigurd. And now Sigurd puts the covers over his head and pretends to be exhausted and lies thus until everyone is asleep and departed. Then he grips Brynhild and takes her virginity in a trice and when it dawns, he takes a ring from her finger and places another one on it instead. And now a hundred men come toward him, first among them King Gunnar, and he goes to the bed, and Sigurd goes to meet him. And they manage it so that they are able to switch their clothes, and no one knows what has happened. Now the banquet has lasted for seven days and nights and now they prepare to ride home. Now King Gunnar places chieftains in command of that castle, and he rides home to the land of the Niflungs with his wife Brynhild. And when he arrives home, he remains there and rules his realm and governs in peace together with his brother-in-law Young Sigurd and his brothers Högni and Gernoz. But King Thidrek and all his men ride home to Verona and they part on the best of terms.

*Here begins the story of the Niflungs and the dealings of Young Sigurd
and Högni and King Gunnar and the battle in Soest and how Grimhild
avenged the dishonor that was done her in the first instance without
cause, and here the chapter begins:*

At this time in the land of the Niflungs in the town called Worms King
Gunnar rules, and with him his brother Högni and as third in the group
their brother-in-law, who was the most distinguished of all warriors and
chieftains both south and north. And this was ensured by his strength
and many accomplishments and daring and intelligence and foresight—
and this man was Young Sigurd who was married to Grimhild, King
Aldrian's daughter and the sister of Gunnar and Högni, the first of whom
was married to Brynhild the powerful and fair. And from the time Sigurd
had married Grimhild, the realm flourished with great glory in every way,
first of all because no match for such courageous and mighty chieftains as
ruled there could be found, and all their enemies feared them. And in
addition they had more wealth and gold and silver than all other kings.
They were a great menace to their enemies, and each of them was such a
good friend to the other that it was as if they were all brothers. Young
Sigurd was preeminent among them in every way. His skin was as hard as
the hide of a wild boar or horn and no weapon could penetrate except
between the shoulders, where his skin was like that of other men.

Concerning Grimhild and Brynhild

Now it happened one time that Queen Brynhild went into her hall and
there Grimhild, King Gunnar's sister, sits before her, and when Brynhild
comes to her seat, she says to Grimhild: "Why are you so arrogant that
you do not rise before your queen?" Then Grimhild answers: "I can tell
you why I do not rise before you. In the first place you are sitting in the
high seat that was my mother's and I am no less entitled to sit there than
you." Then Brynhild said: "Although your mother occupied this seat
and your father this town and this land, still I shall now occupy it and not
you. You might rather run off to the woods and trace the hind tracks after
your husband Sigurd. You are better suited for that than to be queen in
the land of the Niflungs." Then Grimhild said: "You now confront and
reproach and dishonor me with what I thought was an honor and a distinction, namely that Young Sigurd is my husband. Now you have begun a
game that you will want to play out a little longer between us, concerning
what redounds to your honor and dishonor. But now answer the first
question that I put to you: who took your virginity and who was your
first husband?"

Then Brynhild answers: "There you have asked what I can well afford to answer, and there is no dishonor in it for me. A powerful king named Gunnar came to my castle and with him many worthy chieftains, and with the counsel of my friends I took him as a husband, and I was married to him with much pomp, and a most excellent banquet was celebrated with a multitude of guests, and with him I came home here to the land of the Niflungs. And I will make no secret of this to you or anyone if they ask who was my first husband." Now Grimhild answers: "Now you lie about what I asked you, as I expected. That man who first took your virginity is named Young Sigurd." Now Brynhild answers: "I was never Sigurd's wife and he was never my husband." Then Grimhild spoke: "I take to witness this gold ring that he took from your finger and gave me." And when Brynhild sees this gold ring, she recognizes that it is hers, and now she realizes what has happened and regrets sorely that they should have quarreled about this so that many people have heard it and these matters have been revealed in public, of which few people had known before. And Brynhild takes this so much to heart that her skin is as red as newly spilt blood. And now she is silent and says not a word and gets up and goes away and out of the castle.

She sees three men riding to the castle. The first is King Gunnar, then his brother Högni, and the third Gernoz. She goes to meet them and sobs and weeps sorely and tears her clothes. That day King Gunnar and his brother Högni had ridden to the forest to hunt, and when they see Queen Brynhild and how she is acting, they do not know what grieves her, and they stop their horses. Then the queen spoke: "Mighty King Gunnar, I placed myself under your protection and left my realm and my friends and relatives. I did all this for your sake. Will you or any other man avenge my dishonor? And if you will not avenge me, you may at least avenge yourself. Young Sigurd has broken your secret agreement and told his wife Grimhild how you placed your trust in him and, when you could not have me yourself, how you caused Young Sigurd to take my virginity. Grimhild has reproached me with this today before everyone." Then Högni answers: "Mighty Queen Brynhild, weep no longer and say no more about it and act as if this had not happened." Then Brynhild answers: "It is only to be expected that I should act this way," she said. "Young Sigurd came to you here like a beggar, but now he is so proud and mighty that it will not be long before you all serve him. When he first came to me, he didn't know his father or his mother or any of his family." Then King Gunnar said: "Lady, do not weep, and hold your peace. Young Sigurd will not be our lord for long and my sister Grimhild will not be your queen."

Concerning Brynhild and Gunnar

Now Brynhild does as the king asks. King Gunnar and his brother Högni now ride into the castle and to the hall, and his men give him a good reception. And now King Gunnar and Högni and Gernoz act as if they have learned nothing at all, and Brynhild likewise. Young Sigurd had gone to the forest to hunt and enjoy the sport with his men, and he was not at home at this time.

Concerning Högni and Young Sigurd

A few days later in the evening Young Sigurd comes home with his men and when he enters the hall, where King Gunnar is sitting, the king rises and receives his brother-in-law Young Sigurd well, and similarly his brothers Högni and Gernoz and all those who are within. And that evening they drink and are of good cheer. Queen Brynhild is now very dejected. A few days later Högni said to his brother King Gunnar: "Lord, when do you wish to ride out to the forest and hunt with the rest of us?" The king answers that he wishes to ride out some day when there is good weather. And now some days pass. Then Högni goes to the cookhouse and speaks in secret to the cook: "Tomorrow is the day when you should prepare our food and all our choice bits early. Make it as salty as you can manage and serve Young Sigurd the saltiest things you can find." And after this he goes away and calls his butler and says: "Tomorrow morning when we eat early, you are to hold back the drink." Now Högni returns.

Young Sigurd's death

The next day early in the morning King Gunnar and Högni give orders that they wish to ready themselves to ride out and hunt. Then they sit down at table and breakfast. Then Young Sigurd comes and says to King Gunnar: "Where are you riding and why are you breakfasting so early?" Then the king answers: "We want to ride out to hunt and have sport. Do you want to go with us or stay at home?" Then Young Sigurd answers: "Lord, if you want to ride out, I certainly wish to go with you." Then the king said: "Sit down and eat," and so he does. And the cook and butler have done everything that Högni told them. When they have eaten, their horses are ready and they ride out to the forest and pursue the beasts and loose their dogs.

And as soon as Young Sigurd has ridden out from the castle, Grimhild goes to her bed and lies down to sleep because she is so bitter toward Brynhild that she does not want to sit with her or socialize with her in any way. Högni rode from the castle a little later than the others and talked to Brynhild for a long while. And in that private conversation Brynhild asks Högni to manage it in such a way that Young Sigurd does not come home that evening, and that he may die that day. And for this she will give him gold and silver and other treasures as he may ask. But he says that Young Sigurd is such a great champion that he cannot say for certain whether he can contrive his death, but he said he would try to bring it about. And after this Högni rides out to the forest and the queen bids him farewell and enjoins him to keep his word.

Now they ride after the beasts very energetically, sometimes at a gallop. And Young Sigurd is first among them now as always. And now they have killed a large wild boar that they had long pursued. And when the dogs had fastened on the boar, Högni speared it to death. Now they all stand over it and split the boar and take all the innards out and give them to their dogs. And now they are all so warm and tired that they almost think they will burst, and then they come to a place where a brook flows, and King Gunnar throws himself down and drinks, and on the other side his brother Högni. And then Young Sigurd comes up and immediately lies down at the brook like the others. Then Högni stands up when he has drunk and takes his spear with both hands and thrusts it between Young Sigurd's shoulders so that it pierces his heart and emerges from the chest. And Young Sigurd said as he received the thrust: "I did not expect what you have now done from my brother-in-law, and if I had known while I was on my feet that you would do this deed and strike my death wound, then would my shield have been broken and my helmet ruined and my sword notched and more than likely all four of you dead before this was done." And after this Young Sigurd dies.

Now Högni said: "We have hunted a wild boar all this morning and the four of us could hardly bring him down, and now in a short time I alone have hunted down a bear or a bison, and it would have been harder for the four of us to bring down Young Sigurd, if he had been prepared, than to kill a bear or a bison, which is the fiercest of all animals." Now King Gunnar said: "You have indeed hunted well, and we will bring this bison home to my sister Grimhild wherever she is." Now they lift Young Sigurd's corpse and take it home to the castle. And now Queen Brynhild is standing up on the castle walls and sees that King Gunnar and his brothers Högni and Gernoz are riding to the castle, and that they are riding with Young Sigurd's corpse. She goes out of the castle to meet them and says that they are the most blessed of hunters and bids them take him to Grimhild: "She is asleep in her bed. Let her now embrace him dead because he now has what he deserves, and Grimhild too."

They carry the corpse up to the sleeping chamber and find it locked. Immediately they break open the door and carry the corpse in and throw it into the bed and into her arms. And at this she wakes up and sees that Young Sigurd is now there in the bed next to her and is dead. Then Grimhild said to Young Sigurd: "It seems to me that you have sorry wounds. Where did you get them? Here stands your gilded shield whole and unscathed, and your helmet is nowhere broken. How were you so wounded? You must have been murdered, and if I knew who had done it, I would repay him." Then Högni answers: "He was not murdered. We were hunting a wild boar and that same wild boar inflicted his death wounds." Then Grimhild answers: "That wild boar was you, Högni, and no one else." And she weeps sorely.

They leave the sleeping chamber now and go into the hall and are of good cheer, and Brynhild is no less cheerful. But Grimhild calls her men and has them take the corpse of Young Sigurd and prepare it honorably. And when the news is learned that Young Sigurd has been killed, everyone says that no man is left in the world or will ever be born again with such strength, courage, courtesy, daring, or generosity, which he possessed above all other men, and that his name will never die in the German tongue or among the Norsemen.

The Fall of the Burgundians in 'Þiðreks saga'

The following story is translated from *Þiðreks saga*, ed. Bertelsen, 2: 275–328. The most important study of the text is Wisniewski, *Die Darstellung des Niflungenunterganges in der Thidrekssaga*.

King Attila's marriage to Grimhild

King Attila of Soest learns that Young Sigurd is dead and survived by his wife Grimhild, who is the wisest and fairest of women, whereas he is now without a wife. He sends for his relative Osid in Herraland and bids him come to him. And when the duke learns that his relative King Attila wishes to meet with him, he sets out for Soest with a company of twenty knights. King Attila welcomed him warmly and said that he had sent word to him and that he wanted him to carry out a mission in the land of the Niflungs. King Attila wants to send him to woo the woman Grimhild for him, King Gunnar's sister, who was married to Young Sigurd. Duke Osid said that he was willing to make the journey no matter where the king wanted to send him. Now he equips himself for this trip with great courtliness and has with him forty of the most courtly knights and many well-equipped attendants. He pursued his journey until they came to the land of the Niflungs and encountered King Gunnar at Worms. They were warmly welcomed. He remained there for a few days.

One day he takes King Gunnar aside and Högni and Gernoz along with him, and in the course of the discussion Duke Osid said: "King Attila of Soest sends greetings to King Gunnar and his brother Högni. King Attila wishes to marry your sister Grimhild with whatever dowry it befits your honor to send him, and he wishes to be your friend. And before I depart, I am to hear whatever message is to be entrusted to me." Then King Gunnar replies: "King Attila is a powerful man and a mighty chieftain. If my brothers Högni and Gernoz agree with me, we will not refuse him this." Then Högni replies: "It appears to me that it will do us great honor if the powerful King Attila marries our sister. He is the greatest and most powerful of kings. This marriage will make us men of greater prestige than we now are. But it would be well to discuss this with her because she is such a proud woman that neither King Attila nor anyone else in the world can marry her without her consent." Gernoz leaves the decision up to the king and Högni and thinks this is appropriate if it is agreeable to them.

Now King Gunnar and Osid go and meet with Grimhild, and King Gunnar tells her all these tidings and asks what her reaction to this marriage is. And she says that she dares not refuse King Attila as a husband because he is such a powerful king, and because such a distinguished man has been entrusted with his mission, she prefers to accept if her brother King Gunnar so advises. And the king declares that he does not want to reject this marriage as long as it is not against her will. King Gunnar and his brothers discuss the whole matter with Duke Osid so that the decision is reached. And after this Duke Osid prepares to ride home. And when he is ready to leave, King Gunnar takes a gilded shield and a helmet, which had belonged to Young Sigurd and which is the best of weapons, and gives them to Osid, and they part on excellent terms. The duke rides home to the land of the Huns and gives King Attila a full report of his trip. The king thanks him warmly and says that his journey has been an outstanding success.

Soon after King Attila prepares his departure and intends now to journey to the land of the Niflungs to fetch his betrothed, Grimhild. This journey is prepared with great splendor. King Attila has five hundred knights and many attendants. When King Gunnar learns that King Attila and Thidrek have arrived in his country, he rides out to meet them with all his best men, and when they meet, King Gunnar rides up to King Attila and greets him, and his brother Högni greets King Thidrek, and they embrace and meet on the best of terms; now they all ride back together to the town of Worms, and the most sumptuous feast is prepared, and at this feast King Gunnar gives his sister Grimhild to King Attila in marriage. And when the feast is over, King Attila and King Thidrek ride away, and at their parting King Gunnar gave King Thidrek Grani, Young Sigurd's horse, and he gave the sword Gram to the margrave, and to King Attila he gave Grimhild and such an amount of silver as did him honor, and now they part on the best of terms. King Attila and King Thidrek ride home to their realm and [Attila] looks after his realm for a time. But his wife Grimhild weeps every day for her dear husband, Young Sigurd.

How King Attila and Grimhild invite Gunnar and Högni

And when seven years had passed, during which Grimhild had been in the land of the Huns, then it happened one night that she spoke to King

Attila: "Lord Attila, it grieves me greatly that during these seven years I have not seen my brothers. When, lord, will you invite them? I can tell you what you may know already, that Young Sigurd, my husband, possessed so much gold that no king in the world was his equal in wealth, and that great wealth is now in the hands of my brothers, and they begrudge me so much as a penny of it. It would be more fitting for me, lord, to have this wealth, and you can be certain that if I get this gold, you will possess it all in common with me."

And when Attila hears these words, he considers attentively what she says and knows it to be true. And King Attila is the most covetous of men and is ill-pleased not to get the Niflung treasure and answers as follows: "I know, lady, that Young Sigurd possessed much gold, first of all the gold which he took from under the great serpent that he killed, and then the gold that he acquired on plundering expeditions, and, in addition, the gold that belonged to his father King Sigmund. And we are deprived of all this although King Gunnar is our dearest friend. Now it is my wish, lady, that you should invite your brothers if you so desire, and I will not stint in preparing a most magnificent feast."

This was the end of their conversation for the moment. And soon after Grimhild summons two men to her and informs them that she wishes to dispatch them to the land of the Niflungs "to deliver my message, and for this journey I will equip you with gold and silver and good apparel and good horses." And these minstrels say that they are very willing to do whatever she bids them. Now she prepares their journey with the greatest possible splendor and gives them King Attila's and her own letter and seal.

These men proceed on their journey until they come to the land of the Niflungs and encounter King Gunnar in Worms. King Gunnar gives his brother-in-law King Attila's messengers a good reception and they are entertained well. Now when the messengers have been there for a short time, the one entrusted with the message arose and went before King Gunnar and said: "King Attila of Soest and his queen Grimhild send greetings to King Gunnar in Worms and to his brother Högni and to Gernoz and Gislher and to all those who are God's friends and his. We wish to invite you to a feast and friendship in our land. King Attila is now old and failing in the governing of his realm, and his young son Aldrian is still only a few years old. It appears to us that you are most fitting to govern this realm with your relative, his uncle, as long as he is not yet old enough to watch over his own realm. Now you are to come according to our message and share our rule with us to the extent that we determine a division in this matter, and bring with you as many men as will do you honor, and fare you well."

When King Gunnar had read this letter, he called his brothers Högni and Gernoz and Gislher to a conference. He raises the matter and seeks advice from them on what position to take. Then Högni replies: "It may be, lord, that you want to journey to the land of the Huns to the feast of your brother-in-law Attila, but if you travel to the land of the Huns, you will not return, nor will anyone who accompanies you, for Grimhild is a faithless woman and shrewd, and it may be that she is conspiring against us."

Now King Gunnar replies: "My brother-in-law, King Attila, has sent word to me with friendly intent that I should come to the land of the Huns, and these men come with tokens. And it is your advice, Högni, that I should not make the journey, but this advice you give me in the spirit in which your mother gave my father advice, which each time was worse than the time before. Now I will not accept it from you. Now I will indeed journey to the land of the Huns and I expect to return as I desire, and, before I leave the land of the Huns, the whole land of the Huns will be given over to my rule. And you, Högni, may accompany me if you wish, but otherwise stay at home if you do not dare make the journey."

Then Högni spoke: "I do not say this because I am more fearful for my life than you are for yours, and I find it no worse to fight than you do. But I can tell you in truth that if you journey to the land of the Huns, whether you journey with many men or few, none will come back alive to the land of the Niflungs. But if you wish to journey to the land of the Huns, I will [AB: not] choose to remain behind; do you not remember, King Gunnar, how we parted with Young Sigurd? But if you do not remember, I know a person in the land of the Huns who will remember, and that is our sister Grimhild, and she will certainly give you a reminder when you come to Soest." Then King Gunnar replies: "Although you are so frightened of your sister Grimhild that you are afraid to go, I will go all the same." Now Högni is angered at having his birth cast in his teeth repeatedly. He gets up and goes into the hall to his relative Folker and says to him: "You will no doubt want to journey with us to the land of the Huns, as King Gunnar has decided in accordance with Grimhild's message, and all our men will accompany us, and let them arm themselves and make ready quickly, and only those need come who are not afraid to fight."

Then Queen Oda arose, the mother of King Gunnar and Gislher, and went to the king and said to him: "Lord, I dreamt a dream that you should hear. And in this dream I saw so many dead birds in the land of the Huns that our whole country was stripped of birds. Now I hear that you Niflungs intend to journey to the land of the Huns, but I know that this journey will bring about great misfortune for both the Niflungs and the Huns, and it seems to me more likely that if you set out, many men will lose their lives. Be so good, lord, as not to go. Only ill can come of it if you set out."

Then Högni replies: "King Gunnar has now ordered the journey as he sees fit and we care little about the dreams of you old women. You are not much inclined to be optimistic. Your words are not going to stand in the way of our journey." Then the queen replies: "King Gunnar and you, Högni, may determine your own journey and decide whether you will set out for the land of the Huns or not, but my young son Gislher will remain at home." "Now then," says Gislher, "if my brothers set out, then I will certainly not stay behind"—and he jumps up and seizes his arms.

Now King Gunnar sends word around his country that all the men who are boldest and most valiant and best disposed toward him should come to him. And when the expedition is ready, King Gunnar has a thousand men, good fellows and well-equipped with gleaming byrnies and bright helmets and sharp swords and sharp spears and fleet horses, and many a fair and stately lady is left at home by her husband and her son and brother. Now Högni takes King Gunnar's standard in his hand. That standard is gilded at the top and white in the middle with an eagle depicted on it with a crown of red silk, and the bottom part of the standard is green. King Gunnar has a similar eagle on all his arms and Högni also has an eagle on his arms but not with a crown. Gernoz and Gislher have red shields inlaid with a hawk of gold, and that ensign they all have on their arms, and their standards are the same color. Hence one can identify each one by his ensign as they ride. The Niflungs now proceed on their journey until they come to the Rhine, at the point where Danube and Rhine flow together. And it is broad where the rivers meet, and they find no boat. They stay there during the night with their field tents.

In the evening, when they had satisfied their appetites at supper, King Gunnar said to his brother Högni: "Which of our men will mount the watch tonight? Deploy them as you see fit." Then Högni answers: "You may deploy the watch as you see fit upstream, but downstream from the troops I will be the sentinel myself, because then we can be on the lookout to see if we can get some boat." King Gunnar was well pleased with this arrangement.

When the other men went to sleep, Högni took all his weapons and went downstream, and there was bright moonlight and for that reason he could find his way. Now Högni comes to a pond, which is called Mœre, and he sees some people in the water, and he sees that their clothing is lying by the pond, between it and the river. He takes the clothes and hides them. And these people are none other than those who are called mermaids. They are at home on the sea or in lakes. And these mermaids came out of the Rhine and into this pond in order to disport themselves. Now the mermaid calls and asks him to give her the clothes and goes up out of the pond. Now Högni answers: "Tell me first whether we will cross this river and return. If you do not tell me what I ask you, you will never get your clothes." Then she said: "You will all come safely over this river, but never back again, and before all this comes to pass, you will suffer the greatest hardship." Now Högni draws his sword and kills the mermaid and cuts her in half and her daughter likewise.

And he continues downstream for a while. Then he sees a boat out in the middle of the river and a man in it, and he asks him to row to land and fetch one of Elsung's men. And he calls out to him in this way because they have come to the realm of young Earl Elsung, and he thinks that in this way the boatman will row to him more readily. Then the boatman answers: "I am not more likely to pick up one of Elsung's men than anyone else, and I will certainly not row without a fee." Then Högni spoke, taking his gold ring and holding it up: "Look here at your fee, good fellow. Here is a gold ring. I will give it to you as passage money if you ferry me." And when this boatman knows that a gold ring is offered to him as passage money, he is reminded that he has recently married and taken a fair woman to wife and he loves her dearly and wants to get her gold wherever he can. He lays his oars out and rows to shore. Now Högni climbs aboard and gives the ferryman his gold ring and goes out into the boat. Now the ferryman wants to row back across the river, but Högni bids him row upstream along the shore, but the ferryman does not want to row. Högni says that he will row whether he wants to or not. Now the ferryman becomes frightened and rows as Högni wishes, and they both row until they come to the army of the Niflungs.

Now King Gunnar and his whole army are afoot, and they had previously gotten a boat, but a very little one. And with that little boat some men have crossed the river, and as soon as they left the shore, that boat filled and capsized, and they managed to get to shore with great difficulty. But when Högni comes to them with this big boat, the Niflungs rejoice. King Gunnar boards the boat himself, and with him one hundred men. They row to the middle of the river. Högni rows so hard that in one pull of the oars he breaks both oars and oarlocks and says: "May the man who readied these oarlocks for us never prosper"—and he jumped up and drew his sword and cut off the boatman's head as he sat in front of him and put it on the bench.

Then King Gunnar said to Högni: "Why did you do this evil deed? What did you blame him for?" Then Högni answers: "I don't want the news of our journey to precede us into the land of the Huns. Now he can bear no tidings." And then King Gunnar spoke angrily: "You do ill deeds now and always, and you are never happy except when you do ill deeds." Then Högni answers: "Why should I spare ill deeds while we advance? I now know clearly that not a single person in our following will return." King Gunnar steers and now the rudder lines break and the rudder comes loose and the boat drifts at the mercy both of the current and the weather. Now Högni runs back quickly to the rudder and pulls in the rudder lines very firmly. And when he has repaired the rudder lines and gotten hold of the rudder, they have almost reached shore, and at this moment the boat capsizes, and they get to shore in such a condition that every stitch of clothing that they had on board was soaked. They now guide the boat to shore and repair what was broken and send their men back across the river to the army and have them ferried across the river until the whole army is over. And after that they continue their journey that whole day.

In the evening they lie down to sleep and let Högni mount the watch. And when all the men are asleep, Högni goes to patrol alone far from the army. He comes to a place where a man is lying asleep. He is armed and has put his sword under him, and the hilt sticks out. Högni takes hold of the sword, snatches it, and throws it away. He pokes him in the side with his right foot and tells him to wake up. And the man jumps up and reaches for his sword and finds it missing and says: "Woe is me for having fallen asleep. [AB: I lost my sword, and my lord will consider his realm ill-guarded since I fell asleep this way." And now he sees where the army is and he spoke again: "Woe is me for having fallen asleep.] Now an army has entered the land of my lord Margrave Rodingeir. I have now kept watch for three days and three nights, and that is why I fell asleep."

Then Högni spoke to him and found him to be a good fellow: "You seem to be a good fellow. Look here at my gold ring. I will give it to you for your worthy qualities and you will benefit more from it than the fellow to whom it was given before. I will also give you your sword." And so he did. Now this man replies: "May God reward you for your gift, first because you gave me my sword, and then your gold ring." Now Högni spoke: "Have no fear of this army if you are guarding the land of Margrave Rodingeir. He is our friend. King Gunnar of the land of the Niflungs commands our army together with his brothers. Now tell me something else, good fellow: what lodging do you suggest for us tonight, and what is your name?"

"My name is Ekkivard," he said. "And now I am curious about your journey. Are you Högni, the son of Aldrian, who slew my lord Young Sigurd? Be on your guard while you are in the land of the Huns. You will find many enemies here. And I can direct you to no better lodging than in Pöchlarn with Margrave Rodingeir. He is a good chieftain." Then Högni spoke: "You have directed us to the place where we intended to go. Ride home to town now and say that we will come there. And say too that we are rather wet."

Now they part and Ekkivard rides home, and Högni goes back to his men and tells King Gunnar how he fared and bids them get up as quickly as possible and ride to town, and so they did. Ekkivard rides home to town as quickly as he can and when he comes into the hall, Margrave Rodingeir has finished eating and intends to go to bed. Then Ekkivard says that he has met Högni and that King Gunnar has arrived with a great army and intends to ride there to seek lodging. Margrave Rodingeir gets up and calls to all his men, bidding them hasten and dress in the best and most splendid way and prepare his quarters in the same way. And now Margrave Rodingeir himself has his horses brought out and intends to ride out to greet them with many knights, and now all his men are hard at work at the preparations.

And when Margrave Rodingeir rides out of the town, King Gunnar comes toward him with his whole army. Margrave Rodingeir greets the Niflungs warmly and invites them to partake of his hospitality. King Gunnar accepts graciously and Högni asks that God reward Ekkivard for the way in which he carried out their mission.

How Margrave Rodingeir married his daughter to Gislher

Now the Niflungs come to the court of Margrave Rodingeir and dismount from their horses. And Margrave Rodingeir's men take them and care for them well. And following Ekkivard's directions, the margrave has two fires built out in the courtyard because they are wet, and King Gunnar and Högni and their brothers and some of their men sit at one and some of their company at the other. And those who were present follow the margrave into the hall, and he seats them on the benches. Now the Niflungs take off their clothes at the fires. Then the margrave's wife Gudilinda spoke—she was the sister of Duke Naudung, who fell at Gronsport: "The Niflungs have brought here many a bright byrnie and many a hard helmet and sharp sword and new shield; and it is most grievous that Grimhild weeps for her husband Young Sigurd every day." When these fires had burned down, King Gunnar and Högni and their brothers go into the hall and sit that evening and drink with the best of cheer and are in high spirits. And then they go to bed.

Margrave Rodingeir lies in his bed by his wife and they converse. Then Margrave Rodingeir spoke: "Lady, what gift shall I give King Gunnar and his brothers that will be honorable for them to accept and honorable for me to give?" She replies: "Whatever you think advisable, lord. My advice in this matter will be the same as yours." And Margrave Rodingeir spoke again: "I ask you to take note of young Gislher, and if that is your advice, I will give him my young daughter as a first gift." Now Gudilinda answers: "It is well that you give him our daughter if it turns out that he lives to have the benefit, but I am fearful."

Now daylight has come and Margrave Rodingeir gets up and dresses along with his knights, and the Niflungs get up and call for their clothes.

And Margrave Rodingeir bids them stay with him for a few days, but the Niflungs are eager to leave now and not remain. And then Margrave Rodingeir says that he and his knights will ride with them, and now they sit down to table and drink good wine and are in high spirits. Now there are many kinds of entertainment and other amusements. Now Margrave Rodingeir has a helmet brought in, gold-mounted and inlaid with precious gems, and he gives it to King Gunnar, and King Gunnar thanks him warmly for this gift and considers it a great prize. Then Margrave Rodingeir takes a new shield and gives it to Gernoz.

Then the margrave gives Gislher his daughter and says: "Good Sir Gislher, I will give you this maiden to wife if you will accept her." Gislher answers and says that it is the most welcome gift in the world and says that he will gratefully accept. And Margrave Rodingeir spoke again: "I have here a sword, young Sir Gislher, which I wish to give to you. It is called Gram. Young Sigurd was the owner. I believe it will be the best of all weapons in your host." And Gislher thanks him again for this present and wishes that God may reward him for all the honor that he has shown him on this journey. Now Margrave Rodingeir spoke to Högni: "Good friend Högni, what treasure do you see here in my possession that you would most like to receive?" Then Högni answers: "It seems to me," he says, "that I see a shield hanging here. It is dark-colored. It is large and strong as far as I can tell. It is marked by great blows. This is the gift I wish for." Then Margrave Rodingeir replies: "That is fitting because an excellent man bore that shield, Duke Naudung, and he suffered great blows from Vidga the strong, wielding the blade Mimung, before he fell." And when Lady Gudilinda hears this she weeps sorrowfully for her brother Naudung. And this shield was now given to Högni. They thank Margrave Rodingeir in the warmest terms for his gifts and kindness.

Then when they have eaten their fill, they call for their horses and equip themselves, and along with them Margrave Rodingeir, and with him the most valiant knights, and they ride out of the town when they are ready. Then Lady Gudilinda bade them farewell and wished their safe return with honor and distinction. And the margrave kisses his wife Gudilinda before he rides away and bids her govern his realm well until they meet again.

Concerning the Niflungs

Now there is nothing to report from their journey except that they ride day after day. And the day they ride to Soest, the weather is wet and there is a strong wind, and all the Niflungs and their clothes are now wet. And when they advance to a certain town named Dortmund, a man rides toward them. He is King Attila's messenger and was dispatched to Pöchlarn to invite Margrave Rodingeir to the feast, and the margrave is riding ahead of the troop with his men. And when they meet, the margrave asks: "What are the tidings in Soest?" This man answers: "The latest news in Soest is that the Niflungs have come to the land of the Huns and King Attila is now preparing a feast for them, and I was dispatched to you to bid you to the feast. But now I will return with you because now I have carried out my mission."

He now turns back with them and rides with Margrave Rodingeir. Then Margrave Rodingeir spoke to the messenger: "How large a feast does King Attila intend and how many men will he invite?" Then the messenger replies: "It looks to me as though there are not a few men in your train, and King Attila has bidden many men to the feast. But Queen Grimhild has summoned many more of her followers and she is gathering men throughout her whole realm to support her, and such provision has been made for the feast as to anticipate a great attendance, and still it will last for many days." Rodingeir asks this man to ride ahead to the town and say that the Niflungs have now come to King Attila's town. He rides straightway to King Attila and tells him these tidings, that the Niflungs and Margrave Rodingeir have now come to his town.

Now the king sends word all over town that each house be readied, some with tapestries, and in some fires are to be made, and there are now great preparations in the town of Soest. Now King Attila spoke to King Thidrek and bade him ride out to meet them. And he does so and rides out with his men, and when they meet, each greets the other warmly and all ride together to the town.

Concerning Queen Grimhild

Queen Grimhild stands in a tower and sees the procession of her brothers and that they are now riding into the town of Soest. Now she sees many a new shield and many a bright byrnie and many a splendid fellow. Now Grimhild spoke: "Now this is a fair green summer. Now my brothers fare with many a new shield and many a bright byrnie, and now I am reminded how I am grieved by the great wounds of Young Sigurd." Now she wept very sorrowfully for Young Sigurd and went to meet the Niflungs and bade them welcome and kissed the one closest to her and then one after the other. Now the town is almost full of men and horses, and there are already present in Soest many hundreds of men and horses.

Concerning Grimhild's brothers

King Attila receives his in-laws well and they are escorted into the halls, which are readied, and fires are made for them. But the Niflungs do not take off their byrnies and they do not lay aside their weapons for the moment. Now Grimhild comes into the hall, where her brothers are at the fire drying themselves. She sees how they lift their tunics and underneath there are bright byrnies. Now Högni sees his sister Grimhild and straight-way takes his helmet and sets it on his head and straps it tightly, and so does Folker.

Concerning Grimhild and her brothers

Then Grimhild said: "Högni, sit in peace. Now, have you brought me the Niflung treasure that belonged to Young Sigurd?" Then Högni replies: "I bring you," he says, "a formidable enemy, and with him come my shield and my helmet with my sword, and I did not leave my byrnie be-hind." Now King Gunnar said to Grimhild: "Lady sister, come here and sit down." Now Grimhild goes up to her young brother Gislher and kisses him and sits down between him and King Gunnar, and now she weeps sorrowfully. And now Gislher asks: "Why do you weep, lady?" She replies: "I can easily tell you that. I am grieved now as always by the great wounds that Young Sigurd received between the shoulders, and no weapon touched his shield." Then Högni replies: "Let us be silent about Young Sigurd and his wounds and not mention them. Let us now make King Attila of the land of the Huns as dear to you as Young Sigurd was before. He is much more powerful, and Young Sigurd's wounds cannot now be healed. Things must remain as they are." Then Grimhild gets up and goes away.

After that Thidrek of Verona comes and calls the Niflungs to table. And with him comes King Attila's son Aldrian. Now King Gunnar takes the boy Aldrian and carries him out in his arms. And King Thidrek of Verona and Högni are such good friends that each puts his arm around the other and thus they go out of the hall and make their way until they come to the king's hall. And in every tower and every hall and every courtyard and on every wall of the town stand courtly ladies, and all of them want to see Högni because he is so famous in every land for his courage and valor. Now they came to the hall of King Attila.

Concerning King Attila and Grimhild's brothers

King Attila now sits in his high seat and puts his brother-in-law King Gunnar on his right side, and next to him sits young Sir Gislher, then Gernoz, then Högni, then Folker, their relative. On King Attila's left side sit King Thidrek of Verona and Margrave Rodingeir, then Master Hildi-brand. All of these men sit on the dais with King Attila. And now in the hall are seated the noblest men one after the other. That evening they drink good wine and there is the most splendid feast with all sorts of provisions, the best that can be gotten, and they are in good spirits. And now such a multitude of men has come into the town that almost every house in the town is full. And that night they sleep in peace and are in high spirits and are well treated.

When morning comes and the men get up, King Thidrek and Hildibrand and many other knights come to the Niflungs. Now King Thidrek asks how they slept during the night. Then Högni answers and says that he slept well—"and still my mood is no better than middling." Now King Thidrek says: "Be glad and of good cheer and welcome in our midst, my good friend Högni, and be on your guard here in the land of the Huns because your sister Grimhild weeps for Young Sigurd every day, and you will have every reason to be on your guard before you return home." And now Thidrek is the first man who warned the Niflungs. When they are ready, they go out into the court. King Thidrek goes on one side of King Gunnar and Master Hildibrand on the other, and Folker goes with Högni. And now all the Niflungs have gotten up and walk around the town and disport themselves.

And now King Attila gets up and goes out on the balcony and watches where the Niflungs are walking. And many people go now to watch their proud procession and everyone is most eager to ask which one is Högni, such is his fame. Now King Attila sees where Högni and Folker are, and their apparel is no less fine than King Gunnar's, and King Attila is not certain which ones are Högni and Folker because he cannot see them very clearly because they have broad helmets, and he asks who the men are who are walking with King Gunnar and King Thidrek. Then Duke Blodlin answers: "I expect they are probably Högni and Folker." Then the king answers: "I should know Högni very well because he was at my court for a time, and Queen Erka and I dubbed him knight, and at that time he was surely our good friend."

Now Högni and Folker walk about the town and each has his arm over the other's shoulder, and they see many courtly ladies. And now they doff their helmets and let themselves be seen. And Högni is easily recognizable: he is narrow around the waist and broad across the shoulders, he has a long face, pale as ashes, and one eye that is very keen, and nonetheless he is the most distinguished of men. Now the Niflungs stand with their retinue out by the town wall and look at the place and disport themselves. And Thidrek of Verona now goes back to his quarters where business calls him.

Concerning the Gjukungs

King Attila sees now what a multitude has come together here and that he cannot seat all these people in one hall. But now there is good weather and fair sunshine. He orders the feast to be prepared in an apple orchard. At this moment Queen Grimhild goes into the hall of Thidrek of Verona to speak with him alone. He gives her a good reception and asks what she wants. She says, weeping and wailing: "Good friend Thidrek, now I have come to seek your good advice. Now I want to ask you, good sir, to give me assistance in avenging my greatest grief, the death of Young Sigurd. I want to avenge this now against Högni and Gunnar and my other brothers. Now if you wish, good sir, I will give you as much gold and silver as you yourself say. And in addition I will give you aid if you wish to ride across the Rhine and avenge yourself." Then King Thidrek says: "Lady, that I can certainly not do, and whoever does it will do it without my advice and without my consent because they are my best friends and I am more obligated to give them good than bad."

Now she goes away weeping and into the hall where Duke Blodlin was. She spoke again: "Lord Blodlin, will you give me aid in avenging my sorrows? Now I am sorely reminded of how the Niflungs dealt with Young Sigurd. I would avenge this against them if you would give me aid. And if you will do this, I will give you much power and whatever you ask." Then Blodlin answers: "Lady, if I do this, then I will earn the great enmity of King Attila, so great a friend is he of theirs."

Then the queen departs from there, and now she goes to King Attila and she spoke again to him as before: "Lord and king, Attila, where is the gold and where is the silver that my brothers have brought you?" King Attila says that they have not brought him gold or silver, but still he will receive them well since they have sought out his hospitality. Then the queen spoke: "Lord, who will avenge my humiliation if you will not? Now it is still my greatest grief how Young Sigurd was murdered. Be so good now, lord, as to avenge me, and then you can have the treasure of the Niflungs and all the land of the Niflungs." Then the king spoke: "Lady, cease and do not say this again. How should I betray my brothers-in-law, since they have committed themselves to my trust? And neither you nor any man will venture to mistreat them." Now she goes away and has never been so displeased.

Now King Attila goes out into the apple orchard, where the feast is to be, and summons his guests, and now everyone assembles there. Now the queen said to the Niflungs: "You should now give me your weapons for safekeeping. No one should be armed here. You can see yourselves that the Huns act accordingly." Now Högni answers: "You are a queen, and why should you take men's weapons? My father taught me when I was young that I should never entrust my weapons to a woman's care, and as long as I am in the land of the Huns, I will never give up my weapons." Now Högni puts on his helmet and straps it as tightly as he can. And now everyone has the impression that Högni is very angry and in a dark mood, and they do not know the cause. Then Gernoz replies: "Högni has not been in a good mood ever since he began this journey, and it may be that today he will show his valor and wisdom." And now Gernoz suspects treachery and that Högni may have known in advance how the journey would turn out for the Niflungs, and he puts on his helmet and straps it tightly, and thus outfitted he goes into the orchard.

Concerning Högni and Gernoz

Now King Attila perceives that Högni is acting angrily and tightening his helmet, and he asks Thidrek of Verona: "Who are the men who are putting on their helmets and looking wrathful?" Then Thidrek answers: "They look like Högni and his brother Gernoz to me, and they are both stout fellows in a foreign land, and they do this in a great rage." And King Thidrek spoke again: "Indeed they are excellent fellows, and there is reason to think, lord, that you will have a good chance to observe it today if things go as I expect."

Concerning the battle of the Niflungs

Now King Attila gets up and goes to meet King Gunnar and Gislher, and takes King Gunnar by the right hand and young Sir Gislher by the left hand and calls to Högni and Gernoz, and King Attila seats them all honorably on his right side, one after the other as previously described. A large fire was built in the orchard and all around that fire were placed tables and seats. And now all the Niflungs have come into the orchard with their helmets and bright byrnies and sharp swords, but their shields and daggers are given over for safekeeping, and they have assigned their attendants to that job, and they have assigned twenty attendants to guard the men and bring them intelligence if there is any treachery or hostility, and this has been done on the orders of Högni and Gernoz. Folker sits next to the foster father of Aldrian, King Attila's son. Queen Grimhild has her seat placed opposite King Attila, where Duke Blodlin is seated.

At this moment Queen Grimhild goes to her knight, who is in command of the other knights and is named Irung, and speaks to him: "Good friend Irung, will you avenge my humiliation? Now King Attila will not take revenge, nor King Thidrek, nor any of my friends." Then Irung answers: "What do you wish to avenge, lady, and why do you weep so sorely?" Then the queen replies: "Now I am most mindful of how Young Sigurd was murdered. I would like to avenge him now if anyone is willing to help me now." Then she took a gilded shield and said: "Good friend Irung, will you avenge my humiliation? I will give you this shield full of red gold, as full as you can make it, and therewith my undivided friendship."

Then Irung spoke: "Lady, that is a great deal of money, but it is still more valuable to have your friendship"—and he arises immediately and arms himself and calls to his knights and bids them arm themselves, and now he has a hundred knights. Now he raises his standard, and now the queen says that he should first go and kill their attendants and let none of the Niflungs who are outside come inside the orchard, and none of those who are inside come out alive.

And now the queen goes quickly into the orchard, where the feast was, and sits down in her high seat, and now her son Aldrian runs to her and kisses her. And now the queen spoke: "My sweet son, if you are like your relatives and if you have the courage, go to Högni and when he leans forward over the table and takes food from his plate, raise your fist and strike him on the cheek as hard as you can. You will be a brave little fellow if you dare do this." The boy immediately ran over to Högni, and as Högni leans forward over the table, the boy strikes him on the cheek with his fist. And it was a greater blow than one would have expected from such a young fellow.

And now Högni takes the boy by the hair with his left hand and says: "You did not do this on your own or on the advice of your father King Attila, but rather this is at the urging of your mother, and it will be of little avail to you now." And with his right hand Högni seizes the hilt of his sword and draws it from its scabbard and cuts off the boy's head and throws the head at Grimhild, and Högni said: "In this apple orchard we are drinking good wine and we will pay for it dearly. With this I make the first payment on the debt to our sister Grimhild." And once again he aims a blow over Folker's head at the boy's foster father and cuts off his head. "Now the queen has been properly repaid for the way you brought up this boy."

Now King Attila jumps up and calls out: "Let the Huns get up, all my men, and arm themselves and kill the Niflungs." And now every man who was in the orchard jumps up and now the Niflungs draw their swords. On Grimhild's orders raw oxhides were spread in front of the orchard gate. And as the Niflungs run out of the orchard, they fall on the hides and it is thus the lot of many men to be killed. And Irung stands there with his men and kills many excellent men. And now the Niflungs in the orchard kill many men, and there lay a slaughter of many hundreds in the orchard.

Concerning the Niflungs

Now when the Niflungs discover that they are losing the men who go out of the orchard, they turn back and attack once again and fight against the Huns in the orchard, and they do not desist before they have killed the Huns down to the last man, except for those who fled to safety. King Attila now stands on a rampart and from there he urges all his men to attack his in-laws, the Niflungs. But King Thidrek of Verona goes home to his quarters with all his men and is greatly distressed that so many of his good friends should have a falling out and fight with one another. And Queen Grimhild is busy all that day taking the byrnies and helmets and shields and swords that belong to King Attila and arming the men who want to fight, and sometimes she goes out in the town and urges men to attack and calls out that every man who wants to receive gold and silver and valuable prizes from her should attack the Niflungs and kill them. This is her occupation all that day.

Concerning the battle in the orchard

Now there is a fierce battle that day as the Huns attack the orchard and the Niflungs defend it, and the place where the battle is fought is called Homgard, and to this very day it is still called Niflungs' Homgard.* Here there is a great slaughter both of Huns and of Niflungs, but many more Huns fall, and at the same time men gather from the outlying areas and other towns, and now the Huns have a much larger force than when they began.

Now Högni spoke to his brother Gunnar: "It looks to me as though many Huns and Amlungs have fallen, but no matter how many Hunnish men we have killed, many more gather from the country, and it is as if we were doing nothing at all, but the chieftains of the Huns do not come anywhere near us, and we are virtually fighting against their thralls. Now I am greatly angered that we cannot get out of this orchard so that we can choose ourselves against which men to fight. And we can see clearly where this fighting will lead if it is to continue this way. The Niflungs will fall even if they have to endure the spears and missiles of the Huns more than their swords, and we will gain no glory if we cannot take advantage of our swords against the Huns. And now it is my wish," he says, "to make our way out of the orchard manfully."

Now a stone wall was raised around this orchard, limed with mortar like a town wall, and the same stone wall encloses it to this day. Now Högni and his men run to the west side of the orchard. There the stone wall was most dilapidated. Now the Niflungs break down the wall with all their strength and do not stop until there is a breach in the enclosure. And now Högni runs out of the breach straightway, and outside was a broad street and halls on both sides, and there was not much room.

---

*This form must be an error for OS *bômgardo,* MLG *bômgarde* 'orchard.' See Holthausen, "Studien zur Thidrekssaga," p. 457.

Gernoz and Gislher and many Niflungs follow him and rush ahead between the houses. Then Earl Blodlin advanced toward them with his men and now there is a fierce battle between them.

Now the Huns have their trumpets sounded and shout that the Niflungs have broken out of the orchard, and now all the Huns gather there, and now Duke Blodlin has entered the battle against the Niflungs. Now the Huns rally to this battle so that every nearby street is full of Huns, and now the Niflungs are overwhelmed by numbers and retreat into the orchard, but Högni retreats to the hall and puts his back to the door of the hall, and it was locked, and thrusts his shield in front of him and hews with his arm one man after the other, cutting hands and feet off some, heads off some, some in half, and no one attacks him without making this kind of transaction. And there is such a throng that those who are killed hardly have room to fall, and he parries so well with his shield that he suffers no wounds. And on the left side of the Niflungs stands the hall of King Thidrek, and there he stands up on the battlements with his forces all armed. Now Gernoz and Gislher and Folker turn aside from the street and up to the hall and put their backs to it and defend themselves with great valor and kill many men, and now the Huns launch a fierce attack.

Now Gernoz said to King Thidrek: "You might better join the fray with your men and aid us and not let so many men fight against a single man." Now King Thidrek replies: "Good friend Gernoz, I am mightily grieved that this battle was begun. I am losing many good friends here and can do nothing about it. I do not wish to fight against the Huns, the men of King Attila, my lord, and as things stand I wish to do no injury to the Niflungs."

King Gunnar now knows that Högni, Gernoz, and Gislher, his brothers, have gone out of the orchard, and in addition that he is confronted with an overwhelming force fighting against him, and all have deserted him and fled back into the orchard. King Gunnar has stood by and defended the east gate, before which Irung and his men stood. When King Gunnar hears that Högni needs assistance, he heads west in the orchard to the breach broken by the Niflungs and goes out valiantly with his men. And just outside of the orchard stand the Huns fully armed, and there is a very fierce engagement, and King Gunnar presses forward, but none of his men is strong enough to follow him.

And now there advances toward King Gunnar Duke Osid, a relative of King Attila's and a mighty warrior, and the two of them fight with the utmost ferocity for a long time, until the darkness of night descends. And now because King Gunnar has become isolated in the army of the Huns and has to contend with the mightiest warrior, he is overpowered and captured and disarmed and then bound. And when the Huns have won this victory, there was a great outcry, and Attila and the queen call out to bring King Gunnar to them and not to kill him. Osid brings King Gunnar before King Attila. He is cast into a snake pit on the queen's orders, and there he dies, and that tower stands in the middle of Soest.

Now Högni and Gernoz hear the Huns shouting that they have captured King Gunnar. Högni is so furious that he leaps from the door and out onto the street and lays about him on all sides, and there is no getting at him. And Gernoz sees this, heads in his direction on the street, and strikes down Huns on all sides, and his sword cuts right down to the ground. And young Sir Gislher follows and kills many men with his sword Gram, and they exert themselves to such an extent that nothing can withstand them, and all the Huns flee, and some were killed. And now the Niflungs come out of the orchard onto the street and raise a great war cry and shout that the Huns are wretched curs that they run now that the Niflungs want to avenge themselves. And now they run all over town and kill men wherever they go and now the night is pitch dark and the Huns go and fight against them in groups.

King Attila goes now to his halls and orders the courtyard to be closed after him and defended so that the Niflungs can accomplish nothing there. Margrave Rodingeir goes up to the hall of King Thidrek and stays there for a while with him. Duke Blodlin goes into a hall with his men, and Irung with his men. During this night a host of men assembles in the town. And now it is dark.

Högni now orders his trumpet to be blown and summons all the Niflungs, and Högni has now come to the town wall. Now all the Niflungs come to him. Then Högni spoke to Gernoz: "How many men have we lost with King Gunnar?" Gernoz replies that this is well considered: "We should now inspect our men. On the right side from Högni should stand Gislher by his standard, and my men," said Gernoz, "on the left side of Högni, and beyond me those men who followed the standards of King Gunnar, and Folker along with them." And thus the Niflungs order their ranks. Now they count how many men they have lost, and they have lost three hundred men, and seven hundred remain. And then Högni said that they still had a large force and that the Huns would still lose many men before all the Niflungs fell, and they all concur.

Now Högni spoke: "If it were now day and if we could see to fight, since night prevents us now, then we would win the victory. Now King Attila has little more troop strength than we have. But if we are to wait here until it dawns, then men will gather in the town from the country and we will have to contend against such a great force that we will be overpowered. And I do not know whether we will earn any glory before we die. And it is a shame that we can get no fire, because then we would be able to fight." And now Högni goes off with a few men, and nearby

204 Sources and Analogues

was a cookhouse, where they get fire and cast it immediately into the house and burn it down, and now the whole town is illumined.

Concerning the battle of the Niflungs and Huns

Then the Niflungs raise their standards and go around the town shouting and trumpeting, and they urge the Huns to attack them when they arrive at the halls. But the Huns stand up on the battlements and bombard them from a distance, as do the Niflungs, and the Huns do not want to fight before day, and still the Niflungs kill many men that night. And now it dawns. Then the Huns who have come from the country rush up to the town and enter and have a very great host.

The fall of H. [the Huns?]

Now both set up their standards and both sides blow all their trumpets, and after that there is a long and very fierce battle, and the Huns now move to the attack very valiantly. Everyone urges each other and Queen Grimhild urges everyone to kill as many of the Niflungs as possible, and she offers gold and silver for this. That day Duke Blodlin and Irung are in the battle, and now King Attila is nowhere near. Gernoz has his standard borne against Blodlin, and those two battle formations advance against one another very spiritedly. Now Gernoz goes forward in advance of all his men and hews to the left and right and kills many men. And now Duke Blodlin comes against him. And they begin their single combat with mighty blows and attack very valiantly for a long time, and Gernoz puts an end to it by cutting off Earl Blodlin's head. And now the Niflungs exert themselves greatly. And now a chieftain of the Huns has fallen.

And then this comes to the ears of Margrave Rodingeir, and he becomes very wrathful that Duke Blodlin has fallen, and he calls to his men that they should now fight and kill the Niflungs, and he has his standard borne forward in the battle very boldly, and many Niflungs fall before him, and now he has fought for a long time.

Now Högni goes by himself into the middle of the army of the Huns and hews with each arm to the left and to the right and strikes down Huns as far as his sword can reach, and he wreaks much havoc with his spear as well, and now he has his arms bloody up to the shoulders and his whole byrnie is the color of gore. And he has now fought so long and has come so far into the army of the Huns that he is now almost completely worn out, and he does not know now whether he can get back to his men, and he turns aside to a hall and breaks open the hall and enters and turns around in the door and takes his stand there and rests.

Margrave Rodingeir now rushes forward against the Niflungs and there is a great battle. Now the Huns attack the hall in which Högni stands and guards the door and kills many men. Now Grimhild sees where Högni is and that he is killing many men. She calls out in a loud voice to the Huns and bids them put fire to the hall because the roof of the hall was made of wood, and so it was done. Then Grimhild calls her dear friend Irung. "Good Irung," she said, "now you can attack Högni since he is in a house. Bring me his head now and I will fill your shield with red gold." Now Irung makes for the hall smartly, as the queen asked, and now there is smoke in the hall in which Högni stands. Irung runs into the hall very bravely with his sword and when he gets inside he strikes at Högni very boldly with his sword and wounds him on the thigh so that it separates the byrnie and so much of the thigh as the largest piece carved for the kettle. Then he immediately runs out of the hall.

Now Grimhild sees that Högni is bleeding and goes to Irung and says: "Listen, my dear Irung, most excellent fellow, now you have wounded Högni, and the next time you will kill him." She took two gold rings and fastened one to the right side of his helmet strap and one to the left side and said: "Irung, my good man, bring me Högni's head now. You will have as much gold and silver as your shield will hold and then again as much." And now Irung runs into the hall a second time against Högni, and now Högni is on his guard and turns to face him and thrusts his spear under his shield and into his chest so that it splits the byrnie and the torso and comes out at the shoulders. And then Irung collapses at the stone wall, and this stone wall is called Irung's wall to this day. And Högni's spear sticks in the stone wall. Then Högni spoke: "If I had avenged Grimhild's wickedness as I have now avenged my wound against Irung, then I would have made my sword sing bravely in the land of the Huns."

Concerning Gislher's battle

Now there are great tidings. Margrave Rodingeir now presses forward strongly and kills Niflungs, and young Sir Gislher goes against him, and now they avail themselves of their weapons. And Gislher's sword, Gram, bit so well that when he struck shields, byrnies, and helmets, it cut them like cloth. And there Margrave Rodingeir fell to the ground dead before Gislher with great wounds, and all this he received from the same sword that he had given to Gislher as a gift of friendship before.

Now Gernoz and Gislher press forward strongly and penetrate into the hall of King Attila and kill many men there. And now Folker presses forward boldly toward the hall in which Högni stands and he cuts down one man after the other so that he never treads on the bare ground but rather from one trunk to the next. And now Högni sees one of the Niflungs advancing and cutting down Huns and wants to bring him aid. Now Högni asks: "Who is that man who is making his way to me so boldly?" Then he answers: "I am your companion Folker. Look at the path I have cleared here." Then Högni answers: "May God reward you for the way you have made your sword sing on the helmets of the Huns."

Concerning King Thidrek and the Niflungs

Now King Thidrek sees that Margrave Rodingeir is dead. Then he calls out in a loud voice: "Now my best friend is dead, Margrave Rodingeir. Now I can no longer stand aside. Let all my men take up their arms, and I will now fight against the Niflungs." Now Thidrek goes down the street and we are told in German lays that it was not cozy for cowards when Thidrek and the Niflungs joined battle, and it is audible all over the town how Ekkisax sings on the helmets of the Niflungs. And now Thidrek is in a fury, but the Niflungs defend themselves well and valiantly and kill many Amlungs, King Thidrek's men, and many Niflungs fall in this battle.

Now Thidrek presses forward so hard with his men that the valiant man Högni of Troy falls back with his sharp sword. Gislher and Gernoz are inside as well, and King Thidrek pursues them, and Master Hildibrand as well. And now Högni, Gernoz, Gislher, and Folker are inside the hall. Now King Thidrek goes into the hall very boldly, and before him stands Folker in the door and bars his way, and King Thidrek strikes the first blow on his helmet with his sword so that his head flies off. And then Högni moves against him and they engage in single combat. And Master Hildibrand attacks Gernoz and there is a great battle. And now Hildibrand strikes at Gernoz with his great sword Lagulf, and from that Gernoz gets a deadly wound and now falls down dead to the ground. And now there is no one on his feet in the hall able to bear weapons other than these four: Thidrek and Högni with their combat, and Hildibrand and Gislher in another place.

Concerning Högni and his son Aldrian

And now King Attila comes from his tower to the place where they are fighting. Then Högni spoke: "It will be a worthy deed, King Attila, if you grant this boy Gislher his life. He is innocent of the killing of Young Sigurd and I alone inflicted his fatal wound. Do not hold Gislher responsible for it. He will be a worthy man if he is allowed to live." Then Gislher spoke: "I do not say this because I do not dare defend myself. My sister Grimhild knows that when Young Sigurd was killed, I was five years old and I lay in my mother's bed with her and I am innocent of this killing. But I do not care to survive my brothers alone." And now Gislher attacks Master Hildibrand and strikes one blow after the other. But their single combat turns out as one might expect and Master Hildibrand inflicts a fatal wound on Gislher and now he falls.

Now Högni spoke to King Thidrek: "It looks to me as though this is the end of our friendship no matter how great it has been, and now I will fight so hard in defense of my life that it will either turn out that I lose my life or win yours. Let us contest this single combat worthily and let neither reproach the other for his birth." And King Thidrek replies: "I ask no man's assistance in this single combat and I will surely win it with skill and valor."

They fight long and hard and it is difficult to tell which of them has the better of it, and the combat lasts so long that both are tired and wounded. And now King Thidrek becomes so enraged and so wrathful that it infuriates him to have to fight so long against a single man. Then he spoke: "This is surely a great shame that I stand here all day and am confronted and opposed by the son of an elf." Now Högni answers: "What can an elf's son expect worse than the devil himself?" And now King Thidrek becomes so enraged that fire shoots out of his mouth and from that Högni's byrnie gets so hot that he practically melts from it, and it does not protect him but rather it burns him. And now Högni spoke: "Now I am willing to come to terms and surrender my weapons. Now I am burning from my byrnie rings. If I were a fish rather than a man, I am so roasted that some of my flesh would be ready to eat." Now King Thidrek takes ahold of him and pulls off the byrnie.

And now Grimhild goes and takes a great firebrand where the house had burnt and goes to her brother Gernoz and sticks the flaming brand in his mouth and wants to know whether he is dead or alive. But Gernoz is most certainly dead, and now she goes to Gislher and sticks the firebrand in his mouth. He was not dead before, but Gislher dies from this. Now King Thidrek of Verona sees what Grimhild is doing, and he spoke to King Attila: "Look how the devil Grimhild, your wife, torments her brothers, who are worthy men, and how many men have lost their lives because of her and how many good men she has wasted, Huns and Amlungs and Niflungs, and she would like to dispatch you and me to hell in just the same way if she could." Then King Attila spoke: "Indeed she is a devil, and kill her, and that would have been a good deed if you had done it a week ago. Then many an excellent man, who is now dead, would still be alive." Now Thidrek rushes at Grimhild and cuts her in half.

Now King Thidrek goes to Högni and asks if he can be healed. Högni says that he will live a few days but there is no reason to expect that he will not die of these wounds. Now King Thidrek has Högni brought to his hall and has his wounds dressed. Herad was the name of one of King Thidrek's female relations. He gets her to dress his wounds.

And in the evening Högni asks King Thidrek to get him a woman and says that he wishes to sleep with her that night. And Thidrek does so. And in the morning Högni says to this woman: "Now it may happen that when some time has passed you will bear a son, and the boy shall be named Aldrian. And here are some keys that you shall keep and give to the boy when he is full grown. These keys are to Siegfried's [sic] cellar, in which the Niflung treasure is stored." And hereafter Högni dies. And now are ended the lives of the Niflungs and also of all the most powerful men in the land of the Huns except King Attila and King Thidrek and Master Hildibrand. In this battle there fell a thousand Niflungs and four thousand Huns and Amlungs.

German men tell us that no battle was more celebrated in tales of old than this one. And after this battle there was such a depletion of great men in the land of the Huns that during the days of King Attila there was no such elite as before the fighting began. Now has been fulfilled what Queen Erka prophesied to King Attila, that all the Huns would suffer harm if he married in the land of the Niflungs.

Here you may hear the story of German men and what happened according to the account of some who were born in Soest, where these events took place, who many a day saw the same places unchanged where the events happened, where Högni fell or Irung was killed or the snake pit where King Gunnar was killed and the orchard that is still called the orchard of the Niflungs and stands in just the same way as it did when the Niflungs were killed, and the gates—the old gate, the east gate, where the battle first began, and the west gate, which is called Högni's gate, which the Niflungs breached in the enclosure, and that is still called in the same way as then. Those men have told us about this who were born in Bremen or Münster, and none of them knew anything of the others, but they all told the same story, and that is mostly as it is told in old lays in the German tongue, which wise men have composed about those great events in that country.

Reconstructions of the 'Brünhildenlied' and the 'Ältere Not'

The hypothetical source for Part I of the *Nibelungenlied* may be reconstructed by comparing the Siegfried story in *Þiðreks saga* (pp. 169–85 above) with the equivalent narrative in the *Nibelungenlied*, *Vǫlsunga saga*, and *Das Lied vom Hürnen Seyfrid*. I have carried out this comparison in *The Legend of Brynhild* (esp. pp. 151–204) and suggested the following content for the common source.

THE 'BRÜNHILDENLIED'

Kriemhild has a monitory dream about a handsome falcon or hawk, which is identified as her future husband. The story then turns to Siegfried, who is of uncertain parentage and grows up in the wilds. His youthful adventures include the slaying of a dragon and the acquisition of a great treasure. He takes service with a smith, but behaves so destructively that his master wishes to be rid of him and sends him to a dragon's lair on the pretext of burning charcoal. Siegfried kills the dragon and bathes in its blood, thus becoming invulnerable except for a spot between his shoulders that he cannot reach. According to *Þiðreks saga* he takes the treasure from the dragon, but the version in the *Nibelungenlied*, according to which he takes the treasure from the mountain of the mysterious Nibelungs, is more likely to represent the German "Brünhildenlied."

Siegfried now rides out alone and encounters Brünhild, whom he wins with a show of force against her family or guardians. They exchange betrothal vows, but Siegfried rides on to Worms, where he engages in feats of arms with the Burgundian brothers. Oblivious of his earlier vows, he is betrothed to Kriemhild and undertakes to support Gunther's wooing of Brünhild because he is familiar with the location of her home. Here he speaks on Gunther's behalf, and a double wedding is subsequently celebrated. During the bridal night, however, Brünhild resists her husband, and Siegfried is called on to overcome her resistance and take her virginity in disguise. On his departure he removes her ring.

Unaware of what has happened, Brünhild nonetheless grieves over

having the lesser husband and vows to take revenge for Kriemhild's duplicity. It comes to a quarrel over seating precedence in the hall, and the
two queens dispute the relative distinction of their husbands. Angered
over Brünhild's derogation of Siegfried, Kriemhild reveals that he was her
"first husband" and displays the ring that Siegfried took on that occasion
as proof of her contention.

Humiliated by the revelation, Brünhild appeals to Hagen and Gunther
for revenge because Siegfried slept with her and then betrayed the matter
to her rival Kriemhild. She vows not to sleep with Gunther until Siegfried
has been killed. Hagen and Gunther determine to carry out the deed, and
Hagen arranges a hunting party with salted provisions and an inadequate
supply of water. Siegfried must therefore slake his thirst at a spring; as he
does so, Hagen pierces him from behind with a spear thrust in the vulnerable spot. Siegfried, who is unarmed, can only fell the retreating Hagen
with a cast of his shield and upbraid his slayers with his dying words.

Returning from the hunt, the murderers throw his corpse into Kriemhild's bed. She cries aloud so that the whole residence resounds. From the
undamaged condition of his shield she deduces that he has been slain in a
sneak attack, and she confronts Hagen. He claims that Siegfried was
killed by a boar, but she sardonically identifies that boar. While Brünhild
triumphs, Kriemhild prepares the body for burial.

The hypothetical source for Part II of the *Nibelungenlied* can be worked out in
greater detail because the equivalent section of *Þiðreks saga* (pp. 186–208 above)
is fuller. The following reconstruction is based on my analysis in "The Epic
Source of Niflunga saga and the Nibelungenlied."

THE 'ÄLTERE NOT'

The Hunnish king Etzel loses his wife Helche. Learning of Siegfried's
death, he dispatches Rüdeger, richly equipped, to sue for the hand of
Siegfried's widow Kriemhild. Rüdeger is well received at the court of
Worms and is given a favorable hearing. At a council convened to discuss
the matter, Hagen warns of Kriemhild's vengefulness and the danger of
giving her free rein, but he is finally obliged to acquiesce. Kriemhild herself is persuaded by Etzel's power and the prospect it offers for revenge.
Hagen attempts to curtail her capacity for revenge by seizing her treasure. She sets out on her bridal journey down the Danube and arrives in
Hunland, where she is married to Etzel, but after her new marriage she
continues to mourn for Siegfried incessantly.

Kriemhild gives birth to a son called Ortlieb and remains in Hunland for seven years. She continues to reflect on Siegfried's death and the loss of the Nibelung treasure, and she ponders revenge. One night as she and Etzel lie in bed, she expresses a yearning to see her brothers. Etzel readily consents, and she proceeds to dispatch two minstrels to Worms with an invitation and a false offer of a share in Etzel's realm. Their journey and reception are described. Once more Gunther convenes a council to debate the invitation, and once more Hagen opposes it, warning that they will not return alive. Gunther can detect only good intentions, but Hagen repeats his warning, causing Gunther to denounce his low birth. Hagen repeats his prediction once more, and Gunther now mocks his fear of Kriemhild. Hagen must finally submit, and he summons his men, along with Volker, to prepare for the journey. In the meantime, the messengers are detained so that Kriemhild will have no advance notice of the guests' arrival and no time to plot against them. Uote has an ominous dream that Hagen rejects. She then seeks to detain Giselher, but he will not be restrained from accompanying his brothers. The Nibelungs now muster their forces and set out, leaving behind many fair women.

Camping first by the Rhine, they march on to the Danube, where they find no boat to ferry them across. That night Hagen stands watch and patrols downstream in the moonlight. He encounters mermaids bathing in a pond and removes their clothes. When they ask for the return of their clothes, he stipulates a prophecy. According to this prophecy all the Nibelungs will cross the Danube, but only the chaplain will return. Hagen kills the offending mermaid and her daughter.

Continuing downstream, he discovers a ferryman on the river. Hagen identifies himself as Amelrich, a retainer of Else, the local count, but the ferryman refuses to transport him without a fee. Hagen lures him to shore with a gold ring that he is only too eager to earn for his young wife. At first the ferryman refuses Hagen's orders to follow the shoreline to the Nibelung camp, but he is quickly subdued. Having arrived in camp, Hagen takes over the boatman's office but rows so hard that he breaks both oars and oarlocks. In anger he curses the ferryman and kills him. When Gunther asks the reason, he explains that he wishes to prevent a premature report of their arrival. After repairing the boat, he next throws the chaplain overboard in an attempt to drown him and discredit the mermaid's prophecy, but the chaplain survives. Gunther chides Hagen once again, but he retorts by asking why he should refrain from evil deeds when they are all fated to die. When all have reached the other shore, he destroys the boat.

Having crossed the Danube, the Nibelungs now march all day and pitch camp in the evening. Hagen once again holds the watch. Encountering the border guard Eckewart asleep, he disarms him, but when Eckewart bewails his own dereliction, Hagen promptly returns his sword and gives him gold in addition. Eckewart now warns him of the enmity in Hunland and responds to his request for lodging by directing him to Rüdeger in Pöchlarn and proceeding ahead to announce the arrival of the Nibelungs.

Rüdeger makes festive preparations and rides out to receive his guests, who are handsomely feted in the evening before they retire. That night Rüdeger consults with his wife Gotelind on the marriage of their daughter to Giselher. The following day he urges the Nibelungs to prolong their stay, but they are eager to press on. Before they leave, however, there is feasting and entertainment, and Rüdeger bestows gifts on his guests: Gunther receives a helmet (or a coat of mail), Gernot receives a shield, Giselher receives the hand of Rüdeger's daughter in marriage and a sword, and Hagen receives Nuodung's shield. Gotelind bids her guests farewell, and Rüdeger takes leave of Gotelind in order to accompany the Nibelungs on their journey. He also dispatches a messenger ahead to Etzel.

Dietrich rides out to welcome the guests and warn them that Kriemhild still mourns, but Hagen rejects the warning with the comment that Siegfried is dead and buried and should be forgotten. As the procession advances, Kriemhild observes her brothers from a window and the Huns gaze admiringly at Hagen. The Nibelung attendants are given separate lodgings. As Kriemhild now greets and kisses her brother Giselher, Hagen straps his helmet on more tightly. Turning to him, Kriemhild demands to know whether he has brought her treasure. Hagen retorts that he has brought only his weapons. Kriemhild now bids all the Nibelungs lay aside their arms before entering the banquet hall. When Hagen refuses, she surmises that they have been warned and she denounces the culprit. Dietrich promptly claims credit for the warning, and Kriemhild departs in silence. Dietrich and Hagen now converse arm in arm while Etzel observes them from a distance and inquires about Hagen's identity. This leads him to reminisce about Hagen and Walter (of Aquitaine) when they were hostages at his court. As the Nibelungs enter Etzel's hall, he welcomes them from his high seat. After a sumptuous feast the Nibelungs retire to their sleeping quarters.

In the morning Hagen awakens the Nibelungs and they go to church armed. In response to Etzel's inquiry into the meaning of their arms Hagen explains that the bearing of arms is a Nibelung custom. After the church services preparations are made to renew the banquet, and Kriemhild initiates a series of maneuvers. She first appeals to Dietrich for help and is refused. She then turns to Etzel's brother Blœdelin, who refuses at first but eventually consents and is commissioned to kill the unprotected Nibelung attendants.

As this mission is being carried out, the banquet begins, and Kriemhild has her son Ortliep carried into the hall. There she instructs him to strike Hagen in the face, in order to precipitate the hostilities. Hagen responds by striking off the child's head, and that of his tutor as well. Seeing what has happened, Etzel orders his men to attack the Nibelungs and a general melee ensues, in which all the Huns who do not escape from the hall are killed. Outside the hall Etzel orders them to renew the attack, but Dietrich withdraws from the scene. Kriemhild feverishly incites the Hunnish warriors with gold. Blœdelin engages Gernot and falls. Rüdeger, who has previously stood aside, is infuriated at the news of Blœdelin's death and plunges into the fray. Kriemhild persists in her efforts at recruitment by offering Iring gold. He engages Hagen, succeeds in inflicting a wound, and retires. Kriemhild thanks him and encourages him with the sight of blood flowing from Hagen's wound. Iring renews his attack but falls before Hagen's blows. Kriemhild now orders the hall set ablaze, and the Nibelungs pass the night in terrible straits.

The next morning the survivors prepare for a new attack. It is led by Rüdeger, who engages Giselher and succumbs. Gernot and Giselher now lead the counterattack against the remaining Huns. Seeing that Rüdeger is dead, Dietrich abandons his neutrality and orders his men into action on the Hunnish side. A final sequence of single combats ensues and the tide begins to turn decisively against the Nibelungs. Dietrich kills Volker; Hildebrand kills Gernot. Giselher now confronts Hildebrand, but Hagen asks Etzel to spare him; Giselher himself points out that he was only a child at the time of Siegfried's death, but he declines to survive his brothers and succumbs, leaving Hildebrand to contend with Hagen while Dietrich does battle with Gunther. Hagen wounds Hildebrand at about the same moment that Dietrich subdues Gunther. Hagen therefore challenges Dietrich to fight him alone, but the encounter ends in his defeat. Hagen is now bound and delivered to Kriemhild, who bids him surrender the Nibelung treasure. He replies that his lips are sealed as long as any of his lords is alive. Kriemhild counters by bringing him Gunther's severed head. Hagen exults in his sole possession of the secret, Kriemhild beheads him in her fury, and Dietrich executes her in turn.

The Bridal-Quest Stories
in 'Þiðreks saga'

The structure of the "Ältere Not" and the *Nibelungenlied* is determined by the conventions of bridal-quest narrative, as argued in Chapters 4, 5, and 7 above. These conventions emerge from *König Rother* and the following stories from *Þiðreks saga*. Two of the stories ("Osantrix and Oda" and "Attila and Erka") exist in doublet versions recorded by scribes Mb² and Mb³ in the Norwegian parchment of *Þiðreks saga*. On the relationship between Mb² and Mb³ see in particular Klein, "Zur Þiðreks saga," and his references. Because of the difficulties in determining the relationship, both versions have been translated below.

1. THE STORY OF SAMSON AND HILDISVID (1:8–12)

Here begins the story of a knight who was born in the town called Salerno. There an earl ruled whose name was Rodgeir, and his brother was Brunstein. The earl had a daughter whose name was Hildisvid. She was the most beautiful maiden and most accomplished in every possible way, and better to win than to lose. The earl loved her greatly, and his retinue too, because of her beauty, courtesy, generosity, affability, and her multiple skills.

A certain knight was named Samson. He was the most excellent and valiant knight. His hair and beard were black as pitch and both very full. In stature he was like a giant except that his legs and arms were not so long, but his stoutness and strength were like that of the strongest giant. His face was long and wide, tough and fierce. Between his eyes was a span's width, and his brows were large, broad, and black, as if two crows were sitting over his eyes. His coloring was dark, but he was most manly. His neck was very thick and his shoulders very broad and powerful and his arms were hard as logs or stones to the touch. He had fair hands with soft and shapely fingers. And with this great strength he has the agility both to ride horses and to perform all sorts of games involving no less skill than strength. His endowments were beyond any man in the world at that time.

He was somewhat heavy-eyed, gentle and affable toward all men, rich and poor, so that he replied cheerfully to the humblest man, and no one was so poor that he scorned him. He was wise and penetrating and displayed great foresight, and he was so generous and munificent that he withheld neither money nor aid from his friends even when the outlay or the peril was great. He was a very valiant man and never encountered any danger that caused him fright or the fear of any man. He often engaged in battles or combats, one against many, but he never entered battle without having the upper hand. His word was good, whatever he promised for good or ill. Whatever he undertook, he would rather die than abandon it before it was accomplished, whether it be a major or a minor matter.

And for all these reasons he becomes so famous that all his friends and acquaintances love him, and his enemies are afraid of him even if they know him only by reputation. But he never accomplished so great a deed that he would boast of it, but when others praise his deeds, he listens but does not speak. He serves Earl Rodgeir well and is much honored by him, as might be expected. Samson falls greatly in love with the earl's daughter Hildisvid, and as time passes he wishes to gain her love by fair means or foul.

Now one day the earl is sitting at table and Sir Samson before him. Now the earl sends from his table the best delicacies on two gilded silver plates to his daughter Hildisvid. Now Samson takes these plates and bears them aloft on either hand. Now he goes out to Hildisvid, and his attendant with him. He said to the attendant: "Go out and fetch my horse and all my weapons and best treasures and be ready when I leave this courtyard."

Now Samson goes into the courtyard and asks that the castle be opened, and the man who guarded the door opened it. Now Sir Samson goes up into the highest tower, and there the earl's daughter sat at table with a few ladies in attendance. Now Sir Samson went up to her and bowed to her and said: "I greet you, lady, and all of you." They receive him well and bid him eat and drink with them. He does so and tells her his message.

And a little after the tables were removed, she took her best treasures and said to her ladies in waiting tearfully: "Now Sir Samson has come and wishes to take me away without the leave of my father and relatives. And how are we to prevent him from doing what he wishes? Even if a hundred knights were here, still he would take from here what he wants. And I have taken my treasures and all my best clothes, because it is shame enough to leave with a man and thus part with my father and relatives and dear retainers and all honor and standing. Now I wish to request that you hide this from my father as long as possible, because I know that he will ride in pursuit as soon as he knows this and realizes what has happened. But if they meet, Sir Samson is such a valiant man and great champion that before he dies I will see many a man cloven and shield broken and byrnie bloodied, and many of my dear friends and relatives will fall headless to the ground."

Now Sir Samson puts the earl's daughter on his arm and carries her out of the castle, and all her ladies are left behind weeping. His attendant was outside the courtyard with two horses, one with a saddle and the other with their treasures. Now he arms himself and leaps on his horse. He places his lady on his lap and rides from the town for a long way until he comes to a forest. It is vast and uninhabited. There he builds a house, and they stayed in it for a long time. [The story goes on to tell how Samson waged war against Earl Rodgeir and his brother Brunstein and how he eventually became king of Salerno. Samson and Hildisvid have two sons, Ermanaric and Thetmar. Thetmar is the father of Thidrek of Verona.]

2a. THE STORY OF OSANTRIX AND ODA (Mb²: 1:49–56)

There was a king named Melias. He ruled over Hunland. He was a most powerful, liberal, and haughty man. He had a daughter whose name was Oda. She was a very fair and courtly maiden, and the most powerful kings and dukes had wooed her, but her father the king loved the maiden so much that he would marry her to no man.

King Osantrix was now widowed and wanted to make inquiries. He learns of this powerful king Melias and his daughter. Now King Osantrix dispatches twelve well-equipped knights and gives them a letter with his seal. And this was the content of the message: "King Osantrix of Vilkinaland [the land of the Viltsians] sends word to King Melias the Powerful and Broad-Bearded. We have learned of your realm and that your daughter is the fairest maiden. Now we wish to woo her in marriage. Send with her as much dowry as is honorable for her. And send me gold and precious objects to honor me. Receive our thanks if you do so. And if you ignore our message, then we will try who has the greater strength, you or we."

These knights come to Hunland and then to the town where he was residing and meet him there. They show him the letter and seal, and he receives them and looks at them and finds it strange that King Osantrix has sent him a letter, since they have exchanged no tokens of friendship. He reads the letter and then says: "I wonder at King Osantrix' saying I should send him my daughter, for I have not wished to marry her to the most mighty kings and dukes, who have no less power than he, but who spoke humbly and courteously—and still we refused them. Now King Osantrix demands this marriage with arrogance and believes he will intimidate us with his army. But it seems more likely to me that something other than that will befall him." And he has the messengers seized and cast in the dungeon and says that they may wait there for King Osantrix.

At this time two young men come to King Osantrix, his nephews Hertnid and Osid, the sons of Ilias, earl of Greece. Hertnid was eleven years old and Osid ten. Hertnid was the most courteous and valiant man in all the ways of chivalry far and wide in Vilkinaland. King Osantrix made him chieftain within his retinue and gave him the title of earl, which his father held. And now Hertnid is a great man, and he gives him a great fief in Vilkinaland.

Now King Osantrix learns that his knights have been put in irons, and now he takes counsel with his chieftains and knights and tells them how shamefully King Melias has received his message and that he has put his men in irons and in a dungeon. He pleaded the case to move against King Melias and avenge this disgrace. Then a wise man replied to the king. "Lord," he said, "let us adopt a different plan. It may be that King Melias did not think the messengers as noble as they should have been. Send your relative Earl Hertnid to him, and with him his brother Osid and many other courteous knights with great treasures and a great portion of gold and silver. Then he will receive them well." King Osantrix agrees to this and submits it to his relative Hertnid and says that he wishes to send him to Hunland to meet with King Melias. And he says that he is ready to go wherever he wishes to send him.

Now King Osantrix has the journey prepared in as magnificent a way as possible. Then King Osantrix has a letter composed with these words: "Osantrix, king of Vilkinaland, sends word to Melias, king of Hunland. You have done an ill deed and received our communication in an unworthy manner, but you could have acted in such a way as to honor us both, by receiving our words graciously and temperately. But now you have disgraced us and the men you have put in prison. Now we are sending to you our relative Earl Hertnid, and along with him his brother Osid, with the same mission as the previous messengers. Receive them well and send what we request. And if any part is missing, we will be obligated to take revenge against you; then defend yourselves and fortify your towns and castles as best you can."

They set out now for a meeting with King Melias and go before the king. Earl Hertnid now presented the message and delivered a long speech and many fair and eloquent words. The king was unresponsive to his speech. Then Earl Hertnid takes a purple cloth and two large goblets of ruddy gold and a great tent embroidered with gold and says that King Osantrix wishes to give him these things to facilitate his request. Then King Melias answers: "I will send him my bondwomen in exchange for these gifts, but I do not expect that King Osantrix will get my daughter for money. He may have my ill will for his proposition, and you who have presented it likewise." He has the earl and his brother Osid seized and put in irons, as the previous messengers were, and says that they can wait for King Osantrix there.

Now King Osantrix learns of these events. He has a great army mustered, but before moving this army from his realm he addresses his men. He says that the powerful king Melias "has seized my knights and put them in a dungeon, and now I have sent my two nephews to him, and he did the same to them. And how do I avenge this disgrace, and how do you wish to proceed, my friends? Now give me good counsel. Now Melias is so powerful and imposing that it seems likely to me that we will win no victory unless we have some plan." Now his chieftains replied and bade him make the provision that seemed best. But they said they were at his disposal and would gladly follow him in any extremity wherever he wishes to go.

Then King Osantrix sends word to Zealand to King Asplian and said that he should send him his three brothers Etgeir, Aventrod, and Vidolf *mittumstangan* [MHG *mit der stangen* 'with the club'] and all the men he could muster. King Osantrix sets out with the army, and the giants, brothers to King Asplian, join him, and a great army beside. Etgeir and Aventrod led Vidolf *mittumstangan* and carried the stout iron club with iron bands wherever the army went.

King Osantrix told all his men to call him King Frederick and he asked all to conceal his real name, and so they do. And now he bids them be peaceful and do no damage even though they enter the land of their enemies. And so it is done. They come now into Hunland and move across the country in such peace that no man, however humble or ignorant, seeks out this foreign chieftain without having his business brought to a good conclusion. And in this way he becomes popular and gains a good reputation. And whoever learns about him travels to him to bring him provisions and wine, and he gives each much more than it is worth. He proceeds to that town called Vilkinaborg. That was the capital of King Melias. Then King Frederick sent word ahead to King Melias inquiring whether he will give them leave to ride into the town. And he says that this army has come from Spain and that they wish to do homage and serve King Melias.

King Melias replies, and says that he fears such a great army, for they might betray him. King Frederick replied that they are not at all likely to betray him, because he was prepared to place his life and the lives of his men in the king's service. Now many men relate to King Melias how well Frederick has conveyed such a large army in an unfamiliar country and how many men have sought him out and how well he has treated all, and they said that it was most likely that he would be a strong support for King Melias. But he was loath and very skeptical.

The townsmen themselves take counsel with one another and say that their town will not be disgraced by such a good chieftain, but rather considerably strengthened. And on the instigation of the townsmen themselves Frederick rides into the town. And when King Melias saw this force, he was very fearful and would much have preferred that this army not enter the town. King Frederick rides to the king's hall, and all his men with him. Then King Frederick says to Etgeir and Aventrod that they should guard Vidolf mittumstangi [MHG *mit der stange* (here with the strong inflection)] and he tells them to stay outside before the hall. King Frederick goes into the hall and many other knights with him. As he enters, he comes before King Melias's high seat and falls at his feet and says: "Oh powerful King Melias, receive me out of deference to your kingdom, and I will become your man. And I have sought you out all the way from Spain because I wish to offer you my service."

King Melias answered: "Your service looks suspect to me and I do not wish to have it, and you have my ill will for having stormed into our town with such a large army." Then King Frederick said: "I rode into the town with the leave of the townsmen, and I thought that you would not object to our coming. And I would not have come here if I had thought that it would displease you. And I do not wish that anyone should suffer injury from our coming if that is in our power. Now be so good, lord, to raise me from where I lie and all my men will serve you." Then King Melias spoke: "Be certain that I will not receive you. If you and I should quarrel and fall out, such a multitude of your men has come into our town that you will not defer to us, and for that reason I cannot trust you, and I do not wish to hear your words any longer."

Vidolf mittumstangan outside the door learns that his lord is lying inside before King Melias's high seat, and he says that is a great disgrace and becomes very angry and struggles free. . . . [Here the text breaks off because of a missing leaf.]

2b. THE STORY OF OSANTRIX AND ODA (Mb³: 2:71–83)

There was a king named Milias who ruled over Hunland at that time and was a very powerful and haughty king. He had a daughter named Oda. She was a very beautiful woman. The greatest chieftains and kings and earls had wooed her. The king loved her so much that he could never take his eyes off her and he would not marry her to any man who wooed her. And when King Osantrix learned about this king and his daughter, he sent his six knights very well equipped to King Milias and had a letter composed with this substance: "Osantrix, king of the Viltsians, sends greetings to King Milias the Powerful of the Huns. Your daughter Oda is much praised in our country for her beauty and courtesy, and we are told of your power. We wish to woo your daughter in marriage, and send us as much money as is honorable for your daughter's dowry and for our wife, and now send this all to us with worthy knights and in knightly style and with large purses filled with gold and silver and other treasures. And we shall grant you our friendship in return [AB; M corrupt]. We have so determined this arrangement that, if you wish to reject it and dishonor our mission and communication, it will be contested between us with armed troops before we retreat from our proposal."

These knights now ride on their way until they come to Hunland, and then into the presence of King Milias, and they show him King Osantrix' letter and with it King Osantrix' greeting. King Milias accepts King Osantrix' greeting and has the letter read aloud and wishes to hear what the king of the Viltsians wants in his realm since he never knew before that he had been so much his friend that this should be understood as a friendly mission. Nor was he so much his enemy that it seemed likely to the king that he would crave his realm. And when King Milias has heard the letter read and what is at the bottom of King Osantrix' message, then he replies in this way: "My daughter Oda has been raised at my court and she is fifteen years old. Kings from the greatest countries have wooed her, and dukes who are more powerful than kings, and they requested this marriage with diplomacy and courtesy, and we refused them our kinship by marriage because we could hardly keep our eyes off her, this fair maiden Oda, so greatly do I love her. But this king of the Viltsians is so high and mighty that he thinks I would rather give him my daughter than see his army. But he may put this to the test." And he calls his treasurer and tells him to seize these messengers and cast them in the dungeon, and says that there they shall await King Osantrix.

At this time there came to King Osantrix in the land of the Viltsians two young men, the sons of Earl Ilias of Greece and the nephews of King Osantrix. At that time Hertnid was eleven years old and Hirdir ten. Hertnid is a very fair and valiant man in every respect. No knight in all the land of the Viltsians is his equal in tourneying and all knightly endeavors. King Osantrix appoints him chieftain in the retinue and gives him the title of earl, like his father's, and a great fief in the land of the Viltsians. Now King Osantrix learns about the knights he sent to Hunland, and that they have been thrown in a dungeon. He takes counsel with his chieftains and all his wisest men and asks advice on how to proceed. And he says that his knights sit in irons in Hunland and how dishonorably King

Milias has received his message. Now he said that he was most eager to gather an army and march to Hunland and do battle against King Milias, and he said that he would win the daughter of King Milias or die in the attempt.

A wise man replies to the king's words and says that it would be more prudent to attempt this matter once more with diplomatic communications and gifts, and says that King Milias may have found that the previous messengers did not proceed with as much honor as he wished and as was fitting. King Osantrix accepts that advice, that he should send other, much nobler, and more numerous men, and with them a great deal of money and gifts of friendship, to see whether the king will take that into consideration. And if that does not work, then [he urges him] to send other, much more forceful letters than the previous ones, to find out whether he will be swayed in this matter. And the conclusion of the matter is that the king himself and all those who participate agree, and thus the plan is determined.

Now the king summons his relative Hertnid and tells him that he wants to send him to Hunland to meet with King Milias and woo his daughter, first with fair words and gifts of money, and then, if that is of no avail, to tell him to expect war if he will not give the maiden in marriage. And the earl said he was ready to go wherever the king wishes. Now the king has another letter prepared and this is the substance: "King Osantrix sends word to King Milias of the Huns. You have done an ill deed and given our proposal and communication a bad reception. You could have managed it so that there would have been honor for both us and you. But you have disgraced us and our men, and your own dignity suffers, when you seized our men and put innocent men under duress. Now we send you our kinsman Earl Hertnid and eleven other noble knights. Now do his bidding and release our men from the dark dungeon and turn them over to him, and likewise your daughter. Send her to us honorably as a wife. But if you wish to refuse us any part of what we request, it may be that in doing so you will lose your realm and with it your life."

King Osantrix had Hertnid's journey prepared in the most magnificent fashion, and with him eleven knights with gold and silver and all manner of treasures, and he sends many great gifts to King Milias. Earl Hertnid now rides south to Hunland to meet with King Milias, and he comes to the place where the king was when he was sitting at table. They ask for leave to enter and it is granted. Earl Hertnid greets the king and says that King Osantrix of the land of the Viltsians has sent him greetings, and he delivers a long speech and relates his journey and the nature of his mission and speaks with many fair words on this matter. But King Milias was loath to respond to his speech.

Then Hertnid takes a purple cloth and two plates of gold and a silken tent embroidered with gold and says that King Osantrix has sent him these things as gifts of friendship so that the king would allow the earl to convey King Osantrix' desire. Then King Milias replies that the Viltsians cannot buy his daughter with gifts of money, but he is willing to sell his bondwomen and take money for them.

Now Earl Hertnid takes King Osantrix' letter and seal and shows them to King Milias. And when the king has read the letter, and he reads it himself, he speaks angrily: "King Osantrix of the Viltsians is a fool to think that he will win my daughter or my friendship with threats or boasts because I seized his six knights and threw them in a dungeon. And now I will throw his nephew Hertnid into the same place, and all his company. And it may be that King Osantrix will enter this dungeon." Then Earl Hertnid and all his men are seized and placed in irons and thrown into the dungeon.

This news spreads far and wide. And King Osantrix learns that his nephew now lies in irons in the dungeon. Then he sends word throughout his realm and summons every man who can draw a sword or bear a shield or bend a bow. And in all he has ten thousand knights and three thousand footmen. King Aspilian is with him, and his brothers Aventrod and Adgeir and the mighty Vidolf mittumstangi, who is the oldest and the strongest of the brothers.

Now when King Osantrix has come with this great army into Hunland, he changes his name and orders that the chieftain of the army be called Thidrek. He marches peacefully with this army and injures no one. And they do not plunder, and market places are established everywhere so that they can buy everything they need. They meet up with King Milias. Then King Thidrek rides into the town with his army. King Milias is present with a great multitude. Then King Thidrek asks for leave to enter the hall and says that he has a pressing mission to the king. And leave is granted. When King Thidrek has come before King Milias's high seat, he speaks thus: "Greetings to you and all your men." The king answers: "God's greeting to you. What is your name, and what is your family and extraction? Where were you born and where are you journeying?" He answers: "My name is Thidrek. I was born in the land of the Viltsians and I was a duke there before I fell out with King Osantrix. Now he has driven me from his realm and will not tolerate me there. Now I wish to request, lord, that you receive me as your man, and likewise all our men, and we wish to serve you as we have served King Osantrix before." And then Thidrek sank on both knees before King Milias.

Then King Milias replies: "Good fellow, it looks to me as though you are a powerful man in your country. Why were you not reconciled with your king? You should serve him. Go back to your realm and make peace with your king." And the king spoke thus because he could not make out who this man was. Then Thidrek prostrated himself before King Milias and surrendered himself into his power and asked him to receive him. Then the king answers: "You have brought a great army into our land. Now [B: if] you become our man, it may be that this does not serve you well and that we have a disagreement, and that we lose our army before we succeed in driving you out." Now the king's daughter Oda spoke: "Why do you not wish to marry me to a king who is so powerful that he exiled this chieftain from his country? And I believe that this man might conquer your whole land with his sword if he wishes to do battle against you." But still the king does not want to receive Thidrek as he lies there before his feet, and accept him as his man.

Then the giants hear of this, and Vidolf mittumstangi becomes so angry that he wants to kill King Milias. But the other two giants hold him. And now he stamps with both feet up to his ankles in the earth and calls aloud: "Lord, why do you lie prostrate before King Milias when you are a much more distinguished man than he? Let us waste and destroy his town and lay fire to all his realm. Take his daughter and have her as your slave." Now Thidrek hears the giant's shout and realizes that he is angry. Then he sends knights out to tell the giants to tie him to the town wall, and they do this in such a way that he is bound with iron chains both hand and foot. Now Thidrek fell for the third time at King Milias's feet and said: "In God's name and for the sake of that nobility that it is seemly for every chieftain to have, and for the sake of your royal name and manliness, grant peace to me and my men here in your country because I cannot be in my estates because of King Osantrix the Powerful. And if he captures me, I will quickly be hanged." Now King Milias replies: "Stand up, sir, and go away, and leave my realm in peace. This town is all full of warriors. We do not want a foreign army here in our realm. If you fail to do so, we will sound our trumpets, and our knights will then arm themselves and drive you willy-nilly from the town."

King Aspilian hears these words and becomes enraged that his lord lies prostrate at the feet of King Milias and goes into the hall and raises his fist and strikes a blow by King Milias's ear so that he falls unconscious instantly. And now King Osantrix sprang up and drew his sword and likewise all the Viltsians who were inside. And now Vidolf mittumstangi realizes that his brother Aspilian is in a rage. He breaks his iron chains apart, with which he is bound, and grasps his iron club and runs about the town and kills both men and women and children and cattle and everything alive that comes in his way, and calls aloud: "Where are you now, Earl Hertnid? Be glad and in good spirits. I will come straightway to release you."

Earl Hertnid heard the giant's shout and was glad, and they begin to batter about the dungeon, and there was a knight named Hermann who was so strong that he broke open the dungeon, and they all run out and to the place where they hear the giant's shout. And all together the Viltsians kill a multitude of men, but King Milias takes flight and escapes.

Then the Viltsians take King Milias's daughter Oda and all his ready treasure in the town and bring them to the Viltsians' chieftain. Then he said to her: "Now, although your father did not want to give you to King Osantrix, I will now take you to my lord and thus buy my peace with him and have his friendship." She answers: "Lord, things have come to such a pass that it is now up to you to treat me well or ill." Then the chieftain takes a slipper fashioned from pure silver and places the princess on his knee. Then he draws the slipper onto her foot, and it was neither too big nor too small, but rather it was as if made to order. Then he takes off the shoe and puts on another, and it was fashioned from ruddy gold. And he puts it on the same foot and wants to see how it will fit her, and this one fits much better even than the first one. And now the princess smoothed her leg and looked up and said: "God above, when will you be so well disposed to me that I may see the day when I can smooth my leg in the high seat of King Osantrix?" Then the king answered and laughed: "It is today that God is so gracious and well disposed to you that you may smooth your leg in the high seat of King Osantrix of the Viltsians." And thus she realizes that King Osantrix himself has come, and she welcomes him gladly.

King Osantrix now journeys home with no more ado and takes the princess with him. A little later King Osantrix sends men to meet with King Milias and wishes to be reconciled with him. King Milias has given half his kingdom to his daughter and the man who marries her. Now King Osantrix wants to have Oda as his wife, but does not wish to diminish the kingdom of his father-in-law King Milias, and is willing to surrender [B: the realm] to his stewardship as long as he lives. But after King Milias he wants to inherit the whole realm together with his wife Oda. And in this way the kings are reconciled. King Osantrix prepares a worthy wedding feast. After that King Osantrix rules over his realm and King Milias over Hunland. King Osantrix has a daughter named Erka with his wife, and she was a very beautiful and courteous maiden in every way that befits a woman.

3a. THE STORY OF ATTILA AND ERKA (Mb²: 1:57–73)

It befalls at one time that King Attila summons his kinsman Osid and tells him that he wishes to send him to King Osantrix in the land of the Viltsians to woo his daughter on the king's behalf. His journey is prepared splendidly and twenty of the courtliest knights in the retinue ride with him.

Now they ride to the land of the Viltsians with great pomp and meet with King Osantrix. The king gives King Attila's envoys a good reception even though they are not friends. He bears in mind that it does not befit a king to injure a chieftain's messengers who carry out their lord's mission faithfully [*vaket* = *vakrliga?*]. And he wishes to know what King Attila wants from him that he should send such noble men to him. And now Osid delivers his message, to wit, that King Attila wishes to have his daughter Erka. King Osantrix replied in these words: "King Attila is not our friend and has declared his hostility toward us. He has done great damage to the Viltsians, and it is not to be expected now that I will marry my daughter to him. But you are welcome here as long as you wish to stay." Osid now returns home and conveys the message to the king and says that there is no hope that King Attila will win King Osantrix' daughter. And Osid reports that his eyes have never rested on such a fair maiden as the princess Erka, and, next after her, Berta, her courteous sister.

There was a town named Pöchlarn. There a margrave named Rodolf ruled, a great chieftain and a friend of King Attila's. Now King Attila sends word to the margrave to come to him. He comes accordingly. King Attila says that he wishes to send him to the land of the Viltsians to meet with King Osantrix on the same mission on which he had previously sent his kinsman Osid to woo his daughter on his behalf. "And if he still does not want to listen to our words and would rather scorn them as before, then tell him to ready himself and all his realm and all his men, and we will come to encounter him and pitilessly take from him everything we have asked for."

The margrave declares himself ready and his expedition was splendidly outfitted, as was appropriate, for no man was so praised in all Hunland for chivalry and courtliness and courtesy. He sets out, and with him sixty knights and many attendants. He came to the land of the Viltsians and was well received wherever he went. King Osantrix learns of his journey and has a feast prepared for his coming, and is most willing to welcome such a chieftain as the margrave. And he accepts the feast in friendship as soon as he arrives.

Now Margrave Rodolf delivers his message and says that the powerful King Attila has sent him there, "and he wishes you to send him your daughter as his queen with as much honor as befits a king's child. And King Attila thought that I would not deliver his message precisely and that I would scarcely have the courage for it, but that is not the case. He said that if you deny him any part of this, he will come with his army. He has a great force and great power won by the might of his sword, and it is better to have his friendship than to engage in hostilities."

Then King Osantrix replied: "You are a great chieftain, Margrave, and you are much praised, and you deliver your lord's message in a courtly manner. But King Attila's message seems odd to me, and it is strange that he dares to woo my daughter since he has occupied the realm that I can claim by right. And he has magnified himself only with what my father-in-law King Melias possessed. And even if we were unreconciled, I would still be obligated to avenge him if I could. In addition, King Attila is not from such a distinguished family as our kinsmen the Russians. And that he has threatened me and my men with war inspires me with no fear at all. And even if he engages in hostilities with us, everyone will say that his cause is less just. And our great power will count for little if King Attila seizes what he asks for against our will. Our relatives would be ill pleased if they knew that he proceeded in this way, but you shall be welcome here as long as you wish to stay. But I do not expect that your mission will turn out as you wish." The margrave now wishes to return home, and King Osantrix takes leave of him with good gifts.

He comes into the presence of King Attila and tells him that there is no hope that he will win his [Osantrix'] daughter. Then King Attila answered laughing: "Let the child have what he whines for. Listen, all my men, we will not fear to enter the land of the Viltsians, and let each knight ready himself, and the Huns will make trial of themselves. And the Viltsians will find out whether we can color our swords in their blood or endure cold steel in our flesh now as formerly. And that message shall be delivered in every house before we return home." Now a great army is gathered, and now King Attila is fully prepared to ride to the land of the Viltsians against King Osantrix and avenge the dishonor he has suffered in not getting his daughter. He now leads the army out of Soest and has six thousand knights and a great army of those who are called "sergeants" [i.e., attendants]. Now he comes to the land of the Viltsians and burns and wastes it, fares with point and blade over all the land, reduces castles, and burns settlements.

King Osantrix learns of this hostility and sends word to Zealand to his tributary king Asplian and his brothers the giants and wants to post them in advance while he prepares his army. And now they meet and there is a great battle and loss of life. King Asplian has a small force but is confident in it because of his brothers. Vidolf mittumstangan was now released with his great iron club, and he lays about him with both arms, kills both men and horses, and maims everything in his way. And they are overwhelmed by numbers and obliged to flee, but first they kill five hundred knights. Vidolf kills three hundred alone. And now King Attila pursues the fugitives a long distance and kills off many of them. But Vidolf runs so fast that no horse can overtake him. Now and then he turns to strike a blow and injures many men. And now King Asplian and his brothers, the giants, rejoin King Osantrix and tell him that they cannot withstand King Attila because of the numbers in his army.

After this, King Osantrix sets out with a great army against King Attila, and he has no fewer than ten thousand knights and a great army besides. Now the kings meet and there is a great battle and bloodshed, and Vidolf mittumstangan and his brothers advance so forcefully that they disable and kill everything in their way. And now the day comes to an end and King Attila is overcome by numbers and flees in the evening into a forest and through the forest. And King Osantrix pursues the fugitives to the forest, but the forest is large and he is loath to ride into the forest at night. And for this reason he pitches his tents and sets up camp and remains there during the night. And King Attila stays on the other side of the forest with the remnants of his army.

And when the night is darkest, Margrave Rodolf gets up, and five hundred knights with him, and they arm themselves. And now the margrave rides to the forest and through the forest, and now they come upon King Osantrix' tents. They catch them unawares and kill many knights, and before they can reach their weapons, they have killed six hundred of them, some with their weapons and some under their horses' hooves. And when King Osantrix' army manages to arm itself, Rodolf flees back to King Attila and tells him this news and bids him return to Hunland and guard his realm carefully. He says that they will get nothing more done for the present. The king thanks him warmly and takes this advice and returns now to his realm. And at this point things are quiet for a very long time, so that neither makes war on the other.

Now it happens one day that the excellent envoy Margrave Rodolf tells his lord King Attila that he wants three hundred knights from his retinue, the most valiant that can be found, and with them the king's nephew Osid. And he wishes to ride off and says that there is no need to expect him back before three years are up. The king does as he asks and gives him an armed force and numerous troops to accompany him. They now ride off. Margrave Rodolf shows the way and lets it be known that he is going to ride to Spain to woo a wife for King Attila there, the daughter of the king who rules over Spain.

But instead he rides to the land of the Viltsians night after night through woods and wilderness and wild trails, but during the day they sleep. And they do not halt their journey until they come to the realm of King Osantrix and enter a great forest a short distance from the king's residence. There Margrave Rodolf bids his companions build houses and good quarters and secretly gather from the country provisions and what they have need of. And he bids Osid take command of them while he is gone. And so he does. Now Rodolf rides away alone and comes to King Osantrix' retinue and disguises his appearance as much as he can. Now he goes before King Osantrix as he sat at table and has a wide hood on and greets the king courteously.

The king asks who he is and where he comes from and what he wants. He replied: "My name is Sigurd and I come in search of you, lord, and I wish to offer you my service." Then King Osantrix answered: "You speak like our enemies the Huns, and you are not unlike King Attila's envoy Margrave Rodolf who killed six hundred of our knights in one night and thus rewarded our gifts and the honor we did him here." Then Sigurd replies: "I do not know Rodolf, although he has done great harm to me as well as to many others, and he has committed many evil deeds for King Attila's sake. And I was born in Hunland and I was together with King Melias in good cheer for many a day, and I cannot conceal that I was against you then to the full extent of my power as long as you were enemies. But when King Attila wantonly seized power and conquered King Melias, I did not wish to serve him, nor did any of my brothers, because I discouraged them all. But when King Attila saw and realized that I did not wish to serve him, he deprived me of all my lands and property and killed my four brothers, and he outlawed me. But I took some little vengeance in return. I killed a hundred of his men, and then I saw no better alternative than to seek you out for whatever mercy you would show me. And now my case is in your power, and I expect of you such mercy that I may rather profit from than pay for my relationship to King Melias. I expect this both of you, lord, and also of your queen, his daughter. And if she had not been so young when she parted from her father and all her kinsmen, then she would clearly recognize me. I am now also most eager to serve his descendant and your highness rather than any other chieftain. And I pray God, lord," he said, "that Margrave Rodolf might have come into your power as I have now come, and that you had rewarded his treachery and evil deeds."

Then King Osantrix spoke. "I expect, my good man," he said, "that Margrave Rodolf will take good care not to enter our presence under these circumstances. But you shall be welcome here and have thanks that you killed King Attila's men, and all my men will make you welcome." Then Sigurd said, "If your men are kindly disposed toward me, I will be pleased and will reward them well." Now Sigurd remains in King Osantrix' retinue for two years. He wears a wide hood and says that he has very poor sight. And during this period he has not spoken with the maiden in any way that satisfies him.

At this time a king arrives from Swabia whose name is Nordung. He woos King Osantrix' daughter Erka, and many good men speak in his support. The maiden resides in a castle and with her the courteous Berta, her sister, and many other noble maidens too, and it is not allowed that men visit them. Then King Osantrix said to Sigurd: "I have come to know you as a good and faithful man. I wish to send you to the castle to convey King Nordung's message and represent his case to her in such a courteous manner as you know best." Sigurd says that he will do everything the king bids him. King Osantrix and King Nordung go out onto the town wall.

Now Sigurd goes to meet with the princess and asks that the castle be opened for him. And when she learns that her father has sent him there, she receives him well and bids him welcome. "And you are a wise and discreet man. And no man has come to my father before who has conducted himself as discreetly as you and not asked more than is permitted, and you have never come to see us." Then Sigurd answers: "It is not customary in our country that a man should enter conversation with a maiden unless the king himself so directs him. And foreign men should not speak with young maidens, and this discretion I learned at a young age. But because the king your father bade me transact a private matter with you, we must now converse a short time."

Then the maiden said: "Good sister Berta, go out from the castle, and the rest of you as well, and we two will remain inside so that he can convey his message." Sigurd answers: "Let us proceed differently, and that is more courteous. Let us go onto your lawn and let everyone see our conversation. Then the king and all the others can see what we are about, and no one will have suspicions about what we are saying, but no one will know what is said. And I want no one to speak ill of you because of me, for many are eager for slander and inclined to speak ill of women and one must guard carefully against evil tongues." Now the maiden has two cushions brought out on the lawn and says: "It is certain that you are a good fellow and most prudent, and a courtly man, and you have learned great discretion at an early age. Let us go out onto the grass and sit down under an apple tree." The weather was fair and the sunshine mild. The kings sit on the town wall and are in good spirits, and King Nordung thinks that Sigurd is supporting his case, but Sigurd thinks that he has more important matters to attend to and for this reason no mention is made of King Nordung.

Now Sigurd takes off his hood and says: "Maiden, I deceive men and I deceive women and I deceive King Osantrix and I deceive you. I am not Sigurd, but rather I am Margrave Rodolf, King Attila's messenger. Make him your friend and lord and take him as a husband. He will give you land and power and many courteous knights, great towns and many fine stuffs. And great dukes will accompany you and bear your train. And you will yourself be queen of all Hunland and all your maidens will be the daughters of powerful men and wear costly stuffs."

Then the maiden answered in great anger and called out: "Good sister Berta," she said, "come here and listen to this man's message." Berta goes there and asks what she wants. Erka answers: "This is not Sigurd, as he claims. He now admits that he is rather Margrave Rodolf, King Attila's messenger. He deceived me and my father and now he speaks on behalf of King Attila. Now go after my father, and he will kill him because in one battle he slew five [*recte:* six?] hundred of my father's knights, and for that he shall be hanged today." Again Margrave Rodolf speaks: "Do as I say, maiden, give your love to King Attila and be queen over that realm which your grandfather King Melias possessed, and your young sister Berta will be my wife in great honor and high favor."

Then the maiden Berta spoke. She says: "You are of royal blood. You should not denounce or defame a man from abroad because he has placed himself in your power. That befits your nobility. Let him go wherever he pleases. And tell me, sister, did you not once say words to this effect: 'Lord God in heaven, grant me my prayer that I may be queen of all Hunland'? Now what you have asked for has come to pass, and God has now granted your prayer. Do not denounce a foreign man. Be King Attila's queen, and I will go with you." But before Berta had spoken her piece, Rodolf had wanted to depart, thinking that she would tell the king as she threatened. Then the maiden calls to Rodolf: "Listen, good knight, do not go away so quickly. I wish to be King Attila's queen and I will give you a gold ring as a pledge, and my sister and I will take good care to conceal your presence here from my father, but you should make a plan for our escape."

Now Sigurd leaves the castle and goes into the town before the kings, and they have witnessed their whole conversation. Then King Nordung spoke: "Good friend, you have faithfully executed our mission, and if you have brought it to a successful conclusion I will reward you well. You will be my earl in my realm and govern many castles and great lands." Then Sigurd answered: "In confidence she told me that she did not want to marry or take a husband for a year, and as a pledge she gave me her gold ring, and here is the ring, lord. But I could not present the case more successfully than that, and, so help me God, I conveyed it to the best of my ability. And I believe that few foreigners would have executed a mission better or more boldly before such noble persons in a strange land." Then King Nordung answered and said that he would gladly wait, and asked him to bend his efforts that this might come to pass in a year's time, and he promises him his friendship if it is achieved. And now King Nordung rides home.

King Osantrix sat on his high seat and summoned Sigurd, and when he came before his high seat, the king spoke: "Good friend, you have now been in my realm for two years and I have learned by experience that you are a more courtly and courteous knight than any other in this retinue, and I surmise that you are a powerful man and of good family in your country. And I wish to give you some authority if you choose to stay here. You shall be the first officer in the retinue and govern the king's business and ride with the army to defend the realm." Then Sigurd answered and thanked the king for his offer and said he would accept it. "But it grieves. me, lord, that I cannot repay King Attila for killing my brothers and driving me from my lands and honor. And this would have come about if I had not come to such an excellent chieftain as I have. And King Attila would be far from being ruler over all Hunland. And he has sacrificed nothing for the time being, no matter what wrongs he has committed. They have all turned out well for him whenever he takes revenge." Then King Osantrix answers: "He will be stopped in the long run. We will visit him in Hunland." Then Sigurd said: "I should wish to be a part of that [expedition?—word missing in MS]. I have a brother, lord, whose name is Alibrand. He is the most courteous and valiant of men in every way, and he was wounded when we parted. And those wounds he got from King Attila. And it is not pleasing to me that he does not come to you to serve your honor. Now I wish to ask you, lord, to give me leave to search him out." The king gives him leave for this journey.

Now Margrave Rodolf, who called himself Sigurd, rode away into the forest alone to join his men. And they have maintained themselves well there. Now Margrave Rodolf says to Osid, King Attila's nephew: "You must ride with me to King Osantrix' court, and I have said there that you are my brother, and you should say so too and call yourself Alibrand." Osid says it is up to him. Now they ride to King Osantrix and go before him and greet him warmly and honorably, and he receives them with kindness and great distinction. And the king does not think that Sigurd has praised his brother more than he deserves. Now they remain there as long as they wish and are well entertained.

One evening Sigurd sent a trusted man to the maiden telling her to be ready in seven days, and her sister Berta too, with all their most valuable treasures. Now these seven days pass, and one evening when the king and all his men had gone to sleep after drinking much wine, Sigurd and

Alibrand harness six of the best horses and ride to the castle, and there the women are ready with all their best treasures. And some horses they load and some they ride, and they leave the castle and ride all that night and the following day and do not stop until they come to the forest to their companions, and they now have five hundred good knights. Now they turn toward Hunland and think they have succeeded well.

Now King Osantrix becomes aware of this great betrayal and deception, and he is furious. He gathers a great army and rides in pursuit of them. And Margrave Rodolf and his men become aware of this and see that there is no chance to escape. And they have not the resources to fight and there is no possibility of a truce, for this was not how matters stood [?—text unclear]. And they flee now to a castle and take shelter in it. And King Osantrix besieges it with his whole army, constructs catapults, and launches heavy attacks against the castle. But they defend themselves well and stoutly. And now Margrave Rodolf addresses his men and tells them that they are in dire straits, as was the truth, and asks if any of his men is so bold and valiant that he dares ride to King Attila "and tell him of our straits and what a turn this expedition has taken, so that some help may be lent us. That man's honor will be great."

And for this mission two of the most valiant knights volunteer, and they ride out from the castle one night in pitch darkness. And King Osantrix' sentinels are aware of them, but think they are their own attendants who ride so boldly at night. And thus they get away from the king's tents and do not stop until they reach King Attila and tell him everything concerning the margrave's expedition. Now when King Attila hears this, he says: "I have never heard of such a knight as Margrave Rodolf, and he has now achieved great honor for me if I can hold onto it myself. And this prey will not escape my grasp, so well has it now been proffered to me. Let all my men now arm themselves and let us come to the margrave's aid." And an enormous army is gathered there.

King Attila leads this army out of Soest and marches to join the margrave. And on the other front we can tell of the encounter between King Osantrix and the margrave and Osid that they do battle every day. And they attack so vigorously that in King Osantrix' army three hundred knights fell, and the defenders of the castle lose sixty knights. Now men hasten to King Osantrix and tell him that King Attila is a short distance from the castle with an enormous army. Now King Osantrix sees that he cannot withstand King Attila for the moment because of his shortage of troops, because there had been such haste to set out in pursuit that the king had assembled fewer troops than were needed. Then King Osantrix' advisers counseled him that he should flee and gather troops and march against King Attila with sufficient force another time. And King Osantrix accepts this advice and has the signal sounded for retreat, and they break camp and flee.

Now Margrave Rodolf and all the defenders of the castle see this and surmise King Attila's expedition. They mount their horses and ride out of the castle and kill two hundred knights of King Osantrix' force. And then they hear a great war cry and clamor of arms and blare of trumpets from King Attila's army, and now they turn back. King Attila and Margrave Rodolf and Osid meet and greet each other warmly.

Now King Attila returns home to his realm with great honor. He now organizes a splendid feast with all the best provisions in the land and marries King Osantrix' daughter Erka. And he marries her courteous sister Berta to Rodolf, and gives him great authority. And everyone who learns of it praises his expedition and wisdom and guile. Now Erka is queen of all Hunland, and Margrave Rodolf enjoys the greatest honor from King Attila, as is proper. From that time on and for a long period there was great hostility between the Huns and the Viltsians, as may be heard before this story is concluded.

3b. THE STORY OF ATTILA AND ERKA (Mb³: 2:87–105)

One time it happens that King Attila summons his kinsman Osid and tells him that he wishes to send him north to the land of the Viltsians to King Osantrix with the mission of wooing his daughter Erka for King Attila. For this journey King Attila secures a second chieftain, who was a duke in the retinue and in command of King Attila's knights. His name is Rodolf. And King Attila gives them a company of twenty knights chosen from his retinue for courtliness and courtesy, and each has two well-equipped attendants. And now this journey is prepared splendidly in every way.

Osid and Rodolf press their journey until they come to the land of the Viltsians; the trip proceeds without incident. They meet King Osantrix in Sweden. He gives good receptions to the messengers of foreign kings and wishes to know their mission even though King Attila is his enemy. Osid gives King Osantrix a full report and says that King Attila wants to marry his daughter Erka. But King Osantrix is not favorably disposed and says that King Attila has despoiled his realm and demonstrated great hostility to the Viltsians. But King Osantrix says that the envoys are welcome and should remain as long as they wish. But when Osid and Rodolf see that their mission will come to naught, they wish to ride home, and so they do. And as they ride home, they discuss together that they have never seen so fair a woman as Erka, and second to her Berta, her sister, King Osantrix' other daughter. Now Osid and Rodolf arrive home and tell King Attila how their expedition has fared and how King Osantrix responded negatively to his message asking him to give his daughter in marriage.

Now King Attila sends word to Margrave Rodingeir, who rules over the town called Pöchlarn. He is the greatest chieftain in King Attila's realm. And when the margrave comes to Soest to meet with King Attila, King Attila says that he wishes to send him north to the land of the Viltsians to meet with King Osantrix and woo his daughter Erka for King Attila. "And if he refuses us his daughter and disgraces us in this way, you should make it no secret that he must prepare himself and his realm for the army of the Huns."

Margrave Rodingeir now journeys until he arrives in the land of the Viltsians. He has with him sixty knights and many attendants and he is well received wherever he goes, because he is the most famous and popular chieftain in all the world and most outstanding in the generosity that he practices above all other men. He is the boldest of men in tourneying. And when he comes to the land of the Viltsians, he meets with King Osantrix. The king receives him very warmly, as is fitting, and organizes a rich feast and invites many friends. And when this feast had lasted three days, Margrave Rodingeir said to King Osantrix: "You must hear a message that has come to you from Hunland. The powerful King Attila has sent greetings to King Osantrix and asked God to let you and your realm prosper. And he asks too to have your daughter Erka in marriage with as much wealth and honor as befits both you and him. And he will reward you with both gifts and other tokens of friendship, and he rules now over all Hunland with great honor and is now the most renowned of kings."

Then King Osantrix replies: "You are an excellent chieftain, Margrave Rodingeir, and you deliver the message of your lord King Attila ably. But it seems strange to us that King Attila is so bold as to dare to woo our daughter when he despoiled our realm by force of arms, and only by virtue of this [scil. conquest] does he now enjoy honor. But his father Osid was a petty king and his family is not so distinguished as that of our Russian kinsmen. Why should I honor him so greatly as to give him my fair daughter Erka, whom I love more than a great part of my realm? Now travel in peace in our country and be welcome to stay with us. But King Attila can have no hope that I will give him my daughter Erka in marriage."

Now Margrave Rodingeir answers. "Lord," he said, "King Attila intended, when he sent us, that we should execute his mission as he said, and so it shall be. King Attila is a great warrior and has many thousands of knights who are keen to do battle. If you do not wish to marry your daughter to King Attila, it may be expected that he will do great damage to your realm, and be prepared for him to waste your land whether it is fated that he or you emerge victorious over the other." Now King Osantrix answers laughing: "You are a good fellow, Margrave Rodingeir. You deliver your message as you are instructed and you shall suffer no blame from us for this. But let King Attila come to the land of the Viltsians with his army as soon as he wishes. We fear him not at all. And before he returns, he will say that the Viltsians have keen swords and tough shields and hard byrnies and good horses, and they are not loath to fight."

Now Margrave Rodingeir departs and King Osantrix gives him good gifts. And he pursues his journey until he comes to King Attila in Soest and tells him of his expedition and that there is no hope that King Osantrix will give him his daughter. Now when King Attila hears this news, he sends word throughout his realm, and an army is gathered. And he wishes to ride to the land of the Viltsians to avenge his disgrace. And when King Attila rides out of Soest, he has five thousand knights and a great army in addition. And he rides with this army north to the land of the Viltsians and burns and plunders wherever he goes. Then the giant Aspilian comes against him with his army. Then a great battle takes place. Before it is over, the Viltsians flee and have lost five hundred men in the process, and now King Attila pursues them all the way to the land of the Viltsians. Then the giant Aspilian and his brother Edgeir flee to the east, and Widolf mittrimstanghan and his brother Aventrod flee to King Osantrix. But King Attila takes all of Aspilian's movable possessions and much booty besides.

And when King Osantrix learns that Attila is harrying in his realm, he gathers an army and marches against him, and when he arrives south in Jutland, he has ten thousand knights and many troops besides and wants now to do battle against King Attila. But King Attila rides away south to Hunland, and King Osantrix rides after him with his whole army. Now when King Attila comes to the forest that lies between Denmark and Hunland, he pitches his tents and waits to see if King Osantrix will ride out of his realm and into Hunland.

The worthy knight Rodolf was reconnoitering in the forest when King Osantrix arrives there with his army. He halts his army and has his tents pitched. Now when Rodolf is aware of this, he rides back to the army of King Attila and gets three hundred fully armed knights. Then night began to fall and it was almost dark. Now Rodolf and his men ride back through the forest and encounter twelve of King Osantrix' sentinels by the forest and kill all of them. And now they ride among King Osantrix' tents and blow all their trumpets and kill everything that comes in their way, both men and horses. Then Rodolf and his companions have done great damage to the army, but its numbers are difficult to contend with. He rides off and back to the forest, and now he inspects his men; and he has lost none, and none is severely wounded. But he has killed five hundred of King Osantrix' men. Now Rodolf rides back to King Attila's army and tells him of his expedition. Attila wishes him God's reward for this and says that he will reward him well for it too. After that King Attila goes home to Soest, but King Osantrix returns to his realm and they part with nothing more accomplished.

And when King Attila is at home in Soest, it happens one time that Duke Rodolf goes before him and says: "Lord, I want to request of you that you give me three hundred knights for an expedition, and as much gold and silver as I think necessary for this expedition." King Attila replies: "Where are you going that you should need so many troops?" Then Rodolf answers: "How does it concern you where I intend to go? But if I do not return when three years have passed, I will be dead." And King Attila said that he would give him what he asked.

Now Rodolf leaves Soest with three hundred knights and heads north for the land of the Viltsians. And now they come to a trackless forest and pitch their tents and stay there for a night. Then Rodolf summons all his men to parley and speaks thus: "This forest is uninhabited and no men pass near it. Here you shall live, my men, and build houses for yourselves until I come to you. And this gold and silver that I give you, you shall keep for provisions and clothes and drink in ample style and measure, and send your men into the country to buy what you require. And if I do not come to you when three years have passed, go home and tell King Attila that I am dead." Then he takes a wide hood and a horse and rides now to the land of the Viltsians and calls himself Sigifrid or, as we say, Sigurd. And nothing is told of his journey until he comes to King Osantrix. And now when he comes to the king's hall, he asks for leave to enter the hall. He is [disguised as] an old man with poor sight and he has a wide hood so that one can hardly see his face.

Now when he comes before the king, he falls at his feet and says: "Lord Osantrix, for the love of God and your kingdom, show me mercy." Then King Osantrix answers: "Who are you and where are you headed and where have you come from? You speak like our enemies. Why have you come here?" Rodolf answers: "Lord, I was born in Hunland. There I have kinsmen, and I was a powerful man there, and my father too. My name is Sigurd, and I have fled my estates because of my enemies." King Osantrix answers: "You are of Hunnish descent and your appearance makes you most like King Attila's man Rodolf, who once did us such harm that he killed five hundred men in a single encounter, and if I could put my hands on him, he would hang before my castle."

Then Sigurd answers: "King Attila and I were never cordial. I was King Milias's man and I had three other brothers. But King Attila hanged one of them and another he killed with his sword and the third one he wounded, and this one was still disabled with his wounds when I rode away. And I do not know whether he will die or not. And after that I killed five hundred of his men and burned five of his estates. Then I fled from Hunland." Then the king answers: "That was a valiant deed—may God reward you for it. And you are welcome here. And if what you say is true, I will give you an earldom and such authority as you yourself may determine." Then Sigurd answers: "Lord, I wish to be some years in your retinue, and if your men are well disposed toward me and it seems congenial to me here, I would like to accept this from you." This seemed well spoken to the king and he wished to grant it. And there he stayed for two years and during all this time he did not speak to the king's daughter Erka.

Then a king from Swabia, named Nordung, came to the king. He comes to woo Erka, the daughter of King Osantrix. He is a powerful king. This suit is vigorously supported by Earl Hertnid and his brother Hirdir. Nordung is a great friend of theirs. King Osantrix gives the suit a good reception, stipulating his daughter's consent, and organizes a great and splendid feast for the time King Nordung stays with him. But the princess Erka resides in a castle, where no man is allowed to come to her, and with her were forty noble maidens.

Now King Osantrix speaks to his friend Sigurd: "You have been in my realm for two years. You are a wise man and a good fellow, faithful and eloquent, and I wish to send you to meet my daughter Erka in her castle and to tell her that King Nordung is wooing her and to discuss whether she will accept his suit." King Osantrix and King Nordung are sitting out on the town wall as this transpires. At the king's request Sigurd goes to the princess and asks that the castle be opened. And when the princess learns that this is her father's messenger, she gives him a good reception and welcomes him and asks what business he has there. And she went on: "You must be a wise and discreet man. No man has been with my father for twice twelve months and conducted himself as you have, for you have inquired only about what is proper and permissible, and you have never tried to speak with us during the time you have been here."

Then Sigurd answers: "Lady, it is not customary in our country that a man should enter the presence of his queen early or late, indeed never unless the king himself permits. And foreigners should not speak to noble maidens. These forms of courtesy I learned in Hunland, but because the king himself sent me to speak with you, we should speak in secret." Now Erka spoke to her sister Berta: "Go out of the castle, all of you, and the two of us will stay here, and he shall deliver his message to me." Sigurd answers: "Lady, let us go out onto the lawn—that would be much more courteous—and have our discussion there, because the king is sitting on his wall and he may then see what we are about, but still no one will be able to hear our words. Then no one will have suspicions about a foreigner's talking to the king's daughter or about the nature of my message." Now Erka answers: "You are certainly a courteous knight and you have learned discreet behavior at an early age." Then Erka calls her sister Berta and tells her to take two cushions and put them in the apple orchard. And now they go and sit down under a fair tree. But King Osantrix and King Nordung see where they are sitting. Now all the maidens have left them.

Now Sigurd said: "Lady, look here as I take off my hood. I deceived men, I deceived women, I deceived King Nordung, I deceived King Osantrix, and I have deceived you, lady. I am not Sigurd. Instead I am Duke Rodolf, King Attila's man. He has sent me to ask you to be gracious enough to vow to make him your lord and take him as husband and be his lady. Then he will give you sons and many courteous knights, great towns, much gold and silver, and you shall wear gold-embroidered purple, and all your maidens and ladies in waiting will be nobly born and wear gold-embroidered stuff. Powerful dukes will bear your train, and you yourself will be the greatest queen in all the world."

Now Erka replies in great wrath and anger and calls out: "My sweet sister, listen now to this man's message; he is not Sigurd but rather King Attila's man Duke Rodolf. And he deceived me and he deceived my father. Go fetch my father and tell him this news so that he can quickly kill him, because he slew five hundred of my father's men. And for that reason he shall quickly be hanged." Then Rodolf answers: "Do rather as I say. Go with me and be King Attila's wife and queen. And your young sister Berta will be my wife." Then Berta answers and says to Erka: "Lady, you are of royal blood and you should not defame this man because he has placed himself in your power on trust, and that honors you. Let him depart if he wishes. But didn't you say once, sister Erka, in my hearing, words to this effect: 'Lord God in heaven, grant me that I may become the queen of Hunland and the queen of King Attila'? That you will now become. Now God has granted you what you asked for. You should not defame a foreigner. You should be the most powerful queen of Hunland, and I will go with you."

And before Berta had said this, Rodolf wanted to get up and depart, because he thought that Erka would tell her father as she threatened. Now she cries out: "Listen now, good Rodolf, come back and do not leave. I wish to be King Attila's queen, and Berta your wife. And I give you now my gold ring as a pledge that it shall be as I tell you." And King

Nordung and King Osantrix see that she gives him a gold ring. Now they think that she must be willing to marry King Nordung, but he was in fact not mentioned in this conversation. And then Sigurd went away from there to the kings.

Now King Nordung said: "Good friend Sigurd, have you faithfully executed my mission? And if you have brought it to a successful conclusion, I will reward you. You shall become my earl and vassal and I will give you great authority." Then Sigurd answers: "Lord, she tells me in confidence that she does not want to take a husband for twelve months, and in confirmation of this arrangement she gave me this gold ring. And as God is my witness, I executed my mission as best I could, and I cannot do it better. And few, I think, would execute it better or more boldly, foreigner though I am in the presence of such noble men." Now King Nordung answers and says that he will gladly wait "if our arrangement will be concluded in another twelve months." And he thanks Sigurd profusely for his intercession. And following this conversation, King Nordung makes ready for his journey and returns to his realm.

King Osantrix summons his friend Sigurd, and when Sigurd comes before the king's high seat, King Osantrix says: "Good friend Sigurd, you have now been in my realm for two years, and I have learned by experience that you are a courteous knight, and I surmise that by lineage you are a powerful man in your country, and now I wish to confer some authority on you. You shall be the leader of my retinue and ride with my army and defend my land." Now Sigurd answers: "I have not been able to repay King Attila for killing my brothers and driving me from my estates. And my young brother Alibrand was wounded. He has now recovered, and I wish to seek him out, lord, and he should be in your service. He is a much more valiant man and a better knight than I. He is fit to serve you." Then King Osantrix answers and thinks it is appropriate that he should ride after his brother and that they should both become his men.

And after that Rodolf rides away until he comes to the forest where his knights are, and they have maintained themselves well since they parted. He then takes Osid, the younger brother of King Attila, as his companion. They ride all the way to the land of the Viltsians and into the presence of King Osantrix. Now Sigurd goes before the king's high seat and bows to him and addresses him honorably. And the king greets Sigurd well and asks him how he has fared. And he answers: "My young brother Alibrand has come here now and you may see what a fair man he is." King Osantrix welcomes them both and says that he will make both of them great chieftains in his realm.

And when they have stayed there for seven days, one evening when the king has gone to bed, after collecting all their weapons and money Sigurd and Alibrand go to their horses and ride now to Queen Erka's castle. And when they arrive at the castle, Queen Erka and her sister Berta come to them and are ready to depart with them. They ride that night as hard as they can, and they ride both day and night as hard as they can and as the horses can stand.

Now when King Osantrix realizes that he has been betrayed, he orders all his knights to arm, and arms himself, and rides after them as hard as he can both day and night. And now both ride as hard as they can, and Rodolf meets up with his men and they are very glad to see him because they think that they have very nearly lost him. They now ride on their way to Hunland, and King Osantrix rides after them with his army. And now he comes so close on their heels that Rodolf and his men see that they cannot get away, and they ride to a castle called Markstein in the Falster Forest and close the castle after them.

Now King Osantrix comes to the castle with his whole army and encircles it with field quarters. But Rodolf has sent two men to Hunland to tell King Attila where the expedition stands. And as soon as these men come to Soest and into the presence of King Attila, and when he hears how Rodolf has carried out his business and in what state he finds himself, he calls out immediately and asks for his weapons and has all his trumpets sounded and dispatches men throughout the realm and assembles an enormous army and rides day and night as hard as he can until he comes to Falster Forest.

And Rodolf and Osid have fought every day against King Osantrix and have killed many of his troops, sometimes making sallies from the castle and sometimes fighting from the ramparts. And before King Attila arrives to relieve them, they have lost forty men, but King Osantrix has lost a hundred men. And this castle is so strong that King Osantrix cannot reduce it, and when he gets the intelligence that King Attila is approaching with an enormous army, he breaks camp and rides home to his realm. And thus they part.

And when King Osantrix has ridden away with this army, Rodolf tells his men to take their weapons and horses and ride to meet King Attila, and this they do. And they meet with King Attila on a fair plain, and he has an army numbering no fewer than twenty thousand knights. And Rodolf presents King Osantrix' daughter Erka to King Attila, and there is a joyous meeting. Then King Attila turns back home with his whole army to Soest. And some time later he celebrated a splendid wedding with Erka, and then he marries King Osantrix' other daughter Berta to his duke Rodolf and gives him great estates in Hunland. This celebration is arranged with great magnificence and a multitude of guests and all kinds of entertainment and gifts, and the celebration lasts seven days. Now

King Attila rules over his kingdom with his wife Erka. They have two sons, Erp and Ortvin. From this time on there was great warfare between Hunland and the land of the Viltsians. And King Attila fights many battles against King Osantrix of the Viltsians and against King Valdamar of the Russians, and they have alternating successes. And now these realms continue in this way for some time.

4. THE STORY OF HERBURT AND HILD (2:47–60)

Herburt now becomes a very accomplished man in every respect so that his match can hardly be found in any exercise or other knightly endeavor. Now King Thidrek has no woman as his wife because he has nowhere seen or heard of a woman so fair that he might wish to marry her. And now he is told of a woman whose name is Hild, daughter of King Arthur of Brittany. She is the fairest woman he has heard of.

Now King Thidrek sends his men throughout the world in search of a courtly woman for him, and these men come to King Arthur in Brittany. And they are told that his daughter is the fairest woman in the world, but she is so closely guarded that the messengers can never see her as long as they stay there. But still all those who have seen her say that no man has seen so fair or beautiful a woman, and with this they return to Verona and tell King Thidrek how much has been told them of this woman—that she was more courteous and beautiful than any other woman who might be found, even if the whole world were searched. And they also say that she is so closely guarded that no foreigner may view her, nor any of her countrymen except the king's closest friends.

And when King Thidrek has heard this news, he conceives a great desire to find a way to win this woman. Now he summons his kinsman Herburt and tells him to undertake a mission to Brittany and woo King Arthur's daughter Hild for him. And Herburt said he would go wherever he sent him. Now King Thidrek has his journey readied and gives him twenty-four knights and provides them with good weapons and good horses and good clothes. Now Herburt pursues his journey until they come to Brittany, and there they are well received by King Arthur.

Now when Herburt has been there for some time, he goes before the king and tells him his business, namely that King Thidrek of Verona, his uncle, has sent him there to woo his daughter Hild for King Thidrek. Then King Arthur answers and asks why King Thidrek did not come himself to woo his daughter if he wishes to marry her. Herburt replies that other men of King Thidrek's had been there for a time and had not gotten to see her. And for this reason he has now sent his nephew, in whom he has great confidence, to see the woman on his behalf. Then the king answers that he could still not see her, and that it was not customary that foreigners should see her except on that one day when she was accustomed to go to church.

Now Herburt stays with King Arthur for a long time, and the king makes him his man, and he is to serve the king. And now he remains for a time. Herburt is such a courtly knight that the king and the other men think they have hardly ever seen his equal. And now when the king sees how well he serves, he increases his honor and appoints him cupbearer and puts him in charge of the mead and lets him provide for the guests and serve those to whom he is most obligated. And now he performs this service with such great skill that no one had seen such service before. Now the king again has his status honorably enhanced, so that now the king appoints him steward. And now he is to serve the king himself. And he is so adroit at this service that it seems to the king himself and all his men that no man has come there, native or foreign, who equals him in courtesy and courtliness or all those matters that are advantageous. And one time he does the following when he has taken a bath and serves at the king's table: he does not want to use a towel, but rather he holds his hands in the sunbeam and dries them thus.

Herburt now stays with the king until a great feast day comes. Then there was a great banquet in the king's hall, and on that day Hild is to attend church. And now Herburt goes ahead and wishes to see her. And as Hild goes from her hall, twelve counts go with her, six on each side, who bear her train, and after them twelve monks, six on each side, who bear her cloak. And there follow twelve earls with byrnies and helmets and shields and swords, and they are to guard against anyone's being bold enough to address her. And her headdress was arranged as if two peacocks surmounted her head, and they were raised so high with their adornment that they shield her against the heat of the sun, so that the sun could not burn her fair complexion. And her head is swathed in silken kerchiefs so that no one can see her face, and thus she enters the church and sits down on her chair and takes her book and sings and never lets her eyes wander.

Now Herburt goes to church and gets as close to where the king's daughter sits as he can, but does not see her face because the guards who have accompanied her stand in front of her. The twelve counts and twelve monks and twelve earls who are to guard her with weapons stand outside the church. Now Herburt has captured two mice and adorned one with gold and one with silver. Now he lets loose the mouse decorated with gold, and that mouse runs to the stone wall and close to where the princess is sitting. And as the mouse runs toward her, she looks up quickly and looks where the mouse is running. And now Herburt gets a glimpse of her face. A little later he lets loose the mouse that was decorated with silver, and this mouse follows the same path as the previous one, toward the wall where the princess was, and again the princess looks up from her book and at where the mouse is running. And now she sees an exceptionally courtly man and smiles at him, and he at her.

A little later she sends her lady in waiting to ask who he is and where he comes from and what his mission is. He answers: "My name is Herburt and I am a kinsman of King Thidrek of Verona, and I have been sent here. But I cannot tell you my mission. But if your mistress wishes to know, I may tell her alone." And now the girl returns and tells the princess everything that was told her, and that this man wishes to meet with her. Now she replies and says that she does not dare say a word to a foreign man as long as her mother and father are present, and she asks him to wait for them to depart and stand behind the church door. Now the girl goes a second time and tells him what the princess has said. And he does as she says and waits by the door until the king has departed.

Now the princess follows the king out to the door, but turns aside behind the door, and Herburt bows to her and greets her. And she bids him welcome and asks him what his business is with her. He answers: "It is a long story to tell of our business. I have now been in this place for three months and never succeeded in seeing you or talking to you before this. But I have a message for you, and I would wish you to arrange it that I might speak to you at leisure so that you might know our business." And she replies and says that she will arrange it. A monk, who was her guard, goes between them and pushes him away and asks why he, a foreigner, is so bold that he dares speak to his mistress. And he will get his reward without delay. But Herburt grasps his beard with his right hand and shakes him so hard that the skin is loosened with the beard, and says that will teach him once and for all to push foreigners.

And now the princess goes away with her attendants and ladies in waiting, and Herburt returns to the king's table and serves. But the princess drinks with her father in the hall because this is a great feast. Now Herburt stands before the king's table and serves. Then the princess speaks to her father: "Lord, will you give me a gift that I desire from you?" The king answers: "What do you wish? Everything in my power that you wish for is at your disposal." She answers: "I wish you to give me this courteous steward as my servant." The king answers: "You shall have the steward, but I promised your request before I knew what you would ask for." And when this feast was over, the princess goes to her castle, and young Herburt goes with her to serve her.

Now Herburt sends twelve knights home to Verona to tell King Thidrek that the matter has now progressed to the point that he may speak with her, and that he has seen her, and that she is truly the most beautiful woman, and that he is keeping the other twelve knights to await the out-

come of the mission. Now the messengers travel until they arrive home in
Verona. And they tell King Thidrek all this news, and he expresses great
pleasure about their mission.

Herburt often speaks with King Arthur's daughter Hild and says that
his uncle King Thidrek has sent him to woo her as his wife. She asks:
"What kind of man is Thidrek of Verona?" She asks: "And what does he
look like?" Now Herburt replies: "King Thidrek is the greatest champion
in the world and most generous. And if you become his wife, you will
have no lack of gold or silver or treasures." She answers: "Can you draw
his face here on the stone wall?" He answers: "Lady, I can draw him by
hand so that a man who has seen King Thidrek will recognize him." And
now he drew on the stone wall a large and fearful face, and then he said:
"Lady, look now at the face of King Thidrek of Verona, and as God is my
witness, King Thidrek's face is much more fearful."

Now she answers: "May God not be so wroth with me that I should
marry this fearful demon." And then she spoke again: "Lord, why do you
woo me for King Thidrek of Verona and not for yourself?" Then Herburt
said: "I wish to carry out King Thidrek's mission as I was instructed. But
if you do not wish to have him, I would gladly ask you to have me. And
even if I am not a king, my family is nonetheless noble and I have a suffi-
ciency of gold and silver to give you. And I fear no man, neither King
Arthur and his men, nor King Thidrek of Verona, nor any man in the
world. And I will do everything I can to accomplish this, if you wish it."
Now she replies: "Lord, of all the men I have seen, I would choose you
first. And I do not know whether King Thidrek of Verona is more powerful than you, but I want you and not him." And before they part, they
join their hands together and each swears to the other that nothing but
death will part them.

And now Herburt remains there in her hall for a time, until he spoke to
the princess early one day: "Lady, I advise that we should ride away before the king gets suspicious about this matter." And she says that he
should make all decisions regarding her and that she is as glad to obey
him as to live. Now he takes two horses and saddles one for her and one
for himself. They ride out of town and ride hastily to the forest. But when
the watchmen who guard the town gates see Herburt riding off and suspect who is accompanying him, they go quickly to the king and tell him
what they have seen. And when the king hears this, he sends men to the
princess's castle. And when the men learn that the princess has ridden
away, and Herburt with her, they go swiftly to the king's hall and tell the
king what they have learned. Then the king summons his knight Hermann
and bids him ride after Herburt and not to return until he has Herburt's
head and brings it to the king.

Hermann quickly takes his weapons and his horse, and thirty knights and thirty attendants accompany him with weapons and byrnies, and they ride the same way that Herburt had ridden before. And they come so close on his heels that Herburt can see them. And he spoke to his mistress: "The king's knights are riding after us, and the king must think that you have departed with little honor. For this reason he is probably sending his knights after you so that they may serve you, and me as well." Then she answers as follows: "Lord, I think they have a commission different from the one you mention, because they surely want your life." Then he answers: "Lady, why would they want the life of an innocent man? And if their commission is as you say, then, as God is my witness, never shall I die by the hand of these men without cause. Nor will I run or flee any longer." And now he dismounts and lifts her down and ties the horses to a tree. And he lies down with the princess and takes her virginity.

And a little later King Arthur's kinsman Hermann and his men arrive, and Herburt bade them welcome and Hermann replied that he would never get a pardon. And Hermann spoke again: "Tell me, wicked cur, before you die, and so help me God you had better not lie, whether Hild still has her virginity." Herburt answers: "This morning when the sun rose, she was a virgin, but now she is my wife." Then Hermann attacked him and aimed his spear at his breast, but at the same time Herburt drew his sword and chopped the spear shaft in half. And with a second blow he struck his helmet so that he split the helmet and byrnie and neck, and he falls to the ground dead. And immediately he delivers another blow on the thigh of the second knight so that he split the thigh, and that man falls off the other side of the horse. And the third he thrusts through with his sword, and then a hard battle ensues and lasts for a long time until twelve knights and fourteen attendants are killed. And those who remain flee back to the town. And Herburt has eleven wounds, all major ones, and his shield and byrnie are rent and hewn apart so as to be useless. And now she takes her kerchief [AB: and tears it in strips] and binds his wounds. After that he mounts his horse and they ride on their way for a long distance until they come to a certain king, and he stays with him for a long time and was a duke there in his retinue to defend the land. And he enjoyed great honor there, and there are many stories to tell of him.

5. THE STORY OF APOLLONIUS AND HERBORG (2:111–20)

King Salomon was a very powerful and valiant and wealthy king. His wife was named Herborg. They had a daughter, who was named Herborg like her mother. She is a very fair maiden and the king loved her greatly.

Many princes and dukes had wooed her. But King Salomon loves her so much that he does not wish to marry her to anyone.

Duke Apollonius learns of this maiden and sends his men to France, to King Salomon, to woo his daughter for him. These knights ride as the earl had ordered them. They are well received there, but he is unresponsive to their mission and they return home with nothing more accomplished and tell Apollonius. He is ill pleased and goes to meet his brother Iron and tells him how this matter has turned out, and at the same time that he desires nothing so keenly as to win this maiden, and asks his brother to help him, and is eager to assemble an army and thus win the woman.

Earl Iron tells him how powerful King Salomon is and that he is so powerful and has so many troops that they cannot win his daughter by force of arms. Then Earl Iron's wife Isolde, who was very beautiful and wise and distinguished in every way, said: "I will offer you advice, Apollonius and Earl Iron. You should not march with an army against France. Even if you dispatch great champions and are great champions yourselves, King Salomon is much more powerful than both of you and you cannot stand against his army. Take a few knights and equip them honorably and ride to France to meet King Salomon with a few knights and ask him to give Apollonius his daughter. If the suit succeeds, all is well, but if King Salomon refuses the woman, I have another counsel. I will give you a little gold ring, Apollonius. My father gave it to my mother with her dowry. In this gold ring there is a stone, and it is the nature of this stone and setting that if a man puts this ring on a woman's finger, she will love him so greatly that she will want him at any cost, whether that is the wish of her kinsmen or not."

Earl Iron and Apollonius thank Isolde warmly for her good counsel and accept this plan. They ready themselves and their men and ride all the way to France to King Salomon. The king gives a good reception to those who now visit him and invites many people and organizes a great feast. Earl Iron and his brother ask if he will marry his daughter to Earl Apollonius. But King Salomon refuses and will not marry his only daughter to Earl Apollonius because he is an earl and not a king. But the discussion went on for many days.

Earl Apollonius saw Herborg and was exceedingly well pleased by her appearance, as he had been led to expect. And now he is much more eager than he was before to win her. He presents his case to her, but she says that her father may arrange whatever he wishes for her. She does not refuse that man who seems to her father to be an honorable son-in-law. Nor does she want to accept a man whom the king has already rejected. Apollonius replies: "It may be that your father will not give you to me in marriage, but you are certainly a courteous maiden and I love you greatly.

And even if I never win you, I still wish to give you a token of my love." And he now takes the gold ring and puts it on her finger and says that he wishes to give it to her as a sign of how he is minded. He bids her prosper and she bids him farewell.

After this the earls prepare to leave and are dissatisfied with their journey. When Earl Apollonius has mounted his horse, and all his men with him, he said: "King Salomon has given our journey an altogether dishonorable and rather disgraceful conclusion, since he thinks it a shame to marry his daughter to us. And now it might come to pass that I will get his daughter in a way that discredits him, and it might also come to pass that his realm will not be long at peace." King Salomon cares not at all if the earl threatens him with enmity or arms, and they part as matters stand. The earls return home. Lady Herborg has the gold ring that Earl Apollonius gave her, and after she received it, she loved him so much that she would rather live with him at night than at home with her father in daylight.

When Apollonius rode off from town and had parted from King Salomon, the queen and the maiden Herborg came toward him. And they both go up and kiss the earl. The maiden Herborg kissed Apollonius and laid an apple in his hand, red as blood and fair to see. The earl rode that day and played with this apple. He tosses it into the air and catches it as it falls. And once he catches it so hard as it flew down to him that the apple splits in half. He puts the parts in his palm and looks at them. He sees that inside the apple is a letter. He took the letter and read it. This is what was in the letter, that the maiden Herborg sends Earl Apollonius her greeting. She wants to swear in the name of God that if Apollonius loves her, she loves him much more, and if he can arrange to come secretly when she sends him word, she will come to meet him without her father's consent, and he should not waste King Salomon's realm.

The earl is now rather better pleased than before, but he pretends to all his men that he is dissatisfied with his journey. He remains at home in his town of Tyre for some time. Earl Iron stays in his town and wants to be prepared to harry if that is what his brother wishes. Earl Apollonius says that they should wait six months and make preparations, and this they do. Before the six months have passed, it happens one evening in Tyre that a man arrives dressed as a minstrel. He came to the earl secretly and gave him a letter in secret. And Lady Herborg sent this to him. She sends her greeting to Earl Apollonius. "King Salomon has departed from his realm to a feast in Rome at the court of King Ermanaric. Now you should take ten or twelve of your knights and ride as swiftly as you can, but secretly, to France. Then I can arrange it so that we can meet."

When the earl has seen the letter, he is very glad, and first thing in the morning he orders ten knights to make ready and says where he intends to ride. They ride for the most part through uninhabited regions and forests, as much as they can, and most often in the early morning or at night, until they come to France. They ride along the outskirts of a town where there is some scrub growth to the place where the lady arranged that they should meet. There they encounter no one, dismount, and hide there in the brush. Now the earl does not know what it means that no one comes to him. They remain there during the night. In the morning the earl said that the men should wait there while he goes out to reconnoiter alone to find out what he can.

He proceeds until he comes to a little village and finds a woman in a house. And he said to the woman that she should give him her kerchief and cloak, and he gave her his gold ring and good cloak. He took the kerchief and wrapped it around his head and put on the cloak and went to the town rather late in the day. And there the town gate was open and he heads for the queen's hall. And he joins the women, and the women there ask who this woman is, and he calls himself Heppa. The queen remembers that she has often heard mention of Heppa the vagrant woman [MHG: *varndez wîp* 'wandering woman'], or, as we say, beggar woman. She had been the greatest whore. She was also a very big woman, so that no man was taller or stouter. For that reason the earl called himself by her name.

Many of the maidens spoke to the woman and found it amusing and thought it was a novelty that she had come. Lady Herborg went up to her and spoke to her laughingly, as the other maidens did: "Tell us now, how many men have you taken in a single night?" The woman felt she could not answer properly in the French tongue as was appropriate in answering a princess, and she raised all ten fingers over her head. Then the princess and all the maidens laughed. The lady thought she could tell from this how many men he had taken with him, but the other maidens laugh and think that ten men slept with her in a single night.

A little later the lady took some apples and gave one to each woman who was present, and when she had given everybody one, she tosses an apple to the beggar woman. She caught the apple and cut it open and ate it, as did the other women who were there. In it he found a letter folded up. He gathers now that the lady has recognized him. He gets up and leaves, bidding the princess and all the others farewell. The queen took a valuable and ample shift and a kerchief and gave them to her. And with this they part.

He reads the letter the first opportunity he gets, and it says that that night the lady will come to him at the place arranged between them. The earl goes back to his men and spends the night there. In the middle of the night they hear two people coming, and as they come to the brushwood, one said: "Are you here, my dearest love? Or where are you?" Then the earl answers, "I am here with my sons [AB: knights]," and then the earl jumped up and went toward her and put his arms around her neck and kissed her. Then he called to his knights to ready their horses as quickly as possible.

Now when Apollonius has mounted his horse together with his lady, and all the knights are ready, the earl spoke to the woman who had accompanied her and asks who she is. She said she was a poor woman from the town. Then the earl took the shift and kerchief that Herborg had given him and gave them to the woman. He gave her a letter and told her to give it to the queen, and the woman does so. The queen is very sorrowful and grieved now that her daughter is gone. In the letter it says that Herborg should [B: she should] not be sad because of this, and that her daughter is well taken care of; she is in Tyre with Earl Apollonius. Thus the whole matter is revealed.

The earl now returns home with all the others. Everyone is glad that he and his brother Iron and all the others are back in Tyre. Earl Apollonius now speaks to his lady and says that he wishes to marry her, but she bids him wait and send men to King Salomon and be reconciled with him, and their marriage will then be more honorable. The earl does not want to deviate from her wishes. When King Salomon learns of these events, he is mightily displeased. When the lady has been in Tyre for a month, men were dispatched to King Salomon [to say that] Earl Apollonius wishes to be reconciled. King Salomon gives this message a good reception and arranges a place where they can meet and be reconciled. When the messengers return to Tyre, the maiden has been taken seriously ill and a few days later she dies. And with this their reconciliation is cancelled. Forever after there was hostility between King Salomon and Earl Apollonius and his brother Earl Iron.

6. THE STORY OF IRON AND BOLFRIANA (2:147–53)

King Attila of Soest is to attend a feast south in Rome at the court of King Ermanaric. He is accompanied by many of his chieftains. Earl Iron of Brandenburg also makes the trip and altogether they have a hundred knights and many attendants. King Attila now arrives in the south of the land of the Amelungs at a town called Fritila, and Aki, known as Pillar of the Amelungs and the brother of King Ermanaric, prepares a feast for them. The most splendid feast takes place there.

In the evening they drink excellent wine. That evening the duke's wife Bolfriana entertains. She is a very beautiful woman. She entertains noble men. There she sees with the king a tall man. He has hair as full and fair as beaten gold, a pale beard, and a bright complexion, fair in every way. He has fair eyes and white hands, and there is not his equal in fairness in that gathering. This is Earl Iron of Brandenburg. She often glances at Earl Iron, when she thinks no one else is paying attention, to dwell on him fondly. Iron too sees how fair this woman is. He does not indulge much in drink that evening. He conceives a great affection for the woman so that he becomes ill from it. Everyone else drinks and is merry, and finally they all lie down dead drunk except Earl Iron and Bolfriana. Then they converse together about how each feels about the other. Earl Iron gives Bolfriana the gold ring that his brother Apollonius had owned and had given to King Salomon's daughter Herborg.

The next morning King Attila goes on to the feast in Rome. At this feast King Thidrek of Verona and Vidga and Heimir were present. On this occasion Thettleif the Dane and Walter of the Vosges contested as was previously described. When King Attila returns from the feast, he rides to a feast in Fritila with Duke Aki, and they banquet there. And at this feast Earl Iron contrives to talk with Bolfriana, and when they part, they pledge with tokens that each will love the other whether they can meet or not. King Attila and all his men now return north to their realm in Hunland. Earl Iron also goes home to Brandenburg with his men. He continues to ride out frequently to the forest to hunt with his dogs.

Sometime later it happens that Earl Iron prepares for a journey, and with him his hunter Nordian and some other knights, and they take with them many dogs. Now they make their preparations as if they are going to be away from home for two months. They ride now far off into the wilderness and hunt and have their sport. The earl now rides south through the forests and wilderness until they come to the land of the Amelungs and the realm of Aki and to Fritila. Then Earl Iron learns that King Ermanaric has prepared a great feast in Rome and invited King Thidrek of Verona. And Duke Aki is also to attend. Then Earl Iron sends a knight to the town. He takes his letter with him to Bolfriana, in which Earl Iron sends her word on how they can meet when Aki has left home. This knight gets minstrel's clothing and dresses like a minstrel and enters town in this guise.

There is a great drinking party in the hall. Lady Bolfriana stands and serves the duke. And when she goes toward the goblet that the cupbearer has brought in, the messenger comes to her and gives her the letter and the recognition signs. She puts the letter in her purse and said that Earl Iron should enter town when Aki has ridden away that night. The knight leaves the hall hastily.

Lady Bolfriana picks up the goblet and serves the duke. He takes the goblet and drinks to Bolfriana and says, "Here now, lady, drink half a draught with me." She takes the goblet and finishes it off. That evening the duke has her drink half draughts with him. And before it was over

Bolfriana had had so much to drink that she fell sound asleep. The duke tells his knights to lift her up and carry her to bed, and he himself retires. The knights put Bolfriana on her bed with all her clothes on. Then he tells the knights to go to bed. And six candles were there that were supposed to burn at the duke's head and feet. When his personal attendant had undressed him, he bade him leave. He closes the door securely, then goes to where his wife is lying.

He takes her purse and empties it. There he finds a letter. He unfolds it and reads. This is what it said: "Earl Iron of Brandenburg sends his beloved Bolfriana greetings. He has come to the forest that is nearby. If Duke Aki departs from his realm tomorrow, we should meet tomorrow evening at sunset in the grove outside the town. He will then stay with you for some little time. If Duke Aki delays his departure, send me a clear message with someone you trust and I shall await that." The duke folds the letter as it was before, puts it in the purse, lies down in his bed, and sleeps.

Now when the duke has slept for a long time, he gets up early in the morning and goes to where Bolfriana is sleeping. He awakens her and acts very cheerful and bids her get up with him. He intends to ride on his way and bids twelve knights come to him. He orders them to get ready early, for he is now ready to ride south to Rome. They all make ready in the worthiest fashion with good weapons, and they have excellent horses. Before midday they ride out of the town of Fritila and continue on their way until they come to the forest. They now ride all day until the middle of the afternoon. Then Duke Aki spoke to his men: "It is certain that I have ridden with an ill grace if I do not wait for my kinsman King Thidrek of Verona and ride with him to the feast. It is badly arranged if he comes to Fritila and we are not at home."

He now turns his horse around, and the rest of them too, and when they reenter the forest, they ride on for a time. And a little after sundown they see a man riding. Two dogs run ahead of him and on his left wrist he carries a hawk. He has a fair and handsome shield with a hawk of gold and a dog painted on it. Aki recognizes that this is Earl Iron of Brandenburg, and he calls out to his men that they should overtake and kill him. Then Aki draws his sword and all his knights ride toward him. Earl Iron now recognizes the first man. He has a red shield with a gold lion painted on it, and he knows that this is Duke Aki of Fritila, who was the greatest of champions and combatants. They meet by the road and fight immediately. Earl Iron defends himself well and valiantly, but before it was over he fell from his horse and slumped to the ground with many great wounds. Duke Aki now rides away with his men and leaves Earl Iron dead.

Saxo Grammaticus'
'Lay of Grimhild's Perfidy'

The following episode is translated from Saxo Grammaticus, *Gesta Danorum*, 13.5.14–6.9, ed. Olrik and Ræder (pp. 353–55). The background of the narrative is that jealous rivals of Cnut Lavard at the Danish court have slandered him with charges of royal ambition at the expense of his uncle King Niels. The king demands an explanation, and Cnut clears himself in an eloquent speech. But the slanderers, including Niels's son Magnus and nephew Henry, persist in their conspiracy, which culminates in Cnut's murder on Epiphany in the year 1131. See also Müllenhoff, "Zeugnisse und Excurse," pp. 335–36.

Soothed by this speech, the king [King Niels], displaying a more smiling countenance, put aside on the spot a displeasure so wrongly conceived, and, despising those who would basely abuse his credulity, he vowed henceforth to close his ears to such accusatory whisperings. When, however, Henry [Henrik Skadelaar, nephew of King Niels] saw the whole force of his slander undermined by Cnut's thoughtful reply, he plied the king with the danger of threats to his family, professing his own tender affection for the realm and the uncertainty of Magnus's succession to the throne if he should become involved in a dispute over supreme rule with the people standing in judgment. For Cnut would be preferred to the other men of royal blood, were the choice left to the general public. For which reason the father should assign the law of succession to his own discretion rather than the discretion of others, and eliminate a hereditary rival from the designated position if he wished to be an arbiter of his son's affairs. Thus he might judge whether he should strive to anticipate Cnut's suspicious good fortune by the use of steel. These words tormented the mind of the king, so often importuned and already beset by worry, with even graver suspicions than before.

Then Magnus, availing himself of his father's permission to aid his own fortunes as well as to remove a rival, forced those who had already associated themselves with Henry's villainous intentions to swear an oath that they would conceal the undertaking in loyal silence. They were joined by Hakon, the Jute by cognomen and extraction. Nor were there any doubts about this word although he was known to have married Cnut's sister. Thus the conspirators, after lengthy and secret discussions on what whirlwinds of peril or decree of death they would conjure up against Cnut's sacred life, wove the snares of their hellish plans as they lay on the ground so that if it should happen that the matter were exposed, they could safely swear that they had never conspired against his life either sitting or standing, and could, with the aid of their posture, claim a pretext of innocence, never thinking that a man swearing an oath with a verbal trick would be liable for perjury. Their false and errant guilelessness placed the burden of crime in the godlessness of the word rather than the act and constituted a violation of religion through the temerity of their lips instead of their hands.

When, however, Hakon the Jute realized that the outcome of the quietly contracted oath was directed against Cnut's life, he withdrew from participation in this hellish conspiracy and departed from the conclave, lest he appear to play the part of a brigand rather than a kinsman. Then, admonished by the author of the conspiracy not to break the bonds of the oath, he replied that he would be neither a promoter of nor a traitor to the scheme—although it would have been better to prevent the danger to an innocent man by revealing it than to tolerate it in silence.

When Magnus had thus hidden the nature of the scheme with the aid of his family connections and avoided any sign of suspicion by his cunning, he determined above all to institute the feigned equality of friendship with the man for whose blood he most ardently thirsted by means of a sworn pact (intending to strengthen the bond of kinship with the authority of religion as well), and in order to disguise all signs of ill will with a pretense of piety and not to seem to harbor any perfidious or covert designs, he obscured his wicked enterprise with an insidious affectation of religion. Consequently, having gathered a meeting of noblemen on Zealand and having invited Cnut to Roskilde to celebrate Christmas, he professed the desire to undertake a holy pilgrimage. Furthermore, he appointed Cnut guardian of his wife and children and gave him full authority over his family affairs. But Ingiborg [Cnut's wife] had gotten some inkling of the scheme, perhaps through the hints of some of the conspirators, and immediately sent a letter to warn her husband to avoid the designs prepared against his life. But, thinking that the messenger had set out not so much because of any certain discovery as because of a woman's fearfulness, he rejected the warning and declared that he had no less faith in Magnus than in his wife. If fate had counseled him as prudently as his wife, he would have avoided the snares of perfidy laid in his path and would not have offered his credulity to be caught on the hooks of another man's malice.

Thus it was that when the lords of Roskilde had celebrated for four days, Cnut and Magnus dissolved the general assembly and spent the remainder of the holy season in separate residences. At that time, as it happened, one of Cnut's distant relatives killed in his presence an officer, with whom he had fallen out, with a blow of his fist, and, under orders to leave the court for this reason, he sought out Magnus. Fearing that through him some hint of the plan might reach Cnut, Magnus set out in the night appointed for this horrid and bloody office, and, having ordered the others to follow, rejected as a companion only this one man, who was suspect because of his former association with Cnut. Then he obliged the participants in the design, already bound by an oath, to swear to remain silent about everything. After this he hid his troop and laid his ambush with the aid afforded by the darkness of the place.

Then, dispatching one of the conspirators, a Saxon by lineage and a singer by avocation, he sent word to Cnut, who had been housed near the town of Haraldsted by Erik, the governor of Falster, to come to him without witnesses. As a meeting place he designated a grove near the residence. Cnut, suspecting no treachery and accompanied only by two fighting men and as many grooms, mounted without arms and did not so much as gird a sword to his side. When one of his servants remonstrated with him for departing without a sword, he replied that he had no need of a sword to protect his life. For he attributed such good faith and such peaceful intentions to Magnus that it did not occur to him that he might use a sword in a meeting with him. But his adviser insisted that he not leave his sword behind, and he grudgingly took up a weapon.

Then the singer, because he knew Cnut to be fond of Saxons and Saxon customs, and wishing to caution him discreetly, although the bond of his oath seemed to prevent him from committing an open violation, tried to expose the matter by implication, balancing his integrity between the faithful keeping of a secret and the pious preservation of innocence. Therefore, sedulously rehearsing the well-known perfidy of Grimhild against her brothers in the words of a very polished lay, he attempted to inspire in him a comparable fear through the example of this notorious deceit. But he was unable to shake the firmness of his confidence with indirect warnings. For he had such faith in his kinship with Magnus that he preferred to risk his own life rather than to doubt Magnus's friendship. Wishing to bring even more obvious hints to bear, the singer then discovered the border of the corselet that he wore beneath his cloak. But not even with this incitement to suspicion was he able to constrict with cowardice a breast bursting with courage. Thus this retainer wished to perform his duty diligently with a loyalty free of perjury and perfectly guiltless.

Cnut was just entering the woods when he was received by Magnus, seated on the trunk of a felled tree, with false cheer and feigned kisses. When, as he embraced him, he became aware that his chest was sheathed in steel, he inquired into the meaning of this manner of dress. But Magnus, wishing to explain his attire by a feigned desire to commit some evil deed, stated that there was a man dwelling in the country whose home he wished to waste. Cnut, considering the wickedness of the undertaking and the religious season (for they were celebrating Epiphany), begged him not to stain a solemn holiday with his private wrath. Without dismissing his vengeance or abjuring his intentions, he undertook in response to Cnut's admonition to put off his just demands for satisfaction.

When there was a clamor from those lodged in ambush, Cnut looked around and asked the meaning of this armed band. Magnus replied that it was time to consider the succession to the throne and the most pressing questions. Then Cnut expressed the wish that his father's majesty might yet for some time hold a prosperous course with sails cheerfully spread to the winds of good fortune, and he denied that the season for such discussions had arrived. As he spoke, Magnus leaped forward and, as his only retort, took aim at his head. Then Cnut, with the treachery revealed for all to see, put his hand on his hilt and tried to draw his sword from the scabbard. He had already half unsheathed the sword when Magnus split his skull and laid him low. The other conspirators stabbed the fallen man with repeated spear thrusts. But his blood, absorbed in the earth, supplies the salutary gush of a spring for the perpetual uses of mankind.

Summary of the 'Klage'

The *Klage* is a poem of 4,360 verses in Bartsch's edition, composed in the standard rhymed couplets of Middle High German epic. It is appended to the *Nibelungenlied* in all the main manuscripts but one and describes the aftermath of the cataclysm in Hunland. For a survey of the relevant scholarship see W. Hoffmann, *Das Nibelungenlied* (1982), pp. 116–28, and Günzburger, *Studien zur Nibelungenklage*. On the disputed relationship between *Klage* and *Nibelungenlied* see especially Curschmann, "'Nibelungenlied' und 'Nibelungenklage,'" Voorwinden, "Nibelungenklage und Nibelungenlied," and Wachinger, "Die 'Klage' und das Nibelungenlied." The following summary is based on *Diu Klage, mit den Lesarten sämtlicher Handschriften*, ed. Bartsch. References are to lines.

The following story would be appropriate to tell were it not the source of such grief. An author had it put down in writing for the greater glory of the Burgundians. King Dankrat and Queen Uote had three sons and a daughter, Kriemhild, who married a warrior destined to die for his pride [C: because of the pride of others]. She then married the all-powerful king of Hunland, Etzel, but suffered from exile and the constant thought that her kinsmen had killed her husband. She had a great following among the Huns. Eventually, when her power permitted, she conceived of revenge for Siegfried. Siegfried's relatives also imagined how she might avenge him if she were only a man. Therefore no one should censure her, for she acted only out of loyalty. (1–158)

Etzel arranges a great banquet, at which Kriemhild also contrives to include those she is eager to see. Accordingly her kinsmen also come from the Rhine, but without her treasure. King Etzel welcomes them, and his retainers too, not realizing that the day of reckoning has come. No matter how well disposed Etzel was, Hagen's deed required atonement, but before he died, forty thousand others fell. Kriemhild was helpless to prevent it. She would have been satisfied with the death of one man and had no designs against her brothers, but no one was spared. The slaughter could have been prevented had Etzel been told the truth, but the Burgundians failed to tell him because of their pride, and Kriemhild because of her guile. Despite Etzel's good intentions everyone succumbed. (159–316)

A wondrous number of heroes died because of a woman's wrath. Six hundred of Dietrich's and Hildebrand's men died. Blœdelin lost thirteen hundred men; he sacrificed life and honor in the loyal service of Kriemhild. Herman of Pœlan and Sigeher of Walachen lost two thousand. Walber, who had come from Turkey through Greece, lost twelve hundred men. Irnfrid of Thuringia, Hawart of Denmark, and Iring of Lotharingia, who were under imperial ban, were also among the victims. Irnfrid succumbed to Volker, Iring to Hagen, and Hawart to Dankwart. Gernot performed miracles of valor and slew Rüdeger, to whose dying blow he also succumbed. No one could bear the death of Giselher, who was innocent of Siegfried's murder. Gunther, however, had counseled Siegfried's death and earned his sister's hatred. Kriemhild's child was also slain, a loss avenged by the Huns. Even she was killed by Hildebrand, to Etzel's profound grief. Now everyone capable of fighting had fallen. Many people believe that Kriemhild had forfeited her soul, but her fidelity has earned her a place in heaven. (317–586)

Etzel grieves mightily, and a host of women with him. People gather from the countryside to join in the lamentation. The corpses are cleared away so that the hall can be reached, and the arms of the dead are gathered up. The women tear their hair and wail. Many tears are shed in particular for Kriemhild, who died by Hildebrand's hand because she killed Hagen. Many people can hardly believe that she was the slayer of such a hero as Hagen. Dietrich arrives on the scene, pronounces a eulogy, and has her placed on a bier. Etzel's lamentations are so intemperate that Dietrich chides him. He also laments the death of his brother Blœdelin at great length (887–1,007), at the same time repenting his heathen apostasy after spending five years as a Christian. (587–1,012)

Dietrich once more seeks to calm Etzel, who continues to lament the loss of everything but life itself. Dietrich asks in turn for consolation now that all those men have fallen who were prepared to help him [scil. to regain his realm]. Etzel now has his child and his brother laid next to Kriemhild on the bier. He and Dietrich then lament the death of Iring and have him laid on a bier. Next they lament Gunther, and Dietrich explains at length how he was obliged to subdue Gunther and turn him over to Kriemhild; he had no idea that she would have him killed. Etzel renews his lament and expresses his regret that no one informed him of the imminent hostilities. Hildebrand injects the view that Hagen bears the responsibility for the disaster and that Siegfried's killers prepared their own fate. Hagen is laid on a bier amid the curses of the people, but the poet explains that he would have abstained from battle if Blœdelin had not slain his brother Dankwart. (1,013–1,318)

Dietrich next finds the body of Volker of Alzey, and Hildebrand sings his praises. The scene repeats itself with Dankwart. Etzel in turn laments the death of Wolfbrant, and Dietrich laments Sigestab. The list is extended to include Wolfwin, son of Nere, who was slain by Giselher along with Nitger and Gerbart, and Wicnant, who was slain by Gunther along with Sigeher and Wichart. (1,319–1,576)

The bodies are now gathered in a hall and disarmed amidst continued mourning. Hildebrand finds his nephew Wolfhart slain by Giselher; both lie together. Hildebrand and Dietrich can hardly pry the sword loose from Wolfhart's hand. Dietrich speaks his eulogy, and both lament the passing of Giselher, so recently betrothed. He is deposited near Kriemhild. Next Gernot is discovered and praised; Etzel laments in particular that his son did not survive to inherit the good qualities of the Burgundians. (1,577–1,966)

When Rüdeger's body is found, Dietrich reminisces at length about the time his friend interceded to save him from Etzel's wrath [after Etzel's sons were killed at the battle of Ravenna, during Dietrich's attempt to regain his kingdom]. Etzel joins the lament for his faithful vassal. Dietrich solicits Etzel's care for Rüdeger's orphaned daughter. Hildebrand brings Rüdeger's lady to the hall, but, being wounded himself, collapses in the effort and must be revived. The mourning spreads to the people at large and is joined by many women from Helche's former retinue, a number of whom are identified. Dietrich has the three Burgundian kings placed in separate coffins. Etzel prepares coffins for his wife, son, and brother. The leading heroes are provided for similarly. (1,967–2,382)

The burials go on for three days, with many dead consigned to a common grave. Dietrich again tries to console Etzel for his losses. Hildebrand advises Dietrich that they should depart with Dietrich's wife Herrat, leaving all the clothes and weapons of the dead with Etzel. These are to be returned to the countries from which the warriors came, together with news of their deaths. Etzel dispatches a mission led by Swemmelin to Burgundy to inform Brünhild and Uote. Etzel urges the messengers to assure them that his invitation was issued in good faith. Dietrich instructs them not to divulge Rüdeger's death until they arrive in Pöchlarn. (2,383–2,708)

Swemmelin and his following set out and adhere carefully to Dietrich's instructions along the way. In Vienna they are entertained by a Duchess Isalde, who learns the truth and precipitates general mourning in the city. The messengers ride on to Traismauer and Pöchlarn. Their small number inspires Rüdeger's daughter [named Dietlind in the *Klage*] with foreboding, and she and her mother speak of their ominous dreams. Swemmelin at first deceives them with a series of misrepresentations, but the messengers finally cannot suppress their grief and the truth comes out. Gotelind and Dietlind fall in a swoon. Revived, they break into lamentations and learn the details of the tragedy from Swemmelin. (2,709–3,286)

Swemmelin now rides on to Passau, the seat of Bishop Pilgrim, uncle to the Burgundians. He makes the messengers welcome and learns the news. People and clergy mourn alike, and church services are held. Swemmelin reports in greater detail to Pilgrim, expressing the wish that Kriemhild had allowed Giselher and Gernot to live so that only Hagen might have paid the penalty for his deed. Pilgrim reinforces the idea that the Burgundians died for their own pride, because they did not restore Kriemhild's treasure to her. He also extracts a promise from Swemmelin to stop on his way back so that he can collect information for a written version of "the greatest event the world has ever seen." (3,287–3,484)

As they ride on through Bavaria, they cannot refrain from spreading the news. Count Else learns of it, and his grief is tempered by the knowledge that his brother [Gelpfrat] has been avenged, whatever the manner. In Worms Swemmelin appears before Brünhild and asks for permission to deliver his message in security. She assures him that messengers are sacred, and Swemmelin delivers Etzel's and Dietrich's greetings and an account of the terrible events. The lamentations recommence and spread the news to Uote at Lorsch. Wiser heads try to moderate Brünhild's grief, and Swemmelin recounts the order of events in greater detail. Mourning breaks out anew and Uote succumbs to her grief a week later. Brünhild reflects on her relations with Kriemhild. Eventually calm is restored and the people call for Gunther's son to be knighted and crowned. In a retrospective lament Rumold attributes the responsibility for the tragedy to Hagen's pride and exculpates Kriemhild and Siegfried. (3,485–4,099)

Swemmelin now returns to Hunland. Here Dietrich and Hildebrand take leave of Etzel and set out with Herrat. On the way they stop at Pöchlarn for a mournful reunion with Dietlind, since Gotelind has died in the meantime. Dietrich gives generous assurances of aid, and they part. Bishop Pilgrim, using the information provided by Swemmelin and others, has the whole story set down in Latin by his scribe Master Konrad. It has often been composed in German since then. The poet concludes by stating that he has no certain knowledge of Etzel's fate. (4,100–4,360)

Reference Matter

Abbreviations

The following abbreviations are used in the Notes and the Works Cited:

ABäG   *Amsterdamer Beiträge zur älteren Germanistik.*
ANF   *Arkiv för nordisk filologi.*
ATB   Altdeutsche Textbibliothek.
BGDSL   *Beiträge zur Geschichte der deutschen Sprache und Literatur.*
DMA   Dictionary of the Middle Ages. Ed. Joseph R. Strayer. 13 vols. New York, 1982–.
DVLG   *Deutsche Vierteljahrsschrift für Literaturwissenschaft und Geistesgeschichte.*
GLL   *German Life and Letters.*
GR   *Germanic Review.*
GRM   *Germanisch-romanische Monatsschrift.*
"Hohenemser Studien"   "Hohenemser Studien zum Nibelungenlied." In *Montfort: Vierteljahresschrift für Geschichte und Gegenwart Vorarlbergs*, 32 (1980), 181–381 [7–207].
ÍF   Íslenzk Fornrit.
JEGP   *Journal of English and Germanic Philology.*
JIG   *Jahrbuch für internationale Germanistik.*
MGH   Monumenta Germaniae Historica.
MHG   Middle High German.
MLG   Middle Low German.
MLR   *Modern Language Review.*
MScan   *Mediaeval Scandinavia.*
MTU   Münchener Texte und Untersuchungen zur deutschen Literatur des Mittelalters.
Nibelungenlied   Das Nibelungenlied. Ed. Helmut de Boor. 21st ptg. Rev. Roswitha Wisniewski. Wiesbaden, 1979.
OE   Old English.
ON   Old Norse.
OS   Old Saxon.
PLAC   Poetae Latini Aevi Carolini.

Rupp   *Nibelungenlied und Kudrun.* Ed. Heinz Rupp. Wege der Forschung, 54. Darmstadt, 1976.
Verfasserlexikon   Die deutsche Literatur des Mittelalters: Verfasserlexikon. Ed. Kurt Ruh. Vols. 1–. Berlin, 1978–.
WW   *Wirkendes Wort.*
ZDA   *Zeitschrift für deutsches Altertum und deutsche Literatur.*
ZDP   *Zeitschrift für deutsche Philologie.*
Þiðreks saga   Þiðriks saga af Bern. Ed. Henrik Bertelsen. Samfund til Udgivelse af Gammel Nordisk Litteratur, 34. 2 vols. Copenhagen, 1905–11.

Notes

Only the author's surname and an abbreviated form of the relevant title are supplied in the Notes. Complete references appear in the list of Works Cited, pp. 281–97.

Chapter 1

1. The classic survey of this material is Heusler, *Die altgermanische Dichtung*, pp. 150–200. The best modern survey is von See, *Germanische Heldensage*.

2. For a general evaluation of the *Hildebrandslied* and its analogues see Hatto, "On the Excellence of the 'Hildebrandslied.'"

3. For a survey of the problems connected with this text see Fry, *Finnsburh: Fragment and Episode*.

4. See *Hervarar saga*, ed. and trans. Tolkien, and von See, *Germanische Heldensage*, pp. 69–74.

5. Von See, *Germanische Heldensage*, pp. 68–69.

6. Paul the Deacon, *Historia Langobardorum*, ed. Bethmann and Waitz, 2.28 (pp. 87–89); trans. Foulke, pp. 81–83.

7. Jordanes, *Getica*, ed. Mommsen, pp. 90–91; trans. Mierow, p. 87.

8. This view is taken, for example, by Brady, *The Legends of Ermanaric*, p. 17, and von See, *Germanische Heldensage*, p. 62. Haug, "Andreas Heuslers Heldensagenmodell," derives the story not from history but from a literary stereotype serving to explain the fall of a nation on the basis of the ruler's moral failure.

9. I have argued this view in "Cassiodorus and the Gothic Legend of Ermanaric." Cf. *The Poetic Edda*, ed. Dronke, pp. 192–96, and Gschwantler, "Ermanrich, sein Selbstmord und die Hamdirsage."

10. The sources are conveniently summarized in Dronke's edition of *The Poetic Edda*, pp. 35–36.

11. The fullest Germanic commentary on *Germania* is Much, *Die Germania des Tacitus*. On Much's commentary and modern views of Tacitus' *Germania* in general see von See, "Der Germane als Barbar."

12. The best-known modern proponent of such heroic poetry is Höfler, *Siegfried, Arminius und die Symbolik*, p. 26. The idea is perpetuated in such books as Mackensen, *Die Nibelungen*, p. 39. Norden, *Die germanische Urgeschichte in Tacitus Germania*, pp. 273–74, believed that the reference implied poems but identified them as contemporary panegyric poems. Koestermann still maintains

the reality of these poems in *Cornelius Tacitus: Annalen*, 1:415, but Goodyear, *The Annals of Tacitus*, 2:448, is skeptical.

13. Reitzenstein, "Philologische Kleinigkeiten," p. 271. See also Münzer, "Zu dem Nachruf des Tacitus auf Arminius," p. 617.

14. See *The Fourth Book of the Chronicle of Fredegar*, ed. and trans. Wallace-Hadrill, p. 4.

15. Cassiodorus, *Variae*, ed. Mommsen, p. 239; trans. Hodgkin, pp. 353–54. The passage goes on to relate how Gensimundus surrendered his own claim to the throne in favor of the minor heirs of the Amali. The incident is referred to heroic poetry for example by Naumann, "Die Zeugnisse der antiken und frühmittelalterlichen Autoren zur germanischen Poesie," p. 271, and Heusler, *Die altgermanische Dichtung*, p. 152.

16. There are, for example, unrevealing references to Germanic *cantus* in Tacitus' *Annales* 1.65 and 4.47, and his *Historiae* 4.18 and 5.15. The key references from Ammianus, Julian the Apostate, Ausonius, Sidonius Apollinaris, Procopius, Gregory the Great, Bede, and so forth, have been collected and discussed, notably by Naumann, "Die Zeugnisse der antiken und frühmittelalterlichen Autoren zur germanischen Poesie" and *Frühgermanisches Dichterbuch*, and by Baesecke, *Vor- und Frühgeschichte des deutschen Schrifttums*, 1:77–95. Some of the examples are reviewed for English readers by Opland, *Anglo-Saxon Oral Poetry*, pp. 40–73.

17. Jordanes, *Getica*, ed. Mommsen, pp. 61, 65, 112–13, and 124; trans. Mierow, pp. 58, 62, 111, and 124.

18. Jordanes, *Getica*, ed. Mommsen, p. 104; trans. Mierow, p. 101.

19. See Gillespie, *A Catalogue of Persons Named in German Heroic Literature*, pp. 145–47 (s.v. Witege).

20. Paul the Deacon, *Historia Langobardorum*, ed. Bethmann and Waitz, 1.27 (p. 70); trans. Foulke, p. 52.

21. Altfrid, *Vita Sancti Liudgeri*, ed. Pertz, p. 412.

22. Alcuin, *Epistolae*, ed. Dümmler, p. 183.

23. Einhard, *Vita Karoli magni*, ed. Pertz p. 458.

24. Meissburger, "Zum sogenannten Heldenliederbuch Karls des Grossen." Meissburger based his view on a passage from the Poeta Saxo's *Annales de gestis Caroli magni imperatoris*, 5.117–20 (ed. von Winterfeld, p. 58) from about 890. The passage alleges "vulgaria carmina" celebrating Charlemagne's ancestors, although two of the six names mentioned belong to his successors, not his ancestors. Von See, *Germanische Heldensage*, p. 149, accepted Meissburger's view. Assuming a collection of heroic poems, von der Leyen, *Das Heldenliederbuch Karls des Grossen*, extrapolated from various sources the plots of twenty-five Gothic, Langobardic, Frankish, Burgundian, Thuringian, Anglian, Frisian, and Danish heroic lays that might have been included.

25. Theganus, *Vita Hludowici imperatoris*, ed. Pertz, p. 594.

26. Otfrid von Weissenburg, *Evangelienbuch*, ed. Erdmann, p. 4.

27. Harris has argued for a second heroic recitation, albeit of German origin, in "*Guðrúnarbrögð* and the Saxon Lay of Grimhild's Perfidy."

28. The episode is first reported in the so-called *Legendary Saga of St. Olaf* (*Olafs saga hins helga*, ed. Heinrichs et al., p. 183), from the beginning of the thirteenth century. Snorri Sturluson gives a fuller account in his version of the saga in *Heimskringla* (ed. Aðalbjarnarson, 2:361–62), from about 1230.

29. Olrik attempted an approximate reconstruction of the complete original in

The Heroic Legends of Denmark, pp. 66–150. Von See has expressed doubts about the age and authenticity of the incident at Stiklarstaðir in "Hastings, Stiklastaðir und Langemarck" and "Húskarla hvǫt."

30. The narrative is conveniently translated in Bury, *History of the Later Roman Empire*, 1:279–88.

31. Heusler, *Die altgermanische Dichtung*, p. 114, identified the singers as Goths, but E. A. Thompson, *A History of Attila and the Huns*, p. 216, sensibly argued that Attila was unlikely to have had his praises sung in a language other than his own.

32. Scholars have frequently entertained the idea that heroic poetry grew out of panegyric poetry, but it seems more likely that the two genres were quite distinct. See Heusler, *Die altgermanische Dichtung*, p. 156, and von See, *Germanische Heldensage*, pp. 83–95.

33. E. A. Thompson, *The Early Germans*.

34. Kuhn expressed doubts about Tacitus' meaning in "Die Grenzen der germanischen Gefolgschaft." See also von See, "Der Germane als Barbar," p. 57, but cf. Lindow, *Comitatus, Individual and Honor*, pp. 19–26.

35. Ihlenburg, "Die gesellschaftliche Grundlage des germanischen Heldene-thos."

Chapter 2

1. This chapter of German philology is reviewed by Hoffmann, *Das Nibelungenlied* (1982), pp. 7–12. An English account is provided by Thorp, *The Study of the Nibelungenlied*.

2. Heusler, *Lied und Epos*, esp. pp. 24–25.

3. In his article "Andreas Heuslers Heldensagenmodell," Haug criticizes Heusler's emphasis on the mechanics of the conversion from lay to epic and calls for more attention to the reconceptualization of epic, but this literary-historical viewpoint does not seem to me to be in conflict with Heusler's premises. Bäuml and Ward, "Zur mündlichen Überlieferung des Nibelungenliedes," replace Heusler's literary evolution with an oral evolution, but they do not discuss the nature of Heusler's evidence.

4. The proposals are conveniently summarized by Haymes, *Das mündliche Epos*. The standard work on Yugoslav epic is Lord, *The Singer of Tales*.

5. Magoun, "The Oral-Formulaic Character of Anglo-Saxon Narrative Poetry."

6. Benson, "The Literary Character of Anglo-Saxon Formulaic Poetry."

7. Heusler, *Lied und Epos*, pp. 51–52.

8. *Egils saga Skalla-Grímssonar*, ed. Nordal, p. 183.

9. Snorri Sturluson, *Heimskringla*, ed. Aðalbjarnarson, 2:361.

10. Saxo, *Gesta Danorum*, ed. Olrik and Ræder, 2.7.4–28 (pp. 53–61). The case for deliberative composition and memorial transmission has been made by Lönnroth, "Hjálmar's Death-Song," and Harris, "Eddic Poetry as Oral Poetry." More recently Walter Haug, "Mittelalterliche Epik," p. 2, assumes that the short heroic lay was composed on the oral-formulaic model.

11. Magoun, "Béowulf B: A Folk-Poem on Béowulf's Death," p. 128.

12. Haymes, *Mündliches Epos in mittelhochdeutscher Zeit*, pp. 2–3.

13. Niles, *Beowulf: The Poem and Its Tradition*, pp. 56–57.

14. Ibid., pp. 74–79.

15. Niles allows two and a half centuries for the growth of the epic form by

dating *Beowulf* in the second quarter of the tenth century (*Beowulf*, pp. 96–117), but such a late dating is very much in dispute. In general see *The Dating of Beowulf*, ed. Colin Chase. I adhere to an early date in "The Dating of *Beowulf*." See also Fulk, "Review Article: Dating *Beowulf* to the Viking Age."

16. Harris, "Die altenglische Heldendichtung," pp. 266–67.

17. Haymes, *Das mündliche Epos*, pp. 18–21.

18. Ibid., p. 20.

19. I propose this scenic morphology in "Tradition and Design in *Beowulf*."

20. See Heusler, *Die altgermanische Dichtung*, p. 194. A comparison of *Genesis A* to the original is facilitated by the arrangement of facing texts in A. N. Doane's edition of *Genesis A*.

21. Heusler, *Lied und Epos*, p. 5.

22. I have argued this development in *The Legend of Brynhild*, pp. 24–77, "The Lays in the Lacuna of *Codex Regius*," and "Beyond Epic and Romance: *Sigurðarkviða in meiri*." Sperberg-McQueen, "The Legendary Form of *Sigurðarkviða in Skamma*," opposes my chronology of the texts and argues that the composition of *Meiri* precedes that of *Skamma* (esp. pp. 35–40).

23. Ker, *Epic and Romance*, p. 155 (see also p. 92).

24. I carry out the comparison more fully in "Did the Poet of *Atlamál* Know *Atlaqviða*?"

25. See de Boor, "Die Bearbeitung m des Nibelungenliedes (Darmstädter Aventiurenverzeichnis)," p. 180.

Chapter 3

1. The text is printed in PLAC, 1:366–79. A facing German translation and useful background essays are provided by Beumann, Brunhölzl, and Winkelmann, *Karolus Magnus et Leo Papa*.

2. See Ebenbauer, *Carmen historicum*, pp. 101–49. The text is printed in PLAC, 2:4–79. A facing French translation is provided by E. Faral, *Ermold le noir*.

3. See Ebenbauer, *Carmen historicum*, pp. 150–74. The text is printed in PLAC, 4:79–121. A facing French translation is provided by Waquet, *Le Siège de Paris par les normands*.

4. See Ebenbauer, *Carmen historicum*, pp. 199–211. The text is printed in PLAC, 4:7–71.

5. The text is printed in PLAC, 4:24–83. A facing translation is provided in *Waltharius and Ruodlieb*, ed. and trans. Kratz. For literary assessments see Katscher, "Waltharius—Dichtung und Dichter," and Kratz, *Mocking Epic*.

6. The best English guide to these texts is Bostock, *A Handbook on Old High German Literature* (rev. 1976), pp. 168–83 and 190–212.

7. The only attempts at epic during this period were the biblical *Genesis* (ca. 1070) and *Exodus* (ca. 1120). For an extensive analysis of the latter in English see Green, *The Millstätter Exodus*. See also Ursula Hennig's articles "Altdeutsche Exodus" and "Altdeutsche Genesis" in the *Verfasserlexikon*, 2:276–84.

8. The report of such a recitation in Saxo Grammaticus' *Gesta Danorum* (13.6.7) is translated on pp. 252–55. See also Müllenhoff, "Zeugnisse und Excurse zur deutschen Heldensage," pp. 335–36. That such short poems were

still performed in the middle of the thirteenth century is shown by the famous heroic repertory of der Marner. See *Der Marner*, ed. Strauch, pp. 124–25.

9. The text is edited by M. Roediger in MGH: *Deutsche Chroniken*, 1:115–32. A facing German translation is provided in *Das Annolied*, ed. and trans. Nellmann. A thorough study of the *Annolied* in the context of eleventh-century historiography is Knab, *Das Annolied*. Knab favors a date between 1080 and 1085 (p. 122), but other critics have preferred a date after 1105. On the special regionalism of the *Annolied* compared to other histories of the period see Knab, pp. 85 and 92 in particular. See also Nellmann, "Annolied" in the *Verfasserlexikon*, 1:366–71.

10. On this apparent disproportion see Knab, *Das Annolied*, p. 93.

11. This commonplace can be traced to early Christian epic, for example Juvencus and Sedulius. See Juvencus, *Libri evangeliorum IIII*, ed. Marold, p. 2, and Sedulius, *Opera omnia*, ed. Huemer, pp. 16–17. For further examples: Huemer, *De Sedulii poetae vita et scriptis commentatio*, pp. 62–64. The same commonplace is echoed in the Carolingian period, for example in Otfrid's "Epistola ad Liutbertum" (*Otfrids Evangelienbuch*, ed. Erdmann, p. 4) and an anonymous *Vita Sancti Remacli*, ed. Mabillon in *Acta Sanctorum*, 2:489. The life of Remaclus was reworked in the same circle and along the same lines as the *Annolied* (Knab, *Das Annolied*, pp. 91–93). See MGH: *Scriptores*, vol. 7, ed. G. H. Pertz, pp. 180–89.

12. See Nellmann's edition of *Das Annolied*, pp. 75–76. Nellmann comments on the topos and understands the passage to refer to Germanic traditions. See also Eggers, *Deutsche Sprachgeschichte*, 2:90–91, Gillespie, "Spuren der Heldendichtung," pp. 237–38, and Haug, *Literaturtheorie*, p. 61.

13. On the background of the legend see Grau, *Der Gedanke der Herkunft*, Bollnow, "Die Herkunftssagen der germanischen Stämme," and Hachmann, *Die Goten und Skandinavien*, pp. 15–35.

14. The text is edited by E. Schröder in MGH: *Deutsche Chroniken*, 2:79–392. The standard treatise on the sources is Ohly, *Sage und Legende in der Kaiserchronik*. See also Gellinek, *Die deutsche Kaiserchronik* and "The German Emperors' Chronicle." On the dating discussion see Nellmann, "Kaiserchronik" in the *Verfasserlexikon*, 4:949–64.

15. The *Homilies* and *Recognitions* are edited by Rehm, *Die Pseudoklementinen*. An English translation is available in *The Ante-Nicene Fathers*, 8:75–211. For a summary see Perry, *The Ancient Romances*, pp. 285–93. On the relationship of the *Recognitiones* and *Vita* to the *Kaiserchronik* see Ohly, *Sage und Legende*, pp.74–84.

16. On the tale in general see Schlauch, *Chaucer's Constance and Accused Queens*. On the German versions see Baasch, *Die Crescentialegende*. Baasch reinforces the argument that the Crescentia tale existed in a prior version that was incorporated into the *Kaiserchronik*. On the relationship of the story to the version of the Siegfried legend in *Þiðreks saga* (translated on pp. 169–85 above), see Wild, *Sisibesage und Genovefalegende*.

17. Baasch, *Die Crescentialegende*, pp. 110–22.

18. See Ohly, *Sage und Legende*, p. 156.

19. See the edition of Frings and Schieb, *Die epischen Werke des Henric van Veldeken*, vol. 1.

20. The basic information on Heinrich von Veldeke is presented by Schieb,

Henric van Veldeken; Heinrich von Veldeke. For an English account see Sinnema, *Hendrik Van Veldeke.*

21. See *Die epischen Werke des Henric van Veldeken,* ed. Frings and Schieb, pp. xlii and xlvi–xlvii, but cf. L. Wolff and W. Schröder, "Heinrich von Veldeke" in the *Verfasserlexikon,* 3:906.

22. See the edition of Kinzel, *Lamprechts Alexander nach den drei Texten.* A modern German retelling of the *Strassburger Alexander* is provided in *Das Alexanderlied des Pfaffen Lamprecht,* ed. Ruttmann.

23. Fischer, *Die Alexanderliedkonzeption.*

24. See Urbanek, "Umfang und Intention von Lamprechts Alexanderlied."

25. The pertinent passages are reviewed by W. Schröder, "Zum Vanitas-Gedanken," esp. pp. 49–54. See also Fischer, *Die Alexanderliedkonzeption,* pp. 48 and 63.

26. On the medieval legend in general see Cary, *The Medieval Alexander,* and W. T. H. Jackson, "Alexander Romances" in *DMA,* 1:149–52.

27. For the text see *Das Rolandslied des Pfaffen Konrad,* ed. Wesle, rev. Wapnewski. A facing German translation is provided in *Das Rolandslied des Pfaffen Konrad,* ed. and trans. Kartschoke. On the dating see Kartschoke, *Die Datierung des deutschen Rolandsliedes.*

28. Kartschoke, *Die Datierung,* p. 165.

29. The classic exposition of crusade rhetoric in the *Rolandslied* is Wentzlaff-Eggebert, *Kreuzzugsdichtung des Mittelalters,* pp. 77–98. The effort to down-play this component by Ott-Meimberg, *Kreuzzugsepos oder Staatsroman?,* esp. pp. 51–62, does not seem to me convincing. On the crusade component in the *Song of Roland* see Kloocke, "Kreuzzugsideologie und Chansons de Geste."

30. A convenient edition with facing translation is *The Song of Roland,* ed. and trans. Brault.

31. For the French text see *Enéas: Texte critique,* ed. Salverda de Grave. For the German text see *Henric van Veldeken: Eneide,* ed. Schieb and Frings. An English translation with a very helpful introduction is *Eneas,* trans. Yunck.

32. On Virgil and Augustus see the elegant essay by Pöschl, "Virgil und Augustus."

33. See *Enéas,* ed. Salverda de Grave, pp. xxxvii–lxii.

34. In general see Schieb, *Henric van Veldeken: Heinrich von Veldeke,* pp. 49–58.

35. See van Dam, *Zur Vorgeschichte des höfischen Epos,* pp. 85–111, and L. Wolff and W. Schröder in the *Verfasserlexikon,* 3:899–918.

36. See for example the topical references to Almeria and Tortosa discussed by Kartschoke, *Die Datierung,* pp. 98–129.

37. Cf. the passages in *Enéas,* ed. Salverda de Grave, pp. 57 (vv. 1,520–26) and 335 (vv. 9,035–45).

38. The standard edition is *Þiðriks saga af Bern,* ed. Bertelsen. For a German translation see *Die Geschichte Thidreks von Bern,* trans. Erichsen.

39. Storm, *Sagnkredsene om Karl den store og Didrik af Bern*; Hempel, "Sächsische Nibelungendichtung und sächsischer Ursprung der Thidrikssaga." I have presented my view in "An Interpretation of *Þiðreks saga,*" but Thomas Klein maintains the view that *Þiðreks saga* was composed in Norway in his important study "Zur Þiðreks saga," esp. pp. 538–43.

40. See Droege, "Die Vorstufe unseres Nibelungenliedes," p. 203.

41. A popular German book by Heinz Ritter-Schaumburg, *Die Nibelungen*

zogen nordwärts, argues that the location is historical, but another popular book (Mackensen, *Die Nibelungen,* p. 197) rightly views the scene at Soest as a relocation based on regional pride. See also Hofmann, "'Attilas Schlangenturm' und der 'Niflungengarten' in Soest."

42. On the geography of *Þiðreks saga* see Holthausen, "Studien zur Thidrekssaga," and Paff, *The Geographical and Ethic Names in the Þiðriks Saga.*

43. For a survey of this question see Szklenar, "Die Jagdszene von Hocheppan—ein Zeugnis der Dietrichsage?" pp. 427–42 and notes.

44. See especially E. Schröder, "Die deutschen Alexander-Dichtungen des 12ten Jahrhunderts," pp. 83–86.

45. *Þiðriks saga af Bern,* ed. Bertelsen, 1:318, and *Lamprechts Alexander,* ed. Kinzel, pp. 50–53. See Gillespie, "Spuren der Heldendichtung," p. 39.

Chapter 4

1. Schneider, *Heldendichtung, Geistlichendichtung, Ritterdichtung.*

2. On the dating of Fredegar see Goffart, "The Fredegar Problem Reconsidered," esp. pp. 232–41, and Erikson, "The Problem of Authorship in the Chronicle of Fredegar."

3. *Chronicarum quae dicuntur Fredegarii scholastici libri IV,* ed. Krusch, 3.18 (pp. 99–100), and *Liber historiae Francorum,* ed. Krusch, 1.11–13 (pp. 253–59).

4. *Historia Langobardorum,* ed. Bethmann and Waitz, pp. 109–10; trans. Foulke, pp. 137–40.

5. Frings, "Die Entstehung der deutschen Spielmannsepen."

6. For translations of the skaldic stanzas and Snorri's account see Hollander, *The Skalds,* pp. 31–37.

7. See in particular Loomis, *Tristan and Isolt.*

8. Gallais, *Genèse du roman occidental.*

9. Frings and Braun, "Brautwerbung," and Geissler, *Brautwerbung in der Weltliteratur.* The general form had been outlined already by Baesecke, *Der Münchener Oswald,* pp. 266–72.

10. See *Þiðriks saga af Bern,* ed. Bertelsen, 1:8–22 ("Samson and Hildisvid"), 1:49–56 = 2:71–83 ("Osantrix and Oda"), 1:58–73 = 2:87–104 ("Attila and Erka"), 2:43–60 ("Herburt and Hild"), 2:109–20 ("Apollonius and Herborg"), and 2:147–55 ("Iron and Bolfriana"). These texts are translated on pp. 214–51 above.

11. *König Rother,* ed. Frings and Kuhnt; rev. Köppe-Benath. For an English translation see *King Rother,* trans. Lichtenstein. On the narrative structure of this and other minstrel epics see Benath, "Vergleichende Studien."

12. See de Vries's edition of *Rother,* pp. lxxviii–xciv, and Panzer, *Italische Normannen,* pp. 27–33. After the completion of my manuscript I learned of Thomas Klein's detailed study "Zur Þiðreks saga." Klein argues that Mb³ stands closer to the German original than Mb² and concludes that Mb³ and *König Rother* are both based on a common German original that is more faithfully reproduced in *Rother* (Klein, pp. 490–500).

13. See Baesecke, *Der Münchener Oswald,* p. 291; de Vries in *Rother,* pp. lxxxiii–lxxxix; Panzer, *Italische Normannen,* pp. 35–36; Klein, "Zur Þiðreks saga," pp. 495–500.

14. See Urbanek, *Kaiser, Grafen und Mäzene,* pp. 14–21.

15. Urbanek, *Kaiser, Grafen und Mäzene,* pp. 87–88; Meves, *Studien zu König Rother,* p. 71; Klein, "Zur Þiðreks saga," pp. 505–12.

16. On the discrepancies between the two parts see Meves, *Studien zu König Rother,* pp. 62–68.

17. Aimon de Varennes, *Florimont,* ed. Hilka.

18. *Dukus Horant,* ed. Ganz, Norman, and Schwarz.

19. On the reconstruction of the *version commune* see Bédier, *Le Roman de Tristan par Thomas,* and Álfrún Gunnlaugsdóttir, *Tristán en el norte.* On the relationship of Eilhart to the French original see Loomis, *Tristan and Isolt.* See also Delbouille, "Le Premier *Roman de Tristan.*" Delbouille argues for a date around 1165 for the original (pp. 433–35). H. Bussmann has edited the texts of Eilhart synoptically so that the twelfth-century fragments can be readily compared with the fifteenth-century versions in *Tristrant: Synoptischer Druck.* An English translation is *Eilhart von Oberge's Tristrant,* trans. Thomas.

20. The same alteration of the plot is found in "Herburt and Hild" in *Þiðreks saga* (pp. 241–44 above). On this story see Frings, "Herbort." A reconstruction of the "Brünhildenlied" is given on pp. 209–10 above.

21. See most recently U. Müller, "Das Nachleben der mittelalterlichen Stoffe," pp. 441–43.

22. See for example Frappier, *Chrétien de Troyes,* pp. 105–6, and Gallais, *Genèse du roman occidental,* pp. 60–64.

23. See for example the reading by Freeman, *The Poetics of translatio studii and conjointure,* pp. 112–34.

24. *Piramus et Tisbé* has been edited with a facing English translation by Cormier (*Three Ovidian Tales*). For the text of the Apollonius fragment see Schulze, "Ein Bruchstück des altfranzösischen Apolloniusromanes."

25. *Le Conte de Floire et Blancheflor,* ed. Leclanche; trans. Hubert, *The Romance of Floire and Blanchefleur.*

26. *Aucassin et Nicolette,* ed. Dufournet (with facing French translation); *Amadas et Ydoine,* ed. Reinhard; *Guillaume de Palerne,* ed. Michelant; Jean Renart, *L'Escoufle,* ed. Sweetser.

27. Urbanek, *Kaiser, Grafen und Mäzene,* pp. 190–215, makes a strong case for believing that the *Rother* poet did not make firsthand use of the *Kaiserchronik,* but he may well have known of its existence (p. 213).

28. Claude Luttrell dates Chrétien's work a decade later in *The Creation of the First Arthurian Romance.* On the traditional date of *Cligès* see pp. 33–46.

29. See *Salman und Morolf,* ed. Vogt, pp. cxii–cxiii, and Curschmann, *Der Münchener Oswald,* p. 100.

30. Curschmann, *Der Münchener Oswald,* esp. p. 83 and pp. 156–66. Hermann Schneider speculated that bridal-quest narrative was not written down in the thirteenth century because it could not meet the competition from other genres (*Die Gedichte und die Sage von Wolfdietrich,* p. 217). One reason bridal-quest epic was noncompetitive surely was that it was ideologically outdated.

31. See, for example, W. J. Schröder, *Spielmannsepik,* and Curschmann, "Spielmannsepik."

32. Bugge, *Helgedigtene,* pp. 218–317; trans. Schofield, pp. 234–348.

33. Heinzel, "Ueber die ostgothische Heldensage," pp. 83–84.

34. *Þiðriks saga,* ed. Bertelsen 2:111 (lines 10–11). This motif also found its way into *Oswald;* see Curschmann's ed., pp. 15–16 (vv. 315–22).

35. Mickel, "Theme and Narrative Structure in *Guillaume d'Angleterre,*" p. 64, note 1, observes an odd contradiction: "It is curious that the prevalent

opinion is against the text's authenticity, even though nearly all the evidence points to the contrary conclusion." A modern French translation of the text is *Guillaume d'Angleterre*, trans. Trotin.

36. Gautier d'Arras, *Oeuvres*, ed. Löseth. *Ille et Galeron* has also been edited by F. A. G. Cowper, and *Eracle* by G. Raynaud de Lage.

37. See Fourrier, *Le Courant réaliste*, pp. 257–75.

38. See Duby, *Le Chevalier, la femme et le prêtre*, p. 96.

39. See the survey by Boase, *The Origin and Meaning of Courtly Love*. For a brief orientation and bibliography see Diane Bornstein, "Courtly Love" in *DMA*, 3 : 668–74. See also Ferrante, "*Cortes'Amor* in Medieval Texts."

40. Duby's *Le Chevalier, la femme et le prêtre* has been translated by B. Bray as *The Knight, the Lady, and the Priest*.

41. Duby, *Medieval Marriage*, p. 13.

42. Köhler, "Der Roman in der Romania," p. 246.

43. Duby, *Medieval Marriage*, p. 79.

44. Hartmann's romances are conveniently printed with modern German retellings in Schwarz's edition, *Erec; Iwein. Iwein* has been edited with a facing English translation by P. M. McConeghy.

45. There are English translations of Wolfram's *Parzival* by Mustard and Passage (*Parzival: A Romance of the Middle Ages*) and Hatto (*Parzival*).

Chapter 5

1. Dürrenmatt, *Das Nibelungenlied im Kreis der höfischen Dichtung*.

2. In Bräuer's *Literatursoziologie und epische Struktur* there is some comparison of the *Nibelungenlied* with bridal-quest epic in the course of the author's sifting of evidence for the municipal roots of Middle High German epic. Hugo Kuhn compared the structure of the *Nibelungenlied* and *Tristan* briefly in "Tristan, Nibelungenlied, Artusstruktur."

3. On the bridging of Parts I and II in the *Nibelungenlied* see Richter, "Beiträge zur Deutung des Mittelteils des Nibelungenliedes," and Wachinger, *Studien zum Nibelungenlied*, pp. 116–27.

4. On the hearsay motif see Reuschel, "Saga und Wikinglied," esp. pp. 333–45.

5. Friese, *Thidrekssaga und Dietrichepos*, p. 42, notes four occurrences of the stereotype in *Þiðreks saga* alone.

6. Kriemhild's role as secluded princess has perhaps most in common with the role of Romadanaple in the Old French *Florimont*.

7. See Heinrich von Veldeke's *Eneide*, vv. 9,749–900.

8. This narrative sequence has been the subject of endless debate. See for example Falk, *Das Nibelungenlied in seiner Epoche*, pp. 40–45 and references.

9. This motif recurs not only in Aimon's *Florimont* but also in *König Rother*, vv. 1,804–32.

10. On the positive side see Panzer, *Das Nibelungenlied*, pp. 289–91, and Nagel, *Das Nibelungenlied*, p. 51. Curschmann was more skeptical in "Spielmannsepik," p. 600. For verbal parallels see particularly Mohr's review of Kralik, *Die Sigfridtrilogie*, pp. 113–16. Possible parallels to the *Nibelungenlied* may also be found in *Orendel*, ed. W. J. Schröder, vv. 876–81 and 1,440–1,500.

11. See especially Wachinger, *Studien zum Nibelungenlied*, pp. 128–30.

12. The fullest biographical argument is presented by W. Schröder, "Die Tragödie Kriemhilts im Nibelungenlied."

13. Ihlenburg, *Das Nibelungenlied: Problem und Gehalt*.

274 Notes to Pages 93–103

14. On Kriemhild in redaction C see in particular Hoffmann, "Die Fassung *C des Nibelungenliedes," pp. 126–29. For various medieval assessments of Kriemhild's character see Grimm, *Deutsche Heldensage*, pp. 124, 158, 181, 187, 314, 361, 477, and Gillespie, "'Die Klage' as a Commentary on 'Das Nibelungenlied,'" pp. 157–58.

15. Heusler, *Nibelungensage und Nibelungenlied*, p. 29.

16. Jordan, *Heinrich der Löwe*, pp. 188–91.

17. See Voorwinden, "Nibelungenklage und Nibelungenlied," p. 284 (110) and note 60.

18. See Lunzer, "Kleine Nibelungenstudien," pp. 225–37, and Panzer, *Das Nibelungenlied*, p. 320. Eis's caveats in "Die angebliche Bayernfeindlichkeit des Nibelungendichters" do not seem convincing to me.

19. See Weller, "Die Nibelungenstrasse."

20. Heusler, *Nibelungensage und Nibelungenlied*, p. 44.

21. Meves, *Studien zu König Rother*, pp. 45–54. The English reader may survey the background in Pacaut, *Frederick Barbarossa*, esp. pp. 70, 112, and 121–22.

22. Urbanek, *Kaiser, Grafen und Mäzene*. See also Meves, *Studien zu König Rother*, pp. 63–99.

23. Urbanek, *Kaiser, Grafen und Mäzene*, pp. 73–82.

24. See Jordan, *Heinrich der Löwe*, p. 163, and Birkhan, "Zur Entstehung und Absicht des Nibelungenliedes," p. 10.

25. Ihlenburg, *Das Nibelungenlied: Problem und Gehalt*.

26. The pattern is explored from Homer to the *Nibelungenlied* by W. T. H. Jackson, *The Hero and the King*. See also Liberman's "Introduction" to Propp, *Theory and History of Folklore*, p. lxxii. It might be added that the Icelandic *Egils saga*, written twenty to forty years after the *Nibelungenlied*, is preoccupied with the same sort of political strain.

27. Panzer, "Nibelungische Problematik," p. 7.

28. On the Frankish name Siegfried see de Boor, "Hat Siegfried gelebt?"

29. On the Pilgrim stanzas see Hempel, "Pilgerin und die Altersschichten des Nibelungenliedes," Münz, "Zu den Passauer Strophen und der Verfasserfrage des Nibelungenliedes," and W. Hoffmann, *Das Nibelungenlied*, pp. 123–26.

30. Kralik, *Wer war der Dichter des Nibelungenliedes?* Oral forms of the lecture were delivered in November of 1950 and May of 1951.

31. Birkhan, "Zur Entstehung und Absicht des Nibelungenliedes," p. 16, doubts that Leopold would have been flattered by an identification with a mere vassal.

32. See the critique by Meves, "Bischof Wolfger von Passau."

33. Similarities in phrasing were collected by Kettner, *Die österreichische Nibelungendichtung*, pp. 4–45.

34. See Heusler, "Die Lieder der Lücke im Codex Regius der Edda," pp. 258–59, and *Lied und Epos*, pp. 8–13.

35. Heusler began his book *Nibelungensage und Nibelungenlied* with an approving reference to the manuscript heading. See also W. Schröder, "Die Tragödie Kriemhilts," p. 48, and Neumann, *Das Nibelungenlied in seiner Zeit*, p. 120.

36. Gillespie, "Spuren der Heldendichtung," p. 239.

37. Ott-Meimberg, *Kreuzzugsepos oder Staatsroman?*, pp. 108–63, esp. 112, 130, and 134.

38. Chrétien de Troyes, *Cligés*, ed. Micha, p. 1.

Chapter 6

1. I have reviewed their work in *The Legend of Brynhild.*
2. Heusler, "Die Lieder der Lücke," and Kralik, *Die Sigfridtrilogie.*
3. See for example Haug, "Normatives Modell oder hermeneutisches Experiment," p. 212 (38) and note 2.
4. Wilmanns, "Der Untergang der Nibelunge in alter Sage und Dichtung."
5. Panzer, *Studien zum Nibelungenliede*, pp. 109–78.
6. Schneider, "Forschungsbericht: Die Quellen des Nibelungenliedes"; Lohse, "Die Beziehungen zwischen der Thidrekssaga und den Handschriften des Nibelungenliedes"; Wisniewski, *Die Darstellung des Niflungenunterganges.* Lohse showed that the variant readings in *Þiðreks saga* cannot be reconciled with any known redaction of the *Nibelungenlied* and must therefore reflect an anterior redaction. Wisniewski noted in particular (p. 20) that the *Nibelungenlied* poet regularly elaborates a scene as it stands in *Þiðreks saga*, and that some scenes in the saga are missing at equivalent points in the *Nibelungenlied* but appear as fragments scattered in other passages; such scenes must be derived from the source and cannot be invented by the saga writer. Hoffmann, *Das Nibelungenlied*, pp. 53–54, has lent support to Wisniewski's book.
7. Hoffmann, *Das Nibelungenlied*, pp. 38–67 (on Panzer, see p. 54). It should be noted, however, that Panzer's view persists as recently as 1984 in U. Schulze's "Nibelungen und Kudrun," p. 128.
8. MGH: Auctores Antiquissimi, vol. 9: *Chronica minora saeculorum IV, V, VI, VII*, vol. 1, ed. Theodor Mommsen (Berlin, 1892), p. 475.
9. MGH: Leges Nationum Germanicarum, vol. 2, pt. 1: *Leges Burgundionum*, ed. Ludwig Rudolf von Salis (Hannover, 1892), p. 43.
10. See Noreen, *Altisländische und altnorwegische Grammatik*, par. 127[b], note (p. 97). The name Gibeche is used for one of Etzel's tributary kings in the *Nibelungenlied* (stanzas 1,343, 1,352, and 1,880).
11. See especially the Poeta Saxo, *Annales de gestis Caroli Magni imperatoris*, Bk. 3, vv. 25–39, in PLAC, 4:31–32.
12. On dating see Harris, "Eddic Poetry," pp. 93–111. On West Germanic traces in Eddic poetry see Kuhn, "Zur Wortstellung und -betonung im Altgermanischen," "Die Negation des Verbs in der altnordischen Dichtung," and "Westgermanisches in der altnordischen Verskunst."
13. The case for an early date around 900 was made by Genzmer, "Der Dichter der Atlakviða," and supplemented by Reichardt, "Der Dichter der Atlakviða." Genzmer's arguments were criticized by Dronke in her edition of *The Poetic Edda* (1:42–43). Despite her reservations she too favored an early date (1:44).
14. I have argued the details in "*Niflunga saga* in the Light of German and Danish Materials" and "Did the Poet of *Atlamál* Know *Atlaqviða?*"
15. I have argued for this reconstruction in "*Niflunga saga* in the Light of German and Danish Materials."
16. Saxo, *Gesta Danorum*, ed. Olrik and Ræder, 1:355 (13.6.7). For a translation of the episode see pp. 252–55 above.
17. Schneider, *Germanische Heldensage*, 1:214–38; Stephens, "An Examination of the Sources of the Thidrikssaga," pp. 124–71; Zink, *Les Légendes héroïques de Dietrich et d'Ermrich*, pp. 64–131.
18. I deviate from Schneider by including the encounter with Else and Amelung.

My reasons are given in "The Encounter between Burgundians and Bavarians."

19. See Hungerland, "Zeugnisse zur Vǫlsungen- und Niflungensage aus der Skaldendichtung," and Harris, "Eddic Poetry," pp. 88–89.

20. I have argued the details of my view in *The Legend of Brynhild,* esp. pp. 24–77. Cf. Sperberg-McQueen, "The Legendary Form of *Sigurðarkviða in skamma.*"

21. There is a facing English translation of *Vǫlsunga saga* in *The Saga of the Volsungs,* ed. and trans. Finch.

22. The classic analysis of the problem was made by Heusler in "Die Lieder der Lücke im Codex Regius der Edda." I have reviewed his findings in "The Lays in the Lacuna of *Codex Regius*" and arrive at only marginally different conclusions.

23. Heusler, "Die Lieder der Lücke," p. 266.

24. The synopsis follows my analysis of Heusler in *The Legend of Brynhild,* pp. 26–27.

25. Most recently Heinrichs argued in "Über das Alter und die deutsche Vorlage des Bruchstücks vom sogenannten alten Sigurdlied" that *Forna* implies Gudrun's revenge for Sigurd's death and therefore presupposes the late German version of the story.

26. De Vries, *Altnordische Literaturgeschichte,* 1:301–2.

27. The following is based on my reconstruction of *Sigurðarkviða in meiri* in *The Legend of Brynhild,* pp. 36–70.

28. My arguments for this reconstruction are provided in *The Legend of Brynhild,* pp. 151–204. On *Das Lied vom Hürnen Seyfrid* see Hoffmann, *Mittelhochdeutsche Heldendichtung,* pp. 95–107.

29. The shared phrasing of "Niflunga saga" and the *Nibelungenlied* may be surveyed in Lohse's "Die Beziehungen zwischen der Thidrekssaga und den Handschriften des Nibelungenliedes." See also Draeger, *Die Bindungs- und Gliederungsverhältnisse der Strophen des Nibelungenliedes,* pp. 51–53, and my "The Epic Source of Niflunga saga and the Nibelungenlied."

30. On memorial transmission in Germany see Heinzle, *Mittelhochdeutsche Dietrichepik,* pp. 79–92.

31. Heusler, "Die Quelle der Brünhildsage in Thidreks saga und Nibelungenlied," p. 85.

32. Ibid., p. 86.

33. The translation of the last half line has been disputed; it could also mean "he knew how to kill." See my references in *The Legend of Brynhild,* p. 31, note 15.

34. See Heinrichs, "Über das Alter und die deutsche Vorlage des Bruchstücks vom sogenannten alten Sigurdlied," and my discussion in *The Legend of Brynhild,* pp. 31 (note 14), 45, 48–53, and 68.

35. Von See argued that the wall of flame was a late Norse borrowing from the Eddic poem *Skírnismál.* See "Die Werbung um Brünhild," esp. pp. 209–13.

Chapter 7

1. On compositional schemes in the *Nibelungenlied* see for example Maurer, "Die Formkunst des Dichters unseres Nibelungenlieds"; Wachinger, *Studien zum Nibelungenlied,* pp. 56–102; Nagel, *Das Nibelungenlied,* pp. 97–136 (review of earlier proposals on pp. 97–101). An interesting analysis of smaller narrative units is provided by Fenik, *Homer and the Nibelungenlied.*

2. Hoffmann, "Zur Situation der gegenwärtigen Nibelungenforschung," pp. 85–87.

3. On this passage see Panzer, "Nibelungische Problematik," p. 22.

4. On the interpretation of this passage see Hans Kuhn, "Der Teufel im Nibelungenlied," and W. Schröder, "Zum Problem der Hortfrage im Nibelungenlied."

5. I have traced the theme of nocturnal combat in "The Discovery of Darkness in Northern Literature."

6. On the symbolism of his gesture see Wynn, "Hagen's Defiance of Kriemhilt."

7. I have altered the punctuation given in the edition of Bartsch, de Boor, and Wisniewski (*Nibelungenlied*, p. 284).

8. Dürrenmatt, *Das Nibelungenlied im Kreis der höfischen Dichtung*, p. 178.

9. It should be noted that he never concealed the deed. The lie that brigands killed Siegfried is concocted by unidentified retainers (stanza 1,000), and when Kriemhild confronts Hagen, it is Gunther who denies the deed (stanza 1,045).

10. Wapnewski, "Rüdigers Schild."

11. Ibid., p. 397; rpt. p. 159.

12. Heusler, "Die deutsche Quelle der Ballade von Kremolds Rache," esp. pp. 111 and 128.

13. Wapnewski, "Rüdigers Schild," p. 407; rpt. p. 174.

14. See Masser, "Von Alternativstrophen und Vortragsvarianten im *Nibelungenlied*," p. 304 (130): "die als Boten vorgesehenen Spielleute eilen kaum mitten in der Nacht ins königliche Schlafgemach, *dâ der künec saz* (!) *bî der küneginne.*"

15. See Neumann, *Das Nibelungenlied in seiner Zeit*, p. 103 and note 50.

16. Heusler, "Die Quelle der Brünhildsage," rpt. p. 85.

17. On the possibility that Part II was composed first see Droege, "Zur Geschichte des Nibelungenliedes," p. 500; Richter, "Beiträge zur Deutung des Mittelteils des Nibelungenliedes," p. 11; Krausse, "Die Darstellung von Siegfrieds Tod," pp. 375–76.

18. De Boor, "Die Bearbeitung m des Nibelungenliedes," p. 180.

19. The comparison is carried out fully by Nagel, *Das Nibelungenlied*, pp. 121–23.

20. On this passage see Wailes, "Bedroom Comedy in the Nibelungenlied."

21. See Reichert, "Zum Sigrdrífa-Brünhild-Problem," pp. 251–52.

22. See Sayce, "Abortive Motivation in Part I of the *Nibelungenlied*." I have reviewed various solutions to the problem in "Why Does Siegfried Die?"

23. The best analysis of the problem is by Wachinger, *Studien zum Nibelungenlied*, pp. 116–27.

Chapter 8

1. Dürrenmatt, *Das Nibelungenlied im Kreis der höfischen Dichtung*; Panzer, *Studien zum Nibelungenliede*.

2. Heusler, "Die Lieder der Lücke im Codex Regius" and *Die altgermanische Dichtung*, 2d rev. ed.

3. See note 6 to Chapter 6.

4. Compare Dürrenmatt, p. 7, with Panzer, *Studien zum Nibelungenliede*, p. 3, and *Das Nibelungenlied*, pp. 11–13.

5. Mergell, "Nibelungenlied und höfischer Roman." On Dürrenmatt see pp. 5–6.

6. Mergell bases his view of Hagen on stanza 2,371, but cf. W. J. Schröder, "Das Nibelungenlied: Versuch einer Deutung," p. 125, note 1; rpt. p. 127, note 1. Also Gentry, "Trends in 'Nibelungenlied' Research since 1949," p. 128.

7. W. J. Schröder, "Das Nibelungenlied," p. 58; rpt. p. 60.

8. Heusler, Nibelungensage und Nibelungenlied, p. 58: "Heroische Geschichten bequemen sich ungern einem lehrhaften Leitsatz."

9. W. Schröder, "Die Tragödie Kriemhilts," pp. 41–43; rpt. pp. 49–51.

10. Tonnelat, La Chanson des Nibelungen.

11. Maurer, Leid.

12. Ibid., pp. 21 and 31.

13. W. Schröder, "Die Tragödie" rpt. pp. 73, 80, 86, 93, 98–99, 149.

14. Bostock, "The Message of the 'Nibelungenlied.'"

15. On the often meaningless use of übermuot in the Nibelungenlied see Wachinger, Studien zum Nibelungenlied, p. 105, and Sacker, "On Irony and Symbolism," pp. 271–72.

16. Mowatt, "Studies towards an Interpretation of the 'Nibelungenlied.'"

17. Sacker, "On Irony and Symbolism."

18. In general see Hoffmann's just assessment of the Anglo-American contributions in "Die englische und amerikanische Nibelungenforschung 1959–62."

19. Panzer, Das Nibelungenlied: Entstehung und Gestalt.

20. Menéndez Pidal, La Chanson de Roland y el neotradicionalismo.

21. Wachinger, Studien zum Nibelungenlied.

22. Weber, Das Nibelungenlied: Problem und Idee.

23. A similar suggestion had already been made by W. J. Schröder, "Das Nibelungenlied: Versuch einer Deutung," pp. 142–43; rpt. pp. 144–45.

24. Nagel, "Zur Interpretation und Wertung des Nibelungenliedes."

25. Nagel, Das Nibelungenlied: Stoff—Form—Ethos.

26. Ibid., e.g., pp. 81, 97, 118, 128.

27. Representative of this aftermath are Mowatt and Sacker, The Nibelungenlied: An Interpretative Commentary; Bekker, The Nibelungenlied: A Literary Analysis; Gentry, Triuwe and vriunt in the Nibelungenlied. It might be noted, however, that Mowatt's and Sacker's Commentary grew out of their articles from 1961 and that Bekker's book built on articles from 1966 and 1967: "Kingship in the Nibelungenlied" and "The 'Eigenmann'-Motif in the Nibelungenlied."

28. Von See, "Die Werbung um Brünhild" and "Freierprobe und Königinnenzank."

29. Bumke, "Sigfrids Fahrt ins Nibelungenland"; "Die Eberjagd im Daurel und in der Nibelungendichtung"; "Die Quellen der Brünhildfabel im Nibelungenlied."

30. Wapnewski, "Rüdigers Schild."

31. Lohse, "Die Beziehungen zwischen der Thidrekssaga und den Handschriften des Nibelungenliedes"; Wisniewski, Die Darstellung des Niflungenunterganges in der Thidrekssaga.

32. Hoffmann, Das Nibelungenlied, p. 54.

33. King, "The Message of the 'Nibelungenlied.'"

34. Neumann, Das Nibelungenlied in seiner Zeit.

35. Neumann, "Schichten der Ethik im Nibelungenliede." Cf. Nagel's essay "Stoffzwang der Überlieferung in mittelhochdeutscher Dichtung."

36. Heusler, Nibelungensage und Nibelungenlied, p. 57; Neumann, Das Nibelungenlied in seiner Zeit, p. 29.

37. Neumann, Das Nibelungenlied in seiner Zeit, pp. 65–105 and 109–21.

38. Falk, *Das Nibelungenlied in seiner Epoche*, p. 20.
39. A briefer example of the "crime and punishment hypothesis" from this period is Wisniewski's "Das Versagen des Königs." Wisniewski concentrates on the disastrous consequences of Gunther's weakness, which she places in the context of medieval *speculum regale* literature.
40. Beyschlag, "Das Motiv der Macht bei Siegfrieds Tod."
41. Szövérffy, "Das Nibelungenlied: Strukturelle Beobachtungen und Zeitgeschichte."
42. Ihlenburg, *Das Nibelungenlied: Problem und Gehalt.*
43. Müller, "Sivrit: *künec—man—eigenholt.*" Müller criticizes Ihlenburg on p. 116.
44. Birkhan, "Zur Entstehung und Absicht des Nibelungenliedes."
45. Konecny, "Das Sozialgefüge am Burgundenhof." A more likely source for Sigemund's abdication would seem to be King Latinus' abdication in favor of Aeneas in Veldeke's *Eneide*, vv. 13,287–91.
46. Czerwinski, "Das Nibelungenlied: Widersprüche höfischer Gewaltreglementierung."
47. Kaiser, "Deutsche Heldenepik."
48. "Hohenemser Studien zum Nibelungenlied" in *Montfort: Vierteljahresschrift für Geschichte und Gegenwart Vorarlbergs*, 32 (1980), 181–381 (7–207).
49. Hennig, "Herr und Mann: Zur Ständegliederung im Nibelungenlied."
50. For earlier reactions to the oral-formulaic theory in Germany see Fromm, "Der oder die Dichter des Nibelungenliedes?"; W. Hoffmann, *Mittelhochdeutsche Heldendichtung*, pp. 53–59; Heinzle, *Mittelhochdeutsche Dietrichepik*, pp. 67–92; von See, "Was ist Heldendichtung?," esp. rpt. pp. 168–76.
51. Curschmann, "'Nibelungenlied' und 'Nibelungenklage'"; Voorwinden, "Nibelungenklage und Nibelungenlied."
52. Wachinger, "Die 'Klage' und das Nibelungenlied."
53. Masser, "Von Alternativstrophen und Vortragsvarianten im Nibelungenlied."
54. Stein, "Orendel 1512: Probleme und Möglichkeiten der Anwendung der *theory of oral-formulaic poetry* bei der literaturhistorischen Interpretation eines mittelhochdeutschen Textes."
55. Bäuml and Ward, "Zur mündlichen Überlieferung des Nibelungenliedes," and Bäuml, "Zum Verständnis mittelalterlicher Mitteilungen." Since the writing of this report Bäuml has contributed a further article, "Medieval Texts and the Two Theories of Oral-Formulaic Composition."
56. For a history and critique of the oral-formulaic theory as applied to the *Nibelungenlied* see Sperberg-McQueen, "An Analysis of Recent Work on *Nibelungenlied* Poetics."
57. Hoffmann, "Das Nibelungenlied in der Literaturgeschichtsschreibung von Gervinus bis Bertau."
58. Haug, "Normatives Modell oder hermeneutisches Experiment."
59. Wolf, "Die Verschriftlichung der Nibelungensage und die französisch-deutschen Literaturbeziehungen im Mittelalter."
60. Meves, "Bischof Wolfger von Passau, *sîn schrîber, meister Kuonrât* und die Nibelungenüberlieferung."
61. Ehrismann, "Archaisches und Modernes im Nibelungenlied: Pathos und Abwehr."

62. Hoffmann, *Heldendichtung II: Nibelungenlied* (1961; rpt. 1964 and 1968; rev. 1974).

63. A similar shift away from the *Nibelungenlied* as sole arbiter of the tradition and toward greater consideration of other testimony is apparent in Nagel's essay "Noch einmal Nibelungenlied." The same trend is visible in the Anglo-Saxon world in Hatto's "Medieval German" in *Traditions of Heroic and Epic Poetry*, 1 : 177, where he writes, "But it seems to the present writer that studies of Nibelung tradition which assume Heusler's theories to be passé, condemn themselves to swift oblivion."

64. Urbanek, *Kaiser, Grafen und Mäzene im König Rother*, pp. 73–82.

Works Cited

Abbo of St. Germain. *Bella Parisiacae urbis*. Ed. Paul von Winterfeld. PLAC, 4:79–121. Berlin, 1899; rpt. 1964.

———. *Le Siège de Paris par les normands*. Ed. and trans. Henri Waquet. Paris, 1942.

Aimon de Varennes. *Florimont: Ein altfranzösischer Abenteuerroman*. Ed. Alfons Hilka. Gesellschaft für Romanische Literatur, 48. Göttingen, 1932.

Alcuin. *Epistolae*. Ed. Ernst Dümmler. MGH: *Epistolae Karolini aevi*, vol. 2. Berlin, 1895.

Álfrún Gunnlaugsdóttir. See Gunnlaugsdóttir.

Altfrid. *Vita Sancti Liudgeri*. Ed. Georg Heinrich Pertz. MGH: *Scriptores*, vol. 2. Hannover, 1829.

Amadas et Ydoine: Roman du XIIIᵉ siècle. Ed. John R. Reinhard. Les Classiques français du moyen âge, 51. Paris, 1926.

Andersson, Theodore M. "Beyond Epic and Romance: *Sigurðarkviða in meiri*." In *Sagnaskemmtun: Studies in Honour of Hermann Pálsson on His 65th Birthday, 26th May 1986*, ed. Rudolf Simek, Jónas Kristjánsson, and Hans Bekker-Nielsen, pp. 1–11. Vienna, 1986.

———. "Cassiodorus and the Gothic Legend of Ermanaric." *Euphorion*, 57 (1963), 28–43.

———. "The Dating of *Beowulf*." *University of Toronto Quarterly*, 52 (1983), 288–301.

———. "Did the Poet of *Atlamál* Know *Atlaqviða*?" In *Edda: A Collection of Essays*, ed. Robert J. Glendinning and Haraldur Bessason, pp. 243–57. Univ. of Manitoba Icelandic Studies, 4. N.p., 1983.

———. "The Discovery of Darkness in Northern Literature." In *Old English Studies in Honour of John C. Pope*, ed. Robert B. Burlin and Edward B. Irving, Jr., pp. 1–14. Toronto, 1974.

———. "The Encounter Between Burgundians and Bavarians in Adventure 26 of the *Nibelungenlied*." *JEGP*, 82 (1983), 365–73.

———. "The Epic Source of Niflunga saga and the Nibelungenlied." *ANF*, 88 (1973), 1–54.

———. "An Interpretation of *Þiðreks saga*." In *Structure and Meaning in Old Norse Literature: New Approaches to Textual Analysis and Literary Criticism of Edda and Saga Narrative*, ed. John Lindow, Lars Lönnroth, and Gerd Wolfgang Weber. The Viking Collection: Studies in Northern Civilization, 4. Odense, 1986.

————. "The Lays in the Lacuna of *Codex Regius.*" In *Speculum Norroenum: Norse Studies in Memory of Gabriel Turville-Petre*, ed. Ursula Dronke, Guðrún P. Helgadóttir, Gerd Wolfgang Weber, and Hans Bekker-Nielsen, pp. 6–26. Odense, 1981.

————. *The Legend of Brynhild.* Islandica, 43. Ithaca, 1980.

————. "*Niflunga saga* in the Light of German and Danish Materials." *MScan*, 7 (1974), 22–30.

————. "Tradition and Design in *Beowulf.*" In *Old English Literature in Context: Ten Essays*, ed. John D. Niles, pp. 90–105. Cambridge, Eng., 1980.

————. "Why Does Siegfried Die?" In *Germanic Studies in Honor of Otto Springer*, ed. Stephen J. Kaplowitt, pp. 29–39. Pittsburgh, 1978.

Annolied. Ed. Max Roediger. MGH: *Deutsche Chroniken und andere Geschichtsbücher des Mittelalters*, 1:115–32. Hannover, 1895.

————. Ed. and trans. Eberhard Nellmann. Stuttgart, 1975; rev. 1979.

Aucassin et Nicolette. Ed. and trans. Jean Dufournet. [Paris, 1973].

Baasch, Karen. *Die Crescentialegende in der deutschen Dichtung des Mittelalters.* Germanistische Abhandlungen, 20. Stuttgart, 1968.

Baesecke, Georg. *Der Münchener Oswald: Text und Abhandlung.* Germanistische Abhandlungen, 28. Breslau, 1907.

————. *Vor- und Frühgeschichte des deutschen Schrifttums.* Vol. 1: *Vorgeschichte.* Halle, 1940.

Bäuml, Franz H. "Medieval Texts and the Two Theories of Oral-Formulaic Composition: A Proposal for a Third Theory." *New Literary History*, 16 (1984), 31–49.

————. "Zum Verständnis mittelalterlicher Mitteilungen." In the "Hohenemser Studien," pp. 288–98 [114–24].

Bäuml, Franz H., and Donald J. Ward. "Zur mündlichen Überlieferung des Nibelungenliedes." *DVLG*, 41 (1967), 351–90.

Bédier, Joseph. *Le Roman de Tristan par Thomas: Poème du XIIe siècle.* 2 vols. Paris, 1902–5.

Bekker, Hugo. "The 'Eigenmann'-Motif in the *Nibelungenlied.*" *GR*, 42 (1967), 5–15.

————. "Kingship in the *Nibelungenlied.*" *GR*, 41 (1966), 251–63.

————. *The Nibelungenlied: A Literary Analysis.* Toronto, 1971.

Benath, Ingeborg. "Vergleichende Studien zu den Spielmannsepen König Rother, Orendel und Salman und Morolf." *BGDSL* (Halle), 84 (1962), 312–72, and 85 (1963), 374–416.

Benson, Larry D. "The Literary Character of Anglo-Saxon Formulaic Poetry." *PMLA*, 81 (1966), 334–41.

Beumann, Helmut, Franz Brunhölzl, and Wilhelm Winkelmann. *Karolus magnus et Leo papa: Ein Paderborner Epos vom Jahre 799.* Paderborn, 1966.

Beyschlag, Siegfried. "Das Motiv der Macht bei Siegfrieds Tod." *GRM*, 33 (1952), 95–108. Rpt. in *Zur germanisch-deutschen Heldensage: Sechzehn Aufsätze zum neuen Forschungsstand*, ed. Karl Hauck, pp. 195–213. Wege der Forschung, 14. Darmstadt, 1965.

Birkhan, Helmut. "Zur Entstehung und Absicht des Nibelungenliedes." In *Österreichische Literatur zur Zeit der Babenberger: Vorträge der Lilienfelder Tagung 1976*, ed. Alfred Ebenbauer, Fritz Peter Knapp, and Ingrid Strasser, pp. 1–24. Vienna, 1977.

Boase, Roger. *The Origin and Meaning of Courtly Love: A Critical Study of European Scholarship.* Manchester, 1977.

Bollnow, Hermann. "Die Herkunftssagen der germanischen Stämme als Geschichtsquelle." *Baltische Studien*, 54 (1968), 14–25.

Boor, Helmut de. "Die Bearbeitung m des Nibelungenliedes (Darmstädter Aventiurenverzeichnis)." *BGDSL* (Tübingen), 81 (1959), 176–95.

———. "Hat Siegfried gelebt?" *BGDSL*, 63 (1939), 250–71. Rpt. in *Zur germanisch-deutschen Heldensage: Sechzehn Aufsätze zum neuen Forschungsstand*, ed. Karl Hauck, pp. 31–51. Darmstadt, 1965.

Bostock, J. Knight. *A Handbook on Old High German Literature.* Rev. K. C. King and D. R. McLintock. Oxford, 1976.

———. "The Message of the 'Nibelungenlied.'" *MLR* 55 (1960), 200–212. Trans. as "Der Sinn des Nibelungenlieds" in Rupp, pp. 84–109.

Brady, Caroline. *The Legends of Ermanaric.* Berkeley, 1943.

Bräuer, Rolf. *Literatursoziologie und epische Struktur der deutschen "Spielmanns"- und Heldendichtung.* Deutsche Akademie der Wissenschaften zu Berlin, Veröffentlichungen des Instituts für deutsche Sprache und Literatur, 48, Reihe C: Beiträge zur Literaturwissenschaft. Berlin, 1970.

Bugge, Sophus. *Helgedigtene i den ældre Edda: Deres hjem og forbindelser.* Copenhagen, 1896. Trans. by William Henry Schofield as *The Home of the Eddic Poems with Especial Reference to the Helgi-Lays* (London, 1899).

Bumke, Joachim. "Die Eberjagd im Daurel und in der Nibelungendichtung." *GRM*, 41 (1960), 105–11.

———. "Die Quellen der Brünhildfabel im Nibelungenlied." *Euphorion*, 54 (1960), 1–38.

———. "Sigfrids Fahrt ins Nibelungenland: Zur achten aventiure des Nibelungenliedes." *BGDSL* (Tübingen), 80 (1958), 253–68.

Bury, J. B. *History of the Later Roman Empire.* 2 vols. Rpt. New York, 1958.

Cary, George. *The Medieval Alexander.* Cambridge, 1956.

Cassiodorus. *The Letters of Cassiodorus*, trans. Thomas Hodgkin. London, 1886.

———. *Variae.* Ed. Theodor Mommsen. MGH: *Auctores Antiquissimi*, vol. 12. Berlin, 1894.

Chanson de Roland. See *Song of Roland.*

Chase, Colin, ed. *The Dating of Beowulf.* Toronto, 1981.

Chrétien. *Guillaume d'Angleterre: Roman traduit de l'ancien français.* Trans. Jean Trotin. Paris, 1974.

Chrétien de Troyes. *Cligés.* Ed. Alexandre Micha. Les Classiques français du moyen âge, 84. Paris, 1965.

Cormier, Raymond, ed. and trans. *Three Ovidian Tales.* The Garland Library of Medieval Literature, 26. New York, 1986.

Curschmann, Michael. *Der Münchener Oswald und die deutsche spielmännische Epik, mit einem Exkurs zur Kultgeschichte und Dichtungstradition.* MTU, 6. Munich, 1964.

———. "'Nibelungenlied' und 'Nibelungenklage': "Über Mündlichkeit und Schriftlichkeit im Prozess der Episierung." In *Deutsche Literatur im Mittelalter: Kontakte und Perspektiven. Hugo Kuhn zum Gedenken*, ed. Christoph Cormeau, pp. 85–119. Stuttgart, 1979.

———. "'Spielmannsepik': Wege und Ergebnisse der Forschung von 1907–

1965." *DVLG*, 40 (1966), 434–78 and 595–647; sep. rev. version Stuttgart, 1968.

Czerwinski, Peter. "Das Nibelungenlied: Widersprüche höfischer Gewaltreglementierung." In *Einführung in die deutsche Literatur des 12. bis 16. Jahrhunderts*, vol. 1: *Adel und Hof—12./13. Jahrhundert*, ed. Winfried Frey, Walter Raitz, and Dieter Seitz, pp. 49–87. Opladen, 1979.

Dam, Jan van. *Zur Vorgeschichte des höfischen Epos: Lamprecht, Eilhart, Veldeke*. Bonn, 1923.

Delbouille, Maurice. "Le Premier *Roman de Tristan*." *Cahiers de civilisation médiévale*, 5 (1962), 273–86 and 419–35.

Draeger, Fritz. *Die Bindungs- und Gliederungsverhältnisse der Strophen des Nibelungenliedes und ihre Bedeutung für Quellen- und Altersfragen*. Germanische Studien, 28. Berlin, 1923; rpt. Nendeln/Liechtenstein, 1967.

Droege, Karl. "Zur Geschichte des Nibelungenliedes." *ZDA*, 48 (1906–7), 471–503.

——. "Die Vorstufe unseres Nibelungenliedes." *ZDA*, 51 (1909–10), 177–218.

Duby, Georges. *Le Chevalier, la femme et le prêtre: Le Mariage dans la France féodale*. N.p., 1981. Trans. Barbara Bray as *The Knight, the Lady, and the Priest: The Making of Modern Marriage in Medieval France* (New York, 1983).

——. *Medieval Marriage: Two Models from Twelfth-Century France*. Trans. Elborg Forster. Baltimore, 1978.

Dukus Horant. Ed. P. F. Ganz, F. Norman, and W. Schwarz, Tübingen, 1964.

Dürrenmatt, Nelly. *Das Nibelungenlied im Kreis der höfischen Dichtung*. Bern, 1945.

Ebenbauer, Alfred. *Carmen historicum: Untersuchungen zur historischen Dichtung im karolingischen Europa*. Vol. 1. Vienna, 1978.

Edda. See *Poetic Edda*.

Eggers, Hans. *Deutsche Sprachgeschichte II: Das Mittelhochdeutsche*. Munich, 1965.

Egils saga Skalla-Grímssonar. Ed. Sigurður Nordal. ÍF, 2. Reykjavik, 1933.

Ehrismann, Otfrid. "Archaisches und Modernes im Nibelungenlied: Pathos und Abwehr." In the "Hohenemser Studien," pp. 338–48 [164–74].

Eilhart von Oberg. *Eilhart von Oberge's Tristrant*. Trans. J. W. Thomas. Lincoln, 1978.

——. *Tristrant: Synoptischer Druck der ergänzten Fragmente mit der gesamten Parallelüberlieferung*. Ed. Hadumod Bussman. ATB, 70. Tübingen, 1969.

Einhard. *Vita Karoli magni*. Ed. Georg Heinrich Pertz. MGH: *Scriptores*, vol. 2. Hannover, 1829.

Eis, Gerhard. "Die angebliche Bayernfeindlichkeit des Nibelungendichters." *Forschungen und Fortschritte*, 30 (1956), 308–12. Rpt. in his *Kleine Schriften zur altdeutschen weltlichen Dichtung*, pp. 113–24, Amsterdamer Publikationen zur Sprache und Literatur, 38 (Amsterdam, 1979).

Enéas: Texte critique. Ed. Jacques Salverda de Grave. Bibliotheca Normannica, 4. Halle, 1891.

Eneas: A Twelfth-Century French Romance. Trans. John A. Yunck. Records of Civilization: Sources and Studies, 93. New York, 1974.

Erikson, Alvar. "The Problem of Authorship in the Chronicle of Fredegar." *Eranos*, 63 (1965), 47–76.

Ermoldus Nigellus. *Ermold le noir: Poème sur Louis le pieux et épîtres au roi Pépin*. Ed. and trans. Edmond Faral. Paris, 1932.

————. *In honorem Hludowici*. Ed. Ernst Dümmler, pp. 4–79. PLAC, vol. 2. Berlin, 1884; rpt. 1964.

Falk, Walter. *Das Nibelungenlied in seiner Epoche: Revision eines romantischen Mythos*. Heidelberg, 1974.

Fenik, Bernard. *Homer and the Nibelungenlied: Comparative Studies in Epic Style*. Martin Classical Lectures, 30. Cambridge, Mass., 1986.

Ferrante, Joan. "*Cortes'Amor* in Medieval Texts." *Speculum*, 55 (1980), 686–95.

Fischer, Wolfgang. *Die Alexanderliedkonzeption des Pfaffen Lambreht*. Medium Aevum, 2. Munich, 1964.

Floire et Blancheflor. *Le Conte de Floire et Blancheflor*. Ed. Jean-Luc Leclanche. Les Classiques français du moyen âge, 105. Paris, 1980.

————. *The Romance of Floire and Blanchefleur: A French Idyllic Poem of the Twelfth Century*. Trans. Merton Jerome Hubert. Studies in the Romance Languages and Literatures, 63. Chapel Hill, 1966.

Fourrier, Anthime. *Le Courant réaliste dans le roman courtois en France au moyen âge*. Vol. 1: *Les Débuts (XIIᵉ siècle)*. Paris, 1960.

Frappier, Jean. *Chrétien de Troyes*. 2d rev. ed. Paris, 1968. Trans. Raymond J. Cormier as *Chrétien de Troyes: The Man and His Work* (Athens, Ohio, 1982).

Fredegar. *Chronicarum quae dicuntur Fredegarii scholastici libri iv cum continuationibus*. Ed. Bruno Krusch. MGH: *Scriptores Rerum Merovingicarum*, vol. 2. Hannover, 1888.

————. *The Fourth Book of the Chronicle of Fredegar, with Its Continuations*. Ed. and trans. J. M. Wallace-Hadrill. London, 1960.

Freeman, Michelle A. *The Poetics of translatio studii and conjointure: Chrétien de Troyes's Cligés*. French Forum Monographs, 12. Lexington, Ky., 1979.

Friese, Hans. *Thidrekssaga und Dietrichepos: Untersuchungen zur inneren und äusseren Form*. Palaestra, 128. Berlin, 1914.

Frings, Theodor. "Die Entstehung der deutschen Spielmannsepen." *Zeitschrift für deutsche Geisteswissenschaft*, 2 (1939–40), 306–21.

————. "Herbort: Studien zur Thidrekssaga I." In *Berichte über die Verhandlungen der Sächsischen Akademie der Wissenschaften zu Leipzig*. Philol.-hist. Kl., 95 (1943). No. 5. Leipzig, 1943.

Frings, Theodor, and Max Braun. "Brautwerbung." In *Berichte über die Verhandlungen der Sächsischen Akademie der Wissenschaften zu Leipzig*. Philol.-hist. Kl., 96 (1944–48). No. 2. Leipzig, 1947.

Fromm, Hans. "Der oder die Dichter des Nibelungenliedes?" In *Colloquio italo-germanico sul tema: I Nibelunghi*. Atti dei Convegni Lincei, 1 : 63–74. Rome, 1974. Also appeared in *Acta: IV. Congresso Latino-Americano de Estudios Germanísticos* (São Paulo, 1974), pp. 51–66.

Fry, Donald K. *Finnsburh: Fragment and Episode*. London, 1974.

Fulk, R. D. "Review Article: Dating *Beowulf* to the Viking Age." *Philological Quarterly*, 61 (1982), 341–59.

Gallais, Pierre. *Genèse du roman occidental: Essais sur Tristan et Iseut et son modèle persan*. Paris, 1974.

Gautier d'Arras. *Eracle*. Ed. Guy Raynaud de Lage. Classiques français du moyen âge, 102. Paris, 1976.

————. *Ille et Galeron*. Ed. Frederick A. G. Cowper. Société des anciens textes français, 88. Paris, 1956.

————. *Oeuvres*. Ed. E. Löseth. 2 vols. Bibliothèque française du moyen âge, 6–7. Paris, 1890.

Geissler, Friedmar. *Brautwerbung in der Weltliteratur.* Halle, 1955.
Gellinek, Christian. *Die deutsche Kaiserchronik: Erzähltechnik und Kritik.* Frankfurt am Main, 1971.
———. "The German Emperors' Chronicle: An Epic Fiction?" *Colloquia Germanica* (1971), 230–36.
Genesis: A New Edition. Ed. A. N. Doane. Madison, 1978.
Gentry, Francis G. "Trends in 'Nibelungenlied' Research since 1949: A Critical Review." *ABäG*, 7 (1974), 125–39.
———. *Triuwe and vriunt in the Nibelungenlied.* Amsterdamer Publikationen zur Sprache und Literatur, 19. Amsterdam, 1975.
Genzmer, Felix. "Der Dichter der Atlakviða." *ANF*, 42 (1925), 97–134.
Gillespie, George T. *A Catalogue of Persons Named in German Heroic Literature (700–1600) Including Named Animals and Objects and Ethnic Names.* Oxford, 1973.
———. "'Die Klage' as a Commentary on 'Das Nibelungenlied.'" In *Probleme mittelhochdeutscher Erzählformen: Marburger Colloquium 1969*, ed. Peter F. Ganz and Werner Schröder, pp. 153–77. Berlin, 1972.
———. "Spuren der Heldendichtung und Ansätze zur Heldenepik in literarischen Texten des 11. und 12. Jahrhunderts." In *Studien zur frühmittelhochdeutschen Literatur: Cambridger Colloquium 1971*, ed. L. P. Johnson, H.-H. Steinhoff, and R. A. Wisbey, pp. 235–63. Berlin, 1974.
Goffart, Walter. "The Fredegar Problem Reconsidered." *Speculum*, 38 (1963), 206–41.
Goodyear, F. R. D. *The Annals of Tacitus.* Vol. 2. Cambridge, Eng., 1981.
Grau, Anneliese. *Der Gedanke der Herkunft in der deutschen Geschichtschreibung des Mittelalters (Trojasage und Verwandtes).* Würzburg, 1938.
Green, D. H. *The Millstätter Exodus: A Crusading Epic.* Cambridge, Eng., 1966.
Grimm, Wilhelm. *Die deutsche Heldensage.* 4th ed. Darmstadt, 1957.
Gschwantler, Otto. "Ermanrich, sein Selbstmord und die Hamdirsage. Zur Darstellung von Ermanrichs Ende in Getica 24, 129f." In *Die Völker an der mittleren und unteren Donau im fünften und sechsten Jahrhundert. Berichte des Symposions der Kommission für Frühmittelalterforschung 24. bis 27. Oktober 1978, Stift Zwettl, Niederösterreich*, ed. Herwig Wolfram and Falko Daim, pp. 187–204. Vienna, 1980. Also appeared as vol. 145 of the *Denkschriften* of the Österreichische Akademie der Wissenschaften, Philos.-hist. Kl.
Guillaume de Palerne. Ed. H. Michelant. Société des anciens textes français, 5. Paris, 1876.
Gunnlaugsdóttir, Álfrún. *Tristán en el norte.* Reykjavik, 1978.
Günzburger, Angelika. *Studien zur Nibelungenklage: Forschungsbericht— Bauform der Klage—Personendarstellung.* Europäische Hochschulschriften, 685. Frankfurt am Main, 1983.
Hachmann, Rolf. *Die Goten und Skandinavien.* Quellen und Forschungen zur Sprach- und Kulturgeschichte der germanischen Völker, 34 (158). Berlin, 1970.
Harris, Joseph. "Die altenglische Heldendichtung." In *Neues Handbuch der Literaturwissenschaft*, vol. 6: *Europäisches Frühmittelalter*, ed. Klaus von See, pp. 237–76. Wiesbaden, 1985.
———. "Eddic Poetry." In *Old Norse-Icelandic Literature: A Critical Guide*, ed. Carol J. Clover and John Lindow, pp. 68–156. Islandica, 45. Ithaca, 1985.
———. "Eddic Poetry as Oral Poetry: The Evidence of Parallel Passages in the Helgi Poems for Questions of Composition and Performance." In *Edda: A*

Collection of Essays, ed. Robert J. Glendinning and Haraldur Bessason, pp. 210–42. Univ. of Manitoba Icelandic Studies, 4. N.p., 1983.

———. "Guðrúnarbrögð and the Saxon Lay of Grimhild's Perfidy." *MScan*, 9 (1976), 173–80.

Hartmann von Aue. *Erec; Iwein*. Ed. Ernst Schwarz. Darmstadt, 1967.

———. *Iwein*. Ed. and trans. Patrick M. McConeghy. The Garland Library of Medieval Literature, 19. New York, 1984.

Hatto, A. T. "Medieval German." In *Traditions of Heroic and Epic Poetry*, vol. 1: *The Traditions*, ed. A. T. Hatto, pp. 165–95. London, 1980.

———. "On the Excellence of the 'Hildebrandslied': A Comparative Study in Dynamics." *MLR*, 68 (1973), 820–38. Rpt. in his *Essays on Medieval German and Other Poetry* (Cambridge, Eng., 1980), pp. 93–116.

Haug, Walter. "Andreas Heuslers Heldensagenmodell: Prämissen, Kritik und Gegenentwurf." *ZDA*, 86 (1975), 273–92.

———. *Literaturtheorie im deutschen Mittelalter von den Anfängen bis zum Ende des 13. Jahrhunderts: Eine Einführung*. Darmstadt, 1985.

———. "Mittelalterliche Epik: Ansätze, Brechungen und Perspektiven." In *Epische Stoffe des Mittelalters*, ed. Volker Mertens and Ulrich Müller, pp. 1–19. Stuttgart, 1984.

———. "Normatives Modell oder hermeneutisches Experiment: Überlegungen zu einer grundsätzlichen Revision des Heuslerschen Nibelungen-Modells." In the "Hohenemser Studien," pp. 212–26 [38–52].

Haymes, Edward R. *Das mündliche Epos: Eine Einführung in die 'Oral Poetry' Forschung*. Stuttgart, 1977.

———. *Mündliches Epos in mittelhochdeutscher Zeit*. Diss. Erlangen-Nürnberg, 1969.

Heinrichs, Heinrich Matthias. "Über das Alter und die deutsche Vorlage des Bruchstücks vom sogenannten alten Sigurdlied (Brot af Sigurðarkviðo)." In *In diutscher diute: Festschrift für Anthonÿ van der Lee zum sechzigsten Geburtstag*, ed. M. A. van den Broek und G. J. Jaspers [=*AbäG*, 20 (1983)], pp. 1–6. Amsterdam, 1983.

Heinzel, Richard. "Ueber die ostgothische Heldensage." In *Sitzungsberichte der Kaiserlichen Akademie der Wissenschaften*, pp. 17–98. Philos.-hist. Cl., 119. Vienna, 1889.

Heinzle, Joachim. *Mittelhochdeutsche Dietrichepik: Untersuchungen zur Tradierungsweise, Überlieferungskritik und Gattungsgeschichte später Heldendichtung*. MTU, 62. Munich, 1978.

Hempel, Heinrich. "Pilgerin und die Altersschichten des Nibelungenliedes." *ZDA*, 69 (1932), 1–16. Rpt. in his *Kleine Schriften*, ed. Heinrich Matthias Heinrichs (Heidelberg, 1966), pp. 195–208.

———. "Sächsische Nibelungendichtung und sächsischer Ursprung der Thidrikssaga." In *Edda, Skalden, Saga: Festschrift zum 70. Geburtstag von Felix Genzmer*, ed. Hermann Schneider, pp. 138–56. Heidelberg, 1952. Rpt. in his *Kleine Schriften*, pp. 209–25.

Hennig, Ursula. "Herr und Mann: Zur Ständegliederung im Nibelungenlied." In the "Hohenemser Studien," pp. 349–59 [175–85].

Hervarar saga ok Heiðreks konungs. Ed. and trans. Christopher Tolkien. London, 1960.

Heusler, Andreas. *Die altgermanische Dichtung*. 2d rev. ed. Potsdam, 1941; rpt. Darmstadt, 1957.

————. "Die deutsche Quelle der Ballade von Kremolds Rache." In *Sitzungs-berichte der Preussischen Akademie der Wissenschaften*, pp. 445–69. Philos.-hist. Kl. (1921). Rpt. in his *Kleine Schriften*, vol. 1, ed. Helga Reuschel, pp. 103–31. Berlin, 1969.

————. "Die Lieder der Lücke im Codex Regius der Edda." In *Germanistische Abhandlungen, Hermann Paul dargebracht*, pp. 1–98. Strasbourg, 1902. Rpt. in his *Kleine Schriften*, vol. 2, ed. Stefan Sonderegger, pp. 223–91.

————. *Lied und Epos in germanischer Sagendichtung*. Dortmund, 1905.

————. *Nibelungensage und Nibelungenlied: Die Stoffgeschichte des deutschen Heldenepos*. 6th ed. Dortmund, 1965.

————. "Die Quelle der Brünhildsage in Thidreks saga und Nibelungenlied." In *Aufsätze zur Sprach- und Literaturgeschichte Wilhelm Braune dargebracht*, pp. 47–84. Dortmund, 1920. Rpt. in his *Kleine Schriften*, vol. 1, pp. 65–102.

Hoffmann, Werner. "Die englische und amerikanische Nibelungenforschung 1959–62: Überschau und Kritik." *ZDP*, 84 (1965), 267–78.

————. "Die Fassung * C des Nibelungenliedes und die 'Klage,'" In *Festschrift Gottfried Weber: Zu seinem 70. Geburtstag überreicht von Frankfurter Kollegen und Schülern*, ed. Heinz Otto Burger and Klaus von See, pp. 109–43. Frankfurter Beiträge zur Germanistik, 1. Bad Homburg, 1967.

————. *Mittelhochdeutsche Heldendichtung*. Grundlagen der Germanistik, 14. Berlin, 1974.

————. *Das Nibelungenlied*. 5th ed. Stuttgart, 1982.

————. *Das Nibelungenlied: Interpretation*. Munich, 1969.

————. "Das Nibelungenlied in der Literaturgeschichtsschreibung von Gervinus bis Bertau." In the "Hohenemser Studien," pp. 193–211 [19–37].

————. *Das Siegfriedbild in der Forschung*. Erträge der Forschung, 127. Darmstadt, 1979.

————. "Zur Situation der gegenwärtigen Nibelungenforschung: Probleme, Ergebnisse, Aufgaben." *WW*, 12 (1962), 79–91.

Höfler, Otto. *Siegfried, Arminius und die Symbolik*. Heidelberg, 1961.

Hofmann, Dietrich. "'Attilas Schlangenturm' und der 'Niflungengarten' in Soest: Zur Geschichtsauffassung des Volkes im Mittelalter." *Niederdeutsches Jahrbuch: Jahrbuch des Vereins für niederdeutsche Sprachforschung*, 104 (1981), 31–46.

Hollander, Lee M. *The Skalds: A Selection of Their Poems with Introduction and Notes*. New York, 1945; rpt. Ann Arbor, Mich., 1968.

Holthausen, Ferdinand. "Studien zur Thidrekssaga." *BGDSL*, 9 (1884), 451–503.

Huemer, Johann. *De Sedulii poetae vita et scriptis commentatio*. Vienna, 1878.

Hungerland, Heinz. "Zeugnisse zur Volsungen- und Niflungensage aus der Skaldendichtung." *ANF*, 20 (1904), 1–43 and 105–42.

Ihlenburg, Karl Heinz. "Die gesellschaftliche Grundlage des germanischen Heldenethos und die mündliche Überlieferung heroischer Stoffe." *Weimarer Beiträge: Zeitschrift für Literaturwissenschaft, Ästhetik und Kulturtheorie*, 17 (1971), 140–69.

————. *Das Nibelungenlied: Problem und Gehalt*. Berlin, 1969.

Jackson, W. T. H. *The Hero and the King: An Epic Theme*. New York, 1982.

Jean Renart. *L'Escoufle: Roman d'aventure*. Ed. Franklin Sweetser. Textes littéraires français, 21. Geneva, 1974.

Jordan, Karl. *Heinrich der Löwe: Eine Biographie.* Munich, 1979.
Jordanes. *Getica.* Ed. Theodor Mommsen. MGH: *Auctores Antiquissimi*, vol. 5, pt. 1. Berlin, 1882.
———. *Getica.* Trans. Charles C. Mierow. Princeton, N.J., 1915.
Juvencus. *Libri evangeliorum IIII.* Ed. Carolus Marold. Leipzig, 1886.
Kaiser, Gert. "Deutsche Heldenepik." In *Neues Handbuch der Literatur-wissenschaft*, vol. 7: *Europäisches Hochmittelalter*, ed. Henning Krauss, pp. 181–205. Wiesbaden, 1981.
Kaiserchronik. Ed. Edward Schröder, MGH: *Deutsche Chroniken und andere Geschichtsbücher des Mittelalters*, 1:79–392. Hannover, 1895.
Kalinke, Marianne E. *King Arthur North-by-Northwest: The matière de Bretagne in Old Norse-Icelandic Romances.* Bibliotheca Arnamagnaeana, 37. Copenhagen, 1981.
Karolus magnus et Leo papa. Ed. Ernst Dümmler. PLAC, 1:366–79. Berlin, 1881; rpt. 1964.
Kartschoke, Dieter. *Die Datierung des deutschen Rolandsliedes.* Stuttgart, 1965.
Katscher, Rosemarie. "Waltharius—Dichtung und Dichter." *Mittellateinisches Jahrbuch*, 9 (1973), 48–120.
Ker, W. P. *Epic and Romance: Essays on Medieval Literature.* London, 1896; rpt. New York, 1957.
Kettner, Emil. *Die österreichische Nibelungendichtung: Untersuchungen über die Verfasser des Nibelungenliedes.* Berlin, 1897.
King, K. C. "The Message of the 'Nibelungenlied'—A Reply." *MLR*, 57 (1962), 541–50. Trans. as "Der Sinn des Nibelungenlieds—Eine Entgegnung" in Rupp, pp. 218–36.
Klage. Diu Klage, mit den Lesarten sämtlicher Handschriften. Ed. Karl Bartsch. Leipzig, 1875; rpt. Darmstadt, 1964.
Klein, Thomas. "Zur Þiðreks saga." In *Arbeiten zur Skandinavistik. 6. Arbeitstagung der Skandinavisten des Deutschen Sprachgebietes: 26.9–1.10.1983 in Bonn*, ed. Heinrich Beck, pp. 487–565. Frankfurt am Main, 1985.
Kloocke, Kurt. "Kreuzzugsideologie und Chansons de Geste." In *Beiträge zur vergleichenden Literaturgeschichte: Festschrift für Kurt Wais zum 65. Geburtstag*, ed. Johannes Hösle, pp. 1–18. Tübingen, 1972.
Knab, Doris. *Das Annolied: Probleme seiner literarischen Einordnung.* Hermaea, 11. Tübingen, 1962.
Koestermann, Erich. *Cornelius Tacitus: Annalen.* Vol. 1. Heidelberg, 1963.
Köhler, Erich. "Der Roman in der Romania." In *Neues Handbuch der Literaturwissenschaft*, vol. 7: *Europäisches Hochmittelalter*, ed. Henning Krauss, pp. 243–82. Wiesbaden, 1981.
Konecny, Sylvia. "Das Sozialgefüge am Burgundenhof." In *Österreichische Literatur zur Zeit der Babenberger: Vorträge der Lilienfelder Tagung 1976*, ed. Alfred Ebenbauer, Fritz Peter Knapp, and Ingrid Strasser, pp. 97–116. Vienna, 1977.
Konrad. *Das Rolandslied des Pfaffen Konrad.* Ed. Carl Wesle, rev. Peter Wapnewski. Tübingen, 1967.
———. *Das Rolandslied des Pfaffen Konrad.* Ed. and trans. Dieter Kartschoke. Frankfurt am Main, 1971.
Kralik, Dietrich von. *Die Sigfridtrilogie im Nibelungenlied und in der Thidreks-saga.* Vol. 1. Halle, 1941.

———. *Wer war der Dichter des Nibelungenliedes?* Vienna, 1954.

Kratz, Dennis M. *Mocking Epic: Waltharius, Alexandreis and the Problem of Christian Heroism.* Madrid, 1980.

Krausse, Helmut K. "Die Darstellung von Siegfrieds Tod und die Entwicklung des Hagenbildes in der Nibelungendichtung." *GRM*, 21 (1971), 369–78.

Kuhn, Hans. "Die Grenzen der germanischen Gefolgschaft." *Zeitschrift der Savigny-Stiftung für Rechtsgeschichte: Germanistische Abteilung,* 86 (1956), 1–83. Rpt. in his *Kleine Schriften: Aufsätze und Rezensionen aus den Gebieten der germanischen und nordischen Sprach-, Literatur- und Kulturgeschichte,* ed. Dietrich Hofmann (Berlin, 1971), pp. 420–83.

———. "Die Negation des Verbs in der altnordischen Dichtung." *BGDSL,* 60 (1936), 431–44. Rpt. in his *Kleine Schriften,* vol. 1 (1969), pp. 124–34.

———. "Der Teufel im Nibelungenlied: Zu Gunthers und Kriemhilds Tod." *ZDA,* 94 (1965), 280–306. Rpt. in his *Kleine Schriften,* 2:158–82.

———. "Westgermanisches in der altnordischen Verskunst." *BGDSL,* 63 (1939), 178–263. Rpt. in his *Kleine Schriften,* 1:485–527.

———. "Zur Wortstellung und -betonung im Altgermanischen." *BGDSL,* 57 (1933), 1–109. Rpt. in his *Kleine Schriften,* 1:18–103.

Kuhn, Hugo. "Tristan, Nibelungenlied, Artusstruktur." In *Colloquio italogermanico sul tema: I Nibelunghi,* Atti dei Convegni Lincei, 1:7–17. Rome, 1974. Also appeared in the *Sitzungsberichte der Bayerischen Akademie der Wissenschaften,* Philos.-hist. Kl. (1973), no. 5.

Lamprecht. *Das Alexanderlied des Pfaffen Lamprecht.* Ed. Irene Ruttmann. Darmstadt, 1974.

———. *Lamprechts Alexander nach den drei Texten mit dem Fragment des Alberic von Besançon und den lateinischen Quellen.* Ed. Karl Kinzel. Halle, 1884.

Leyen, Friedrich von der. *Das Heldenliederbuch Karls des Grossen.* Munich, 1954.

Liber historiae Francorum. Ed. Bruno Krusch. MGH: *Scriptores Rerum Merovingicarum,* vol. 2. Hannover, 1888.

Liberman, Anatoly. "Introduction." In Vladimir Propp, *Theory and History of Folklore,* trans. Ariadna Y. Martin and Richard P. Martin, pp. vii–lxxxi. Theory and History of Literature, 5. Minneapolis, Minn., 1984.

Lindow, John. *Comitatus, Individual and Honor: Studies in North Germanic Institutional Vocabulary.* Univ. of California Publications in Linguistics, 83. Berkeley, 1976.

Lohse, Gerhart. "Die Beziehungen zwischen der Thidrekssaga und den Handschriften des Nibelungenliedes." *BGDSL* (Tübingen), 81 (1959), 295–347.

Lönnroth, Lars. "Hjálmar's Death-Song and the Delivery of Eddic Poetry." *Speculum,* 46 (1971), 1–20.

Loomis, Gertrude Schoepperle. *Tristan and Isolt: A Study of the Sources of the Romance.* 2 vols. 2d ed. New York, 1960.

Lord, Albert B. *The Singer of Tales.* Harvard Studies in Comparative Literature, 24. Cambridge, Mass., 1960.

Lösel-Wieland-Engelmann, Berta. "Verdanken wir das *Nibelungenlied* einer Niedernburger Nonne?" *Monatshefte für deutschen Unterricht, deutsche Sprache und Literatur,* 72 (1980), 5–25.

Lunzer, Justus. "Kleine Nibelungenstudien." *ZDA,* 69 (1932), 71–89, 225–37, 277–95.

Luttrell, Claude. *The Creation of the First Arthurian Romance: A Quest.* London, 1974.

McConnell, Winder. *The Nibelungenlied.* Twayne World Authors Series, 712. Boston, 1984.

Mackensen, Lutz. *Die Nibelungen: Sage, Geschichte, ihr Lied und sein Dichter.* Stuttgart, 1984.

Magoun, Francis P., Jr. "Béowulf B: A Folk-Poem on Béowulf's Death." In *Early English and Norse Studies Presented to Hugh Smith in Honour of His Sixtieth Birthday*, ed. Arthur Brown and Peter Foote, pp. 127–40. London, 1963.

———. "The Oral-Formulaic Character of Anglo-Saxon Narrative Poetry." *Speculum*, 28 (1953), 446–67.

Marner, Der. Ed. Philipp Strauch. Strasbourg, 1876; rpt. Berlin, 1965.

Masser, Achim. "Von Alternativstrophen und Vortragsvarianten im Nibelungenlied." In the "Hohenemser Studien," pp. 299–311 [125–37].

Maurer, Friedrich. "Die Formkunst des Dichters unseres Nibelungenlieds." *Der Deutschunterricht*, 6 (1954), 77–83. Rpt. in his *Dichtung und Sprache des Mittelalters: Gesammelte Aufsätze* (Bern, 1963), pp. 70–79. Also in Rupp, pp. 40–52.

———. *Leid: Studien zur Bedeutungs- und Problemgeschichte besonders in den grossen Epen der staufischen Zeit.* Bern, 1951; 4th ed. 1969.

Meissburger, Gerhard. "Zum sogenannten Heldenliederbuch Karls des Grossen." *GRM*, 44 (1963), 105–19.

Menéndez Pidal, Ramón. *La Chanson de Roland y el neotradicionalismo: Orígenes de la épica románica.* Madrid, 1959. Rev. by the author with René Louis and trans. by Irénée-Marcel Cluzel as *La Chanson de Roland et la tradition épique des Francs* (Paris, 1960).

Mergell, Bodo. "Nibelungenlied und höfischer Roman." *Euphorion*, 45 (1950), 305–36. Rpt. in Rupp, pp. 3–39.

Meves, Uwe. "Bischof Wolfger von Passau, *sîn schrîber, meister Kuonrât* und die Nibelungenüberlieferung." In the "Hohenemser Studien," pp. 246–63 [72–89].

———. *Studien zu König Rother, Herzog Ernst und Grauer Rock (Orendel).* Europäische Hochschulschriften, 181. Frankfurt am Main, 1976.

Mickel, Emanuel J., Jr. "Theme and Narrative Structure in *Guillaume d'Angleterre.*" In *The Sower and His Seed: Essays on Chrétien de Troyes*, ed. Rupert T. Pickens. French Forum Monographs, 44 (Lexington, Ky., 1983), pp. 52–65.

Mohr, Wolfgang. Review of Dietrich von Kralik, *Die Sigfridtrilogie im Nibelungenlied und in der Thidrekssaga*, vol. 1 (Halle, 1941). In *Dichtung und Volkstum*, 42 (1942), 83–123.

Mowatt, D. G. "Studies Towards an Interpretation of the 'Nibelungenlied.'" *GLL*, 14 (1961), 257–70. Trans. as "Zur Interpretation des Nibelungenlieds" in Rupp, pp. 179–200.

Mowatt, D. G., and Hugh Sacker. *The Nibelungenlied: An Interpretative Commentary.* Toronto, 1967.

Much, Rudolf. *Die Germania des Tacitus.* Rev. Herbert Jankuhn and Wolfgang Lange. Heidelberg, 1967.

Müllenhoff, Karl. "Zeugnisse und Excurse zur deutschen Heldensage." *ZDA*, 12 (1865), 253–386.

Müller, Jan-Dirk. "Sivrit: *künec—man—eigenholt.* Zur sozialen Problematik des Nibelungenliedes." *ABäG*, 7 (1974), 85–124.

Müller, Ulrich. "Das Nachleben der mittelalterlichen Stoffe." In *Epische Stoffe des Mittelalters*, ed. Volker Mertens and Ulrich Müller. Stuttgart, 1984.

Münz, Walter. "Zu den Passauer Strophen und der Verfasserfrage des Nibelungenliedes." *Euphorion*, 65 (1971), 345–67.

Münzer, F. "Zu dem Nachruf des Tacitus auf Arminius." *Hermes*, 48 (1913), 617–19.

Nagel, Bert. "Zur Interpretation und Wertung des Nibelungenliedes." *Neue Heidelberger Jahrbücher* (1954), pp. 1–89. Rev. and rpt. as "Widersprüche im Nibelungenlied" in Rupp, pp. 367–431.

———. *Das Nibelungenlied: Stoff—Form—Ethos.* Frankfurt am Main, 1965.

———. "Noch einmal Nibelungenlied." In *Studien zur deutschen Literatur des Mittelalters*, ed. Rudolf Schützeichel with Ulrich Fellmann, pp. 264–318. Bonn, 1979. [This volume is sometimes referred to as *Festgabe für Gerhart Lohse* but is so identified only in an editor's note on p. 773.] Rpt. in his *Kleine Schriften zur deutschen Literatur*, Göppinger Arbeiten zur Germanistik, 310 (Göppingen, 1981), pp. 129–96.

———. "Stoffzwang der Überlieferung in mittelhochdeutscher Dichtung." In *Philologische Studien: Gedenkschrift für Richard Kienast*, ed. Ute Schwab and Elfriede Stutz, pp. 54–95. Heidelberg, 1978. Rpt. in his *Kleine Schriften zur deutschen Literatur*, pp. 67–128.

Naumann, Hans. *Frühgermanisches Dichterbuch: Zeugnisse und Texte für Übungen und Vorlesungen über ältere germanische Poesie.* Trübners Philologische Bibliothek, 13. Berlin, 1931.

———. "Die Zeugnisse der antiken und frühmittelalterlichen Autoren zur germanischen Poesie." *GRM*, 15 (1927), 258–73.

Neumann, Friedrich. *Das Nibelungenlied in seiner Zeit.* Göttingen, 1967.

———. "Schichten der Ethik im Nibelungenliede." In *Festschrift Eugen Mogk zum 70. Geburtstag, 19. Juli 1924*, pp. 119–45. Halle, 1924. Rpt. in his *Das Nibelungenlied in seiner Zeit*, pp. 9–34.

Niles, John D. *Beowulf: The Poem and Its Tradition.* Cambridge, Mass., 1983.

Norden, Eduard. *Die germanische Urgeschichte in Tacitus Germania.* 3d ed. Leipzig, 1923.

Noreen, Adolf. *Altisländische und altnorwegische Grammatik.* 3d ed. Halle, 1903.

Ohly, Ernst Friedrich. *Sage und Legende in der Kaiserchronik: Untersuchungen über Quellen und Aufbau der Dichtung.* Forschungen zur deutschen Sprache und Dichtung, 10. Münster, 1940; rpt. Darmstadt, 1968.

Olafs saga hins helga. Die "Legendarische Saga" über Olaf den Heiligen (Hs. Delagard. saml. nr. 8^{11}). Ed. and trans. Anne Heinrichs, Doris Janshen, Elke Radicke, and Hartmut Röhn. Heidelberg, 1982.

Olrik, Axel. *The Heroic Legends of Denmark.* Trans. Lee M. Hollander. New York and London, 1919.

Opland, Jeff. *Anglo-Saxon Oral Poetry: A Study of the Traditions.* New Haven, 1980.

Orendel. See Schröder, Walter Johannes.

Oswald. Der Münchner Oswald. Ed. Michael Curschmann. ATB, 76. Tübingen, 1974. See also Schröder, Walter Johannes.

Otfrid von Weissenburg. *Evangelienbuch.* Ed. Oskar Erdmann. 2d ed. rev. Edward Schröder. 3d ed. rev. Ludwig Wolff. ATB, 49. Tübingen, 1957.

Ott-Meimberg, Marianne. *Kreuzzugsepos oder Staatsroman? Strukturen adeliger Heilsversicherung im deutschen Rolandslied.* MTU, 70. Munich, 1980.

Pacaut, Marcel. *Frederick Barbarossa.* New York, 1970.

Paff, William J. *The Geographical and Ethnic Names in the Þiðriks Saga: A Study in Germanic Heroic Legend.* Harvard Germanic Studies, 2. Cambridge, Mass., 1959.

Panzer, Friedrich. *Italische Normannen in deutscher Heldensage.* Deutsche Forschungen, 1. Frankfurt am Main, 1925; rpt. Hildesheim, 1974.

————. "Nibelungische Problematik: Siegfried und Xanten; Hagen und die Meerfrauen; Magyaren und Hunnen." In *Sitzungsberichte der Heidelberger Akademie der Wissenschaften.* Philos.-hist. Kl. (1953–54). No. 3. Heidelberg, 1954.

————. *Das Nibelungenlied: Entstehung und Gestalt.* Stuttgart, 1955.

————. *Studien zum Nibelungenliede.* Frankfurt am Main, 1945.

Paul the Deacon. *Historia Langobardorum.* Ed. L. Bethmann and G. Waitz. MGH: *Scriptores rerum Langobardicarum et Italicarum saec. VI–IX.* Hannover, 1878.

————. *History of the Lombards.* Trans. William Dudley Foulke. Philadelphia, 1907; rpt. 1974.

Perry, Ben Edwin. *The Ancient Romances: A Literary-Historical Account of Their Origins.* Berkeley, 1967.

Poeta Saxo. *Annales de gestis Caroli magni imperatoris,* ed. Paul von Winterfeld. PLAC, 4:7–71. Berlin, 1899; rpt. 1964.

Poetic Edda, The. Ed. Ursula Dronke. Vol. 1: *Heroic Poems.* Oxford, 1969.

Pöschl, Viktor. "Virgil und Augustus." In *Aufstieg und Niedergang der römischen Welt: Geschichte und Kultur Roms im Spiegel der neueren Forschung,* 2: *Principat.* Vol. 31, pt. 2, ed. Wolfgang Haase, pp. 709–27. Berlin, 1981.

Pseudo-Clementine Recognitions and Homilies. Ed. Bernhard Rehm. *Die Pseudoklementinen.* Vol. 1: *Homilien.* Berlin, 1953; 2d rev. ed. Franz Paschke, 1969. Vol. 2: *Rekognitionen in Rufins Übersetzung.* Berlin, 1965.

————. Trans. Thomas Smith, Peter Peterson, and James Donaldson. In *Ante-Nicene Fathers,* vol. 8, ed. Alexander Roberts and James Donaldson, rev. A. Cleveland Coxe, pp. 75–346. New York, 1903.

Reichardt, Konstantin. "Der Dichter der Atlakviða." *ANF,* 42 (1925), 323–26.

Reichert, Hermann. "Zum Sigrdrífa-Brünhild-Problem." In *Antiquitates Indogermanicae: Studien zur indogermanischen Altertumskunde und zur Sprach- und Kulturgeschichte der indogermanischen Völker; Gedenkschrift für Hermann Güntert zur 25. Wiederkehr seines Todestages am 23. April 1973,* ed. Manfred Mayrhofer, Wolfgang Meid, Bernfried Schlerath, and Rüdiger Schmitt, pp. 251–65. Innsbrucker Beiträge zur Sprachwissenschaft, 12. Innsbruck, 1974.

Reitzenstein, R. "Philologische Kleinigkeiten." *Hermes,* 48 (1913), 250–73.

Reuschel, Helga. "Saga und Wikinglied: Ein Beitrag zur Hildesage." *BGDSL,* 56 (1932), 321–45.

Richter, Werner. "Beiträge zur Deutung des Mittelteils des Nibelungenliedes." *ZDA,* 72 (1935), 9–47.

Ritter-Schaumburg, Heinz. *Die Nibelungen zogen nordwärts.* Munich, 1981.

Rother. King Rother. Trans. Robert Lichtenstein. Univ. of North Carolina Studies in the Germanic Languages and Literatures, 36. Chapel Hill, N.C., 1962.

————. *König Rother*. Ed. Theodor Frings and Joachim Kuhnt. Altdeutsche Texte für den akademischen Unterricht, 2. Halle, 1954; rev. Ingeborg Köppe-Benath, 1968.

————. *Rother*. Ed. Jan de Vries. Germanische Bibliothek, 2d section, vol. 13. Heidelberg, 1922.

Sacker, Hugh. "On Irony and Symbolism in the *Nibelungenlied*: Two Preliminary Notes." *GLL*, 14 (1961), 271–81. Trans. as "Über Ironie und Symbolismus im Nibelungenlied: Zwei vorläufige Studien" in Rupp, pp. 201–17.

Salman und Morolf. Ed. Friedrich Vogt. Halle, 1880. See also Schröder, Walter Johannes.

Saxo Grammaticus. *Gesta Danorum*. Ed. J. Olrik and H. Ræder. Copenhagen, 1931.

Sayce, Olive. "Abortive Motivation in Part I of the *Nibelungenlied*." *Medium Aevum*, 23 (1954), 36–38.

Schieb, Gabriele. *Henric van Veldeken; Heinrich von Veldeke*. Stuttgart, 1965.

Schlauch, Margaret. *Chaucer's Constance and Accused Queens*. New York, 1927.

Schneider, Hermann. "Forschungsbericht: Die Quellen des Nibelungenliedes. Zu Friedrich Panzers Studien zum Nibelungenlied 1945." *Euphorion*, 45 (1950), 493–98.

————. *Die Gedichte und die Sage von Wolfdietrich: Untersuchungen über ihre Entstehungsgeschichte*. Munich, 1913.

————. *Germanische Heldensage*. Vol. 1: *Deutsche Heldensage*. Grundriss der germanischen Philologie, 10/1. Berlin, 1928; rpt. 1962.

————. *Heldendichtung, Geistlichendichtung, Ritterdichtung*. Heidelberg, 1925.

Schröder, Edward. "Die deutschen Alexander-Dichtungen des 12ten Jahrhunderts." In *Nachrichten von der Gesellschaft der Wissenschaften zu Göttingen*, pp. 45–92. Philol.-hist. Kl. (1928). Pt. 1.

Schröder, Walter Johannes. "Das Nibelungenlied: Versuch einer Deutung." *BGDSL* (Halle), 76 (1954–55), 56–143. Rpt. in his *rede und meine: Aufsätze und Vorträge zur deutschen Literatur des Mittelalters* (Cologne, 1978), pp. 58–145.

————. *Spielmannsepik*. Stuttgart, 1962.

Schröder, Walter Johannes, ed. *Spielmannsepen*. Vol. 2: *Sankt Oswald, Orendel, Salman und Morolf*. Darmstadt, 1976.

Schröder, Werner. "Zum Problem der Hortfrage im Nibelungenlied." In his *Nibelungenlied-Studien*, pp. 157–84. Stuttgart, 1968.

————. "Die Tragödie Kriemhilts im Nibelungenlied." *ZDA*, 90 (1960–61), 41–80 and 123–60. Rpt. in his *Nibelungenlied-Studien*, pp. 48–156.

————. "Zum Vanitas-Gedanken im deutschen Alexanderlied." *ZDA*, 91 (1961–62), 38–55.

Schulze, A. "Ein Bruchstück des altfranzösischen Apolloniusromanes." *Zeitschrift für romanische Philologie*, 33 (1909), 226–29.

Schulze, Ursula. "Nibelungen und Kudrun." In *Epische Stoffe des Mittelalters*, ed. Volker Mertens and Ulrich Müller, pp. 111–40. Stuttgart, 1984.

Sedulius. *Opera omnia*. Ed. Johann Huemer. Corpus Scriptorum Ecclesiasticorum Latinorum, 10. Vienna, 1885.

See, Klaus von. *Edda, Saga, Skaldendichtung: Aufsätze zur skandinavischen Literatur des Mittelalters*. Heidelberg, 1981.

————. "Freierprobe und Königinnenzank in der Sigfridsage." *ZDA*, 89 (1959), 163–72. Rpt. in his *Edda, Saga, Skaldendichtung*, pp. 214–23.

———. "Der Germane als Barbar." *JIG*, 13 (1981), 42–72.
———. *Germanische Heldensage: Stoffe, Probleme, Methoden.* Frankfurt am Main, 1971.
———. "Hastings, Stiklastaðir und Langemarck: Zur Überlieferung vom Vortrag heroischer Lieder auf dem Schlachtfeld." *GRM*, 57 (1976), 1–13. Rpt. in his *Edda, Saga, Skaldendichtung*, pp. 259–71.
———. "Húskarla hvǫt: Nochmals zum Alter der Bjarkamál." In *Speculum Norroenum: Norse Studies in Memory of Gabriel Turville-Petre*, ed. Ursula Dronke, Guðrún P. Helgadóttir, Gerd Wolfgang Weber, and Hans Bekker-Nielsen, pp. 421–31. Odense, 1981. Rpt. in his *Edda, Saga, Skaldendichtung*, pp. 272–82.
———. "Was ist Heldendichtung?" In *Europäische Heldendichtung*, ed. Klaus von See, pp. 1–38. Wege der Forschung, 500. Darmstadt, 1978. Rpt. in his *Edda, Saga, Skaldendichtung*, pp. 154–93.
———. "Die Werbung um Brünhild." *ZDA*, 88 (1957), 1–20. Rpt. in his *Edda, Saga, Skaldendichtung*, pp. 194–213, with *Nachträge* on pp. 516–21.
Sinnema, John R. *Hendrik Van Veldeke.* Twayne World Authors Series, 223. New York, 1972.
Snorri Sturluson. *Heimskringla.* Ed. Bjarni Aðalbjarnarson. 3 vols. ÍF, 26–28. Reykjavik, 1941–51.
Song of Roland. The Song of Roland: An Analytical Edition. Ed. and trans. Gerard J. Brault. Vol. 1: *Introduction and Commentary.* Vol. 2: *Oxford Text and English Translation.* University Park, Pa., 1978.
Sperberg-McQueen, Christopher Michael. "An Analysis of Recent Work on *Nibelungenlied* Poetics." Diss. Stanford, 1985.
———. "The Legendary Form of *Sigurðarkviða in Skamma*." *ANF*, 101 (1986), 16–40.
Stein, Peter K. "Orendel 1512: Probleme und Möglichkeiten der Anwendung der *theory of oral-formulaic poetry* bei der literaturhistorischen Interpretation eines mittelhochdeutschen Textes." In the "Hohenemser Studien," pp. 322–37 [148–63].
Stephens, W. E. D. "An Examination of the Sources of the Thidrikssaga." M.A. Thesis University College, London, 1937.
Storm, Gustav. *Sagnkredsene om Karl den store og Didrik af Bern hos de nordiske folk.* Kristiania, 1874.
Szklenar, Hans. "Die Jagdszene von Hocheppan—ein Zeugnis der Dietrichsage?" In *Deutsche Heldenepik in Tirol: König Laurin und Dietrich von Bern in der Dichtung des Mittelalters. Beiträge der Neustifter Tagung 1977 des Südtiroler Kulturinstitutes*, ed. Egon Kühebacher, pp. 407–65. Bozen, 1979.
Szövérffy, Josef. "Das Nibelungenlied: Strukturelle Beobachtungen und Zeitgeschichte." *WW*, 15 (1965), 233–38. Rpt. in Rupp, pp. 322–32.
Theganus. *Vita Hludowici imperatoris.* Ed. Georg Heinrich Pertz. MGH: *Scriptores*, vol. 2. Hannover, 1829.
Thompson, E. A. *The Early Germans.* Oxford, 1965.
———. *A History of Attila and the Huns.* Oxford, 1948.
Thorp, Mary. *The Study of the Nibelungenlied: Being the History of the Study of the Epic and Legend from 1755 to 1937.* Oxford, 1940.
Tonnelat, Ernest. *La Chanson des Nibelungen: Etude sur la composition et la formation du poème épique.* Publications de la Faculté des Lettres de l'Université de Strasbourg, 30. Paris, 1926.

Urbanek, Ferdinand. *Kaiser, Grafen und Mäzene im König Rother*. Philologische Studien und Quellen, 71. Berlin, 1976.

———. "Umfang und Intention von Lamprechts Alexanderlied." *ZDA*, 99 (1970), 96–120.

Veldeke. *Die epischen Werke des Henric van Veldeken*. Ed. Theodor Frings and Gabriele Schieb. Vol. 1: *Sente Servas; Sanctus Servatius*. Halle, 1956.

———. *Henric van Veldeken: Eneide*. Ed. Gabriele Schieb and Theodor Frings. Vol. 1. Deutsche Texte des Mittelalters, 58. Berlin, 1964.

Vita Sancti Remacli. Ed. Jean Mabillon. *Acta Sanctorum ordinis Benedicti*, 2:489–503. Paris and Venice, 1733; rpt. 1936.

Voorwinden, Norbert. "Nibelungenklage und Nibelungenlied." In the "Hohenemser Studien," pp. 276–87 [102–13].

Vries, Jan de. *Altnordische Literaturgeschichte*. 2d rev. ed. Vol. 1. Grundriss der germanischen Philologie, 15. Berlin, 1964.

Vǫlsunga saga. The Saga of the Volsungs. Ed. and trans. R. G. Finch. London, 1965.

Wachinger, Burghart. "Die 'Klage' und das Nibelungenlied." In the "Hohenemser Studien," pp. 264–75 [90–101].

———. *Studien zum Nibelungenlied: Vorausdeutungen, Aufbau, Motivierung*. Tübingen, 1960.

Wailes, Stephen L. "Bedroom Comedy in the Nibelungenlied." *Modern Language Quarterly*, 32 (1971), 365–76.

Waltharius. Ed. Karl Strecker. PLAC, 6:24–83. Weimar, 1951.

Waltharius and Ruodlieb. Ed. and trans. Dennis M. Kratz. Garland Library of Medieval Literature, 13. New York, 1984.

Wapnewski, Peter. "Rüdigers Schild: Zur 37. Aventiure des 'Nibelungenliedes.'" *Euphorion*, 54 (1960), 380–410. Rpt. in Rupp, pp. 134–78.

Weber, Gottfried, with Werner Hoffmann. *Heldendichtung II: Nibelungenlied*. Stuttgart, 1961; rpt. 1964, 1968; rev. 1974.

———. *Das Nibelungenlied: Problem und Idee*. Stuttgart, 1963.

Weller, Karl. "Die Nibelungenstrasse." *ZDA*, 70 (1933), 49–66.

Wentzlaff-Eggebert, Friedrich-Wilhelm. *Kreuzzugsdichtung des Mittelalters: Studien zu ihrer geschichtlichen und dichterischen Wirklichkeit*. Berlin, 1960.

Wild, Andreas. *Sisibesage und Genovefalegende*. Bamberg, 1970.

Wilmanns, Wilhelm. "Der Untergang der Nibelunge in alter Sage und Dichtung." In *Abhandlungen der Königlichen Gesellschaft der Wissenschaften zu Göttingen*, pp. 1–43. Philol.-hist. Kl. (1903). No. 2.

Wisniewski, Roswitha. *Die Darstellung des Niflungenunterganges in der Thidrekssaga: Eine quellenkritische Untersuchung*. Hermaea, 9. Tübingen, 1961.

———. "Das Versagen des Königs: Zur Interpretation des Nibelungenliedes." In *Festschrift für Ingeborg Schröbler zum 65. Geburtstag*, ed. Dietrich Schmidtke and Helga Schüppert [=*BGDSL*, 95 (1973)], pp. 170–86. Tübingen, 1973.

Wolf, Alois. "Die Verschriftlichung der Nibelungensage und die französisch-deutschen Literaturbeziehungen im Mittelalter." In the "Hohenemser Studien," pp. 227–45 [53–71].

Wolfram von Eschenbach. *Parzival*. Trans. A. T. Hatto. Harmondsworth, 1980.

———. *Parzival: A Romance of the Middle Ages*. Trans. Helen M. Mustard and Charles E. Passage. New York, 1961.

Wynn, Marianne. "Hagen's Defiance of Kriemhilt." In *Mediaeval German Studies Presented to Frederick Norman*, pp. 104–14. No ed. London, 1965.

Zink, Georges. *Les Légendes héroïques de Dietrich et d'Ermrich dans les littératures germaniques*. Lyons, 1950.

Þiðreks saga. *Die Geschichte Thidreks von Bern*. Trans. Fine Erichsen. Thule, 22. Jena, 1924; rev. Helmut Voigt, 1967.

Index

Names of minor characters in the translations and synopses of medieval stories are not indexed. The reader should consult the general references under the author or title of these works.

Baasch, Karen, 269
Baesecke, Georg, 266, 271
Baltic, 95, 97
Barcelona, 30
Barditus, 10
Barnabas (saint), 35
Basel, 41
Basel manuscript of *Alexanderlied,* 42–43
Basques, 30
Bäuml, Franz H., 162, 267, 279
Bavaria, 32, 37, 40, 62, 94, 96, 100, 160
Bede, 21, 266
Bédier, Joseph, 151, 272
Bekker, Hugo, 278
Benath (Köppe-Benath), Ingeborg, 271
Benson, Larry D., 18, 267
Beowulf, 3, 5, 11–13, 18, 20, 50, 62, 162;
  literary provenance, 21–27; as generic
  mosaic, 22; interstitial expansion, 23–
  24
Bergen, 51
Bertelsen, Henrik, 60–61
Beyschlag, Siegfried, 156, 158, 279
Bible, 26
Biblical epic, 21, 26
Birkhan, Helmut, 159–60, 274, 279
Bjarkamál in fornu, 12, 20
Boase, Roger, 273
Boethius, 38, 40
Bollnow, 269
Boor, Helmut de, 105, 146, 268, 274, 277
Bornstein, Diane, 273
Bosnia, 38
Bostock, J. K., 150, 153, 156, 268, 278
Brady, Caroline, 265
Bragi Boddason (*Ragnarsdrápa*), 58
Bräuer, Rolf, 273
Brault, Gerard J., 270
Braun, Max, 58, 271
Bretons, 30
Bridal-quest epic, 56–60, 62; French, 63–
  67; absence of French influence on Ger-
  man bridal-quest epic, 68, 72; later de-
  velopment in Germany, 71; symbolism of
  rings, 73; Wolfram's commentary, 77;
  stereotypes of, and influence on the *Ni-
  belungenlied,* 81, 82–88, 91, 164, 273
  (n. 2); influence on the *Eneide,* 90; pattern absent in the "Brünhildenlied," 135
Bridal quest gone awry, 65
"Brünhildenlied" (lost source of Part I of
  the *Nibelungenlied*), 57, 60, 65, 104,
  116–17, 144–45, 163, 165; summary,
  84, 115; length, 135; accepted by Panzer, 151; reconstruction, 209–10
Brynhild, 5–6; her legend, 112–17

Bucephalus, 54
Bugge, Sophus, 272
Bumke, Joachim, 146, 155, 278
Bury, J. B., 13, 267
Bussmann, Hadumod, 272

Caesar, Julius, 14–15; in the *Annolied* and
  Kaiserchronik, 34–35
Candacis (queen), 43
Carolingian epic, 26, 30–32
Carolingian Renaissance, 32
Cary, George, 270
Cassiodorus, lost Gothic history: 8–9,
  265; *Variae,* 11, 266
Chanson de Guillaume, 98
Chansons de geste, 9, 144
Charlemagne, 7, 9, 12, 30–35, 41, 45–46,
  52, 61
Chase, Colin, 268
Chaucer ("Man of Law's Tale"), 36
Chrétien de Troyes, 3, 42, 47, 56, 58, 72,
  76, 93, 127; dating, 272; *Cligès,* 59–60,
  65–66, 68–72, 75, 77, 102, 103, 272;
  Erec et Enide, 68, 72, 77, 128; *Lan-
  celot,* 75, 77; *Yvain,* 73, 77
Claudius (emperor), 35
Clement (*Life of Clement*), 35
Clitophon, 103
Clotilda (wife of Clovis), 56, 59
Clovis, 56–60, 68, 71
Cluniac Reform, 32
Cnut Lavard, 109–10, 112, 252–55
Cnut VI (Danish king), 95
Codex Regius 2365,4°, 4; the great lacuna,
  113
Cologne, 33–34, 41, 52, 99
Constance, *see* Crescentia story
Constantinople, 38, 86
"Courtly" romance, 75
Crescentia story in the *Kaiserchronik,* 36–
  37, 39, 44, 55, 91, 164, 269
Curschmann, Michael, 71, 162, 257, 272–
  73, 279
Czerwinski, Peter, 160, 279

Dam, Jan van, 270
Daniel, 26
Danube, 108
Darius, 42–43
Darmstädter Aventiurenverzeichnis, 28
Daurel et Beton, 144, 155, 278
David and Goliath, 39
Delbouille, Maurice, 272
Delegate wooer in bridal-quest epic, 58–
  60, 65–66, 71, 82–88, 135, 155, 164
Denmark, 52, 96

Library of Congress Cataloging-in-Publication Data

Andersson, Theodore Murdock, 1934–
  A preface to the Nibelungenlied.

  Bibliography: p.
  Includes index.
  1. Nibelungenlied. I. Nibelungenlied. II. Title.
PT1589.A5 1987   831'.2   86-23064
ISBN 0-8047-1362-6 (alk. paper)